C#:
A Beginner's Guide

Herb Schildt

Osborne/**McGraw-Hill**

New York   Chicago   San Francisco
Lisbon   London   Madrid   Mexico City   Milan
New Delhi   San Juan   Seoul   Singapore   Sydney   Toronto

Osborne/**McGraw-Hill**
2600 Tenth Street
Berkeley, California 94710
U.S.A.

To arrange bulk purchase discounts for sales promotions, premiums, or fund-raisers, please contact Osborne/**McGraw-Hill** at the above address. For information on translations or book distributors outside the U.S.A., please see the International Contact Information page immediately following the index of this book.

1234567890 FGR FGR 01987654321

ISBN 0-07-213329-5

Publisher   Brandon A. Nordin
Vice President and Associate Publisher   Scott Rogers
Acqusition Editor   Ann Sellers
Project Editor   Laura Stone
Acquisitions Coordinator   Tim Madrid
Technical Editor   Forrest Houlette
Copy Editor   Jan Jue
Proofreader   Pamela Vevea
Indexer   Sheryl Schildt
Computer Designers   Carie Abrew, John Patrus
Illustrators   Lyssa Wald, Michael Mueller
Series Design   Gary Corrigan
Cover Design   Greg Scott
Cover Illustration   Eliot Bergman

This book was composed with Corel VENTURA™ Publisher.

Contents at a Glance

1 C# Fundamentals 1

2 Introducing Data Types and Operators 47

3 Program Control Statements 99

4 Introducing Classes, Objects, and Methods 145

5 More Data Types and Operators 189

6 A Closer Look at Methods and Classes 241

7 Operator Overloading, Indexers, and Properties 299

8 Inheritance 345

9 Interfaces, Structures, and Enumerations 403

10 Exception Handling 437

11 Using I/O 471

12 Delegates, Events, Namespaces, and Advanced Topics 519

A Answers to Mastery Checks 579

Index 613

About the Author

Herbert Schildt is the world's leading programming author. He is an authority on the C, C++, Java, and C# languages, and is a master Windows programmer. His programming books have sold more than 3 million copies worldwide and have been translated into all major foreign languages. He is the author of numerous bestsellers, including *C++: The Complete Reference*, *Java 2: The Complete Reference*, *Java 2: A Beginner's Guide*, *Windows 2000 Programming from the Ground Up*, and *C: The Complete Reference*. Schildt holds a master's degree in computer science from the University of Illinois. He can be reached at his consulting office at (217) 586-4683.

Contents

PREFACE xv

1 C# Fundamentals 1
  C#'s Family Tree 2
      C: The Beginning of the Modern Age of Programming 2
      The Creation of OOP and C++ 3
      The Internet and Java Emerge 4
      The Creation of C# 5
  How C# Relates to the .NET Framework 7
      What Is the .NET Framework? 7
      How the Common Language Runtime Works 8
      Managed vs. Unmanaged Code 9
      The Common Language Specification 9
  Object-Oriented Programming 10
      Encapsulation 11
      Polymorphism 12
      Inheritance 13
  A First Simple Program 14
      Using csc.exe, the C# Command-Line Compiler 15
      Using the Visual C++ IDE 16
      The First Sample Program Line by Line 21
  Handling Syntax Errors 25

A Small Variation 26
A Second Simple Program 27
Another Data Type 29
Project 1-1: Converting Fahrenheit to Celsius 32
Two Control Statements 33
    The if Statement 34
    The for Loop 36
Using Blocks of Code 38
Semicolons and Positioning 39
Indentation Practices 40
Project 1-2: Improving the Temperature Conversion Program ... 41
    The C# Keywords 42
Identifiers 43
The C# Class Library 44
Mastery Check 45

2 Introducing Data Types and Operators 47
Why Data Types Are Important 48
C#'s Value Types 48
    Integers 49
Floating-Point Types 52
The decimal Type 53
Characters 54
The bool Type 56
Some Output Options 57
Project 2-1: Talking to Mars 60
Literals 62
    Hexadecimal Literals 63
    Character Escape Sequences 63
    String Literals 64
A Closer Look at Variables 67
    Initializing a Variable 67
    Dynamic Initialization 68
The Scope and Lifetime of Variables 68
Operators 72
Arithmetic Operators 72
    Increment and Decrement 74
Relational and Logical Operators 75
    Short-Circuit Logical Operators 77
Project 2-2: Display a Truth Table for the Logical Operators ... 78
The Assignment Operator 82
    Compound Assignments 82

Type Conversion in Assignments 83
Casting Incompatible Types 85
Operator Precedence 87
Expressions 88
Type Conversion in Expressions 88
Spacing and Parentheses 92
Project 2-3: Compute the Regular Payments on a Loan 92
Mastery Check 96

3 Program Control Statements 99
Inputting Characters from the Keyboard 100
The if Statement 101
Nested ifs 103
The if-else-if Ladder 104
The switch Statement 106
Nested switch Statements 111
Project 3-1: Start Building a C# Help System 112
The for Loop 115
Some Variations on the for Loop 117
Missing Pieces 118
Loops with No Body 120
Declaring Loop Control Variables Inside the for Loop ... 121
The while Loop 123
The do-while Loop 125
Project 3-2: Improve the C# Help System 128
Using break to Exit a Loop 131
Using continue 133
The goto 134
Project 3-3: Finish the C# Help System 136
Nested Loops 141
Mastery Check 143

4 Introducing Classes, Objects, and Methods 145
Class Fundamentals 146
The General Form of a Class 146
Defining a Class 148
How Objects Are Created 153
Reference Variables and Assignment 154
Methods 155
Adding a Method to the Vehicle Class 156
Returning from a Method 159
Returning a Value 160

Using Parameters 163
Adding a Parameterized Method to Vehicle 165
Project 4-1: Creating a Help Class 167
Constructors 174
Parameterized Constructors 176
Adding a Constructor to the Vehicle Class 177
The new Operator Revisited 179
Garbage Collection and Destructors 180
Destructors 181
Project 4-2: Demonstrate Destructors 181
The this Keyword 184
Mastery Check 187

5 More Data Types and Operators 189
Arrays 190
One-Dimensional Arrays 190
Project 5-1: Sorting an Array 196
Multidimensional Arrays 198
Two-Dimensional Arrays 198
Arrays of Three or More Dimensions 200
Initializing Multidimensional Arrays 200
Jagged Arrays 202
Assigning Array References 205
Using the Length Property 206
Project 5-2: A Queue Class 209
The foreach Loop 214
Strings 217
Constructing Strings 218
Operating on Strings 218
Arrays of Strings 221
Strings Are Immutable 222
The Bitwise Operators 224
The Bitwise AND, OR, XOR, and NOT Operators 224
The Shift Operators 230
Bitwise Compound Assignments 232
Project 5-3: A ShowBits Class 232
The ? Operator 236
Mastery Check 239

6 A Closer Look at Methods and Classes 241
Controlling Access to Class Members 242
C#'s Access Specifiers 242

Project 6-1: Improving the Queue Class 248
Pass Objects to Methods 250
    How Arguments Are Passed 252
Using ref and out Parameters 255
    Using ref 255
    Using out 257
Using a Variable Number of Arguments 261
Returning Objects 265
Method Overloading 267
Overloading Constructors 275
    Invoking an Overloaded Constructor Through this 277
Project 6-2: Overloading the Queue Constructor 279
The Main( ) Method 283
    Returning Values from Main( ) 283
    Passing Arguments to Main( ) 283
Recursion 286
Understanding static 289
Project 6-3: The Quicksort 293
Mastery Check 297

7 Operator Overloading, Indexers, and Properties 299
Operator Overloading 300
    The General Forms of an Operator Method 300
    Overloading Binary Operators 301
    Overloading Unary Operators 304
    Adding Flexibility 309
    Overloading the Relational Operators 315
    Operator Overloading Tips and Restrictions 317
Indexers 319
    Multidimensional Indexers 325
Properties 328
    Property Restrictions 333
Project 7-1: Creating a Set Class 333
Mastery Check 344

8 Inheritance 345
Inheritance Basics 346
    Member Access and Inheritance 350
Using Protected Access 353
Constructors and Inheritance 355
    Calling Base Class Constructors 357
Inheritance and Name Hiding 363

Using base to Access a Hidden Name 364
Project 8-1: Extending the Vehicle Class 367
Creating a Multilevel Hierarchy 371
When Are Constructors Called? 374
Base Class References and Derived Objects 376
Virtual Methods and Overriding 382
    Why Overridden Methods? 385
    Applying Virtual Methods 386
Using Abstract Classes 391
Using sealed to Prevent Inheritance 396
The object Class 396
    Boxing and Unboxing 399
Mastery Check 402

9 Interfaces, Structures, and Enumerations 403
Interfaces 404
    Implementing Interfaces 405
Using Interface References 410
Project 9-1: Creating a Queue Interface 413
Interface Properties 419
Interface Indexers 421
Interfaces Can Be Inherited 424
Explicit Implementations 426
Structures 430
Enumerations 432
    Initialize an Enumeration 434
    Specifying the Base Type of an Enumeration 435
Mastery Check 436

10 Exception Handling 437
The System.Exception Class 438
Exception Handling Fundamentals 439
    Using try and catch 439
    A Simple Exception Example 440
    A Second Exception Example 441
The Consequences of an Uncaught Exception 443
Exceptions Let You Handle Errors Gracefully 445
Using Multiple catch Statements 446
Catching All Exceptions 448
try Blocks Can Be Nested 449
Throwing an Exception 450
    Rethrowing an Exception 452

Using finally 453
A Closer Look at Exception 455
    Commonly Used Exceptions 457
Deriving Exception Classes 458
Catching Derived Class Exceptions 460
Project 10-1: Adding Exceptions to the Queue Class 462
Using checked and unchecked 466
Mastery Check 470

11 Using I/O 471
C#'s I/O Is Built upon Streams 472
    Byte Streams and Character Streams 472
    The Predefined Streams 473
The Stream Classes 473
    The Stream Class 474
    The Byte Stream Classes 475
    The Character Stream Wrapper Classes 475
    Binary Streams 477
Console I/O 478
    Reading Console Input 478
    Writing Console Output 480
FileStream and Byte-Oriented File I/O 481
    Opening and Closing a File 481
    Reading Bytes from a FileStream 483
    Writing to a File 485
Character-Based File I/O 488
    Using StreamWriter 488
    Using a StreamReader 491
Redirecting the Standard Streams 492
Project 11-1: A File Comparison Utility 495
Reading and Writing Binary Data 497
    BinaryWriter 498
    BinaryReader 499
    Demonstrating Binary I/O 500
Random Access Files 502
Converting Numeric Strings to Their Internal Representation 505
Project 11-2: Creating a Disk-Based Help System 511
Mastery Check 518

12 Delegates, Events, Namespaces, and Advanced Topics 519
Delegates 520
    Multicasting 525

Why Delegates 528
Events 528
A Multicast Event Example 531
Namespaces 535
Declaring a Namespace 535
using 538
A Second Form of using 540
Namespaces Are Additive 542
Namespaces Can Be Nested 544
The Default Namespace 545
Project 12-1: Putting Set into a Namespace 546
Conversion Operators 549
The Preprocessor 555
#define 555
#if and #endif 556
#else and #elif 558
#undef 560
#error 561
#warning 561
#line 561
#region and #endregion 562
Attributes 562
The Conditional Attribute 563
The Obsolete Attribute 564
Unsafe Code 565
A Brief Look at Pointers 566
Using unsafe 569
Using fixed 570
Runtime Type Identification 571
Testing a Type with is 571
Using as 573
Using typeof 573
Other Keywords 574
The internal Access Modifier 574
sizeof 574
lock 575
readonly 575
stackalloc 576
The using Statement 576
const and volatile...................................... 577
What Next? 577
Mastery Check 578

A Answers to Mastery Checks 579
　Module 1: C# Fundamentals 580
　Module 2: Introducing Data Types and Operators 581
　Module 3: Program Control Statements 583
　Module 4: Introducing Classes, Objects, and Methods 587
　Module 5: More Data Types and Operators 588
　Module 6: A Closer Look at Methods and Classes 591
　Module 7: Operator Overloading, Indexers, and Properties 597
　Module 8: Inheritance 599
　Module 9: Interfaces, Structures, and Enumerations 601
　Module 10: Exception Handling 605
　Module 11: Using I/O 608
　Module 12: Delegates, Events, Namespaces, and Advanced Topics 611

　Index 613

Preface

In the past few years, computing has undergone a major paradigm shift away from a landscape dominated by stand-alone systems to an on-line, networked environment. In an age in which for many "the network is the computer," computer languages, operating systems, and development tools have struggled to keep up. In response to the need for a modern programming language that could meet the demands of the interconnected world, C# was invented.

C# represents the next step in the evolution of programming languages. It takes the best of the past and incorporates the latest in modern computer language design. For example, C# borrows features from both C++ and Java—two of the world's most important languages. It adds innovations such as delegates and indexers. Because C# utilizes the .NET Framework, code produced by C# is highly portable and allows for mixed-language use. For example, software components created using C# are compatible with code created by other languages as long as it too is targeted for the .NET Framework.

The purpose of this book is to teach you the fundamentals of C# programming. It uses a step-by-step approach complete with numerous examples, self-tests, and projects. It assumes no previous programming experience. The book starts with the basics, such as how to compile and run a C# program. It then discusses the keywords, features, and constructs that comprise the C# language. By the time you finish, you will have a firm grasp of the essentials of C# programming.

It is important to state at the outset that this book is just a starting point. C# programming involves more than just the keywords and syntax that define the language. It also involves the use of a sophisticated set of libraries called the .NET Framework Class Library. The .NET Framework Class Library is very large and a complete discussion would require a book of its own. Although several of the classes defined by this library are discussed in this book, because of space limitations, most are not. To be a top-notch C# programmer implies mastery of this library, too. After completing this book you will have the knowledge to pursue any and all other aspects of C#.

One last point: C# is a new language. Like all new computer languages, C# will go through a period of enhancement and change. You will want to watch for new features and new techniques. Also, don't be surprised if a few things change over time. The history of C# is just beginning.

How This Book is Organized

This book presents an evenly paced tutorial in which each section builds upon the previous one. It contains 12 modules, each discussing an aspect of C#. This book is unique because it includes several special elements that reinforce what you are learning.

Goals

Each module begins with a set of goals that tell you what you will be learning.

Mastery Check

Each module concludes with a Mastery Check, a self-test that lets you test your knowledge. The answers are in the Appendix.

1-Minute Drills

At the end of each major section, 1-Minute Drills are presented which test your understanding of the key points of the preceding section. The answers to these questions are at the bottom of the page.

Ask the Expert

Sprinkled throughout the book are special "Ask the Expert" boxes. These contain additional information or interesting commentary about a topic. They use a Question/Answer format.

Projects

Each Module contains one or more projects that show you how to apply what you are learning. These are real-world examples that you can use as starting points for your own programs.

No Previous Programming Experience Required

This book assumes no previous programming experience. Thus, if you have never programmed before, you can use this book. Of course, in this day and age, most readers will have at least a little prior programming experience. For many, this previous experience will be in C++ or Java. As you will learn, C# is related to both of these languages. Therefore, if you already know C++ or Java, then you will be able to learn C# easily.

Required Software

To compile and run the programs in this book you will need Visual Studio.NET 7 (or later) and the .NET Framework must be installed on your computer. The code in this book was tested using Visual Studio.NET 7.0, Beta 2.

Don't Forget: Code on the Web

Remember, the source code for all of the examples and projects in this book is available free-of-charge on the Web at **www.osborne.com**.

For Further Study

C#: A Beginner's Guide is your gateway to the Herb Schildt series of programming books. Here are some others that you will find of interest.

To learn more about C#, try

C#: The Complete Reference

To learn about C++, you will find these books especially helpful.

C++: The Complete Reference

C++: A Beginner's Guide

Teach Yourself C++

C++ from the Ground Up

STL Programming from the Ground Up

The C/C++ Programming Annotated Archives

To learn about Java programming, we recommend the following:

Java 2: A Beginner's Guide

Java 2: The Complete Reference

Java 2: Programmer's Reference

To learn about Windows programming we suggest the following Schildt books:

Windows 98 Programming from the Ground Up

Windows 2000 Programming from the Ground Up

MFC Programming from the Ground Up

The Windows Programming Annotated Archives

If you want to learn about the C language, which is the foundation of all modern programming, then the following titles will be of interest.

C: The Complete Reference

Teach Yourself C

When you need solid answers, fast, turn to Herbert Schildt, the recognized authority on programming.

Module 1

C# Fundamentals

The Goals of This Module

- Understand the history behind C#
- See how C# relates to and uses the .NET Framework
- Learn the three principles of object-oriented programming
- Create, compile, and run C# programs
- Use variables
- Work with the if and for statements
- Apply code blocks
- Know the C# keywords

The quest for the perfect programming language is as old as the discipline of programming itself. In this quest, C# has become the current standard bearer. Created by Microsoft to support development for its .NET Framework, C# leverages time-tested features with cutting-edge innovations. It provides a highly usable, efficient way to write programs for the modern enterprise computing environment, which includes Windows, the Internet, components, and so on. In the process, C# has redefined the programming landscape. In the course of this book you will learn to program using it.

The purpose of this module is to introduce C#, including the forces that drove its creation, its design philosophy, and several of its most important features. By far, the hardest thing about learning a programming language is the fact that no element exists in isolation. Instead, the components of the language work together. It is this interrelatedness that makes it difficult to discuss one aspect of C# without involving others. To help overcome this problem, this module provides a brief overview of several C# features, including the general form of a C# program, some basic control statements, and operators. It does not go into too many details, but rather concentrates on the general concepts common to any C# program.

C#'s Family Tree

Computer languages do not exist in a void. Rather, they relate to one another, with each new language influenced in one form or another by the ones that came before. In a process akin to cross-pollination, features from one language are adapted by another, a new innovation is integrated into an existing context, or an older construct is removed. In this way, languages evolve and the art of programming advances. C# is no exception.

C# inherits a rich programming legacy. It is directly descended from two of the world's most successful computer languages: C and C++. It is closely related to another: Java. Understanding the nature of these relationships is critical to understanding C#. Thus, we begin our examination of C# by placing it in the historical context of these three languages.

C: The Beginning of the Modern Age of Programming

The creation of C marks the beginning of the modern age of programming. C was invented by Dennis Ritchie in the 1970s on a DEC PDP-11 that used the

UNIX operating system. While some earlier languages, most notably Pascal, had achieved significant success, it was C that established the paradigm that still charts the course of programming today.

C grew out of the *structured programming* revolution of the 1960s. Prior to structured programming, large programs were difficult to write because the program logic tended to degenerate into what is known as "spaghetti code," a tangled mass of jumps, calls, and returns that is difficult to follow. Structured languages addressed this problem by adding well-defined control statements, subroutines with local variables, and other improvements. Using structured languages, it became possible to write moderately large programs.

Although there were other structured languages at the time, C was the first to successfully combine power, elegance, and expressiveness. Its terse yet easy-to-use syntax coupled with its philosophy that the programmer (not the language) was in charge quickly won many converts. It can be a bit hard to understand from today's perspective, but C was a breath of fresh air that programmers had long awaited. As a result, C became the most widely used structured programming language of the 1980s.

However, even the venerable C language had its limits. One of the most troublesome was its inability to handle large programs. The C language hits a barrier once a project reaches a certain size. After that point, C programs are difficult to understand and maintain. Precisely where this limit is depends upon the program, the programmer, and the tools at hand, but it can be encountered with as few as 5,000 lines of code.

The Creation of OOP and C++

By the late 1970s, the size of many projects was near or at the limits of what structured programming methodologies and the C language could handle. To solve this problem, a new way to program began to emerge. This method is called *object-oriented programming* (OOP for short). Using OOP, a programmer could handle much larger programs. The trouble was that C, the most popular language at the time, did not support object-oriented programming. The desire for an object-oriented version of C ultimately led to the creation of C++.

C++ was invented by Bjarne Stroustrup beginning in 1979, at Bell Laboratories in Murray Hill, New Jersey. He initially called the new language "C with Classes." However, in 1983 the name was changed to "C++." C++ contains the entire C language. Thus, C is the foundation upon which C++ is built. Most of the additions that Stroustrup made to C were designed to support object-oriented programming.

In essence, C++ is the object-oriented version of C. By building upon the foundation of C, Stroustrup provided a smooth migration path to OOP. Instead of having to learn an entirely new language, a C programmer needed to learn only a few new features before reaping the benefits of the object-oriented methodology.

C++ simmered in the background during much of the 1980s, undergoing extensive development. By the beginning of the 1990s, C++ was ready for mainstream use, and its popularity exploded. By the end of the decade, it had become the most widely used programming language. Today, C++ is still the preeminent language for software development for nondistributed systems.

It is critical to understand that the invention of C++ was not an attempt to create a new programming language. Instead, it was an enhancement to an already highly successful language. This approach to language development— beginning with an existing language and moving it forward—established a trend that continues today.

The Internet and Java Emerge

The next major advance in programming languages was Java. Work on Java, which was originally called Oak, began in 1991 at Sun Microsystems. The main driving force behind Java's design was James Gosling. Patrick Naughton, Chris Warth, Ed Frank, and Mike Sheridan also played a role.

Java is a structured, object-oriented language with a syntax and philosophy derived from C++. The innovative aspects of Java were driven not so much by advances in the art of programming (although some certainly were), but rather by changes in the computing environment. Prior to the mainstreaming of the Internet, most programs were written, compiled, and targeted for a specific CPU and a specific operating system. While it has always been true that programmers like to reuse their code, the ability to easily port a program from one environment to another took a backseat to more pressing problems. However, with the rise of the Internet, in which many different types of CPUs and operating systems are connected, the old problem of portability became substantially more important. To solve the problem of portability, a new language was needed, and this new language was Java.

Although the single most important aspect of Java (and the reason for its rapid acceptance) is its ability to create cross-platform, portable code, it is interesting to note that the original impetus for Java was not the Internet, but rather the need for a platform-independent language that could be used to create software for embedded controllers. In 1993, it became clear that the issues of cross-platform portability found when creating code for embedded controllers are also encountered when attempting to create code for the Internet. Remember, the Internet is a vast, distributed computing universe in which many different types of computers live. The same techniques that solved the portability problem on a small scale could be applied to the Internet on a large scale.

Java achieved portability by translating a program's source code into an intermediate language called *bytecode*. This bytecode was then executed by the Java Virtual Machine (JVM). Therefore, a Java program could run in any environment for which a JVM was available. Also, since the JVM is relatively easy to implement, it was readily available for a large number of environments.

Java's use of bytecode differed radically from both C and C++, which were nearly always compiled to executable machine code. Machine code is tied to a specific CPU and operating system. Thus, if you wanted to run a C/C++ program on a different system, it needed to be recompiled to machine code specifically for that environment. To create a C/C++ program that would run in a variety of environments, several different executable versions of the program were needed. Not only was this impractical, but it also was expensive. Java's use of an intermediate language was an elegant and cost-effective solution. It was also a solution that C# would adapt for its own purposes.

As mentioned, Java is descended from C and C++. Its syntax is based on C, and its object model is evolved from C++. Although Java code is neither upwardly nor downwardly compatible with C or C++, its syntax is sufficiently similar that the large pool of existing C/C++ programmers could move to Java with very little effort. Furthermore, because Java built upon and improved an existing paradigm, Gosling, et al., were free to focus their attentions on the new and innovative features. Just as Stroustrup did not need to "reinvent the wheel" when creating C++, Gosling did not need to create an entirely new language when developing Java. Moreover, with the creation of Java, C and C++ became the accepted substrata upon which new computer languages are built.

The Creation of C#

While Java has successfully addressed many of the issues surrounding portability in the Internet environment, there are still features that it lacks. One is *cross-language interoperability*, also called *mixed-language programming*. This is the ability for the code produced by one language to work easily with the code produced by another. Cross-language interoperability is crucial for the creation of large, distributed software systems. It is also desirable for programming software components because the most valuable component is one that can be used by the widest variety of computer languages, in the greatest number of operating environments.

Another feature lacking in Java is full integration with the Windows platform. Although Java programs can be executed in a Windows environment (assuming that the Java Virtual Machine has been installed), Java and Windows are not closely coupled. Since Windows is the most widely used operating system in the world, lack of direct support for Windows is a drawback to Java.

To answer these and other needs, Microsoft developed C#. C# was created at Microsoft late in the 1990s and was part of Microsoft's overall .NET strategy. It was first released in its alpha version in the middle of 2000. C#'s chief architect was Anders Hejlsberg.

C# is directly related to C, C++, and Java. This is not by accident. These are three of the most widely used—and most widely liked—programming languages in the world. Furthermore, nearly all professional programmers today know C and C++, and most know Java. By building C# upon a solid, well-understood foundation, C# offers an easy migration path from these languages. Since it was neither necessary nor desirable for Hejlsberg to "reinvent the wheel," he was free to focus on specific improvements and innovations.

The family tree for C# is shown in Figure 1-1. The grandfather of C# is C. From C, C# derives its syntax, many of its keywords, and operators. C# builds upon and improves the object model defined by C++. If you know C or C++, then you will feel at home with C#.

C# and Java have a bit more complicated relationship. As explained, Java is also descended from C and C++. It, too, shares the C/C++ syntax and object model. Like Java, C# is designed to produce portable code. However, C# is not descended from Java. Instead, C# and Java are more like cousins, sharing a common ancestry, but differing in many important ways. The good news, though, is that if you know Java, then many C# concepts will be familiar. Conversely, if in the future you need to learn Java, then many of the things you learn about C# will carry over. C# contains many innovative features that we will examine at length throughout the course of this book, but some of its most important features relate to its built-in support for software components. In fact, C# has been characterized as being a component-oriented language because it contains integral support for the writing of software components. For example, C# includes features that directly support the constituents of components, such as properties, methods, and events. However, C#'s ability to work in a mixed-language environment is perhaps its most important component-oriented feature.

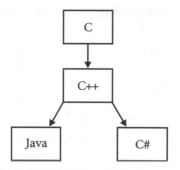

Figure 1-1   The C# family tree

How C# Relates to the .NET Framework

Although C# is a computer language that can be studied on its own, it has a special relationship to its runtime environment, the .NET Framework. The reason for this is twofold. First, C# was initially designed by Microsoft to create code for the .NET Framework. Second, the libraries used by C# are the ones defined by the .NET Framework. Thus, even though it is possible to separate C# the language from the .NET environment, for now the two are closely linked. Because of this, it is important to have a general understanding of the .NET Framework and why it is important to C#.

What Is the .NET Framework?

In a sentence, the .NET Framework defines an environment that supports the development and execution of platform-independent applications. It enables differing computer languages to work together and provides for security, program portability, and a common programming model for the Windows platform. It is important to state, however, that the .NET Framework is not limited to Windows (although this is the only environment that is currently available), which means that programs written for it might be portable to non-Windows environments in the future.

As it relates to C#, the .NET Framework defines two very important entities. The first is the *Common Language Runtime*. This is the system that manages the execution of your program. Along with other benefits, the common language runtime is the part of the .NET Framework that enables programs to be portable, supports mixed-language programming, and provides for security.

The second entity is the .NET *class library*. This library gives your program access to the runtime environment. For example, if you want to perform I/O, such as displaying something on the screen, you will use the .NET class library to do it. If you are new to programming, then the term *class* may be new. Although it will be explained in detail a bit later, briefly, a class is an object-oriented construct that helps organize programs. As long as your program restricts itself to the features defined by the .NET class library, it can run anywhere that the .NET runtime system is supported. Since C# automatically uses the .NET class library, C# programs are automatically portable to all .NET environments.

How the Common Language Runtime Works

The Common Language Runtime (CLR) manages the execution of .NET code. Here is how it works. When you compile a C# program, the output of the compiler is not executable code. Instead, it is a file that contains a special type of pseudocode called Microsoft Intermediate Language, or MSIL for short. MSIL defines a set of portable instructions that are independent of any specific CPU. In essence, MSIL defines a portable assembly language. One other point: although MSIL is similar in concept to Java's bytecode, the two are not the same.

It is the job of the CLR to translate the intermediate code into executable code when a program is run. Thus, any program compiled to MSIL can be run in any environment for which the CLR is implemented. This is part of how the .NET Framework achieves portability.

Microsoft Intermediate Language is turned into executable code using a *JIT* compiler. JIT stands for "just in time." The process works like this: When a .NET program is executed, the CLR activates the JIT compiler. The JIT compiler converts MSIL into native code on a demand basis, as each part of your program is needed. Thus, your C# program actually executes as native code even though it is initially compiled into MSIL. This means that your program runs nearly as

1

fast as it would if it had been compiled to native code in the first place, but it gains the portability benefits of MSIL.

In addition to MSIL, one other thing is output when you compile a C# program: *metadata*. Metadata describes the data used by your program and enables your code to interact with other code. The metadata is contained in the same file as the MSIL.

Fortunately, for the purposes of this book, and for the majority of programming tasks, it is not necessary to know any more about the CLR, MSIL, or metadata. C# handles the details of these things for you.

Managed vs. Unmanaged Code

In general, when you write a C# program, you are creating what is called *managed code*. Managed code is executed under the control of the Common Language Runtime as just described. Because it is running under the control of the CLR, managed code is subject to certain constraints—and derives several benefits. The constraints are easily described and met: the compiler must produce an MSIL file targeted for the CLR (which C# does) and use the .NET Framework libraries (which C# does). The benefits of managed code are many, including modern memory management, the ability to mix languages, better security, support for version control, and a clean way for software components to interact.

The opposite of managed code is *unmanaged* code. Unmanaged code does not execute under the Common Language Runtime. Thus, all Windows programs prior to the creation of the .NET Framework use unmanaged code. It is possible for managed code and unmanaged code to work together, so the fact that C# generates managed code does not restrict its ability to operate in conjunction with preexisting programs.

The Common Language Specification

Although all managed code gains the benefits provided by the CLR, if your code will be used by other programs written in different languages, then for maximum usability, it should adhere to the Common Language Specification (CLS). The CLS describes a set of features, such as data types, that different languages have in common. CLS compliance is especially important when creating software components that will be used by other languages. Although we won't need to worry about the CLS for the purposes of this book, it is something that you will want to look into when you begin writing commercial code.

Ask the Expert

Question: To address the issues of portability, security, and mixed-language programming, why was it necessary to create a new computer language such as C#? Couldn't a language like C++ be adapted to support the .NET Framework?

Answer: Yes, it is possible to adapt C++ so that it produces .NET-compatible code that runs under the CLR. In fact, Microsoft did just that, by adding what are called the *managed extensions* to C++. Although the managed extensions to C++ make it possible to port existing code to the .NET Framework, new .NET development is much easier in C#. Remember, C# is optimized for the .NET environment, and it includes several built-in features that greatly streamline .NET development.

1-Minute Drill

● To what languages is C# related?

● What is the Common Language Runtime?

● What is a JIT compiler?

Object-Oriented Programming

At the center of C# is object-oriented programming (OOP). The object-oriented methodology is inseparable from C#, and all C# programs are to at least some extent object-oriented. Because of its importance to C#, it is useful to understand OOP's basic principles before you write even a simple C# program.

OOP is a powerful way to approach the job of programming. Programming methodologies have changed dramatically since the invention of the computer, primarily to accommodate the increasing complexity of programs. For example, when computers were first invented, programming was done by toggling in the

---

● C# is descended from C and C++ and is a cousin of Java.
● The Common Language Runtime manages the execution of .NET programs.
● JIT stands for just in time, and a JIT compiler converts MSIL code into native code as needed, on demand while your program is executing.

binary machine instructions using the computer's front panel. As long as programs were just a few hundred instructions long, this approach worked. As programs grew, assembly language was invented so that a programmer could deal with larger, increasingly complex programs, using symbolic representations of the machine instructions. As programs continued to grow, high-level languages such as FORTRAN and COBOL were introduced that gave the programmer more tools with which to handle complexity. When these early languages began to reach their breaking point, structured programming was invented.

Consider this: At each milestone in the development of programming, techniques and tools were created to allow the programmer to deal with increasingly greater complexity. Each step of the way, the new approach took the best elements of the previous methods and moved forward. The same is true of object-oriented programming. Prior to OOP, many projects were nearing (or exceeding) the point where the structured approach no longer works. A better way to handle complexity was needed, and object-oriented programming was the solution.

Object-oriented programming took the best ideas of structured programming and combined them with several new concepts. The result was a different and better way of organizing a program. In the most general sense, a program can be organized in one of two ways: around its code (what is happening) or around its data (who is being affected). Using only structured programming techniques, programs are typically organized around code. This approach can be thought of as "code acting on data."

Object-oriented programs work the other way around. They are organized around data, with the key principle being "data controlling access to code." In an object-oriented language, you define the data and the routines that are permitted to act on that data. Thus, a data type defines precisely what sort of operations can be applied to that data.

To support the principles of object-oriented programming, all OOP languages, including C#, have three traits in common: encapsulation, polymorphism, and inheritance. Let's examine each.

Encapsulation

Encapsulation is a programming mechanism that binds together code and the data it manipulates, and that keeps both safe from outside interference and misuse. In an object-oriented language, code and data can be bound together in such a way that a self-contained *black box* is created. Within the box are all necessary data and code. When code and data are linked together in this fashion, an object is created. In other words, an object is the device that supports encapsulation.

Within an object, code, data, or both may be *private* to that object or *public*. Private code or data is known to and accessible by only another part of the object. That is, private code or data cannot be accessed by a piece of the program that exists outside the object. When code or data is public, other parts of your program can access it even though it is defined within an object. Typically, the public parts of an object are used to provide a controlled interface to the private elements of the object.

C#'s basic unit of encapsulation is the *class*. A class defines the form of an object. It specifies both the data and the code that will operate on that data. C# uses a class specification to construct *objects*. Objects are instances of a class. Thus, a class is essentially a set of plans that specifies how to build an object.

The code and data that constitute a class are called *members* of the class. Specifically, the data defined by the class is referred to as *member variables* or *instance variables*. The code that operates on that data is referred to as *member methods* or just *methods*. "Method" is C#'s term for a subroutine. If you are familiar with C/C++, it may help to know that what a C# programmer calls a *method,* a C/C++ programmer calls a *function*. Because C# is a direct descendent of C++, the term "function" is also sometimes used when referring to a C# method.

Polymorphism

Polymorphism (from the Greek, meaning "many forms") is the quality that allows one interface to access a general class of actions. A simple example of polymorphism is found in the steering wheel of an automobile. The steering wheel (the interface) is the same no matter what type of actual steering mechanism is used. That is, the steering wheel works the same whether your car has manual steering, power steering, or rack-and-pinion steering. Thus, turning the steering wheel left causes the car to go left no matter what type of steering is used. The benefit of the uniform interface is, of course, that once you know how to operate the steering wheel, you can drive any type of car.

The same principle can also apply to programming. For example, consider a stack (which is a first-in, last-out list). You might have a program that requires three different types of stacks. One stack is used for integer values, one for floating-point values, and one for characters. In this case, the algorithm that implements each stack is the same, even though the data being stored differs. In a non–object-oriented language, you would be required to create three different sets of stack routines, with each set using different names. However, because of polymorphism, in C# you can create one general set of stack routines that works for all three specific situations. This way, once you know how to use one stack, you can use them all.

More generally, the concept of polymorphism is often expressed by the phrase "one interface, multiple methods." This means that it is possible to design a generic interface to a group of related activities. Polymorphism helps reduce complexity by allowing the same interface to be used to specify a *general class of action*. It is the compiler's job to select the *specific action* (that is, method) as it applies to each situation. You, the programmer, don't need to do this selection manually. You need only remember and utilize the general interface.

Inheritance

Inheritance is the process by which one object can acquire the properties of another object. This is important because it supports the concept of hierarchical classification. If you think about it, most knowledge is made manageable by hierarchical (that is, top-down) classifications. For example, a Red Delicious apple is part of the classification *apple*, which in turn is part of the *fruit* class, which is under the larger class *food*. That is, the *food* class possesses certain qualities (edible, nutritious, and so on) that also, logically, apply to its subclass, *fruit*. In addition to these qualities, the *fruit* class has specific characteristics (juicy, sweet, and so forth) that distinguish it from other food. The *apple* class defines those qualities specific to an apple (grows on trees, not tropical, and so on). A Red Delicious apple would, in turn, inherit all the qualities of all preceding classes and would define only those qualities that make it unique.

Without the use of hierarchies, each object would have to explicitly define all of its characteristics. Using inheritance, an object need only define those qualities that make it unique within its class. It can inherit its general attributes from its parent. Thus, it is the inheritance mechanism that makes it possible for one object to be a specific instance of a more general case.

1-Minute Drill

● Name the principles of OOP.

● What is the basic unit of encapsulation in C#?

● The principles of OOP are encapsulation, polymorphism, and inheritance.
● The class is the basic unit of encapsulation.

Ask the Expert

Question: You state that object-oriented programming is an effective way to manage large programs. However, it seems that it might add substantial overhead to relatively small programs. Since you say that all C# programs are to some extent object-oriented, does this impose a penalty for smaller programs?

Answer: No. As you will see, for small programs, C#'s object-oriented features are nearly transparent. Although it is true that C# follows a strict object model, you have wide latitude as to the degree to which you employ it. For smaller programs, their "object-orientedness" is barely perceptible. As your programs grow, you will integrate more object-oriented features effortlessly.

A First Simple Program

Before going into any more details, let's start by compiling and running the short sample C# program shown here:

```
/*
   This is a simple C# program.

   Call this program Example.cs.
*/

using System;

class Example {

  // A C# program begins with a call to Main().
  public static void Main() {
    Console.WriteLine("A simple C# program.");
  }
}
```

There are two ways to edit, compile, and run a C# program. First, you can use the command-line compiler, **csc.exe**. Second, you can use the Visual C++ Integrated Development Environment (IDE). Both methods are described here.

Using csc.exe, the C# Command-Line Compiler

Although the Visual C++ IDE is what you will probably be using for your commercial projects, the C# command-line compiler is the easiest way to compile and run most of the sample programs shown in this book. To create and run programs using the C# command-line compiler, you will follow these three steps:

1. Enter the program.

2. Compile the program.

3. Run the program.

Entering the Program

The programs shown in this book are available from Osborne's web site: **www.osborne.com**. However, if you want to enter the programs by hand, you are free to do so. In this case, you must enter the program into your computer using a text editor, such as Notepad. Remember, you must create text-only files, not formatted word-processing files, because the format information in a word processor file will confuse the C# compiler. When entering the program, call the file **Example.cs**.

Compiling the Program

To compile the program, execute the C# compiler, **csc.exe**, specifying the name of the source file on the command line, as shown here:

```
C:\>csc Example.cs
```

The **csc** compiler creates a file called **Example.exe** that contains the MSIL version of the program. Although MSIL is not executable code, it is still contained in an **exe** file. The Common Language Runtime automatically invokes the JIT compiler when you attempt to execute **Example.exe**. Be aware, however, that if you try to execute **Example.exe** (or any other **exe** file that contains MSIL) on a computer for which the .NET Framework is not installed, the program will not execute, because the CLR will be missing.

Note

Prior to running **csc.exe** you may need to run the batch file **vcvars32.bat**, which is typically found in the *\Program Files\Microsoft Visual Studio.NET\Vc7\Bin* directory. Alternatively, you can activate a command-prompt session that is already initialized for C# by selecting *Visual Studio.NET Command Prompt* from the list of tools shown under the *Microsoft Visual Studio.NET 7.0* entry in the *Start | Programs* menu of the task bar.

Running the Program

To actually run the program, just type its name on the command line, as shown here:

```
C:\>Example
```

When the program is run, the following output is displayed:

```
A simple C# program.
```

Using the Visual C++ IDE

Beginning with Visual Studio 7, the Visual C++ IDE can compile C# programs. To edit, compile, and run a C# program using the Visual C++ 7 IDE, you will follow these steps. (If you have a different version of Visual C++, then you may need to follow different steps.)

1. Create a new, empty C# project by selecting File | New | Project. Next, select Visual C# Projects, and then Empty Project, as shown here:

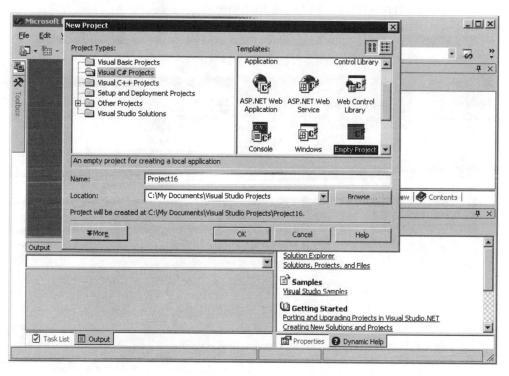

2. Once the project is created, right-click on the project name in the Solution window. Using the pop-up context menu, select Add. Then select Add New Item. Your screen will look like this.

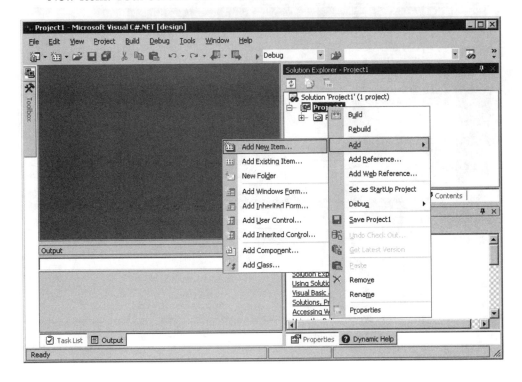

1

3. When you see the Add New Item dialog box, select Local Project Items. Finally, select C# Code File. Your screen will look like this.

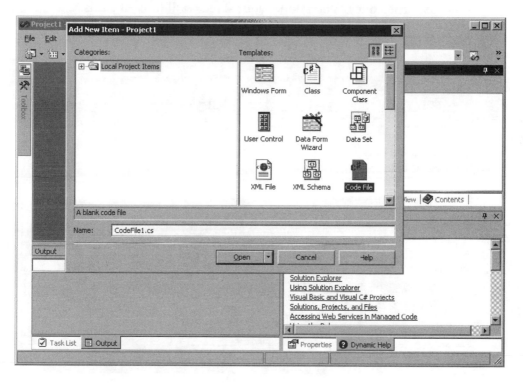

4. Enter the program and save the file using the name **Example.cs**.
(Remember, you can download the programs in this book from
www.osborne.com.) When done, your screen will look like this.

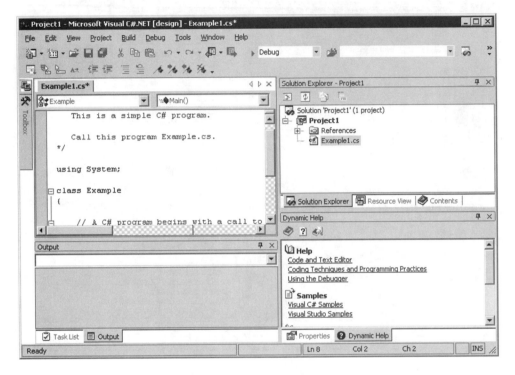

5. Compile the program by selecting Build from the Build menu.

6. Run the program by selecting Start Without Debugging from the
Debug menu.

When you run the program, you will see the window shown
in Figure 1-2.

To compile and run the sample programs in this book, you don't need to
create a new project for each one. Instead, you can use the same C# project.
Just delete the current file and add the new file. Then recompile and run.

As explained, for the short programs shown in the first part of this book,
using the **csc** command-line compiler is by far a much simpler approach.
Of course, the choice is yours.

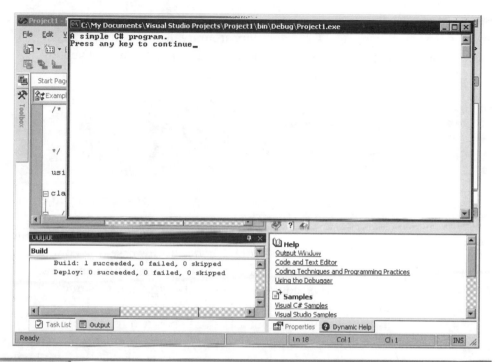

Figure 1-2 Example.exe when run under the Visual C++ IDE

The First Sample Program Line by Line

Although **Example.cs** is quite short, it includes several key features that are common to all C# programs. Let's closely examine each part of the program, beginning with its name.

The name of a C# program can be chosen arbitrarily. Unlike some computer languages (most notably, Java) in which the name of a program file is very important, this is not the case for C#. You were told to call the sample program **Example.cs** so that the instructions for compiling and running the program would apply, but as far as C# is concerned, you could have called the file by another name. For example, the preceding sample program could have been called **Sample.cs**, **Test.cs**, or even **X.cs**.

By convention, C# programs use the **.cs** file extension, and this is a convention that you should follow. Also, many programmers call a file by the name of the principal class defined within the file. This is why the filename **Example.cs** was chosen. Since the names of C# programs are arbitrary, names won't be specified for most of the sample programs in this book. Just use names of your own choosing.

The program begins with the following lines:

```
/*
   This is a simple C# program.

   Call this program Example.cs.
*/
```

This is a *comment*. Like most other programming languages, C# lets you enter remarks into a program's source file. The contents of a comment are ignored by the compiler. Instead, a comment describes or explains the operation of the program to anyone who is reading its source code. In this case, the comment describes the program and reminds you to call the source file **Example.cs**. Of course, in real applications, comments generally explain how some part of the program works or what a specific feature does.

C# supports three styles of comments. The one shown at the top of the program is called a *multiline comment*. This type of comment must begin with /* and end with */. Anything between these two comment symbols is ignored by the compiler. As the name suggests, a multiline comment can be several lines long.

The next line in the program is

```
using System;
```

This line indicates that the program is using the **System** namespace. In C#, a *namespace* defines a declarative region. Although we will look at the namespaces in detail later, a namespace provides a way to keep one set of names separate from another. In essence, names declared in one namespace will not conflict with the same names declared in another. The namespace used by the program is **System**, which is the namespace reserved for items associated with the .NET Framework class library, which is the library used by C#. The **using** keyword simply states that the program is using the names in the given namespace.

The next line of code in the program is shown here:

```
class Example {
```

This line uses the keyword **class** to declare that a new class is being defined. As mentioned, the class is C#'s basic unit of encapsulation. **Example** is the name of the class. The class definition begins with the opening curly brace ({) and ends with the closing curly brace (}). The elements between the two braces are members of the class. For the moment, don't worry too much about the details of a class except to note that in C#, all program activity occurs within one. This is one reason why all C# programs are (at least a little bit) object-oriented.

The next line in the program is the *single-line comment,* shown here:

```
// A C# program begins with a call to Main().
```

This is the second type of comment supported by C#. A *single-line comment* begins with a // and ends at the end of the line. As a general rule, programmers use multiline comments for longer remarks and single-line comments for brief, line-by-line descriptions.

The next line of code is shown here:

```
public static void Main() {
```

This line begins the **Main( )** method. As mentioned earlier, in C#, a subroutine is called a method. As the comment preceding it suggests, this is the line at which the program will begin executing. All C# applications begin execution by calling **Main( )**. (This is similar to the way C/C++ programs begin execution at **main( )**.) The complete meaning of each part of this line cannot be given now, since it involves a detailed understanding of several other C# features. However, since many of the examples in this book will use this line of code, let's take a brief look at it now.

The **public** keyword is an *access specifier.* An access specifier determines how other parts of a program can access a member of a class. When a class member is preceded by **public**, then that member can be accessed by code outside the class in which it is declared. (The opposite of **public** is **private**, which prevents a member from being used by code defined outside of its class.) In this case, **Main( )** is declared as **public** because it will be called by code outside of its class (the operating system) when the program is started.

Note

At the time of this writing, C# does not actually require **Main( )** to be declared as **public**. However, this is the way that many of the examples supplied by Visual Studio.NET declare it. It is also the way that many C# programmers prefer. For these reasons, this book will also declare **Main( )** as **public**. Don't be surprised, though, if you see it declared a bit differently.

The keyword **static** allows **Main( )** to be called before an object of its class has been created. This is necessary since **Main( )** is called at program startup. The keyword **void** simply tells the compiler that **Main( )** does not return a value. As you will see, methods can also return values. The empty parentheses that follow **Main** indicate that no information is passed to **Main( )**. As you will see, it is possible to pass information into **Main( )** or into any other method. The last character on the line is the {. This signals the start of **Main( )**'s body. All of the code that comprises a method will occur between the method's opening curly brace and its closing curly brace.

The next line of code is shown here. Notice that it occurs inside **Main( )**.

```
Console.WriteLine("A simple C# program.");
```

This line outputs the string "A simple C# program." followed by a new line on the screen. Output is actually accomplished by the built-in method **WriteLine( )**. In this case, **WriteLine( )** displays the string that is passed to it. Information that is passed to a method is called an *argument*. In addition to strings, **Write-Line( )** can be used to display other types of information, too. The line begins with **Console**, which is the name of a predefined class that supports console I/O. By connecting **Console** with **WriteLine( )**, you are telling the compiler that **WriteLine( )** is a member of the **Console** class. The fact that C# uses a class to define console output is further evidence of its object-oriented nature.

Notice that the **WriteLine( )** statement ends with a semicolon, as does the **using System** statement earlier in the program. All statements in C# end with a semicolon. The reason that several other lines in the program do not end in a semicolon is that they are not, technically, statements.

The first } in the program ends **Main( )**, and the last } ends the **Example** class definition.

Ask the Expert

Question: You said that C# supports three types of comments, but you only mentioned two. What is the third?

Answer: The third type of comment supported by C# is an *XML comment*. An XML comment uses XML tags to help you create self-documenting code.

1

One last point: C# is case-sensitive. Forgetting this can cause serious problems. For example, if you accidentally type **main** instead of **Main**, or **writeline** instead of **WriteLine**, the preceding program will be incorrect. Furthermore, although the C# compiler *will* compile classes that do not contain a **Main( )** method, it has no way to execute them. So, if you mistype **Main**, the compiler would still compile your program. However, you would also see an error message that states that **Example.exe** does not have an entry point defined.

1-Minute Drill

● Where does a C# program begin execution?

● What does **Console.WriteLine( )** do?

● What is the name of the C# command-line compiler?

Handling Syntax Errors

If you have not yet done so, enter, compile, and run the preceding program. As you may know from your previous programming experience, it is quite easy to accidentally type something incorrectly when entering code into your computer. Fortunately, if you enter something incorrectly, the compiler will report a *syntax error* message when it tries to compile it. The C# compiler attempts to make sense out of your source code no matter what you have written. For this reason, the error that is reported may not always reflect the actual cause of the problem. In the preceding program, for example, an accidental omission of the opening curly brace after the **Main( )** method generates the following sequence of errors when compiled by the **csc** command-line compiler. (Similar errors are generated when compiling using the IDE.)

```
Example.cs(12,28): error CS1002: ; expected
Example.cs(13,22): error CS1519: Invalid token '(' in class,
struct, or interface member declaration
Example.cs(15,1): error CS1022: Type or namespace definition, or
end-of-file expected
```

● **Main( )** begins a C# program's execution.
● **Console.WriteLine( )** outputs information to the console.
● The C# command-line compiler is **csc.exe**.

Clearly, the first error message is completely wrong, because what is missing is not a semicolon, but a curly brace. The second two messages are equally confusing.

The point of this discussion is that when your program contains a syntax error, don't necessarily take the compiler's messages at face value. They may be misleading. You may need to "second guess" an error message in order to find the problem. Also, look at the last few lines of code immediately preceding the one in which the error was reported. Sometimes an error will not be reported until several lines after the point at which the error really occurred.

A Small Variation

Although all of the programs in this book will use it, the statement

```
using System;
```

at the start of the first example program is not technically needed. It is, however, a valuable convenience. The reason it's not necessary is that in C# you can always *fully qualify* a name with the namespace to which it belongs. For example, the line

```
Console.WriteLine("A simple C# program.");
```

can be rewritten as

```
System.Console.WriteLine("A simple C# program.");
```

Thus, the first example could be recoded as shown here:

```
// This version does not include the using System statement.

class Example {

  // A C# program begins with a call to Main().
  public static void Main() {

    // Here, Console.WriteLine is fully qualified.
    System.Console.WriteLine("A simple C# program.");
  }
}
```

Fully qualify **Console.WriteLine**.

Since it is quite tedious to always specify the **System** namespace whenever a member of that namespace is used, most C# programmers include the **using System** statement at the top of their programs, as will all of the programs in this book. It is important to understand, however, that you can explicitly qualify a name with its namespace if needed.

A Second Simple Program

Perhaps no other construct is as important to a programming language as the assignment of a value to a variable. A *variable* is a named memory location that can be assigned a value. Further, the value of a variable can be changed during the execution of a program. That is, the content of a variable is changeable, not fixed.

The following program creates two variables called **x** and **y**:

```
// This program demonstrates variables.

using System;

class Example2 {
  public static void Main() {
    int x; // this declares a variable          ←  Declare variables.
    int y; // this declares another variable

    x = 100; // this assigns 100 to x    ←  This assigns 100 to x.

    Console.WriteLine("x contains " + x);

    y = x / 2;

    Console.Write("y contains x / 2: ");
    Console.WriteLine(y);
  }
}
```

When you run this program, you will see the following output:

```
x contains 100
y contains x / 2: 50
```

This program introduces several new concepts. First, the statement

```
int x; // this declares a variable
```

declares a variable called **x** of type integer. In C#, all variables must be declared before they are used. Further, the kind of values that the variable can hold must also be specified. This is called the *type* of the variable. In this case, **x** can hold integer values. These are whole numbers. In C#, to declare a variable to be of type integer, precede its name with the keyword **int**. Thus, the preceding statement declares a variable called **x** of type **int**.

The next line declares a second variable called **y**.

```
int y; // this declares another variable
```

Notice that its uses the same format as the first except that the name of the variable is different.

In general, to declare a variable you will use a statement like this:

type var-name;

Here, *type* specifies the type of variable being declared, and *var-name* is the name of the variable. In addition to **int**, C# supports several other data types.

The following line of code assigns **x** the value 100:

```
x = 100; // this assigns 100 to x
```

In C#, the assignment operator is the single equal sign. It copies the value on its right side into the variable on its left.

The next line of code outputs the value of **x** preceded by the string "x contains."

```
Console.WriteLine("x contains " + x);
```

In this statement, the plus sign causes the value of **x** to be displayed after the string that precedes it. This approach can be generalized. Using the + operator, you can chain together as many items as you want within a single **WriteLine( )** statement.

The next line of code assigns **y** the value of **x** divided by 2.

```
y = x / 2;
```

This line divides the value in **x** by 2, and then stores that result in **y**. Thus, after the line executes, **y** will contain the value 50. The value of **x** will be unchanged. Like most other computer languages, C# supports a full range of arithmetic operators, including those shown here:

+	Addition
–	Subtraction
*	Multiplication
/	Division

Here are the next two lines in the program:

```
Console.Write("y contains x / 2: ");
Console.WriteLine(y);
```

Two new things are occurring here. First, the built-in method **Write( )** is used to display the string "y contains x / 2:". This string is *not* followed by a new line. This means that when the next output is generated, it will start on the same line. The **Write( )** method is just like **WriteLine( )**, except that it does not output a new line after each call. Second, in the call to **WriteLine( )**, notice that **y** is used by itself. Both **Write( )** and **WriteLine( )** can be used to output values of any of C#'s built-in types.

One more point about declaring variables before we move on: It is possible to declare two or more variables using the same declaration statement. Just separate their names by commas. For example, **x** and **y** could have been declared like this:

```
int x, y; // both declared using one statement
```

Another Data Type

In the preceding program, a variable of type **int** was used. However, a variable of type **int** can hold only whole numbers. Thus, it cannot be used when a fractional component is required. For example, an **int** variable can hold the value 18, but not the value 18.3. Fortunately, **int** is only one of several data types defined by C#. To allow numbers with fractional components, C# defines two floating-point types: **float** and **double**, which represent single- and double-precision values, respectively. Of the two, **double** is probably the most commonly used.

To declare a variable of type **double**, use a statement similar to that shown here:

```
double result;
```

Here, **result** is the name of the variable, which is of type **double**. Because **result** has a floating-point type, it can hold values such as 122.23, 0.034, or −19.0.

To better understand the difference between **int** and **double**, try the following program:

```
/*
   This program illustrates the differences
   between int and double.
*/

using System;

class Example3 {
  public static void Main() {
    int ivar;    // this declares an int variable
    double dvar; // this declares a floating-point variable

    ivar = 100; // assign ivar the value 100

    dvar = 100.0; // assign dvar the value 100.0

    Console.WriteLine("Original value of ivar: " + ivar);
    Console.WriteLine("Original value of dvar: " + dvar);

    Console.WriteLine(); // print a blank line   ←──┐ Output a blank line

    // now, divide both by 3
    ivar = ivar / 3;
    dvar = dvar / 3.0;

    Console.WriteLine("ivar after division: " + ivar);
    Console.WriteLine("dvar after division: " + dvar);
  }
}
```

The output from this program is shown here:

```
Original value of ivar: 100
Original value of dvar: 100

ivar after division: 33
dvar after division: 33.3333333333333
```

As you can see, when **ivar** is divided by 3, a whole-number division is performed and the outcome is 33—the fractional component is lost. However, when **dvar** is divided by 3, the fractional component is preserved.

As the program shows, when you want to specify a floating-point value in a program, you must include a decimal point. If you don't, it will be interpreted as an integer. For example, in C#, the value 100 is an integer, but the value 100.0 is a floating-point value.

There is one other new thing to notice in the program. To print a blank line, simply call **WriteLine( )** without any arguments.

Ask the Expert

Question: Why does C# have different data types for integers and floating-point values? That is, why aren't all numeric values just the same type?

Answer: C# supplies different data types so that you can write efficient programs. For example, integer arithmetic is faster than floating-point calculations. Thus, if you don't need fractional values, then you don't need to incur the overhead associated with types **float** or **double**. Secondly, the amount of memory required for one type of data might be less than that required for another. By supplying different types, C# enables you to make best use of system resources. Finally, some algorithms require (or at least benefit from) the use of a specific type of data. C# supplies a number of built-in types to give you the greatest flexibility.

FtoC.cs

Project 1-1: Converting Fahrenheit to Celsius

Although the preceding sample programs illustrate several important features of the C# language, they are not very useful. Even though you do not know much about C# at this point, you can still put what you have learned to work to create a practical program. In this project we will create a program that converts Fahrenheit to Celsius.

The program declares two **double** variables. One will hold the number of the degrees in Fahrenheit, and the second will hold the number of degrees in Celsius after the conversion. As you may recall, the formula for converting Fahrenheit to Celsius is

$$C = 5/9 * (F - 32)$$

where C is the degrees in Celsius and F is the degrees in Fahrenheit.

Step-by-Step

1. Create a new C# file called **FtoC.cs**. (If you are using the Visual C++ IDE rather than the command line, then you will need to add this file to a C# project, as described earlier in this module.)

2. Enter the following program into the file:

```
/*
   Project 1-1

   This program converts Fahrenheit to Celsius.

   Call this program FtoC.cs.
*/

using System;

class FtoC {
  public static void Main() {
    double f; // holds the temperature in Fahrenheit
    double c; // holds the temperature in Celsius

    f = 59.0; // start with 59 degrees Fahrenheit

    c = 5.0 / 9.0 * (f - 32.0); // convert to Celsius

    Console.Write(f + " degrees Fahrenheit is ");
```

```
    Console.WriteLine(c + " degrees Celsius.");
  }
}
```

3. Compile the program using the Visual C++ IDE (using the instructions shown earlier in this module) or by using the following command line:

```
C>csc FtoC.cs
```

4. Run the program from the Visual C++ IDE or by using this command:

```
C>FtoC
```

You will see this output:

```
59 degrees Fahrenheit is 15 degrees Celsius.
```

5. As it stands, this program converts 59 degrees Fahrenheit to Celsius. However, by changing the value assigned to **f**, you can have the program convert a different temperature.

1-Minute Drill

● What is C#'s keyword for the integer data type?

● What is **double**?

● Is **using System** a necessary part of a C# program?

Two Control Statements

Inside a method, execution proceeds from one statement to the next, top to bottom. However, it is possible to alter this flow through the use of the various program control statements supported by C#. Although we will look closely at control statements later, two are briefly introduced here because we will be using them to write sample programs.

● C#'s keyword for the integer data type is **int**.
● **double** is the keyword for the double floating-point data type.
● No, but it is convenient.

The if Statement

You can selectively execute part of a program through the use of C#'s conditional statement: the **if**. The **if** statement works in C# much like the IF statement in any other language. For example, it is syntactically identical to the **if** statements in C, C++, and Java. Its simplest form is shown here:

if(*condition*) *statement;*

Here, *condition* is a Boolean (that is, true or false) expression. If *condition* is true, then the statement is executed. If *condition* is false, then the statement is bypassed. Here is an example:

```
if(10 < 11) Console.WriteLine("10 is less than 11");
```

In this case, since 10 is less than 11, the conditional expression is true, and **WriteLine( )** will execute. However, consider the following:

```
if(10 < 9) Console.WriteLine("this won't be displayed");
```

In this case, 10 is not less than 9. Thus, the call to **WriteLine( )** will not take place.

C# defines a full complement of relational operators that can be used in a conditional expression. They are shown here:

Operator	Meaning
<	Less than
<=	Less than or equal to
>	Greater than
>=	Greater than or equal to
= =	Equal to
!=	Not equal to

Notice that the test for equality is the double equal sign.

Here is a program that illustrates the **if** statement:

```
// Demonstrate the if.

using System;

class IfDemo {
```

```
public static void Main() {
  int a, b, c;

  a = 2;
  b = 3;

  if(a < b) Console.WriteLine("a is less than b");

  // this won't display anything
  if(a == b) Console.WriteLine("you won't see this");

  Console.WriteLine();                          ┌──────────────┐
                         └────────────────────│ An if statement│
  c = a - b; // c contains -1                   └──────────────┘

  Console.WriteLine("c contains -1");
  if(c >= 0) Console.WriteLine("c is non-negative");
  if(c < 0) Console.WriteLine("c is negative");

  Console.WriteLine();

  c = b - a; // c now contains 1
  Console.WriteLine("c contains 1");
  if(c >= 0) Console.WriteLine("c is non-negative");
  if(c < 0) Console.WriteLine("c is negative");

  }
}
```

The output generated by this program is shown here:

```
a is less than b

c contains -1
c is negative

c contains 1
c is non-negative
```

Notice one other thing in this program. The line

```
int a, b, c;
```

declares three variables, **a**, **b**, and **c**, by use of a comma-separated list. As mentioned earlier, when you need two or more variables of the same type, they can be declared in one statement. Just separate the variable names by commas.

The for Loop

You can repeatedly execute a sequence of code by creating a *loop*. C# supplies a powerful assortment of loop constructs. The one we will look at here is the **for** loop. If you are familiar with C, C++, or Java, then you will be pleased to know that the **for** loop in C# works the same way it does in those languages. The simplest form of the **for** loop is shown here:

for(*initialization*; *condition*; *iteration*) *statement*;

In its most common form, the *initialization* portion of the loop sets a loop control variable to an initial value. The *condition* is a Boolean expression that tests the loop control variable. If the outcome of that test is true, the **for** loop continues to iterate. If it is false, the loop terminates. The *iteration* expression determines how the loop control variable is changed each time the loop iterates. Here is a short program that illustrates the **for** loop:

```
// Demonstrate the for loop.

using System;

class ForDemo {
  public static void Main() {
    int count;                              This loop iterates 5 times.

    for(count = 0; count < 5; count = count+1)
      Console.WriteLine("This is count: " + count);

    Console.WriteLine("Done!");
  }
}
```

The output generated by the program is shown here:

```
This is count: 0
This is count: 1
This is count: 2
This is count: 3
```

```
This is count: 4
Done!
```

In this example, **count** is the loop control variable. It is set to zero in the initialization portion of the **for**. At the start of each iteration (including the first one), the conditional test **count < 5** is performed. If the outcome of this test is true, the **WriteLine( )** statement is executed, and then the iteration portion of the loop is executed. This process continues until the conditional test is false, at which point execution picks up at the bottom of the loop.

As a point of interest, in professionally written C# programs you will almost never see the iteration portion of the loop written as shown in the preceding program. That is, you will seldom see statements like this:

```
count = count + 1;
```

The reason is that C# includes a special increment operator that performs this operation more efficiently. The increment operator is **++** (that is, the double plus sign). The increment operator increases its operand by one. By use of the increment operator, the preceding statement can be written like this:

```
count++;
```

Thus, the **for** in the preceding program will usually be written like this:

```
for(count = 0; count < 5; count++)
```

You might want to try this. As you will see, the loop still runs exactly the same as it did before.

C# also provides a decrement operator, which is specified as **– –** (the double minus sign). This operator decreases its operand by one.

1-Minute Drill

- What does the **if** statement do?
- What does the **for** statement do?
- What are C#'s relational operators?

- **if** is the conditional statement.
- The **for** is one of C#'s loop statements.
- The relational operators are ==, !=, <, >, <=, and >=.

Using Blocks of Code

Another key element of C# is the *code block*. A code block is a grouping of two or more statements. This is done by enclosing the statements between opening and closing curly braces. Once a block of code has been created, it becomes a logical unit that can be used any place that a single statement can. For example, a block can be a target for **if** and **for** statements. Consider this **if** statement:

```
if(w < h) {
  v = w * h;
  w = 0;
}
```

Here, if **w** is less than **h**, then both statements inside the block will be executed. Thus, the two statements inside the block form a logical unit, and one statement cannot execute without the other also executing. The key point here is that whenever you need to logically link two or more statements, you do so by creating a block. Code blocks allow many algorithms to be implemented with greater clarity and efficiency.

Here is a program that uses a block of code to prevent a division by zero:

```
// Demonstrate a block of code.

using System;

class BlockDemo {
  public static void Main() {
    int i, j, d;

    i = 5;
    j = 10;

    // the target of this if is a block
    if(i != 0) {
      Console.WriteLine("i does not equal zero");
      d = j / i;
      Console.WriteLine("j / i is " + d);
    }
  }
}
```

The target of the **if** is this entire block.

Ask the Expert

Question: Does the use of a code block introduce any runtime inefficiencies? In other words, do the { and } consume any extra time during the execution of my program?

Answer: No. Code blocks do not add any overhead whatsoever. In fact, because of their ability to simplify the coding of certain algorithms, their use generally increases speed and efficiency.

The output generated by this program is shown here:

```
i does not equal zero
j / i is 2
```

In this case, the target of the **if** statement is a block of code and not just a single statement. If the condition controlling the **if** is true (as it is in this case), the three statements inside the block will be executed. Try setting **i** to zero and observe the result.

As you will see later in this book, blocks of code have additional properties and uses. However, the main reason for their existence is to create logically inseparable units of code.

Semicolons and Positioning

In C#, the semicolon signals the end of a statement. That is, each individual statement must end with a semicolon.

As you know, a block is a set of logically connected statements that are surrounded by opening and closing braces. A block is *not* terminated with a semicolon. Since a block is a group of statements, with a semicolon after each statement, it makes sense that a block is not terminated by a semicolon; instead, the end of the block is indicated by the closing brace.

C# does not recognize the end of the line as the end of a statement—only a semicolon terminates a statement. For this reason, it does not matter where on a line you put a statement. For example, to C#,

```
x = y;
y = y + 1;
Console.WriteLine(x + " " + y);
```

is the same as

```
x = y;  y = y + 1;  Console.WriteLine(x + " " + y);
```

Furthermore, the individual elements of a statement can also be put on separate lines. For example, the following is perfectly acceptable:

```
Console.WriteLine("This is a long line of output" +
                  x + y + z +
                  "more output");
```

Breaking long lines in this fashion is often used to make programs more readable. It can also help prevent excessively long lines from wrapping.

Indentation Practices

You may have noticed in the previous examples that certain statements were indented. C# is a free-form language, meaning that it does not matter where you place statements relative to each other on a line. However, over the years, a common and accepted indentation style has developed that allows for very readable programs. This book follows that style, and it is recommended that you do so as well. Using this style, you indent one level after each opening brace, and move back out one level after each closing brace. There are certain statements that encourage some additional indenting; these will be covered later.

1-Minute Drill

● How is a block of code created? What does it do?

● In C#, statements are terminated by a _____.

● All C# statements must start and end on one line. True or false?

● A block is started by a {. It is ended by a }. A block creates a logical unit of code.
● A semicolon terminates C# statements.
● False.

FtoCTable.cs

Project 1-2: Improving the Temperature Conversion Program

You can use the **for** loop, the **if** statement, and code blocks to create an improved version of the Fahrenheit-to-Celsius converter that you developed in the first project. This new version will print a table of conversions, beginning with 0 degrees Fahrenheit and ending at 99. After every 10 degrees, a blank line will be output. This is accomplished through the use of a variable called **counter** that counts the number of lines that have been output. Pay special attention to its use.

Step-by-Step

1. Create a new file called **FtoCTable.cs**.

2. Enter the following program into the file:

```
/*
    Project 1-2

    This program displays a conversion
    table of Fahrenheit to Celsius.

    Call this program FtoCTable.cs.
*/

using System;

class FtoCTable {
  public static void Main() {
    double f, c;
    int counter;

    counter = 0;              ◄———— Line counter is initially set to zero.
    for(f = 0.0; f < 100.0; f++) {
      c = 5.0 / 9.0 * (f - 32.0); // convert to Celsius
      Console.WriteLine(f + " degrees Fahrenheit is " +
                        c + " degrees Celsius.");

      counter++;   ◄———— Increment the line counter with each loop iteration.

      // every 10th line, print a blank line
      if(counter == 10) {      ◄———— If counter is 10,
        Console.WriteLine();          output a blank line.
```

```
        counter = 0; // reset the line counter
      }
    }
  }
}
```

3. Compile the program using the Visual C++ IDE or the following command line:

```
C>csc FtoCTable.cs
```

4. Run the program using the Visual C++ IDE or by using this command line:

```
C>FtoCTable
```

Here is a portion of the output that you will see. Notice that results that don't produce an even result include a fractional component.

```
0 degrees Fahrenheit is -17.7777777777778 degrees Celsius.
1 degrees Fahrenheit is -17.2222222222222 degrees Celsius.
2 degrees Fahrenheit is -16.6666666666667 degrees Celsius.
3 degrees Fahrenheit is -16.1111111111111 degrees Celsius.
4 degrees Fahrenheit is -15.5555555555556 degrees Celsius.
5 degrees Fahrenheit is -15 degrees Celsius.
6 degrees Fahrenheit is -14.4444444444444 degrees Celsius.
7 degrees Fahrenheit is -13.8888888888889 degrees Celsius.
8 degrees Fahrenheit is -13.3333333333333 degrees Celsius.
9 degrees Fahrenheit is -12.7777777777778 degrees Celsius.

10 degrees Fahrenheit is -12.2222222222222 degrees Celsius.
11 degrees Fahrenheit is -11.6666666666667 degrees Celsius.
12 degrees Fahrenheit is -11.1111111111111 degrees Celsius.
13 degrees Fahrenheit is -10.5555555555556 degrees Celsius.
14 degrees Fahrenheit is -10 degrees Celsius.
15 degrees Fahrenheit is -9.44444444444444 degrees Celsius.
16 degrees Fahrenheit is -8.88888888888889 degrees Celsius.
17 degrees Fahrenheit is -8.33333333333333 degrees Celsius.
18 degrees Fahrenheit is -7.77777777777778 degrees Celsius.
19 degrees Fahrenheit is -7.22222222222222 degrees Celsius.
```

The C# Keywords

There are currently 77 keywords defined in the C# language (see Table 1-1). These keywords, combined with the syntax of the operators and separators,

abstract	as	base	bool	break
byte	case	catch	char	checked
class	const	continue	decimal	default
delegate	do	double	else	enum
event	explicit	extern	false	finally
fixed	float	for	foreach	goto
if	implicit	in	int	interface
internal	is	lock	long	namespace
new	null	object	operator	out
override	params	private	protected	public
readonly	ref	return	sbyte	sealed
short	sizeof	stackalloc	static	string
struct	switch	this	throw	true
try	typeof	uint	ulong	unchecked
unsafe	ushort	using	virtual	volatile
void	while			

Table 1-1   The C# Keywords

form the definition of the C# language. These keywords cannot be used as names for a variable, class, or method.

Identifiers

In C#, an identifier is a name assigned to a method, a variable, or any other user-defined item. Identifiers can be from one to several characters long. Variable names may start with any letter of the alphabet or with an underscore. Next may be a letter, a digit, or an underscore. The underscore can be used to enhance the readability of a variable name, as in **line_count**. Uppercase and lowercase are different; that is, to C#, **myvar** and **MyVar** are separate names. Here are some examples of acceptable identifiers:

Test	x	y2	MaxLoad
up	_top	my_var	sample23

Remember that you can't start an identifier with a digit. Thus, **12x** is invalid, for example. Good programming practice dictates that you use identifier names that reflect the meaning or usage of the items being named.

Although you cannot use any of the C# keywords as identifier names, C# does allow you to precede a keyword with an @, allowing it to be a legal identifier. For example, **@for** is a valid identifier. In this case, the identifier is actually **for** and the @ is ignored. Frankly, using @-qualified keywords for identifiers is not recommended, except for special purposes. Technically, the @ can precede any identifier, but this is considered bad practice.

1-Minute Drill

● Which is the keyword, **for**, **For**, or **FOR**?

● A C# identifier can contain what type of characters?

● Are **index21** and **Index21** the same identifier?

The C# Class Library

The sample programs shown in this chapter make use of two of C#'s built-in methods: **WriteLine( )** and **Write( )**. As mentioned, these methods are members of the **Console** class, which is part of the **System** namespace, which is defined by the .NET Framework's class library. As explained earlier in this module, the C# environment relies on the .NET Framework class library to provide support for such things as I/O, string handling, networking, and GUIs. Thus, C# as a totality is a combination of the C# language itself, plus the .NET standard classes. As you will see, the class library provides much of the functionality that is part of any C# program. Indeed, part of becoming a C# programmer is learning to use these standard classes. Throughout this book, various elements of the .NET library classes and methods are described. However, the .NET library is quite large, and it is something that you will also want to explore more on your own.

● The keyword is **for**. In C#, all keywords are in lowercase.

● A C# identifier can contain letters, digits, and the underscore.

● No, C# is case-sensitive.

☑ *Mastery Check*

1. What is the MSIL and why is it important to C#?

2. What is the Common Language Runtime?

3. What are the three main principles of object-oriented programming?

4. Where do C# programs begin execution?

5. What is a variable? What is a namespace?

6. Which of the following variable names is invalid?

    A. count

    B. $count

    C. count27

    D. 67count

    E. @if

7. How do you create a single-line comment? How do you create a multiline comment?

8. Show the general form of the **if** statement. Show the general form of the **for** loop.

9. How do you create a block of code?

10. Is it necessary to start each C# program with the following statement?

    ```
    using System;
    ```

11. The moon's gravity is about 17 percent that of Earth's. Write a program that computes your effective weight on the moon.

12. Adapt Project 1-2 so that it prints a conversion table of inches to meters. Display 12 feet of conversions, inch-by-inch. Output a blank line every 12 inches. (One meter equals approximately 39.37 inches.)

Module 2

Introducing Data Types and Operators

The Goals of This Module

- Learn C#'s basic types
- Use literals
- Create initialized variables
- Know the scope rules of a method
- Understand type conversion and casting
- Learn the arithmetic operators
- Learn the relational and logical operators
- Explore the assignment operator
- Examine expressions

At the foundation of any programming language are its data types and operators, and C# is no exception. These elements define the limits of a language and determine the kind of tasks to which it can be applied. As you might expect, C# supports a rich assortment of both data types and operators, making it suitable for a wide range of programming.

Data types and operators are a large subject. We will begin here with an examination of C#'s foundational data types and its most commonly used operators. We will also take a closer look at variables and examine the expression.

Why Data Types Are Important

Data types are especially important in C# because it is a strongly typed language. This means that all operations are type-checked by the compiler for type compatibility. Illegal operations will not be compiled. Thus, strong type-checking helps prevent errors and enhances reliability. To enable strong type-checking, all variables, expressions, and values have a type. There is no concept of a "typeless" variable, for example. Furthermore, the type of a value determines what operations are allowed on it. An operation allowed on one type might not be allowed on another.

C#'s Value Types

C# contains two general categories of built-in data types: *value types* and *reference types*. C#'s reference types are defined by classes, and a discussion of classes is deferred until later. However, at the core of C# are its 13 value types, which are shown in Table 2-1. The value types are also known as *simple types*.

Type	Meaning
bool	Represents true/false values
byte	8-bit unsigned integer
char	Character
decimal	Numeric type for financial calculations
double	Double-precision floating point
float	Single-precision floating point

Table 2-1   The C# Value Types

Type	Meaning
int	Integer
long	Long integer
sbyte	8-bit signed integer
short	Short integer
uint	Unsigned integer
ulong	Unsigned long integer
ushort	Unsigned short integer

Table 2-1   The C# Value Types (*continued*)

C# strictly specifies a range and behavior for each value type. Because of portability requirements, C# is uncompromising on this account. For example, an **int** is the same in all execution environments. There is no need to rewrite code to fit a specific platform. While strictly specifying the size of the value types may cause a small loss of performance in some environments, it is necessary in order to achieve portability.

Integers

C# defines nine integer types: **char**, **byte**, **sbyte**, **short**, **ushort**, **int**, **uint**, **long**, and **ulong**. However, the **char** type is primarily used for representing characters, and it is discussed later in this module. The remaining eight integer types are used for numeric calculations. Their bit-width and ranges are shown here:

Type	Width in Bits	Range
byte	8	0 to 255
sbyte	8	−128 to 127
short	16	−32,768 to 32,767
ushort	16	0 to 65,535
int	32	−2,147,483,648 to 2,147,483,647
uint	32	0 to 4,294,967,295
long	64	−9,223,372,036,854,775,808 to 9,223,372,036,854,775,807
ulong	64	0 to 18,446,744,073,709,551,615

As the table shows, C# defines both signed and unsigned versions of the various integer types. The difference between signed and unsigned integers is in the way the high-order bit of the integer is interpreted. If a signed integer is specified, then the C# compiler will generate code that assumes that the high-order bit of an integer is to be used as a *sign flag*. If the sign flag is 0, then the number is positive; if it is 1, then the number is negative. Negative numbers are almost always represented using the *two's complement* approach. In this method, all bits in the number (except the sign flag) are reversed, and then 1 is added to this number. Finally, the sign flag is set to 1.

Signed integers are important for a great many algorithms, but they have only half the absolute magnitude of their unsigned relatives. For example, as a **short**, here is 32,767:

01111111 11111111

For a signed value, if the high-order bit were set to 1, the number would then be interpreted as –1 (assuming the two's complement format). However, if you declared this to be a **ushort**, then when the high-order bit was set to 1, the number would become 65,535.

Probably the most commonly used integer type is **int**. Variables of type **int** are often employed to control loops, to index arrays, and for general-purpose integer math. When you need an integer that has a range greater than **int**, you have many options. If the value you want to store is unsigned, you can use **uint**. For large signed values, use **long**. For large unsigned values, use **ulong**.

Here is a program that computes the number of cubic inches contained in a cube that is 1 mile long on each side. Because this value is so large, the program uses a **long** variable to hold it.

```
/*
   Compute the number of cubic inches
   in 1 cubic mile.
*/

using System;

class Inches {
  static void Main() {
    long ci;
    long im;

    im = 5280 * 12;
```

```
    ci = im * im * im;

    Console.WriteLine("There are " + ci +
                      " cubic inches in cubic mile.");

  }
}
```

Here is the output from the program:

```
There are 254358061056000 cubic inches in cubic mile.
```

Clearly, the result could not have been held in an **int** or **uint** variable.

The smallest integer types are **byte** and **sbyte**. The **byte** type is an unsigned value between 0 and 255. Variables of type **byte** are especially useful when working with raw binary data, such as a byte stream of data produced by some device. For small signed integers, use **sbyte**. Here is an example that uses a variable of type **byte** to control a **for** loop that produces the summation of the number 100:

```
// Use byte.

using System;

class Use_byte {
  static void Main() {
    byte x;
    int sum;

    sum = 0;
    for(x = 1; x <= 100; x++)
      sum = sum + x;

    Console.WriteLine("Summation of 100 is " + sum);
  }
}
```

The output from the program is shown here:

```
Summation of 100 is 5050
```

Since the **for** loop runs only from 0 to 100, which is well within the range of a **byte**, there is no need to use a larger type variable to control it.

When you need an integer that is larger than a **byte** or **sbyte**, but smaller than an **int** or **uint**, use **short** or **ushort**.

Floating-Point Types

As explained in Module 1, the floating-point types can represent numbers that have fractional components. There are two kinds of floating-point types, **float** and **double**, which represent single- and double-precision numbers, respectively. The type **float** is 32 bits wide and has a range of 1.5E–45 to 3.4E+38. The **double** type is 64 bits wide and has a range of 5E–324 to 1.7E+308.

Of the two, **double** is the most commonly used. One reason for this is that many of the math functions in C#'s class library (which is the .NET Framework library) use **double** values. For example, the **Sqrt( )** method (which is defined by the standard **System.Math** class) returns a **double** value that is the square root of its **double** argument. Here, **Sqrt( )** is used to compute the length of the hypotenuse given the lengths of the two opposing sides:

```
/*
   Use the Pythagorean theorem to
   find the length of the hypotenuse
   given the lengths of the two opposing
   sides.
*/

using System;

class Hypot {
  static void Main() {
    double x, y, z;

    x = 3;
    y = 4;

    z = Math.Sqrt(x*x + y*y);

    Console.WriteLine("Hypotenuse is " + z);
  }
}
```

Notice how **Sqrt( )** is called. It is preceded by the name of the class of which it is a member.

The output from the program is shown here:

```
Hypotenuse is 5
```

Here's another point about the preceding example. As mentioned, **Sqrt( )** is a member of the **Math** class. Notice how **Sqrt( )** is called; it is preceded by the name **Math**. This is similar to the way **Console** precedes **WriteLine( )**. Although not all standard methods are called by specifying their class name first, several are.

The decimal Type

Perhaps the most interesting C# numeric type is **decimal**, which is intended for use in monetary calculations. The **decimal** type utilizes 128 bits to represent values within the range 1E–28 to 7.9E+28. As you may know, normal floating-point arithmetic is subject to a variety of rounding errors when it is applied to decimal values. The **decimal** type eliminates these errors and can accurately represent up to 28 decimal places (or 29 places in some cases). This ability to represent decimal values without rounding errors makes its especially useful for computations that involve money.

Here is a program that uses the **decimal** type in a financial calculation. The program computes a balance after interest has been applied.

```
/*
   Use the decimal type in a financial calculation.
*/

using System;

class UseDecimal {
  public static void Main() {
    decimal balance;
    decimal rate;

    // compute new balance
    balance = 1000.10m;    ◄──────  decimal values must be
    rate = 0.1m;                    followed by an m or M.
    balance = balance * rate + balance;

    Console.WriteLine("New balance: $" + balance);
  }
}
```

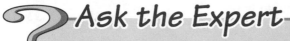

Ask the Expert

Question: The other computer languages that I have worked with do not have a decimal data type. Is it unique to C#?

Answer: The decimal type is not supported by C, C++, or Java. Thus, within its direct line of descent, it is unique.

The output from this program is shown here:

```
New balance: $1100.11
```

In the program, notice that the decimal constants are followed by the **m** or **M** suffix. This is necessary because without the suffix, these values would be interpreted as standard floating-point constants, which are not compatible with the **decimal** data type. (We will look more closely at how to specify numeric constants later in this module.)

1-Minute Drill

● What are C#'s integer types?

● What are the two floating-point types?

● What makes **decimal** important for financial calculations?

Characters

In C#, characters are not 8-bit quantities like they are in many other computer languages, such as C++. Instead, C# uses Unicode. *Unicode* defines a character set that can represent all of the characters found in all human languages. Thus,

---

● The integer types are **byte**, **short**, **int**, **long**, **sbyte**, **ushort**, **uint**, and **ulong**. The **char** type is also technically a numeric type, but it is used mostly for holding characters.
● The floating-point types are **float** and **double**.
● The **decimal** type is valuable for financial calculations because it does not suffer from the rounding errors that can affect **float** and **double**.

in C#, **char** is an unsigned 16-bit type having a range of 0 to 65,535. The standard 8-bit ASCII character set is a subset of Unicode and ranges from 0 to 127. Thus, the ASCII characters are still valid C# characters.

A character variable can be assigned a value by enclosing the character inside single quotes. For example, this assigns X to the variable **ch**:

```
char ch;
ch = 'X';
```

You can output a char value using a **WriteLine( )** statement. For example, this line outputs the value in **ch**:

```
Console.WriteLine("This is ch: " + ch);
```

Although **char** is defined by C# as an integer type, it cannot be freely mixed with integers in all cases. This is because there are no automatic type conversions from integer to **char**. For example, the following fragment is invalid:

```
char ch;

ch = 10; // error, won't work
```

The reason the preceding code will not work is that 10 is an integer value and it won't automatically convert to a **char**. Thus, the assignment involves incompatible types. If you attempt to compile this code, you will see an error message.

Later in this module you will see a way around this restriction.

Ask the Expert

Question: Why does C# use Unicode?

Answer: C# was designed to allow programs to be written for worldwide use. Thus, it needs to use a character set that can represent all of the world's languages. Unicode is the standard character set designed expressly for this purpose. Of course, the use of Unicode is inefficient for languages such as English, German, Spanish, or French, whose characters can be contained within 8 bits. But such is the price of global portability.

The bool Type

The **bool** type represents true/false values. C# defines the values true and false using the reserved words **true** and **false**. Thus, a variable or expression of type **bool** will be one of these two values. Furthermore, there is no conversion defined between **bool** and integer values. For example, 1 does not convert to true, and 0 does not convert to false.

Here is a program that demonstrates the **bool** type:

```
// Demonstrate bool values.

using System;

class BoolDemo {
  static void Main() {
    bool b;

    b = false;
    Console.WriteLine("b is " + b);
    b = true;
    Console.WriteLine("b is " + b);

    // a bool value can control the if statement
    if(b) Console.WriteLine("This is executed.");

    b = false;
    if(b) Console.WriteLine("This is not executed.");

    // outcome of a relational operator is a bool value
    Console.WriteLine("10 > 9 is " + (10 > 9));
  }
}
```

A single **bool** value can control an **if** statement.

The output generated by this program is shown here:

```
b is false
b is true
This is executed.
10 > 9 is true
```

There are three interesting things to notice about this program. First, as you can see, when a **bool** value is output by **WriteLine( )**, "true" or "false" is displayed. Second, the value of a **bool** variable is sufficient, by itself, to control the **if** statement. There is no need to write an **if** statement like this:

```
if(b == true) ...
```

Third, the outcome of a relational operator, such as <, is a **bool** value. This is why the expression 10 > 9 displays the value "true." Further, the extra set of parentheses around 10 > 9 is necessary because the + operator has a higher precedence than the >.

1-Minute Drill

- What is Unicode?
- What values can a **bool** variable have?
- In bits, what is the size of a **char**?

Some Output Options

Before continuing our examination of data types and operators, a small digression will be useful. Up to this point, when outputting lists of data, you have been separating each part of the list with a plus sign, as shown here:

```
Console.WriteLine("You ordered " + 2 + " items at $" + 3 + " each.");
```

While very convenient, outputting numeric information in this way does not give you any control over how that information appears. For example, for a floating-point value, you can't control the number of decimal places displayed. Consider the following statement:

```
Console.WriteLine("Here is 10/3: " + 10.0/3.0);
```

- Unicode is a 16-bit fully international character set.
- Variables of type **bool** can be either **true** or **false**.
- The **char** type is 16 bits wide.

It generates this output:

```
Here is 10/3: 3.33333333333333
```

While this might be fine for some purposes, displaying so many decimal places could be inappropriate for others. For example, in financial calculations, you will usually want to display two decimal places.

To control how numeric data is formatted, you will need to use a second form of **WriteLine( )**, shown here, which allows you to embed formatting information:

WriteLine("*format string*", *arg0, arg1, ... , argN*);

In this version, the arguments to **WriteLine( )** are separated by commas and not + signs. The *format string* contains two items: regular, printing characters that are displayed as-is and format specifiers. Format specifiers take this general form:

{*argnum, width: fmt*}

Here, *argnum* specifies the number of the argument (starting from zero) to display. The minimum width of the field is specified by *width,* and the format is specified by *fmt.*

During execution, when a format specifier is encountered in the format string, the corresponding argument, as specified by *argnum*, is substituted and displayed. Thus, it is the position of a format specification within the format string that determines where its matching data will be displayed. Both *width* and *fmt* are optional. Thus, in its simplest form, a format specifier simply indicates which argument to display. For example, {0} indicates *arg0,* {1} specifies *arg1,* and so on.

Let's begin with a simple example. The statement

```
Console.WriteLine("February has {0} or {1} days.", 28, 29);
```

produces the following output:

```
February has 28 or 29 days.
```

As you can see, the value 28 is substituted for {0}, and 29 is substituted for {1}. Thus, the format specifiers identify the location at which the subsequent arguments, in this case 28 and 29, are displayed within the string. Furthermore, notice that the additional values are separated by commas, not + signs.

Here is a variation of the preceding statement that specifies minimum field widths:

```
Console.WriteLine("February has {0,10} or {1,5} days.", 28, 29);
```

It produces the following output:

```
February has         28 or    29 days.
```

As you can see, spaces have been added to fill out the unused portions of the fields. Remember, a minimum field width is just that: the *minimum* width. Output can exceed that width if needed.

In the preceding examples, no formatting was applied to the values, themselves. Of course, the value of using format specifiers is to control the way the data looks. The types of data most commonly formatted are floating-point and decimal values. One of the easiest ways to specify a format is to describe a template that **WriteLine( )** will use. To do this, show an example of the format that you want, using #s to mark the digit positions. For instance, here is a better way to display 10 divided by 3:

```
Console.WriteLine("Here is 10/3: {0:#.##}", 10.0/3.0);
```

The output from this statement is shown here:

```
Here is 10/3: 3.33
```

In this example, the template is #.##, which tells **WriteLine( )** to display two decimal places. It is important to understand, however, that **WriteLine( )** will display more than one digit to the left of the decimal point if necessary so as not to misrepresent the value.

If you want to display values using a dollars and cents format, use the **C** format specifier. For example,

```
decimal balance;

balance = 12323.09m;
Console.WriteLine("Current balance is {0:C}", balance);
```

The output from this sequence is shown here.

```
Current balance is $12,323.09
```

Mars.cs

Project 2-1: Talking to Mars

At its closest point to Earth, Mars is approximately 34 million miles away. Assuming there is someone on Mars that you want to talk with, what is the delay between the time a radio signal leaves Earth and the time it arrives on Mars? This project creates a program that answers this question. Recall that light travels approximately 186,000 miles per second. Thus, to compute the delay, you will need to divide the distance by the speed of light. Display the delay in terms of seconds and in minutes.

Step-by-Step

1. Create a new file called **Mars.cs**.

2. To compute the delay, you will need to use floating-point values. Why? Because the time interval will have a fractional component. Here are the variables used by the program:

```
double distance;
double lightspeed;
double delay;
double delay_in_min;
```

3. Give **distance** and **lightspeed** initial values, as shown here:

```
distance = 34000000; // 34,000,000 miles
lightspeed = 186000; // 186,000 per second
```

4. To compute the delay, divide **distance** by **lightspeed**. This yields the delay in seconds. Assign this value to **delay** and display the results. These steps are shown here:

```
delay = distance / lightspeed;

Console.WriteLine("Time delay when talking to Mars: " +
                       delay + " seconds.");
```

5. Divide the number of seconds in **delay** by 60 to obtain the delay in minutes; display that result using these lines of code:

```
delay_in_min = delay / 60;

Console.WriteLine("This is " + delay_in_min +
                       " minutes.");
```

Here is the entire **Mars.cs** program listing:

```
/*
   Project 2-1
```

```
   Talking to Mars

   Call this file Mars.cs
*/

using System;

class Mars {
  static void Main() {
    double distance;
    double lightspeed;
    double delay;
    double delay_in_min;

    distance = 34000000; // 34,000,000 miles
    lightspeed = 186000; // 186,000 per second

    delay = distance / lightspeed;

    Console.WriteLine("Time delay when talking to Mars: " +
                      delay + " seconds.");

    delay_in_min = delay / 60;

    Console.WriteLine("This is " + delay_in_min +
                      " minutes.");
  }
}
```

6. Compile and run the program. The following result is displayed:

```
Time delay when talking to Mars: 182.795698924731 seconds.
This is 3.04659498207885 minutes.
```

7. For most people, the program displays too many decimal places. To improve
the readability of the program, substitute the following **WriteLine( )**
statements for the ones shown in the program:

```
Console.WriteLine("Time delay when talking to Mars: {0:###.###} seconds",
                  delay);

Console.WriteLine("This is about {0:###.###} minutes", delay_in_min);
```

8. Recompile and run the program. When you do, you will see this output:

```
Time delay when talking to Mars: 182.796 seconds
This is about 3.047 minutes
```

Now, only three decimal places are displayed.

Literals

In C#, *literals* refer to fixed values that are represented in their human-readable form. For example, the number 100 is a literal. Literals are also commonly called *constants*. For the most part, literals and their usage are so intuitive that they have been used in one form or another by all the preceding sample programs. Now the time has come to explain them formally.

C# literals can be of any of the value types. The way each literal is represented depends upon its type. As explained earlier, character constants are enclosed between single quotes. For example 'a' and '%' are both character constants.

Integer literals are specified as numbers without fractional components. For example, 10 and −100 are integer constants. Floating-point constants require the use of the decimal point followed by the number's fractional component. For example, 11.123 is a floating-point constant. C# also allows you to use scientific notation for floating-point numbers.

Since C# is a strongly typed language, literals, too, have a type. Naturally, this raises the following question: What is the type of a numeric literal? For example, what is the type of 12, 123987, or 0.23? Fortunately, C# specifies some easy-to-follow rules that answer these questions.

First, for integer literals, the type of the literal is the smallest integer type that will hold it, beginning with **int**. Thus, an integer literal is either of type **int**, **uint**, **long**, or **ulong**, depending upon its value. Second, floating-point literals are of type **double**.

If C#'s default type is not what you want for a literal, you can explicitly specify its type by including a suffix. To specify a **long** literal, append an *l* or an *L*. For example, 12 is an **int**, but 12L is a **long**. To specify an unsigned integer value, append a *u* or *U*. Thus, 100 is an **int**, but 100U is a **uint**. To specify an unsigned, long integer, use *ul* or *UL*. For example, 984375UL is of type **ulong**.

To specify a **float** literal, append an *F* or *f* to the constant. For example, 10.19F is of type **float**.

To specify a **decimal** literal, follow its value with an *m* or *M*. For example, 9.95M is a **decimal** literal.

Although integer literals create an **int**, **uint**, **long**, or **ulong** value by default, they can still be assigned to variables of type **byte**, **sbyte**, **short**, or **ushort** as long as the value being assigned can be represented by the target type. An integer literal can always be assigned to a **long** variable.

Hexadecimal Literals

As you probably know, in programming it is sometimes easier to use a number system based on 16 instead of 10. The base 16 number system is called *hexadecimal* and uses the digits 0 through 9 plus the letters A through F, which stand for 10, 11, 12, 13, 14, and 15. For example, the hexadecimal number 10 is 16 in decimal. Because of the frequency with which hexadecimal numbers are used, C# allows you to specify integer constants in hexadecimal format. A hexadecimal literal must begin with 0x (a zero followed by an *x*). Here are some examples:

```
count = 0xFF; // 255 in decimal
incr = 0x1a;  // 26 in decimal
```

Character Escape Sequences

Enclosing character constants in single quotes works for most printing characters, but a few characters, such as the carriage return, pose a special problem when a text editor is used. In addition, certain other characters, such as the single and double quotes, have special meaning in C#, so you cannot use them directly. For these reasons, C# provides special *escape sequences,* sometimes referred to as *backslash character constants,* shown in Table 2-2. These sequences are used in place of the characters that they represent.

For example, this assigns **ch** the tab character:

```
ch = '\t';
```

The next example assigns a single quote to **ch**:

```
ch = '\'';
```

Escape Sequence	Description
\a	Alert (bell)
\b	Backspace
\f	Form feed
\n	New line (linefeed)

Table 2-2   Character Escape Sequences

Escape Sequence	Description
\r	Carriage return
\t	Horizontal tab
\v	Vertical tab
\0	Null
\'	Single quote
\"	Double quote
\\	Backslash

Table 2-2 Character Escape Sequences (*continued*)

String Literals

C# supports one other type of literal: the string. A *string* is a set of characters enclosed by double quotes. For example,

```
"this is a test"
```

is a string. You have seen examples of strings in many of the **WriteLine( )** statements in the preceding sample programs.

In addition to normal characters, a string literal can also contain one or more of the escape sequences just described. For example, consider the following program. It uses the **\n** and **\t** escape sequences.

```
// Demonstrate escape sequences in strings.

using System;

class StrDemo {
  static void Main() {
    Console.WriteLine("First line\nSecond line");
    Console.WriteLine("A\tB\tC");
    Console.WriteLine("D\tE\tF");
  }
}
```

Use \n to generate a new line.

Use tabs to align output.

The output is shown here:

```
First line
Second line
A       B       C
D       E       F
```

Ask the Expert

Question: I know that C++ allows integer literals to be specified in octal (a number system based on 8). Does C# allow octal literals?

Answer: No. C# allows integer literals to be specified only in decimal or hexadecimal form. Octal is seldom used in today's modern programming environments.

Notice how the **\n** escape sequence is used to generate a new line. You don't need to use multiple **WriteLine( )** statements to get multiline output. Just embed **\n** within a longer string at the points at which you want the new lines to occur.

In addition to the form of string literal just described, you can also specify a *verbatim string literal*. A verbatim string literal begins with an @, which is followed by a quoted string. The contents of the quoted string are accepted without modification and can span two or more lines. Thus, you can include newlines, tabs, and so on, but you don't need to use the escape sequences. The only exception is that to obtain a double quote ("), you must use two double quotes in a row (""). Here is a program that demonstrates verbatim string literals:

```
// Demonstrate verbatim literal strings.

using System;

class Verbatim {
  static void Main() {
    Console.WriteLine(@"This is a verbatim
string literal
that spans several lines.
");
    Console.WriteLine(@"Here is some tabbed output:
1    2    3    4
5    6    7    8
");
    Console.WriteLine(@"Programmers say, ""I like C#.""");
  }
}
```

This verbatim quote contains embedded newlines.

This one contains tabs, too.

The output from this program is shown here:

```
This is a verbatim
string literal
that spans several lines.

Here is some tabbed output:
1       2       3       4
5       6       7       8

Programmers say, "I like C#."
```

The important point to notice about the preceding program is that the verbatim string literals are displayed precisely as they are entered into the program.

The advantage of verbatim string literals is that you can specify output in your program exactly as it will appear on the screen. However, in the case of multiline strings, the wrapping will cause the indentation of your program to be obscured. For this reason, the programs in this book will not use verbatim string literals. That said, they are still a wonderful benefit for many formatting situations.

1-Minute Drill

- What is the type of the literal 10? What is the type of the literal 10.0?
- How do you specify 100 as a **long**? How do you specify 100 as a **uint**?
- What is @"testing"?

Ask the Expert

Question: Is a string consisting of a single character the same as a character literal? For example, is "k" the same as 'k'?

Answer: No. You must not confuse strings with characters. A character literal represents a single letter of type **char**. A string containing only one letter is still a string. Although strings consist of characters, they are not the same type.

- 10 is an **int** and 10.0 is a **double**.
- 100 as a **long** is 100L. 100 as a **uint** is 100U.
- @"testing" is a verbatim string literal.

A Closer Look at Variables

Variables were introduced in Module 1. As you learned earlier, variables are declared using this form of statement:

type var-name;

where *type* is the data type of the variable and *var-name* is its name. You can declare a variable of any valid type, including the value types just described. When you create a variable, you are creating an instance of its type. Thus, the capabilities of a variable are determined by its type. For example, a variable of type **bool** cannot be used to store floating-point values. Furthermore, the type of a variable cannot change during its lifetime. An **int** variable cannot turn into a **char** variable, for example.

All variables in C# must be declared prior to their use. This is necessary because the compiler must know what type of data a variable contains before it can properly compile any statement that uses the variable. It also enables C# to perform strict type checking.

C# defines several different kinds of variables. The kinds that we have been using are called *local variables* because they are declared within a method.

Initializing a Variable

You must give a variable a value prior to using it. One way to give a variable a value is through an assignment statement, as you have already seen. Another way is by giving it an initial value when it is declared. To do this, follow the variable's name with an equal sign and the value being assigned. The general form of initialization is shown here:

type var = value;

Here, *value* is the value that is given to *var* when *var* is created. The value must be compatible with the specified type.

Here are some examples:

```
int count = 10; // give count an initial value of 10
char ch = 'X';  // initialize ch with the letter X
float f = 1.2F; // f is initialized with 1.2
```

When declaring two or more variables of the same type using a comma-separated list, you can give one or more of those variables an initial value. For example:

```
int a, b = 8, c = 19, d; // b and c have initializations
```

In this case, only **b** and **c** are initialized.

Dynamic Initialization

Although the preceding examples have used only constants as initializers, C# allows variables to be initialized dynamically, using any expression valid at the time the variable is declared. For example, here is a short program that computes the volume of a cylinder given the radius of its base and its height:

```
// Demonstrate dynamic initialization.

using System;

class DynInit {
    static void Main() {
        double radius = 4, height = 5;

        // dynamically initialize volume
        double volume = 3.1416 * radius * radius * height;

        Console.WriteLine("Volume is " + volume);
    }
}
```

> **volume** is dynamically initialized at runtime.

Here, three local variables—**radius**, **height**, and **volume**—are declared. The first two, **radius** and **height**, are initialized by constants. However, **volume** is initialized dynamically to the volume of the cylinder. The key point here is that the initialization expression can use any element valid at the time of the initialization, including calls to methods, other variables, or literals.

The Scope and Lifetime of Variables

So far, all of the variables that we have been using were declared at the start of the **Main( )** method. However, C# allows a local variable to be declared within any block. As explained in Module 1, a block is begun with an opening curly brace and ended by a closing curly brace. A block defines a *declaration space,* or *scope.* Thus, each time you start a new block, you are creating a new scope.

A scope determines what objects are visible to other parts of your program. It also determines the lifetime of those objects.

The most important scopes in C# are those defined by a class and those defined by a method. A discussion of class scope (and variables declared within it) is deferred until later in this book, when classes are described. For now, we will examine only the scopes defined by or within a method.

The scope defined by a method begins with its opening curly brace. However, if that method has parameters, they, too, are included within the method's scope.

As a general rule, variables declared inside a scope are not visible (that is, accessible) to code that is defined outside that scope. Thus, when you declare a variable within a scope, you are localizing that variable and protecting it from unauthorized access or modification. Indeed, the scope rules provide the foundation for encapsulation.

Scopes can be nested. For example, each time you create a block of code, you are creating a new, nested scope. When this occurs, the outer scope encloses the inner scope. This means that objects declared in the outer scope will be visible to code within the inner scope. However, the reverse is not true. Objects declared within the inner scope will not be visible outside it.

To understand the effect of nested scopes, consider the following program:

```csharp
// Demonstrate block scope.

using System;

class ScopeDemo {
  static void Main() {
    int x; // known to all code within Main()

    x = 10;
    if(x == 10) { // start new scope

      int y = 20; // known only to this block

      // x and y both known here.
      Console.WriteLine("x and y: " + x + " " + y);
      x = y * 2;
    }
    // y = 100; // Error! y not known here ◄────── y is outside of its
                                                   scope, here.

    // x is still known here.
    Console.WriteLine("x is " + x);
  }
}
```

As the comments indicate, the variable **x** is declared at the start of **Main( )**'s scope and is accessible to all subsequent code within **Main( )**. Within the **if** block, **y** is declared. Since a block defines a scope, **y** is visible only to other code within its block. This is why outside of its block, the line y = 100; is commented out. If you remove the leading comment symbol, a compile-time error will occur, because **y** is not visible outside of its block. Within the **if** block, **x** can be used because code within a block (that is, a nested scope) has access to variables declared by an enclosing scope.

Within a block, variables can be declared at any point, but are valid only after they are declared. Thus, if you define a variable at the start of a method, it is available to all of the code within that method. Conversely, if you declare a variable at the end of a block, it is effectively useless, because no code will have access to it.

Here is another important point to remember: variables are created when their scope is entered, and destroyed when their scope is left. This means that a variable will not hold its value once it has gone out of scope. Therefore, variables declared within a method will not hold their values between calls to that method. Also, a variable declared within a block will lose its value when the block is left. Thus, the lifetime of a variable is confined to its scope.

If a variable declaration includes an initializer, then that variable will be reinitialized each time the block in which it is declared is entered. For example, consider this program:

```
// Demonstrate lifetime of a variable.

using System;

class VarInitDemo {
  static void Main() {
    int x;

    for(x = 0; x < 3; x++) {
      int y = -1; // y is initialized each time block is entered
      Console.WriteLine("y is: " + y); // this always prints -1
      y = 100;
      Console.WriteLine("y is now: " + y);
    }
  }
}
```

The output generated by this program is shown here:

```
y is: -1
y is now: 100
y is: -1
y is now: 100
y is: -1
y is now: 100
```

As you can see, **y** is always reinitialized to –1 each time the inner **for** loop is entered. Even though it is subsequently assigned the value 100, this value is lost.

There is one quirk to C#'s scope rules that may surprise you: Although blocks can be nested, no variable declared within an inner scope can have the same name as a variable declared by an enclosing scope. For example, the following program, which tries to declare two separate variables with the same name, will not compile:

```
/*
   This program attempts to declare a variable
   in an inner scope with the same name as one
   defined in an outer scope.

   *** This program will not compile. ***
*/

using System;

class NestVar {
  static void Main() {
    int count;

    for(count = 0; count < 10; count = count+1) {
      Console.WriteLine("This is count: " + count);

      int count; // illegal!!!◀──────  Can't declare count again because
      for(count = 0; count < 2; count++)   it's already declared by Main().
        Console.WriteLine("This program is in error!");
    }
  }
}
```

If you come from a C/C++ background, then you know that there is no restriction on the names that you give variables declared in an inner scope. Thus, in C/C++ the declaration of **count** within the block of the outer **for** loop is completely valid. However, in C/C++, such a declaration hides the outer variable. The designers of C# felt that this *name hiding* could easily lead to programming errors and disallowed it.

1-Minute Drill

● What is a scope? How can one be created?

● Where in a block can variables be declared?

● In a block, when is a variable created? When is it destroyed?

Operators

C# provides a rich operator environment. An operator is a symbol that tells the compiler to perform a specific mathematical or logical manipulation. C# has four general classes of operators: *arithmetic, bitwise, relational,* and *logical.* C# also has several additional operators that handle certain special situations. This module will examine the arithmetic, relational, and logical operators. We will also examine the assignment operator. The bitwise and other special operators are examined later.

Arithmetic Operators

C# defines the following arithmetic operators:

Operator	Meaning
+	Addition
–	Subtraction (also unary minus)
*	Multiplication
/	Division
%	Modulus
++	Increment
– –	Decrement

● A scope defines the visibility and lifetime of an object. A block defines a scope.
● A variable can be defined at any point within a block.
● Inside a block, a variable is created when its declaration is encountered. It is destroyed when the block exits.

2

The operators +, −, *, and / all work the same way in C# as they do in any other computer language (or algebra, for that matter). These can be applied to any built-in numeric data type.

Although the actions of arithmetic operators are well known to all readers, a few special situations warrant some explanation. First, remember that when / is applied to an integer, any remainder will be truncated; for example, 10/3 will equal 3 in integer division. You can obtain the remainder of this division by using the modulus operator %. It works in C# the way that it does in other languages: it yields the remainder of an integer division. For example, 10 % 3 is 1. In C#, the % can be applied to both integer and floating-point types. Thus, 10.0 % 3.0 is also 1. (This differs from C/C++, which allow modulus operations only on integer types.) The following program demonstrates the modulus operator:

```
// Demonstrate the % operator.

using System;

class ModDemo {
  static void Main() {
    int iresult, irem;
    double dresult, drem;

    iresult = 10 / 3;
    irem = 10 % 3;

    dresult = 10.0 / 3.0;
    drem = 10.0 % 3.0;

    Console.WriteLine("Result and remainder of 10 / 3: " +
                      iresult + " " + irem);
    Console.WriteLine("Result and remainder of 10.0 / 3.0: " +
                      dresult + " " + drem);
  }
}
```

The output from the program is shown here:

```
Result and remainder of 10 / 3: 3 1
Result and remainder of 10.0 / 3.0: 3.33333333333333 1
```

As you can see, the % yields a remainder of 1 for both integer and floating-point operations.

Increment and Decrement

Introduced in Module 1, the ++ and the – – are the increment and decrement operators. As you will see, they have some special properties that make them quite interesting. Let's begin by reviewing precisely what the increment and decrement operators do.

The increment operator adds 1 to its operand, and the decrement operator subtracts 1. Therefore,

```
x = x + 1;
```

is the same as

```
x++;
```

and

```
x = x - 1;
```

is the same as

```
--x;
```

Both the increment and decrement operators can either precede (*prefix*) or follow (*postfix*) the operand. For example:

```
x = x + 1;
```

can be written as

```
++x; // prefix form
```

or as

```
x++; // postfix form
```

In the foregoing example, there is no difference whether the increment is applied as a prefix or a postfix. However, when an increment or decrement is used as part of a larger expression, there is an important difference. When an increment or decrement operator *precedes* its operand, C# will perform the operation prior to obtaining the operand's value for use by the rest of the expression. If the operator *follows* its operand, then C# will obtain the operand's value before incrementing or decrementing it. Consider the following:

```
x = 10;
y = ++x;
```

In this case, **y** will be set to 11. However, if the code is written as

```
x = 10;
y = x++;
```

then **y** will be set to 10. In both cases, **x** is still set to 11; the difference is when it happens. There are significant advantages in being able to control when the increment or decrement operation takes place.

Relational and Logical Operators

In the terms *relational operator* and *logical operator, relational* refers to the relationships that values can have with one another, and *logical* refers to the ways in which true and false values can be connected together. Since the relational operators produce true or false results, they often work with the logical operators. For this reason they will be discussed together here.

The relational operators are shown here:

Operator	Meaning
==	Equal to
!=	Not equal to
>	Greater than
<	Less than
>=	Greater than or equal to
<=	Less than or equal to

The logical operators are shown next:

Operator	Meaning
&	AND
|	OR
^	XOR (exclusive OR)
||	Short-circuit OR
&&	Short-circuit AND
!	NOT

The outcome of the relational and logical operators is a **bool** value.

In C#, all objects can be compared for equality or inequality using == and !=. However, the comparison operators, <, >, <=, or >=, can be applied only to those types that support an ordering relationship. Therefore, all of the relational operators can be applied to all numeric types. However, values of type **bool** can only be compared for equality or inequality, since the **true** and **false** values are not ordered. For example, **true > false** has no meaning in C#.

For the logical operators, the operands must be of type **bool** and the result of a logical operation is of type **bool**. The logical operators, **&, |, ^**, and **!**, support the basic logical operations AND, OR, XOR, and NOT, according to the following truth table:

p	q	p & q	p | q	p ^ q	!p
False	False	False	False	False	True
True	False	False	True	True	False
False	True	False	True	True	True
True	True	True	True	False	False

As the table shows, the outcome of an exclusive OR operation is true when exactly one and only one operand is true.

Here is a program that demonstrates several of the relational and logical operators:

```
// Demonstrate the relational and logical operators.

using System;

class RelLogOps {
  static void Main() {
    int i, j;
    bool b1, b2;

    i = 10;
    j = 11;
    if(i < j) Console.WriteLine("i < j");
    if(i <= j) Console.WriteLine("i <= j");
    if(i != j) Console.WriteLine("i != j");
    if(i == j) Console.WriteLine("this won't execute");
    if(i >= j) Console.WriteLine("this won't execute");
    if(i > j) Console.WriteLine("this won't execute");

    b1 = true;
```

```
   b2 = false;
   if(b1 & b2) Console.WriteLine("this won't execute");
   if(!(b1 & b2)) Console.WriteLine("!(b1 & b2) is true");
   if(b1 | b2) Console.WriteLine("b1 | b2 is true");
   if(b1 ^ b2) Console.WriteLine("b1 ^ b2 is true");
  }
}
```

The output from the program is shown here:

```
i < j
i <= j
i != j
!(b1 & b2) is true
b1 | b2 is true
b1 ^ b2 is true
```

Short-Circuit Logical Operators

C# supplies special *short-circuit* versions of its AND and OR logical operators
that can be used to produce more efficient code. To understand why, consider
the following. In an AND operation, if the first operand is false, the outcome is
false no matter what value the second operand has. In an OR operation, if the
first operand is true, the outcome of the operation is true no matter what the
value of the second operand. Thus, in these two cases there is no need to
evaluate the second operand. By not evaluating the second operand, time is
saved and more efficient code is produced.

The short-circuit AND operator is **&&**, and the short-circuit OR operator
is **||**. As described earlier, their normal counterparts are **&** and **|**. The only
difference between the normal and short-circuit versions is that the normal
operands will always evaluate each operand, but short-circuit versions will
evaluate the second operand only when necessary.

Here is a program that demonstrates the short-circuit AND operator. The
program determines if the value in **d** is a factor of **n**. It does this by performing
a modulus operation. If the remainder of **n / d** is zero, then **d** is a factor. However,
since the modulus operation involves a division, the short-circuit form of the
AND is used to prevent a divide-by-zero error.

```
// Demonstrate the short-circuit operators.

using System;
```

```
class SCops {
  static void Main() {
    int n, d;

    n = 10;
    d = 2;
    if(d != 0 && (n % d) == 0)
      Console.WriteLine(d + " is a factor of " + n);

    d = 0; // now, set d to zero

    // Since d is zero, the second operand is not evaluated.
    if(d != 0 && (n % d) == 0)

    /* Now, try same thing without short-circuit operator.
       This will cause a divide-by-zero error.
    */
    if(d != 0 & (n % d) == 0)
      Console.WriteLine(d + " is a factor of " + n);
  }
}
```

The short-circuit operator prevents a division by zero.

Now, both expressions are evaluated, allowing a division by zero to occur.

To prevent a divide-by-zero error, the **if** statement first checks to see if **d** is equal to zero. If it is, the short-circuit AND stops at that point and does not perform the modulus division. Thus, in the first test, **d** is 2 and the modulus operation is performed. The second test fails because **d** is set to zero, and the modulus operation is skipped, avoiding a divide-by-zero error. Finally, the normal AND operator is tried. This causes both operands to be evaluated, which leads to a runtime error when the division-by-zero occurs.

One other point: the short-circuit AND is also known as the *conditional AND*, and the short-circuit OR is also called the *conditional OR*.

LogicOpTable.cs

Project 2-2: Display a Truth Table for the Logical Operators

In this project you will create a program that displays the truth table for C#'s logical operators. You must make the columns in the table line up. This project makes use of several features covered in this module, including one of C#'s escape sequences and the logical operators. It also illustrates the differences in the precedence between the arithmetic + operator and the logical operators.

Step-by-Step

1. Create a new file called **LogicalOpTable.cs**.

2. To ensure that the columns line up, you will use the **\t** escape sequence to embed tabs into each output string. For example, this **WriteLine( )** statement displays the header for the table:

```
Console.WriteLine("P\tQ\tAND\tOR\tXOR\tNOT");
```

3. For each subsequent line in the table, use tabs to properly position the outcome of each operation under its proper heading.

4. Here is the entire **LogicalOpTable.cs** program listing. Enter it at this time.

```
/*
    Project 2-2

    Print a truth table for the logical operators.
*/

using System;

class LogicalOpTable {
  static void Main() {

    bool p, q;

    Console.WriteLine("P\tQ\tAND\tOR\tXOR\tNOT");

    p = true; q = true;
    Console.Write(p + "\t" + q +"\t");
    Console.Write((p&q) + "\t" + (p|q) + "\t");
    Console.WriteLine((p^q) + "\t" + (!p));

    p = true; q = false;
    Console.Write(p + "\t" + q +"\t");
    Console.Write((p&q) + "\t" + (p|q) + "\t");
    Console.WriteLine((p^q) + "\t" + (!p));

    p = false; q = true;
    Console.Write(p + "\t" + q +"\t");
    Console.Write((p&q) + "\t" + (p|q) + "\t");
    Console.WriteLine((p^q) + "\t" + (!p));
```

```
   p = false; q = false;
   Console.Write(p + "\t" + q +"\t");
   Console.Write((p&q) + "\t" + (p|q) + "\t");
   Console.WriteLine((p^q) + "\t" + (!p));
  }
}
```

5. Compile and run the program. The following table is displayed:

P	Q	AND	OR	XOR	NOT
true	true	true	true	false	false
true	false	false	true	true	false
false	true	false	true	true	true
false	false	false	false	false	true

6. Notice the parentheses surrounding the logical operations inside the **Write( )** and **WriteLine( )** statements. They are necessary because of the precedence of C#'s operators. The + operator is higher than the logical operators.

7. On your own, try modifying the program so that it uses and displays 1's and 0's, rather than true and false. This may involve a bit more effort that you might at first think!

Ask the Expert

Question: Since the short-circuit operators are, in some cases, more efficient than their normal counterparts, why does C# still offer the normal AND and OR operators?

Answer: In some cases you will want both operands of an AND or OR operation to be evaluated because of the side-effects produced. Consider the following:

```
// Side-effects can be important.

using System;

class SideEffects {
  static void Main() {
    int i;
```

2

```
    i = 0;

    /* Here, i is still incremented even though
       the if statement fails. */
    if(false & (++i < 100))
       Console.WriteLine("this won't be displayed");
    Console.WriteLine("if statement executed: " + i); // displays 1

    /* In this case, i is not incremented because
       the short-circuit operator skips the increment. */
    if(false && (++i < 100))
       Console.WriteLine("this won't be displayed");
    Console.WriteLine("if statement executed: " + i); // still 1 !!
  }
}
```

As the comments indicate, in the first **if** statement, **i** is incremented whether the **if** succeeds or not. However, when the short-circuit operator is used, the variable **i** is not incremented when the first operand is false. The lesson here is that if your code expects the right-hand operand of an AND or OR operation to be evaluated, then you must use C#'s non–short-circuit forms of these operations.

1-Minute Drill

● What does the **%** operator do? To what types can it be applied?

● What type of values can be used as operands of the logical operators?

● Does a short-circuit operator always evaluate both of its operands?

● The % is the modulus operator, which returns the remainder of an integer division. It can be applied to all of the numeric types.
● The logical operators must have operands of type **bool**.
● No, a short-circuit operator evaluates its second operand only if the outcome of the operation cannot be determined solely by its first operand.

The Assignment Operator

You have been using the assignment operator since Module 1. Now it is time to take a formal look at it. The *assignment operator* is the single equal sign, =. The assignment operator works in C# much as it does in any other computer language. It has this general form:

var = expression;

Here, the type of *var* must be compatible with the type of *expression*.

The assignment operator does have one interesting attribute that you may not be familiar with: it allows you to create a chain of assignments. For example, consider this fragment:

```
int x, y, z;

x = y = z = 100; // set x, y, and z to 100
```

This fragment sets the variables **x**, **y**, and **z** to 100 using a single statement. This works because the = is an operator that yields the value of the right-hand expression. Thus, the value of **z = 100** is 100, which is then assigned to **y**, which in turn is assigned to **x**. Using a "chain of assignment" is an easy way to set a group of variables to a common value.

Compound Assignments

C# provides special compound assignment operators that simplify the coding of certain assignment statements. Let's begin with an example. The assignment statement shown here:

```
x = x + 10;
```

can be written using a compound assignment such as

```
x += 10;
```

The operator pair += tells the compiler to assign to **x** the value of **x** plus 10.

Here is another example. The statement

```
x = x - 100;
```

is the same as

```
x -= 100;
```

Both statements assign to **x** the value of **x** minus 100.

There are compound assignment operators for all the binary operators (that is, those that require two operands). The general form of the shorthand is

var op = expression;

Thus, the arithmetic and logical assignment operators are

+=	–=	*=	/=
%=	&=	|=	^=

Because the compound assignment statements are shorter than their noncompound equivalents, the compound assignment operators are also sometimes called the *shorthand assignment* operators.

The compound assignment operators provide two benefits. First, they are more compact than their "longhand" equivalents. Second, they can result in more efficient executable code (because the operand is evaluated only once). For these reasons, you will often see the compound assignment operators used in professionally written C# programs.

Type Conversion in Assignments

In programming, it is common to assign one type of variable to another. For example, you might want to assign an **int** value to a **float** variable, as shown here:

```
int i;
float f;

i = 10;
f = i; // assign an int to a float
```

When compatible types are mixed in an assignment, the value of the right side is automatically converted to the type of the left side. Thus, in the preceding fragment, the value in **i** is converted into a **float** and then assigned to **f**. However, because of C#'s strict type-checking, not all types are compatible, and thus, not all type conversions are implicitly allowed. For example, **bool** and **int** are not compatible.

When one type of data is assigned to another type of variable, an *automatic type conversion* will take place if:

- The two types are compatible.

- The destination type is larger than the source type.

When these two conditions are met, a *widening conversion* takes place. For example, the **int** type is always large enough to hold all valid **byte** values, and both **int** and **byte** are integer types, so an automatic conversion can be applied.

For widening conversions, the numeric types, including integer and floating-point types, are compatible with each other. For example, the following program is perfectly valid since **long** to **double** is a widening conversion that is automatically performed:

```
// Demonstrate automatic conversion from long to double.

using System;

class LtoD {
  static void Main() {
    long L;
    double D;

    L = 100123285L;
    D = L;          Automatic conversion from
                    long to double

    Console.WriteLine("L and D: " + L + " " + D);
  }
}
```

Although there is an automatic conversion from **long** to **double**, there is no automatic conversion from **double** to **long** since this is not a widening conversion. Thus, the following version of the preceding program is invalid:

```
// *** This program will not compile. ***

using System;

class LtoD {
  static void Main() {
    long L;
    double D;

    D = 100123285.0;
    L = D; // Illegal!!!
    
    Console.WriteLine("L and D: " + L + " " + D);

  }
}
```

No automatic conversion from **double** to **long**

In addition to the restrictions just described, there are no automatic conversions between **decimal** and **float** or **double**, or from the numeric types to **char** or **bool**. Also, **char** and **bool** are not compatible with each other.

Casting Incompatible Types

Although the automatic type conversions are helpful, they will not fulfill all programming needs because they apply only to widening conversions between compatible types. For all other cases you must employ a cast. A *cast* is an instruction to the compiler to convert one type into another. Thus, it requests an explicit type conversion. A cast has this general form:

> (*target-type*) *expression*

Here, *target-type* specifies the desired type to convert the specified expression to. For example, if you want the type of the expression **x/y** to be **int**, you can write

```
double x, y;
// ...
(int) (x / y)
```

Here, even though **x** and **y** are of type **double**, the cast converts the outcome of the expression to **int**. The parentheses surrounding **x / y** are necessary.

Otherwise, the cast to **int** would apply only to the **x**, and not to the outcome of the division. The cast is needed here because there is no automatic conversion from **double** to **int**.

When a cast involves a *narrowing conversion*, information might be lost. For example, when casting a **long** into an **int**, information will be lost if the **long**'s value is greater than the range of an **int** because its high-order bits are removed. When a floating-point value is cast to an integer type, the fractional component will also be lost due to truncation. For example, if the value 1.23 is assigned to an integer, the resulting value will simply be 1. The 0.23 is lost.

The following program demonstrates some type conversions that require casts:

```
// Demonstrate casting.

using System;

class CastDemo {
  static void Main() {
    double x, y;
    byte b;
    int i;
    char ch;

    x = 10.0;
    y = 3.0;

    i = (int) (x / y); // cast double to int
    Console.WriteLine("Integer outcome of x / y: " + i);

    i = 100;
    b = (byte) i;
    Console.WriteLine("Value of b: " + b);

    i = 257;
    b = (byte) i;
    Console.WriteLine("Value of b: " + b);

    b = 88; // ASCII code for X
    ch = (char) b;
    Console.WriteLine("ch: " + ch);
  }
}
```

Truncation will occur in this conversion.

No loss of info here. A byte can hold the value 100.

Information loss this time. A byte cannot hold the value 257.

Cast between incompatible types

The output from the program is shown here:

```
Integer outcome of x / y: 3
Value of b: 100
Value of b: 1
ch: X
```

In the program, the cast of (**x / y**) to **int** results in the truncation of the fractional component and information is loss. Next, no loss of information occurs when **b** is assigned the value 100 because a **byte** can hold the value 100. However, when the attempt is made to assign **b** the value 257, information loss occurs because 257 exceeds a **byte**'s range. Finally, no information is lost, but a cast is needed when assigning a **byte** value to a **char**.

1-Minute Drill

● What is a cast?

● Can a **short** be assigned to an **int** without a cast? Can a **byte** be assigned to a **char** without a cast?

● How can the following statement be rewritten?

```
x = x + 23;
```

Operator Precedence

Table 2-3 shows the order of precedence for all C# operators, from highest to lowest. This table includes several operators that will be discussed later in this book.

● A cast is an explicit conversion.
● Yes. No.
● The statement can be rewritten as
   x += 23;

Highest

()	[]	.	++(postfix)	--(postfix)	checked	new	sizeof	typeof	unchecked
!	~		(cast)	+(unary)	-(unary)	++(prefix)		--(prefix)	

```
*  /   %
+  -
<<   >>
<  >  <=  >=  is
==  !=
&
^
|
&&
||
?:
=  op=
```

Lowest

| **Table 2-3** | The Precedence of the C# Operators |

Expressions

Operators, variables, and literals are the constituents of *expressions*. An expression in C# is any valid combination of those pieces. You might already know the general form of an expression from other programming experience, or from algebra. However, there are a few aspects of expressions that will be discussed now.

Type Conversion in Expressions

Within an expression, it is possible to mix two or more different types of data as long as they are compatible with each other. For example, you can mix **short** and **long** within an expression because they are both numeric types. When

2

different types of data are mixed within an expression, they are converted to the same type, on an operation-by-operation basis.

The conversions are accomplished through the use of C#'s *type promotion rules*. Here is the algorithm that they define for binary operations:

IF one operand is **decimal**, THEN the other operand is promoted to **decimal** (unless it is of type **float** or **double**, in which case an error results).

ELSE IF one of the operands is **double**, the second is promoted to **double**.

ELSE IF one operand is a **float** operand, the second is promoted to **float**.

ELSE IF one operand is a **ulong**, the second is promoted to **ulong** (unless it is of type **sbyte**, **short**, **int**, or **long**, in which case an error results).

ELSE IF one operand is a **long**, the second is promoted to **long**.

ELSE IF one operand is a **uint** and the second is of type **sbyte**, **short**, or **int**, both are promoted to **long**.

ELSE IF one operand is a **uint**, the second is promoted to **uint**.

ELSE both operands are promoted to **int**.

There are a couple of important points to be made about the type promotion rules. First, not all types can be mixed in an expression. Specifically, there is no implicit conversion from **float** or **double** to **decimal**, and it is not possible to mix **ulong** with any signed integer type. To mix these types requires the use of an explicit cast.

Second, pay special attention to the last rule. It states that if none of the preceding rules applies, then all other operands are promoted to **int**. Therefore, in an expression, all **char**, **sbyte**, **byte**, **ushort**, and **short** values are promoted to **int** for the purposes of calculation. This is called *integer promotion*. It also means that the outcome of all arithmetic operations will be no smaller than **int**.

It is important to understand that type promotions apply only to the values operated upon when an expression is evaluated. For example, if the value of a **byte** variable is promoted to **int** inside an expression, outside the expression the variable is still a **byte**. Type promotion only affects the evaluation of an expression.

Type promotion can, however, lead to somewhat unexpected results. For example, when an arithmetic operation involves two **byte** values, the following sequence occurs: First, the **byte** operands are promoted to **int**. Then the operation takes place, yielding an **int** result. Thus, the outcome of an operation involving two **byte** values will be an **int**. This is not what you might intuitively expect. Consider the following program:

```
// A promotion surprise!

using System;

class PromDemo {
  static void Main() {
    byte b;
    int i;

    b = 10;
    i = b * b; // OK, no cast needed

    b = 10;
    b = (byte) (b * b); // cast needed!!

    Console.WriteLine("i and b: " + i + " " + b);
  }
}
```

> No cast needed because result is already elevated to **int.**

> Cast is needed here to assign an **int** to a **byte**!

Somewhat counterintuitively, no cast is needed when assigning **b** * **b** to **i**, because **b** is promoted to **int** when the expression is evaluated. However, when you try to assign **b** * **b** to **b**, you do need a cast—back to **byte**! Keep this in mind if you get unexpected type-incompatibility error messages on expressions that would otherwise seem perfectly okay.

This same sort of situation also occurs when performing operations on **char**s. For example, in the following fragment, the cast back to **char** is needed because of the promotion of **ch1** and **ch2** to **int** within the expression:

```
char ch1 = 'a', ch2 = 'b';

ch1 = (char) (ch1 + ch2);
```

Without the cast, the result of adding **ch1** to **ch2** would be **int**, which can't be assigned to a **char**.

Casts are not only useful when converting between types in an assignment. For example, consider the following program. It uses a cast to **double** to obtain a fractional component from an otherwise integer division.

```
// Using a cast.

using System;
```

```
class UseCast {
  static void Main() {
    int i;

    for(i = 0; i < 5; i++) {
      Console.WriteLine(i + " / 3: " + i / 3);
      Console.WriteLine(i + " / 3 with fractions: {0:#.##}",
                          (double) i / 3);
      Console.WriteLine();
    }
  }
}
```

The output from the program is shown here:

```
0 / 3: 0
0 / 3 with fractions:

1 / 3: 0
1 / 3 with fractions: .33

2 / 3: 0
2 / 3 with fractions: .67

3 / 3: 1
3 / 3 with fractions: 1

4 / 3: 1
4 / 3 with fractions: 1.33
```

Ask the Expert

Question: Do type promotions occur when a unary operation, such as the unary –, takes place?

Answer: Yes. For the unary operations, operands smaller than **int** (**byte**, **sbyte**, **short**, and **ushort**) are promoted to **int**. Also, a **char** operand is converted to **int**. Furthermore, if a **uint** value is negated, it is promoted to **long**.

Spacing and Parentheses

An expression in C# can have tabs and spaces in it to make it more readable. For example, the following two expressions are the same, but the second is easier to read:

```
x=10/y*(127/x);

x = 10 / y * (127/x);
```

Parentheses increase the precedence of the operations contained within them, just like in algebra. Use of redundant or additional parentheses will not cause errors or slow down the execution of the expression. You are encouraged to use parentheses to make clear the exact order of evaluation, both for yourself and for others who may have to figure out your program later. For example, which of the following two expressions is easier to read?

```
x = y/3-34*temp+127;

x = (y/3) - (34*temp) + 127;
```

RegPay.cs

Project 2-3: Compute the Regular Payments on a Loan

As mentioned earlier, the **decimal** type is especially well suited for calculations that involve money. In this project, you will put the **decimal** type to work. You will create a program that computes the regular payments on a loan, such as a car loan. Given the principal, the length of time, number of payments per year, and the interest rate, the program will compute the payment. Since this is a financial calculation, it makes sense to use the **decimal** type to represent the data. This project also demonstrates casting and another of C#'s library methods: **Pow( )**.

To compute the payments, you will use the following formula:

$$\text{Payment} = \frac{\text{IntRate} * (\text{Principal} / \text{PayPerYear})}{1 - ((\text{IntRate} / \text{PayPerYear}) + 1)^{-\text{PayPerYear} * \text{NumYears}}}$$

where IntRate specifies the interest rate, Principal contains the starting balance, PayPerYear specifies the number of payments per year, and NumYears specifies the length of the loan in years.

Notice that in the denominator of the formula, you must raise one value to the power of another. To do this, you will use another C# math method: **Math.Pow( )**. Here is how you will call it:

result = Math.Pow(*base*, *exp*);

Pow( ) returns the value of *base* raised to the *exp* power. The arguments to **Pow( )** must be of type **double**, and it returns a value of type **double**. This means that you will need to use a cast to convert between **double** and **decimal**.

Step-by-Step

1. Create a new file called **RegPay.cs**.

2. Here are the variables that will be used by the program:

```
decimal Principal;      // original principal
decimal IntRate;        // interest rate as a decimal, such as 0.075
decimal PayPerYear;     // number of payments per year
decimal NumYears;       // number of years
decimal Payment;        // the regular payment
decimal numer, denom;   // temporary work variables
double b, e;            // base and exponent for call to Pow()
```

Since most of the calculation will be done using the **decimal** data type, most of the variables are of type **decimal**.

Notice how each variable declaration is followed by a comment that describes its use. They help anyone reading your program understand the purpose of each variable. Although we won't include such detailed comments for most of the short programs in this book, it is a good practice to follow as your programs become longer and more complicated.

3. Add the following lines of code, which specify the loan information. In this case, the principal is $10,000, the interest rate is 7.5 percent, the number of payments per year is 12, and the length of the loan is 5 years.

```
Principal = 10000.00m;
IntRate = 0.075m;
PayPerYear = 12.0m;
NumYears = 5.0m;
```

4. Add the lines that perform the financial calculation:

```
numer = IntRate * Principal / PayPerYear;

e = (double) -(PayPerYear * NumYears);
```

```
b = (double) (IntRate / PayPerYear) + 1;

denom = 1 - (decimal) Math.Pow(b, e);

Payment = numer / denom;
```

Notice how casts must be used to pass values to **Pow( )** and to convert the return value. Remember, there are no automatic conversions between **decimal** and **double** in C#.

5. Finish the program by outputting the regular payment, as shown here:

```
Console.WriteLine("Payment is {0:C}", Payment);
```

6. Here is the entire **RegPay.cs** program listing:

```
/*
   Project 2-3

   Compute the regular payments for a loan.

   Call this file RegPay.cs
*/

using System;

class RegPay {
  static void Main() {
    decimal Principal;      // original principal
    decimal IntRate;        // interest rate as a decimal, such as 0.075
    decimal PayPerYear;     // number of payments per year
    decimal NumYears;       // number of years
    decimal Payment;        // the regular payment
    decimal numer, denom;   // temporary work variables
    double b, e;            // base and exponent for call to Pow()

    Principal = 10000.00m;
    IntRate = 0.075m;
```

2

```
      PayPerYear = 12.0m;
      NumYears = 5.0m;

      numer = IntRate * Principal / PayPerYear;

      e = (double) -(PayPerYear * NumYears);
      b = (double) (IntRate / PayPerYear) + 1;

      denom = 1 - (decimal) Math.Pow(b, e);

      Payment = numer / denom;

      Console.WriteLine("Payment is {0:C}", Payment);
   }
}
```

Here is the output from the program:

```
Payment is $200.38
```

Before moving on, you might want to try having the program compute the regular payments for differing amounts, periods, and interest rates.

☑ *Mastery Check*

1. Why does C# strictly specify the range and behavior of its simple types?

2. What is C#'s character type, and how does it differ from the character type used by many other programming languages?

3. A **bool** value can have any value you like because any nonzero value is true. True or false?

4. Given this output:

   ```
   One
   Two
   Three
   ```

   Using a single string and escape sequences, show the **WriteLine( )** statement that produced it.

5. What is wrong with this fragment?

   ```
   for(i = 0; i < 10; i++) {
     int sum;

     sum = sum + i;
   }
   Console.WriteLine("Sum is: " + sum);
   ```

6. Explain the difference between the prefix and postfix forms of the increment operator.

7. Show how a short-circuit AND can be used to prevent a divide-by-zero error.

8. In an expression, what type are **byte** and **short** promoted to?

9. Which of the following types cannot be mixed in an expression with a **decimal** value?

   A. float

   B. int

   C. uint

   D. byte

☑ *Mastery Check*

2

10. In general, when is a cast needed?

11. Write a program that finds all of the prime numbers between 1 and 100.

12. On your own, rewrite the truth table program from Project 2-2 so that it uses verbatim string literals with embedded tab and newline characters rather than escape sequences.

Module 3

Program Control Statements

The Goals of This Module

- Input characters from the keyboard
- Learn more about if and for
- Examine switch
- Understand while
- Use do-while
- Employ break
- Use continue
- Examine goto

In this module you will learn about the statements that control a program's flow of execution. There are three categories of program control statements: *selection* statements, which include the **if** and the **switch**; *iteration* statements, which include the **for**, **while**, **do-while**, and **foreach** loops; and *jump* statements, which include **break**, **continue**, **goto**, and **return**. Except for **return** and **foreach**, which are discussed later in this book, the remaining control statements, including the **if** and **for** statements to which you have already had a brief introduction, are examined in detail here.

Inputting Characters from the Keyboard

Before examining C#'s control statements, we will make a short digression that will allow you to begin writing interactive programs. Up to this point, the sample programs in this book have displayed information *to* the user, but they have not received information *from* the user. Thus, you have been using console output, but not console (that is, keyboard) input. Here you will begin to use input by reading characters that are typed at the keyboard.

To read a character from the keyboard, call **Console.Read( )**. This method waits until the user presses a key and then returns the result. The character is returned as an integer, so it must be cast into a **char** to assign it to a **char** variable. By default, console input is *line-buffered,* so you must press ENTER before any character that you type will be sent to your program. Here is a program that reads a character from the keyboard:

```
// Read a character from the keyboard.

using System;

class KbIn {
  public static void Main() {
    char ch;

    Console.Write("Press a key followed by ENTER: ");

    ch = (char) Console.Read(); // get a char     ◄——— Read a character
                                                       from the keyboard.

    Console.WriteLine("Your key is: " + ch);
  }
}
```

Here is a sample run:

```
Press a key followed by ENTER: t
Your key is: t
```

The fact that **Read( )** is line-buffered is a source of annoyance at times.
When you press ENTER, a carriage-return, linefeed sequence is entered into the
input stream. Furthermore, these characters are left pending in the input buffer
until you read them. Thus, for some applications, you may need to remove
them (by reading them) before the next input operation. You will see an
example of this later in this module.

1-Minute Drill

● How can you read a character typed at the keyboard?

● What does "line-buffered" mean?

The if Statement

Module 1 introduced the **if** statement. It is examined in detail here. The
complete form of the **if** statement is

if(*condition*) *statement*;
else *statement*;

where the targets of the **if** and **else** are single statements. The **else** clause is
optional. The targets of both the **if** and **else** can be blocks of statements. The
general form of the **if** using blocks of statements is

if(*condition*)
{
  statement sequence
}
else
{

● To read a character, call **Console.Read( )**.
● When input is line-buffered, you must press ENTER before what you type is sent to your program.

statement sequence

}

If the conditional expression is true, the target of the **if** will be executed; otherwise, if it exists, the target of the **else** will be executed. At no time will both of them be executed. The conditional expression controlling the **if** must produce a **bool** result.

To demonstrate the **if**, we will evolve a simple computerized guessing game that would be suitable for small children. In the first version of the game, the program asks the player for a letter between A and Z. If the player presses the right letter on the keyboard, the program responds by printing the message **** Right ****. The program is shown here:

```
// Guess the letter game.

using System;

class Guess {
  public static void Main() {
    char ch, answer = 'K';

    Console.WriteLine("I'm thinking of a letter between A and Z.");
    Console.Write("Can you guess it: ");

    ch = (char) Console.Read(); // read a char from the keyboard

    if(ch == answer) Console.WriteLine("** Right **");
  }
}
```

This program prompts the player and then reads a character from the keyboard. Using an **if** statement, it then checks that character against the answer, which is K in this case. If K was entered, the message is displayed. When you try this program, remember that the K must be entered in uppercase.

Taking the guessing game further, the next version uses the **else** to print a message when the wrong letter is picked.

```
// Guess the letter game, 2nd version.

using System;

class Guess2 {
  public static void Main() {
```

```
    char ch, answer = 'K';

    Console.WriteLine("I'm thinking of a letter between A and Z.");
    Console.Write("Can you guess it: ");

    ch = (char) Console.Read(); // get a char

    if(ch == answer) Console.WriteLine("** Right **");
    else Console.WriteLine("...Sorry, you're wrong.");
  }
}
```

3

Nested ifs

A *nested if* is an **if** statement that is the target of another **if** or **else**. Nested **ifs** are very common in programming. The main thing to remember about nested **ifs** in C# is that an **else** statement always refers to the nearest **if** statement that is within the same block as the **else** and not already associated with an **else**. Here is an example:

```
if(i == 10) {
  if(j < 20) a = b;
  if(k > 100) c = d;     This if goes with this else.          This if goes
  else a = c; // this else refers to if(k > 100)              with this else.
}
else a = d; // this else refers to if(i == 10)
```

As the comments indicate, the final **else** is not associated with **if(j<20)**, because it is not in the same block (even though it is the nearest **if** without an **else**). Rather, the final **else** is associated with **if(i==10)**. The inner **else** refers to **if(k>100)**, because it is the closest **if** within the same block.

You can use a nested **if** to add a further improvement to the guessing game. This addition provides the player with feedback about a wrong guess.

```
// Guess the letter game, 3rd version.

using System;

class Guess3 {
  public static void Main() {
    char ch, answer = 'K';
```

```
   Console.WriteLine("I'm thinking of a letter between A and Z.");
   Console.Write("Can you guess it: ");

   ch = (char) Console.Read(); // get a char

   if(ch == answer) Console.WriteLine("** Right **");
   else {
     Console.Write("...Sorry, you're ");

     // a nested if
     if(ch < answer) Console.WriteLine("too low");     ←  A nested if
     else Console.WriteLine("too high");
   }
 }
}
```

A sample run is shown here:

```
I'm thinking of a letter between A and Z.
Can you guess it: Z
...Sorry, you're too high
```

The if-else-if Ladder

A common programming construct that is based upon the nested **if** is the
if-else-if ladder. It looks like this:

```
if(condition)
  statement;
else if(condition)
  statement;
else if(condition)
  statement;
.
.
.
else
  statement;
```

The conditional expressions are evaluated from the top downward. As soon as a true condition is found, the statement associated with it is executed, and the rest of the ladder is bypassed. If none of the conditions is true, then the final **else** statement will be executed. The final **else** often acts as a default condition; that is, if all other conditional tests fail, then the last **else** statement is performed. If there is no final **else** and all other conditions are false, then no action will take place.

The following program demonstrates the **if-else-if** ladder:

```
// Demonstrate an if-else-if ladder.

using System;

class Ladder {
  public static void Main() {
    int x;

    for(x=0; x<6; x++) {
      if(x==1)
        Console.WriteLine("x is one");
      else if(x==2)
        Console.WriteLine("x is two");
      else if(x==3)
        Console.WriteLine("x is three");
      else if(x==4)
        Console.WriteLine("x is four");
      else
        Console.WriteLine("x is not between 1 and 4");
    }
  }
}
```

This is the default statement.

The program produces the following output:

```
x is not between 1 and 4
x is one
x is two
x is three
x is four
x is not between 1 and 4
```

As you can see, the default **else** is executed only if none of the preceding **if** statements succeed.

1-Minute Drill

● The condition controlling the **if** must be of what type?

● To what **if** does an **else** always associate?

● What is an **if-else-if** ladder?

The switch Statement

The second of C#'s selection statements is the **switch**. The **switch** provides for a multiway branch. Thus, it enables a program to select among several alternatives. Although a series of nested **if** statements can perform multiway tests, for many situations the **switch** is a more efficient approach. It works like this: the value of an expression is successively tested against a list of constants. When a match is found, the statement sequence associated with that match is executed. The general form of the **switch** statement is

```
switch(expression) {
  case constant1:
    statement sequence
    break;
  case constant2:
    statement sequence
    break;
  case constant3:
    statement sequence
    break;
  .
  .
  .
  default:
    statement sequence
    break;
}
```

● The condition controlling an **if** must be of type **bool**.

● An **else** always associates with the nearest **if** in the same block that is not already associated with an **else**.

● An **if-else-if** ladder is a sequence of nested **if-else** statements.

The **switch** expression must be of an integer type, such as **char**, **byte**, **short**, or **int**, or of type **string** (which is described later in this book). Thus, floating-point expressions, for example, are not allowed. Frequently, the expression controlling the **switch** is simply a variable. The **case** constants must be literals of a type compatible with the expression. No two **case** constants in the same **switch** can have identical values.

The **default** statement sequence is executed if no **case** constant matches the expression. The **default** is optional; if it is not present, no action takes place if all matches fail. When a match is found, the statements associated with that **case** are executed until the **break** is encountered.

The following program demonstrates the **switch**:

```
// Demonstrate the switch.

using System;

class SwitchDemo {
  public static void Main() {
    int i;

    for(i=0; i<10; i++)
      switch(i) {
        case 0:
          Console.WriteLine("i is zero");
          break;
        case 1:
          Console.WriteLine("i is one");
          break;
        case 2:
          Console.WriteLine("i is two");
          break;
        case 3:
          Console.WriteLine("i is three");
          break;
        case 4:
          Console.WriteLine("i is four");
          break;
        default:
          Console.WriteLine("i is five or more");
          break;
      }

  }
}
```

3

The output produced by this program is shown here:

```
i is zero
i is one
i is two
i is three
i is four
i is five or more
i is five or more
i is five or more
i is five or more
i is five or more
```

As you can see, each time through the loop, the statements associated with the **case** constant that matches **i** are executed. All others are bypassed. When **i** is five or greater, no **case** constants match, so the **default** statement is executed.

In the preceding example, the **switch** was controlled by an **int** variable. As explained, you can control a **switch** with any integer type, including **char**. Here is an example that uses a **char** expression and **char** case constants:

```
// Use a char to control the switch.

using System;

class SwitchDemo2 {
  public static void Main() {
    char ch;

    for(ch='A'; ch<= 'E'; ch++)
      switch(ch) {
        case 'A':
          Console.WriteLine("ch is A");
          break;
        case 'B':
          Console.WriteLine("ch is B");
          break;
        case 'C':
          Console.WriteLine("ch is C");
          break;
        case 'D':
```

```
        Console.WriteLine("ch is D");
        break;
      case 'E':
        Console.WriteLine("ch is E");
        break;
    }
  }
}
```

The output from this program is shown here:

```
ch is A
ch is B
ch is C
ch is D
ch is E
```

Notice that this example does not include a **default** statement. Remember, the **default** is optional. When not needed, it can be left out.

In C#, it is an error for the statement sequence associated with one **case** to continue on into the next **case**. This is called the *no fall-through rule*. This is why **case** sequences end with a **break** statement. (You can avoid fall-through in other ways, but **break** is by far the most commonly used approach.) When encountered within the statement sequence of a **case**, the **break** statement causes program flow to exit from the entire **switch** statement and resume at the next statement outside the **switch**. One other point: The **default** statement must also not "fall through" and it too usually ends with a **break**.

Although you cannot allow one **case** sequence to fall through into another, you can have two or more **case** statements refer to the same code sequence, as shown in this example:

```
switch(i) {
  case 1:
  case 2:                          These cases refer to the
  case 3: Console.WriteLine("i is 1, 2 or 3");   same code sequence.
    break;
  case 4: Console.WriteLine("i is 4");
    break;
}
```

In this fragment, if **i** has the value 1, 2, or 3, then the first **WriteLine( )** statement executes. If it is 4, then the second **WriteLine( )** statement executes. The *stacking* of **case**s does not violate the no fall-through rule because the **case** statements all use the same statement sequence.

Stacking **case** statements is a commonly employed technique when several **case**s share common code. For example, here it is used to categorize letters of the alphabet into vowels and consonants:

```
// Categorize letters into vowels and consonants.

using System;

class VowelsAndConsonants {
  public static void Main() {
    char ch;

    Console.Write("Enter a letter: ");
    ch = (char) Console.Read();
    switch(ch) {
        case 'a':
        case 'e':
        case 'i':
        case 'o':
        case 'u':
        case 'y':
          Console.WriteLine("Letter is a vowel.");
          break;
        default:
          Console.WriteLine("Letter is a consonant.");
          break;
    }
  }
}
```

If this example were written without **case** stacking, the same **WriteLine( )** statement would have been duplicated six times. The stacking of **case**s prevents this redundant duplication.

Ask the Expert

Question: Under what conditions should I use an if-else-if ladder rather than a switch when coding a multiway branch?

Answer: In general, use an if-else-if ladder when the conditions controlling the selection process do not rely upon a single value. For example, consider the following if-else-if sequence:

```
if(x < 10) // ...
else if(y != 0) // ...
else if(!done) // ...
```

This sequence cannot be recoded into a **switch** because all three conditions involve different variables—and differing types. What variable would control the **switch**? Also, you will need to use an **if-else-if** ladder when testing floating-point values, or testing other objects that are not of types valid for use in a **switch** expression.

Nested switch Statements

It is possible to have a **switch** as part of the statement sequence of an outer **switch**. This is called a *nested switch*. The **case** constants of the inner and outer **switch** can contain common values and no conflicts will arise. For example, the following code fragment is perfectly acceptable:

```
switch(ch1) {
  case 'A': Console.WriteLine("This A is part of outer switch.");
    switch(ch2) {                              A nested switch
      case 'A':
        Console.WriteLine("This A is part of inner switch");
        break;
      case 'B': // ...
    } // end of inner switch
    break;
  case 'B': // ...
```

Ask the Expert

Question: In C, C++, and Java, one case sequence may continue on (that is, fall through) into the next case. Why is this not allowed by C#?

Answer: There are two reasons that C# instituted the no fall-through rule for cases. First, it allows the compiler to freely rearrange the order of the case statements, perhaps for purposes of optimization. Such a rearrangement would not be possible if one case sequence could flow into the next. Second, requiring each case to explicitly end prevents a programmer from accidentally allowing one case to flow into the next.

1-Minute Drill

● The expression controlling the **switch** must be of what type?

● When the **switch** expression matches a **case** constant, what happens?

● Can the statement sequence associated with one **case** constant continue on into the following **case**?

Project 3-1: Start Building a C# Help System

Help.cs

This project builds a simple help system that displays the syntax for the C# control statements. The program displays a menu containing the control statements and then waits for you to choose one. After one is chosen, the syntax of the statement is displayed. In this first version of the program, help is available for only the **if** and **switch** statements. The other control statements are added by subsequent projects.

● The **switch** expression must be of an integer type, or of type **string**.
● When a matching **case** constant is found, the statement sequence associated with that **case** is executed.
● No, because C# contains a "no fall-through" rule for **switch** statements.

Step-by-Step

1. Create a file called **Help.cs**.

2. The program begins by displaying the following menu:

```
Help on:
  1. if
  2. switch
Choose one:
```

To accomplish this, you will use the statement sequence shown here:

```
Console.WriteLine("Help on:");
Console.WriteLine("  1. if");
Console.WriteLine("  2. switch");
Console.Write("Choose one: ");
```

3. The program obtains the user's selection by calling **Console.Read( )**, as shown here:

```
choice = (char) Console.Read();
```

4. Once the selection has been obtained, the program uses the **switch** statement shown here to display the syntax for the selected statement:

```
switch(choice) {
  case '1':
    Console.WriteLine("The if:\n");
    Console.WriteLine("if(condition) statement;");
    Console.WriteLine("else statement;");
    break;
  case '2':
    Console.WriteLine("The switch:\n");
    Console.WriteLine("switch(expression) {");
    Console.WriteLine("  case constant:");
    Console.WriteLine("    statement sequence");
    Console.WriteLine("    break;");
    Console.WriteLine("  // ...");
    Console.WriteLine("}");
```

```
      break;
    default:
      Console.Write("Selection not found.");
      break;
}
```

Notice how the **default** clause catches invalid choices. For example, if the user enters 3, no **case** constants will match, causing the **default** sequence to execute.

5. Here is the entire **Help.cs** program listing:

```
/*
   Project 3-1

   A simple help system.
*/

using System;

class Help {
  public static void Main() {
    char choice;

    Console.WriteLine("Help on:");
    Console.WriteLine("  1. if");
    Console.WriteLine("  2. switch");
    Console.Write("Choose one: ");
    choice = (char) Console.Read();

    Console.WriteLine("\n");

    switch(choice) {
      case '1':
        Console.WriteLine("The if:\n");
        Console.WriteLine("if(condition) statement;");
        Console.WriteLine("else statement;");
        break;
      case '2':
        Console.WriteLine("The switch:\n");
        Console.WriteLine("switch(expression) {");
        Console.WriteLine("  case constant:");
        Console.WriteLine("    statement sequence");
        Console.WriteLine("    break;");
```

```
        Console.WriteLine("  // ...");
        Console.WriteLine("}");
        break;
      default:
        Console.Write("Selection not found.");
        break;
    }
  }
}
```

Here is a sample run:

```
Help on:
  1. if
  2. switch
Choose one: 1

The if:

if(condition) statement;
else statement;
```

The for Loop

You have been using a simple form of the **for** loop since Module 1. You might be surprised at just how powerful and flexible the **for** loop is. Let's begin by reviewing the basics, starting with the most traditional forms of the **for**.

The general form of the **for** loop for repeating a single statement is

for(*initialization*; *condition*; *iteration*) *statement*;

For repeating a block, the general form is

for(*initialization*; *condition*; *iteration*)
{
   statement sequence
}

The *initialization* is usually an assignment statement that sets the initial value of the *loop control variable*, which acts as the counter that controls the loop.

The *condition* is an expression of type **bool** that determines whether the loop will repeat. The *iteration* expression defines the amount by which the loop control variable will change each time the loop is repeated. Notice that these three major sections of the loop must be separated by semicolons. The **for** loop will continue to execute as long as the condition tests true. Once the condition becomes false, the loop will exit, and program execution will resume on the statement following the **for**.

The following program uses a **for** loop to print the square roots of the numbers between 1 and 99. It also displays the rounding error present for each square root.

```
// Show square roots of 1 to 99 and the rounding error.

using System;

class SqrRoot {
  public static void Main() {
    double num, sroot, rerr;

    for(num = 1.0; num < 100.0; num++) {
      sroot = Math.Sqrt(num);
      Console.WriteLine("Square root of " + num +
                        " is " + sroot);

      // compute rounding error
      rerr = num - (sroot * sroot);
      Console.WriteLine("Rounding error is " + rerr);
      Console.WriteLine();
    }
  }
}
```

Notice that the rounding error is computed by squaring the square root of each number. This result is then subtracted from the original number, thus yielding the rounding error. Of course, in some cases, rounding errors occur when the square root is squared, so sometimes the rounding error, itself, is rounded! This example illustrates the fact that floating-point calculations are not always as precise as we sometimes think they should be!

The **for** loop can proceed in a positive or negative fashion, and it can change the loop control variable by any amount. For example, the following program prints the numbers 100 to –100, in decrements of 5:

```
// A negatively running for loop.

using System;

class DecrFor {
  public static void Main() {
    int x;

    for(x = 100; x > -100; x -= 5)
      Console.WriteLine(x);
  }
}
```

Loop control variable is decremented by 5 each time through this loop.

An important point about **for** loops is that the conditional expression is always tested at the top of the loop. This means that the code inside the loop may not be executed at all if the condition is false to begin with. Here is an example:

```
for(count=10; count < 5; count++)
  x += count; // this statement will not execute
```

This loop will never execute because its control variable, **count**, is greater than five when the loop is first entered. This makes the conditional expression, **count<5**, false from the outset; thus, not even one iteration of the loop will occur.

Some Variations on the for Loop

The **for** is one of the most versatile statements in the C# language because it allows a wide range of variations. For example, multiple loop control variables can be used. Consider the following fragment of a program:

```
// Use commas in a for statement.

using System;

class Comma {
  public static void Main() {
    int i, j;

    for(i=0, j=10; i < j; i++, j--)
      Console.WriteLine("i and j: " + i + " " + j);
  }
}
```

Notice the two loop control variables.

The output from the program is shown here:

```
i and j: 0 10
i and j: 1 9
i and j: 2 8
i and j: 3 7
i and j: 4 6
```

Here, commas separate the two initialization statements and the two iteration expressions. When the loop begins, both i and j are initialized. Each time the loop repeats, i is incremented and j is decremented. Multiple loop control variables are often convenient and can simplify certain algorithms. You can have any number of initialization and iteration statements, but in practice, more than two make the **for** loop unwieldy.

The condition controlling the loop can be any valid expression that produces a **bool** result. It does not need to involve the loop control variable. In the next example, the loop continues to execute until the user types **S** at the keyboard.

```
// Loop until an S is typed.

using System;

class ForTest {
  public static void Main() {
    int i;

    Console.WriteLine("Press S to stop.");

    for(i = 0; (char) Console.Read() != 'S'; i++)
      Console.WriteLine("Pass #" + i);
  }
}
```

Missing Pieces

Some interesting **for** loop variations are created by leaving pieces of the loop definition empty. In C#, it is possible for any or all of the initialization, condition, or iteration portions of the **for** loop to be blank. For example, consider the following program:

```
// Parts of the for can be empty.

using System;

class Empty {
  public static void Main() {
    int i;

    for(i = 0; i < 10; ) {          ◄——  The iteration
      Console.WriteLine("Pass #" + i);    expression is missing.
      i++; // increment loop control var
    }
  }
}
```

Here, the iteration expression of the **for** is empty. Instead, the loop control variable
i is incremented inside the body of the loop. This means that each time the loop
repeats, **i** is tested to see whether it equals ten, but no further action takes place.
Of course, since **i** is incremented within the body of the loop, the loop runs
normally, displaying the following output:

```
Pass #0
Pass #1
Pass #2
Pass #3
Pass #4
Pass #5
Pass #6
Pass #7
Pass #8
Pass #9
```

In the next example, the initialization portion is also moved out of the **for**.

```
// Move more out of the for loop.

using System;

class Empty2 {
  public static void Main() {
    int i;
```

```
    i = 0; // move initialization out of loop ◄──── Initialization
    for(; i < 10; ) {                               expression is
      Console.WriteLine("Pass #" + i);              moved out
      i++; // increment loop control var            of the loop.
    }
  }
}
```

In this version, **i** is initialized before the loop begins, rather than as part of the **for**. Normally, you will want to initialize the loop control variable inside the **for**. Placing the initialization outside of the loop is generally done only when the initial value is derived through a complex process that does not lend itself to containment inside the **for** statement.

The Infinite Loop

You can create an *infinite loop* (a loop that never terminates) using the **for** by leaving the conditional expression empty. For example, the following fragment shows the way many C# programmers create an infinite loop:

```
for(;;) // intentionally infinite loop
{
  //...
}
```

This loop will run forever. Although there are some programming tasks, such as operating-system command processors, that require an infinite loop, most "infinite loops" are really just loops with special termination requirements. Near the end of this module you will see how to halt a loop of this type. (Hint: It's done using the **break** statement.)

Loops with No Body

In C#, the body associated with a **for** loop (or any other loop) can be empty. This is because a *null statement* is syntactically valid. Body-less loops are often useful. For example, the following program uses one to sum the numbers 1 through 5:

```
// The body of a loop can be empty.

using System;

class Empty3 {
```

```
public static void Main() {
    int i;
    int sum = 0;

    // sum the numbers through 5
    for(i = 1; i <= 5; sum += i++) ;

    Console.WriteLine("Sum is " + sum);
  }
}
```

No body in this loop!

The output from the program is shown here:

```
Sum is 15
```

Notice that the summation process is handled entirely within the **for** statement and no body is needed. Pay special attention to the iteration expression:

```
sum += i++
```

Don't be intimidated by statements like this. They are common in professionally written C# programs and are easy to understand if you break them down into their parts. In words, this statement says "add to **sum** the value of **sum** plus **i**, then increment **i**." Thus, it is the same as this sequence of statements:

```
sum = sum + i;
i++;
```

Declaring Loop Control Variables Inside the for Loop

Often the variable that controls a **for** loop is needed only for the purposes of the loop and is not used elsewhere. When this is the case, it is possible to declare the variable inside the initialization portion of the **for**. For example, the following program computes both the summation and the factorial of the numbers 1 through 5. It declares its loop control variable **i** inside the **for**.

```
// Declare loop control variable inside the for.

using System;
```

```
class ForVar {
  public static void Main() {
    int sum = 0;
    int fact = 1;

    // compute the factorial of the numbers through 5
    for(int i = 1; i <= 5; i++) {
      sum += i;   // i is known throughout the loop
      fact *= i;
    }

    // but, i is not known here.

    Console.WriteLine("Sum is " + sum);
    Console.WriteLine("Factorial is " + fact);
  }
}
```

The variable **i** is declared inside the **for** statement.

When you declare a variable inside a **for** loop, there is one important point to remember: the scope of that variable ends when the **for** statement does. (That is, the scope of the variable is limited to the **for** loop.) Outside the **for** loop, the variable will cease to exist. Thus, in the preceding example, **i** is not accessible outside the **for** loop. If you need to use the loop control variable elsewhere in your program, you will not be able to declare it inside the **for** loop.

Before moving on, you might want to experiment with your own variations on the **for** loop. As you will find, it is a fascinating loop.

1-Minute Drill

- Can portions of a **for** statement be empty?

- Show how to create an infinite loop using **for**.

- What is the scope of a variable declared within a **for** statement?

- Yes. All three parts of the **for**, initialization, condition, and iteration, can be empty.
- for(; ;)
- The scope of a variable declared within a **for** is limited to the loop. Outside the loop, it is unknown.

The while Loop

Another of C#'s loops is the **while**. The general form of the **while** loop is

while(*condition*) *statement;*

where *statement* can be a single statement or a block of statements, and *condition* defines the condition that controls the loop and may be any valid Boolean expression. The statement is performed while the condition is true. When the condition becomes false, program control passes to the line of code immediately following the loop.

Here is a simple example in which a **while** is used to print the alphabet:

```
// Demonstrate the while loop.

using System;

class WhileDemo {
  public static void Main() {
    char ch;

    // print the alphabet using a while loop
    ch = 'a';
    while(ch <= 'z') {
      Console.Write(ch);
      ch++;
    }
  }
}
```

Here, **ch** is initialized to the letter a. Each time through the loop, **ch** is output and then incremented. This process continues until **ch** is greater than z.

As with the **for** loop, the **while** checks the conditional expression at the top of the loop, which means that the loop code may not execute at all. This eliminates the need to perform a separate test before the loop. The following program illustrates this characteristic of the **while** loop. It computes the integer powers of 2 from 0 to 9.

```
// Compute integer powers of 2.

using System;

class Power {
  public static void Main() {
    int e;
    int result;

    for(int i=0; i < 10; i++) {
      result = 1;
      e = i;
      while(e > 0) {
        result *= 2;
        e--;
      }

      Console.WriteLine("2 to the " + i +
                          " power is " + result);
    }
  }
}
```

The output from the program is shown here:

```
2 to the 0 power is 1
2 to the 1 power is 2
2 to the 2 power is 4
2 to the 3 power is 8
2 to the 4 power is 16
2 to the 5 power is 32
2 to the 6 power is 64
2 to the 7 power is 128
2 to the 8 power is 256
2 to the 9 power is 512
```

Notice that the **while** loop executes only when **e** is greater than 0. Thus, when **e** is zero, as it is in the first iteration of the **for** loop, the **while** loop is skipped.

Ask the Expert

Question: Given the flexibility inherent in all of C#'s loops, what criteria should I use when selecting a loop? That is, how do I choose the right loop for a specific job?

Answer: Use a **for** loop when performing a known number of iterations. Use the **do-while** when you need a loop that will always perform at least one iteration. The **while** is best used when the loop will repeat an unknown number of times.

3

The do-while Loop

The last of C#'s loops is the **do-while**. Unlike the **for** and the **while** loops, in which the condition is tested at the top of the loop, the **do-while** loop checks its condition at the bottom of the loop. This means that a **do-while** loop will always execute at least once. The general form of the **do-while** loop is

```
do {
   statements;
} while(condition);
```

Although the braces are not necessary when only one statement is present, they are often used to improve readability of the **do-while** construct, thus preventing confusion with the **while**. The **do-while** loop executes as long as the conditional expression is true.

The following program loops until the user enters the letter **q**:

```
// Demonstrate the do-while loop.

using System;

class DWDemo {
  public static void Main() {
    char ch;

    do {
      Console.Write("Press a key following by ENTER: ");
```

```
      ch = (char) Console.Read(); // get a char
    } while(ch != 'q');
  }
}
```

Using a **do-while** loop, we can further improve the guessing game program from earlier in this module. This time, the program loops until you guess the letter.

```
// Guess the letter game, 4th version.

using System;

class Guess4 {
  public static void Main() {
    char ch, answer = 'K';

    do {
      Console.WriteLine("I'm thinking of a letter between A and Z.");
      Console.Write("Can you guess it: ");

      // read a letter, but skip cr/lf
      do {
        ch = (char) Console.Read(); // get a char
      } while(ch == '\n' | ch == '\r');

      if(ch == answer) Console.WriteLine("** Right **");
      else {
        Console.Write("...Sorry, you're ");
        if(ch < answer) Console.WriteLine("too low");
        else Console.WriteLine("too high");
        Console.WriteLine("Try again!\n");
      }
    } while(answer != ch);
  }
}
```

Here is a sample run:

```
I'm thinking of a letter between A and Z.
Can you guess it: A
```

```
...Sorry, you're too low
Try again!

I'm thinking of a letter between A and Z.
Can you guess it: Z
...Sorry, you're too high
Try again!

I'm thinking of a letter between A and Z.
Can you guess it: K
** Right **
```

Notice one other thing of interest in this program. The **do-while** loop shown here obtains the next character, skipping over any carriage-return and linefeed characters that might be in the input stream:

```
// read a letter, but skip cr/lf
do {
  ch = (char) Console.Read(); // get a char
} while(ch == '\n' | ch == '\r');
```

Here is why this loop is needed. As explained earlier, console input is line-buffered—you have to press ENTER before characters are sent. Pressing ENTER causes a carriage-return and a linefeed character to be generated. These characters are left pending in the input buffer. This loop discards those characters by continuing to read input until neither is present.

1-Minute Drill

- What is the main difference between the **while** and the **do-while** loops?
- The condition controlling the **while** can be of any type. True or false?

- The **while** checks its condition at the top of the loop. The **do-while** checks its condition at the bottom of the loop. Thus, a **do-while** will always execute at least once.
- False. The condition must be of type **bool**.

Help2.cs

Project 3-2: Improve the C# Help System

This project expands on the C# help system that was created in Project 3-1. This version adds the syntax for the **for**, **while**, and **do-while** loops. It also checks the user's menu selection, looping until a valid response is entered.

Step-by-Step

1. Copy **Help.cs** to a new file called **Help2.cs**.

2. Change the portion of the program that displays the choices so that it uses the loop shown here:

```
do {
  Console.WriteLine("Help on:");
  Console.WriteLine("  1. if");
  Console.WriteLine("  2. switch");
  Console.WriteLine("  3. for");
  Console.WriteLine("  4. while");
  Console.WriteLine("  5. do-while\n");
  Console.Write("Choose one: ");
  do {
    choice = (char) Console.Read();
  } while(choice == '\n' | choice == '\r');
} while( choice < '1' | choice > '5');
```

Notice that a nested **do-while** loop is used to discard any spurious carriage-return or linefeed characters that may be present in the input stream. After making this change, the program will loop, displaying the menu until the user enters a response that is between 1 and 5.

3. Expand the **switch** statement to include the **for**, **while**, and **do-while** loops, as shown here:

```
switch(choice) {
  case '1':
    Console.WriteLine("The if:\n");
    Console.WriteLine("if(condition) statement;");
    Console.WriteLine("else statement;");
    break;
  case '2':
    Console.WriteLine("The switch:\n");
    Console.WriteLine("switch(expression) {");
    Console.WriteLine("  case constant:");
```

```
      Console.WriteLine("    statement sequence");
      Console.WriteLine("    break;");
      Console.WriteLine("  // ...");
      Console.WriteLine("}");
      break;
    case '3':
      Console.WriteLine("The for:\n");
      Console.Write("for(init; condition; iteration)");
      Console.WriteLine(" statement;");
      break;
    case '4':
      Console.WriteLine("The while:\n");
      Console.WriteLine("while(condition) statement;");
      break;
    case '5':
      Console.WriteLine("The do-while:\n");
      Console.WriteLine("do {");
      Console.WriteLine("  statement;");
      Console.WriteLine("} while (condition);");
      break;
  }
```

Notice that no **default** statement is present in this version of the **switch**. Since the menu loop ensures that a valid response will be entered, it is no longer necessary to include a **default** statement to handle an invalid choice.

4. Here is the entire **Help2.cs** program listing:

```
/*
   Project 3-2

   An improved Help system that uses a
   a do-while to process a menu selection.
*/

using System;

class Help2 {
  public static void Main() {
    char choice;

    do {
      Console.WriteLine("Help on:");
      Console.WriteLine("  1. if");
```

```
      Console.WriteLine("  2. switch");
      Console.WriteLine("  3. for");
      Console.WriteLine("  4. while");
      Console.WriteLine("  5. do-while\n");
      Console.Write("Choose one: ");
      do {
        choice = (char) Console.Read();
      } while(choice == '\n' | choice == '\r');
    } while( choice < '1' | choice > '5');

    Console.WriteLine("\n");

    switch(choice) {
      case '1':
        Console.WriteLine("The if:\n");
        Console.WriteLine("if(condition) statement;");
        Console.WriteLine("else statement;");
        break;
      case '2':
        Console.WriteLine("The switch:\n");
        Console.WriteLine("switch(expression) {");
        Console.WriteLine("  case constant:");
        Console.WriteLine("    statement sequence");
        Console.WriteLine("    break;");
        Console.WriteLine("  // ...");
        Console.WriteLine("}");
        break;
      case '3':
        Console.WriteLine("The for:\n");
        Console.Write("for(init; condition; iteration)");
        Console.WriteLine(" statement;");
        break;
      case '4':
        Console.WriteLine("The while:\n");
        Console.WriteLine("while(condition) statement;");
        break;
      case '5':
        Console.WriteLine("The do-while:\n");
        Console.WriteLine("do {");
        Console.WriteLine("  statement;");
        Console.WriteLine("} while (condition);");
        break;
    }
  }
}
```

Using break to Exit a Loop

It is possible to force an immediate exit from a loop, bypassing any code remaining in the body of the loop and the loop's conditional test, by using the **break** statement. When a **break** statement is encountered inside a loop, the loop is terminated and program control resumes at the next statement following the loop. Here is a simple example:

```
// Using break to exit a loop.

using System;

class BreakDemo {
  public static void Main() {
    int num;

    num = 100;

    // loop while i-squared is less than num
    for(int i=0; i < num; i++) {
      if(i*i >= num) break; // terminate loop if i*i >= 100
      Console.Write(i + " ");
    }
    Console.WriteLine("Loop complete.");
  }
}
```

Use **break** to terminate the loop.

This program generates the following output:

```
0 1 2 3 4 5 6 7 8 9 Loop complete.
```

As you can see, although the **for** loop is designed to run from 0 to **num** (which in this case is 100), the **break** statement causes it to terminate early, when **i** squared is greater than or equal to **num**.

The **break** statement can be used with any of C#'s loops, including intentionally infinite loops. For example, the following program simply reads input until the user presses q.

```
// Read input until a q is received.

using System;

class Break2 {
  public static void Main() {
    char ch;

    for( ; ; ) {
      ch = (char) Console.Read(); // get a char
      if(ch == 'q') break;
    }
    Console.WriteLine("You pressed q!");
  }
}
```

This "infinite" loop is terminated by the **break**.

When used inside a set of nested loops, the **break** statement will break out of only the innermost loop. For example:

```
// Using break with nested loops.

using System;

class Break3 {
  public static void Main() {

    for(int i=0; i<3; i++) {
      Console.WriteLine("Outer loop count: " + i);
      Console.Write("    Inner loop count: ");

      int t = 0;
      while(t < 100) {
        if(t == 10) break; // terminate loop if t is 10
        Console.Write(t + " ");
        t++;
      }
      Console.WriteLine();
    }
    Console.WriteLine("Loops complete.");
  }
}
```

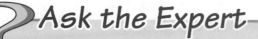

Ask the Expert

Question: I know that in Java, the break and continue **statements** can be used with a label. Does C# support the same feature?

Answer: No. The designers of C# did not give **break** or **continue** that capability. Instead, **break** and **continue** work the same in C# as they do in C and C++. One reason that C# did not follow Java's lead on this issue is that Java does not support the **goto** statement, but C# does. Thus, Java needs to give **break** and **continue** extra power to make up for the lack of the **goto**.

3

This program generates the following output:

```
Outer loop count: 0
    Inner loop count: 0 1 2 3 4 5 6 7 8 9
Outer loop count: 1
    Inner loop count: 0 1 2 3 4 5 6 7 8 9
Outer loop count: 2
    Inner loop count: 0 1 2 3 4 5 6 7 8 9
Loops complete.
```

As you can see, the **break** statement in the inner loop causes only the termination of that loop. The outer loop is unaffected.

Here are two other points to remember about **break**. First, more than one **break** statement may appear in a loop. However, be careful. Too many **break** statements have the tendency to destructure your code. Second, the **break** that terminates a **switch** statement affects only that **switch** statement and not any enclosing loops.

Using continue

It is possible to force an early iteration of a loop, bypassing the loop's normal control structure. This is accomplished using **continue**. The **continue** statement forces the next iteration of the loop to take place, skipping any code in between. Thus, **continue** is essentially the complement of **break**. For example, the following program uses **continue** to help print the even numbers between 0 and 100:

```
// Use continue.

using System;

class ContDemo {
  public static void Main() {
    int i;

    // print even numbers between 0 and 100
    for(i = 0; i<=100; i++) {
      if((i%2) != 0) continue; // iterate  ◄──────  Continue if i is odd.
      Console.WriteLine(i);
    }
  }
}
```

Only even numbers are printed, because an odd one will cause the loop to iterate early, bypassing the call to **WriteLine( )**.

In **while** and **do-while** loops, a **continue** statement will cause control to go directly to the conditional expression and then continue the looping process. In the case of the **for**, the iteration expression of the loop is evaluated, the conditional expression is executed, and then the loop continues.

Good uses of **continue** are rare. One reason is that C# provides a rich set of loop statements that fit most applications. However, for those special circumstances in which early iteration is needed, the **continue** statement provides a structured way to accomplish it.

The goto

The **goto** is C#'s unconditional jump statement. When encountered, program flow jumps to the location specified by the **goto**. The statement fell out of favor with programmers many years ago because it encouraged the creation of "spaghetti code." However, the **goto** is still occasionally—and sometimes effectively— used. This book will not make a judgment regarding its validity as a form of program control. It should be stated, however, that there are no programming situations that require the use of the **goto** statement—it is not an item necessary for making the language complete. Rather, it is a convenience which, if used wisely, can be of benefit in certain programming situations. As such, the **goto** is not used in this book outside of this section. The chief concern most programmers have about the **goto** is its tendency to clutter a program and render it nearly unreadable. However, there are times when the use of the **goto** can clarify program flow rather than confuse it.

The **goto** requires a label for operation. A *label* is a valid C# identifier followed by a colon. Furthermore, the label must be in the same method as the **goto** that uses it. For example, a loop from 1 to 100 could be written using a **goto** and a label, as shown here:

```
x = 1;
loop1:
  x++;
  if(x < 100) goto loop1;        Execution jumps to loop1.
```

One good use for the **goto** is to exit from a deeply nested routine. Here is a simple example.

```
/*
  Demonstrate the goto.
*/

using System;

class Use_goto {
  public static void Main() {
    int i=0, j=0, k=0;

    for(i=0; i < 10; i++) {
      for(j=0; j < 10; j++ ) {
        for(k=0; k < 10; k++) {
          Console.WriteLine("i, j, k: " + i + " " + j + " " + k);
          if(k == 3) goto stop;
        }
      }
    }

stop:
    Console.WriteLine("Stopped! i, j, k: " + i + ", " + j + " " + k);

  }
}
```

The output from the program is shown here.

```
i, j, k: 0 0 0
i, j, k: 0 0 1
i, j, k: 0 0 2
i, j, k: 0 0 3
Stopped! i, j, k: 0, 0 3
```

Eliminating the **goto** would force the use of three **if** and **break** statements. In this case, the **goto** simplifies the code. While this is a contrived example used for illustration, you can imagine situations in which a **goto** might be beneficial.

1-Minute Drill

● Within a loop, what happens when a **break** is executed?

● What does **continue** do?

● What is C#'s unconditional jump statement?

Help3.cs

Project 3-3: Finish the C# Help System

This project puts the finishing touches on the C# help system that was created by the previous projects. This version adds the syntax for **break, continue,** and **goto**. It also allows the user to request the syntax for more than one statement. It does this by adding an outer loop that runs until the user enters a **q** as a menu selection.

Step-by-Step

1. Copy **Help2.cs** to a new file called **Help3.cs**.

2. Surround all of the program code with an infinite **for** loop. Break out of this loop, using **break**, when a **q** is entered. Since this loop surrounds all of the program code, breaking out of this loop causes the program to terminate.

● Within a loop, **break** causes immediate termination of the loop. Execution resumes at the first line of code after the loop.
● The **continue** statement causes a loop to iterate immediately, bypassing any remaining code.
● C#'s unconditional jump statement is **goto**.

3. Change the menu loop as shown here:

```
do {
  Console.WriteLine("Help on:");
  Console.WriteLine("  1. if");
  Console.WriteLine("  2. switch");
  Console.WriteLine("  3. for");
  Console.WriteLine("  4. while");
  Console.WriteLine("  5. do-while");
  Console.WriteLine("  6. break");
  Console.WriteLine("  7. continue");
  Console.WriteLine("  8. goto\n");
  Console.Write("Choose one (q to quit): ");
  do {
    choice = (char) Console.Read();
  } while(choice == '\n' | choice == '\r');
} while( choice < '1' | choice > '8' & choice != 'q');
```

Notice that this loop now includes the **break**, **continue**, and **goto** statements. It also accepts a **q** as a valid choice.

4. Expand the **switch** statement to include the **break**, **continue**, and **goto** statements, as shown here:

```
case '6':
  Console.WriteLine("The break:\n");
  Console.WriteLine("break;");
  break;
case '7':
  Console.WriteLine("The continue:\n");
  Console.WriteLine("continue;");
  break;
case '8':
  Console.WriteLine("The goto:\n");
  Console.WriteLine("goto label;");
  break;
```

5. Here is the entire **Help3.cs** program listing:

```
/*
   Project 3-3

   The finished C# statement Help system
```

```
     that processes multiple requests.
*/

using System;

class Help3 {
  public static void Main() {
    char choice;

    for(;;) {
      do {
        Console.WriteLine("Help on:");
        Console.WriteLine("  1. if");
        Console.WriteLine("  2. switch");
        Console.WriteLine("  3. for");
        Console.WriteLine("  4. while");
        Console.WriteLine("  5. do-while");
        Console.WriteLine("  6. break");
        Console.WriteLine("  7. continue");
        Console.WriteLine("  8. goto\n");
        Console.Write("Choose one (q to quit): ");
        do {
          choice = (char) Console.Read();
        } while(choice == '\n' | choice == '\r');
      } while( choice < '1' | choice > '8' & choice != 'q');

      if(choice == 'q') break;

      Console.WriteLine("\n");

      switch(choice) {
        case '1':
          Console.WriteLine("The if:\n");
          Console.WriteLine("if(condition) statement;");
          Console.WriteLine("else statement;");
          break;
        case '2':
          Console.WriteLine("The switch:\n");
          Console.WriteLine("switch(expression) {");
          Console.WriteLine("  case constant:");
          Console.WriteLine("    statement sequence");
          Console.WriteLine("    break;");
          Console.WriteLine("  // ...");
          Console.WriteLine("}");
```

```
          break;
        case '3':
          Console.WriteLine("The for:\n");
          Console.Write("for(init; condition; iteration)");
          Console.WriteLine(" statement;");
          break;
        case '4':
          Console.WriteLine("The while:\n");
          Console.WriteLine("while(condition) statement;");
          break;
        case '5':
          Console.WriteLine("The do-while:\n");
          Console.WriteLine("do {");
          Console.WriteLine("  statement;");
          Console.WriteLine("} while (condition);");
          break;
        case '6':
          Console.WriteLine("The break:\n");
          Console.WriteLine("break;");
          break;
        case '7':
          Console.WriteLine("The continue:\n");
          Console.WriteLine("continue;");
          break;
        case '8':
          Console.WriteLine("The goto:\n");
          Console.WriteLine("goto label;");
          break;
      }
      Console.WriteLine();
    }
  }
}
```

Here is a sample run:

```
Help on:
  1. if
  2. switch
  3. for
  4. while
  5. do-while
  6. break
```

```
   7. continue
   8. goto

Choose one (q to quit): 1

The if:

if(condition) statement;
else statement;

Help on:
   1. if
   2. switch
   3. for
   4. while
   5. do-while
   6. break
   7. continue
   8. goto

Choose one (q to quit): 6

The break:

break;

Help on:
   1. if
   2. switch
   3. for
   4. while
   5. do-while
   6. break
   7. continue
   8. goto

Choose one (q to quit): q
```

Nested Loops

As you have seen in some of the preceding examples, one loop can be nested inside another. Nested loops are used to solve a wide variety of programming problems and are an essential part of programming. So, before leaving the topic of C#'s loop statements, let's look at one more nested loop example. The following program uses a nested **for** loop to find the factors of the numbers from 2 to 100:

3

```
/*
   Use nested loops to find factors of numbers
   between 2 and 100.
*/

using System;

class FindFac {
  public static void Main() {

    for(int i=2; i <= 100; i++) {
      Console.Write("Factors of " + i + ": ");
      for(int j = 2; j < i; j++)
        if((i%j) == 0) Console.Write(j + " ");
      Console.WriteLine();
    }
  }
}
```

Here is a portion of the output produced by the program:

```
Factors of 2:
Factors of 3:
Factors of 4: 2
Factors of 5:
Factors of 6: 2 3
Factors of 7:
Factors of 8: 2 4
Factors of 9: 3
Factors of 10: 2 5
Factors of 11:
```

```
Factors of 12: 2 3 4 6
Factors of 13:
Factors of 14: 2 7
Factors of 15: 3 5
Factors of 16: 2 4 8
Factors of 17:
Factors of 18: 2 3 6 9
Factors of 19:
Factors of 20: 2 4 5 10
```

In the program, the outer loop runs i from 2 through 100. The inner loop successively tests all numbers from 2 up to i, printing those that evenly divide i.

☑ *Mastery Check*

1. Write a program that reads characters from the keyboard until a period is received. Have the program count the number of spaces. Report the total at the end of the program.

2. In the **switch**, can the code sequence from one **case** run into the next?

3. Show the general form of the **if-else-if** ladder.

4. Given

```
if(x < 10)
  if(y > 100) {
    if(!done) x = z;
    else y = z;
  }
else Console.WriteLine("error"); // what if?
```

to what **if** does the last **else** associate?

5. Show the **for** statement for a loop that counts from 1,000 to 0 by –2.

6. Is the following fragment valid?

```
for(int i = 0; i < num; i++)
  sum += i;

count = i;
```

7. Explain what **break** does.

8. In the following fragment, after the **break** statement executes, what is displayed?

```
for(i = 0; i < 10; i++) {
  while(running) {
    if(x<y) break;
    // ...
  }
  Console.WriteLine("after while");
}
Console.WriteLine("After for");
```

☑ Mastery Check

9. What does the following fragment print?

```
for(int i = 0; i<10; i++) {
  Console.Write(i + " ");
  if((i%2) == 0) continue;
  Console.WriteLine();
}
```

10. The iteration expression in a **for** loop need not always alter the loop control variable by a fixed amount. Instead, the loop control variable can change in any arbitrary way. Using this concept, write a program that uses a **for** loop to generate and display the progression 1, 2, 4, 8, 16, 32, and so on.

11. The ASCII lowercase letters are separated from the uppercase letters by 32. Thus, to convert a lowercase letter to uppercase, subtract 32 from it. Use this information to write a program that reads characters from the keyboard. Have it convert all lowercase letters to uppercase, and all uppercase letters to lowercase, displaying the result. Make no changes to any other character. Have the program stop when the user presses period. At the end, have the program display the number of case changes that have taken place.

Module 4

Introducing Classes, Objects, and Methods

The Goals of This Module

- Learn the fundamentals of the class
- Understand how objects are created
- Create a method
- Add parameters to a method
- Return a value from a method
- Utilize constructors
- Examine new and understand garbage collection
- Understand destructors
- Gain an overview of the this keyword

Before you can go much further in your study of C#, you need to learn about the class. The class is the essence of C# because it defines the nature of an object. The class is the foundation upon which the entire C# language is built. As such, the class forms the basis for object-oriented programming in C#. Within a class are defined data and the code that acts upon that data. The code is contained in methods. Because classes, objects, and methods are fundamental to C#, they are introduced in this module. Having a basic understanding of these features will allow you to write more sophisticated programs and to better understand certain key C# elements described in the following module.

Class Fundamentals

Because all C# program activity occurs within a class, we have been using classes since the start of this book. Of course, only extremely simple classes have been used, and we have not taken advantage of the majority of their features. As you will see, classes are substantially more powerful than the limited ones presented so far.

Let's begin by reviewing the basics. A class is a template that defines the form of an object. It specifies both the data and the code that will operate on that data. C# uses a class specification to construct *objects*. Objects are *instances* of a class. Thus, a class is essentially a set of plans that specifies how to build an object. It is important to be clear on one issue: A class is a logical abstraction. It is not until an object of that class has been created that a physical representation of that class exists in memory.

One other point: recall that the methods and variables that constitute a class are called *members* of the class.

The General Form of a Class

When you define a class, you declare the data that it contains and the code that operates on it. While very simple classes might contain only code or only data, most real-world classes contain both.

In general terms, data is contained in instance variables defined by the class and code is contained in methods. It is important to state at the outset, however, that C# defines several specific flavors of data and code members, which include instance variables, static variables, constants, methods, constructors, destructors, indexers, events, operators, and properties. For now, we will limit our discussion of the class to its essential elements: instance variables and methods. Later in this module constructors and destructors are discussed. The other types of members are described in later modules.

A class is created by using the keyword **class**. The general form of a **class** definition that contains only instance variables and methods is shown here:

```
class classname {
    // declare instance variables
    access type var1;
    access type var2;
    // ...
    access type varN;

    // declare methods
    access ret-type method1(parameters) {
        // body of method
    }
    access ret-type method2(parameters) {
        // body of method
    }
    // ...
    access ret-type methodN(parameters) {
        // body of method
    }
}
```

Notice that each variable and method is preceded with *access*. Here, *access* is an access specifier, such as **public**, which specifies how the member can be accessed. As mentioned in Module 1, class members can be private to a class, or more accessible. The access specifier determines what type of access is allowed. The access specifier is optional, and if absent, then the member is private to the class. Members with private access can be used only by other members of their class. For the examples in this module, all members will be specified as **public**, which means that they can be used by all other code—even code defined outside the class. We will return to the topic of access specifiers in a later module.

Although there is no syntactic rule that enforces it, a well-designed class should define one and only one logical entity. For example, a class that stores names and telephone numbers will not normally also store information about the stock market, average rainfall, sunspot cycles, or other unrelated information. The point here is that a well-designed class groups logically connected information. Putting unrelated information into the same class will quickly destructure your code!

Up to this point, the classes that we have been using have only had one method: **Main( )**. Soon you will see how to create others. However, notice that the general form of a class does not specify a **Main( )** method. A **Main( )** method is required only if that class is the starting point for your program.

Defining a Class

To illustrate classes, we will be evolving a class that encapsulates information about vehicles such as cars, vans, and trucks. This class is called **Vehicle**, and it will store three items of information about a vehicle: the number of passengers that it can carry, its fuel capacity, and its average fuel consumption (in miles per gallon).

The first version of **Vehicle** is shown here. It defines three instance variables: **passengers**, **fuelcap**, and **mpg**. Notice that **Vehicle** does not contain any methods. Thus, it is currently a data-only class. (Subsequent sections will add methods to it.)

```
class Vehicle {
  public int passengers; // number of passengers
  public int fuelcap;    // fuel capacity in gallons
  public int mpg;        // fuel consumption in miles per gallon
}
```

The instance variables defined by **Vehicle** illustrate the way that instance variables are declared in general. The general form for declaring an instance variable is shown here:

access type var-name;

Here, *access* specifies the access, *type* specifies the type of variable, and *var-name* is the variable's name. Thus, aside from the access specifier, you declare an instance variable in the same way that you declare local variables. For **Vehicle**, the variables are preceded by the **public** access modifier. As explained, this allows them to be accessed by code outside of **Vehicle**.

A **class** definition creates a new data type. In this case, the new data type is called **Vehicle**. You will use this name to declare objects of type **Vehicle**.

Remember that a **class** declaration is only a type description; it does not create an actual object. Thus, the preceding code does not cause any objects of type **Vehicle** to come into existence.

To actually create a **Vehicle** object, you will use a statement like the following:

```
Vehicle minivan = new Vehicle(); // create a Vehicle object called minivan
```

After this statement executes, **minivan** will be an instance of **Vehicle**. Thus, it will have "physical" reality. For the moment, don't worry about the details of this statement.

Each time you create an instance of a class, you are creating an object that contains its own copy of each instance variable defined by the class. Thus, every **Vehicle** object will contain its own copies of the instance variables **passengers**, **fuelcap**, and **mpg**. To access these variables, you will use the *dot* (.) operator. The dot operator links the name of an object with the name of a member. The general form of the dot operator is shown here:

object.member

Thus, the object is specified on the left, and the member is put on the right. For example, to assign the **fuelcap** variable of **minivan** the value 16, use the following statement:

```
minivan.fuelcap = 16;
```

In general, you can use the dot operator to access both instance variables and methods.

Here is a complete program that uses the **Vehicle** class:

```
/* A program that uses the Vehicle class.

   Call this file UseVehicle.cs
*/

using System;

class Vehicle {
  public int passengers; // number of passengers
  public int fuelcap;    // fuel capacity in gallons
  public int mpg;        // fuel consumption in miles per gallon
}
```

4

```
// This class declares an object of type Vehicle.
class VehicleDemo {
  public static void Main() {
    Vehicle minivan = new Vehicle();          Create an instance of
    int range;                                 Vehicle called minivan.

    // assign values to fields in minivan
    minivan.passengers = 7;
    minivan.fuelcap = 16;                      Notice the use of the dot
    minivan.mpg = 21;                          operator to access a member.

    // compute the range assuming a full tank of gas
    range = minivan.fuelcap * minivan.mpg;

    Console.WriteLine("Minivan can carry " + minivan.passengers +
                     " with a range of " + range);
  }
}
```

This program consists of two classes: **Vehicle** and **VehicleDemo**. Inside **VehicleDemo**, the **Main( )** method creates an instance of **Vehicle** called **minivan**. Then the code within **Main( )** accesses the instance variables associated with **minivan**, assigning them values and using those values. It is important to understand that **Vehicle** and **VehicleDemo** are two separate classes. The only relationship they have to each other is that one class creates an instance of the other. Although they are separate classes, code inside **VehicleDemo** can access the members of **Vehicle** because they are declared **public**. If they had not been given the **public** access specifier, their access would have been limited to the **Vehicle** class, and **VehicleDemo** would not have been able to use them.

Assuming that you call the preceding file **UseVehicle.cs**, compiling this program creates a file called **UseVehicle.exe**. Both the **Vehicle** and **Vehicle-Demo** classes are automatically part of the executable file. The program displays the following output:

```
Minivan can carry 7 with a range of 336
```

It is not necessary for both the **Vehicle** and the **VehicleDemo** classes to actually be in the same source file. You could put each class in its own file, called **Vehicle.cs** and **VehicleDemo.cs**, for example. Just tell the C# compiler to compile both files and link them together. For example, you could use this command line to compile the program if you split it into two pieces as just described:

```
csc Vehicle.cs VehicleDemo.cs
```

If you are using the Visual C++ IDE, you will need to add both files to your program and then build.

Before moving on, let's review a fundamental principle: each object has its own copies of the instance variables defined by its class. Thus, the contents of the variables in one object can differ from the contents of the variables in another. There is no connection between the two objects except for the fact that they are both objects of the same type. For example, if you have two **Vehicle** objects, each has its own copy of **passengers**, **fuelcap**, and **mpg**, and the contents of these can differ between the two objects. The following program demonstrates this fact:

```
// This program creates two Vehicle objects.

using System;

class Vehicle {
  public int passengers; // number of passengers
  public int fuelcap;    // fuel capacity in gallons
  public int mpg;        // fuel consumption in miles per gallon
}

// This class declares an object of type Vehicle.
class TwoVehicles {
  public static void Main() {
    Vehicle minivan = new Vehicle();
    Vehicle sportscar = new Vehicle();

    int range1, range2;

    // assign values to fields in minivan
    minivan.passengers = 7;
    minivan.fuelcap = 16;
```

Remember, **minivan** and **sportscar** refer to separate objects.

4

```
   minivan.mpg = 21;

   // assign values to fields in sportscar
   sportscar.passengers = 2;
   sportscar.fuelcap = 14;
   sportscar.mpg = 12;

   // compute the ranges assuming a full tank of gas
   range1 = minivan.fuelcap * minivan.mpg;
   range2 = sportscar.fuelcap * sportscar.mpg;

   Console.WriteLine("Minivan can carry " + minivan.passengers +
                     " with a range of " + range1);

   Console.WriteLine("Sportscar can carry " + sportscar.passengers +
                     " with a range of " + range2);
  }
}
```

The output produced by this program is shown here:

```
Minivan can carry 7 with a range of 336
Sportscar can carry 2 with a range of 168
```

As you can see, **minivan**'s data is completely separate from the data contained in **sportscar**. Figure 4-1 depicts this situation.

1-Minute Drill

- A class contains what two things?
- What operator is used to access the members of a class through an object?
- Each object has its own copies of the class' _____.

- A class contains code and data.
- The dot operator is used to access the members of a class through an object.
- Each object has its own copies of the class' instance variables.

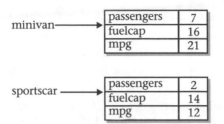

Figure 4-1   One object's instance variables are separate from another's.

How Objects Are Created

In the preceding programs, the following line was used to declare an object of type **Vehicle**:

```
Vehicle minivan = new Vehicle();
```

This declaration performs two functions. First, it declares a variable called **minivan** of the class type **Vehicle**. This variable does not define an object. Instead, it is simply a variable that can *refer to* an object. Second, the declaration creates an actual, physical copy of the object and assigns to **minivan** a reference to that object. This is done by using the **new** operator. Thus, after the line executes, **minivan** refers to an object of type **Vehicle**.

The **new** operator *dynamically allocates* (that is, allocates at runtime) memory for an object and returns a reference to it. This reference is, more or less, the address in memory of the object allocated by **new**. This reference is then stored in a variable. Thus, in C#, all class objects must be dynamically allocated.

The two steps combined in the preceding statement can be rewritten like this to show each step individually:

```
Vehicle minivan; // declare reference to object
minivan = new Vehicle(); // allocate a Vehicle object
```

The first line declares **minivan** as a reference to an object of type **Vehicle**. Thus, **minivan** is a variable that can refer to an object, but it is not an object, itself. At this point, **minivan** contains the value **null**, which means that it does not refer to an object. The next line creates a new **Vehicle** object and assigns a reference to it to **minivan**. Now, **minivan** is linked with an object.

The fact that class objects are accessed through a reference explains why classes are called *reference types*. The key difference between value types and reference types is what a variable of each type means. For a variable of a value type, the variable, itself, contains the value. For example, given

```
int x;
x = 10;
```

x contains the value 10 because **x** is a variable of type **int**, which is a value type. However, in the case of

```
Vehicle minivan = new Vehicle();
```

minivan does not, itself, contain the object. Instead, it contains a reference to the object.

Reference Variables and Assignment

In an assignment operation, reference variables act differently than do variables of a value type, such as **int**. When you assign one value type variable to another, the situation is straightforward. The variable on the left receives a *copy* of the *value* of the variable on the right. When you assign an object reference variable to another, the situation is a bit more complicated because you are changing the object that the reference variable refers to. The effect of this difference can cause some counterintuitive results. For example, consider the following fragment:

```
Vehicle car1 = new Vehicle();
Vehicle car2 = car1;
```

At first glance, it is easy to think that **car1** and **car2** refer to different objects, but this is not the case. Instead, **car1** and **car2** will both refer to the *same* object.

The assignment of **car1** to **car2** simply makes **car2** refer to the same object as does **car1**. Thus, the object can be acted upon by either **car1** or **car2**. For example, after this assignment executes,

```
car1.mpg = 26;
```

both of these **WriteLine( )** statements display the same value, 26:

```
Console.WriteLine(car1.mpg);
Console.WriteLine(car2.mpg);
```

4

Although **car1** and **car2** both refer to the same object, they are not linked in any other way. For example, a subsequent assignment to **car2** simply changes the object to which **car2** refers. For example:

```
Vehicle car1 = new Vehicle();
Vehicle car2 = car1;
Vehicle car3 = new Vehicle();

car2 = car3; // now car2 and car3 refer to the same object.
```

After this sequence executes, **car2** refers to the same object as **car3**. The object referred to by **car1** is unchanged.

1-Minute Drill

● Explain what occurs when one reference variable is assigned to another.

● Assuming a class called **MyClass**, show how an object called **ob** is created.

● How do value types and reference types differ?

Methods

As explained, instance variables and methods are two of the primary constituents of classes. So far, the **Vehicle** class contains data but no methods. Although

---

● When one reference variable is assigned to another reference variable, both variables will refer to the same object. A copy of the object *is not* made.
● `MyClass ob = new MyClass();`
● A variable of a value type contains its value, itself. A variable of a reference type refers to another object.

data-only classes are perfectly valid, most classes will have methods. Methods are subroutines that manipulate the data defined by the class and, in many cases, provide access to that data. Typically, other parts of your program will interact with a class through its methods.

A method contains one or more statements. In well-written C# code, each method performs only one task. Each method has a name, and this name is used to call the method. In general, you can name a method whatever you please. However, remember that **Main( )** is reserved for the method that begins execution of your program. Also, don't use C#'s keywords for method names.

When denoting methods in text, this book has used and will continue to use a convention that has become common when writing about C#. A method will have parentheses after its name. For example, if a method's name is **getval**, then it will be written **getval( )** when its name is used in a sentence. This notation will help you distinguish variable names from method names in this book.

The general form of a method is shown here:

```
access ret-type name(parameter-list) {
    // body of method
}
```

Here, *access* is an access modifier that governs what other parts of your program can call the method. As explained earlier, the access modifier is optional. If not present, then the method is private to the class in which it is declared. For now, we will declare all methods as **public** so that they can be called by any other code in the program. The *ret-type* specifies the type of data returned by the method. This can be any valid type, including class types that you create. If the method does not return a value, its return type must be **void**. The name of the method is specified by *name*. This can be any legal identifier other than those already used by other items within the current scope. The *parameter-list* is a sequence of type and identifier pairs separated by commas. Parameters are essentially variables that receive the value of the *arguments* passed to the method when it is called. If the method has no parameters, then the parameter list will be empty.

Adding a Method to the Vehicle Class

As just explained, the methods of a class typically manipulate and provide access to the data of the class. With this in mind, recall that **Main( )** in the preceding examples computed the range of a vehicle by multiplying its fuel consumption rate by its fuel capacity. While technically correct, this is not the best way to handle this computation. The calculation of a vehicle's range is something that is best handled by the **Vehicle** class, itself. The reason for this conclusion is easy to understand: The range of a vehicle is dependent upon the capacity of the fuel tank and the rate of fuel consumption, and both of these quantities are encapsulated by **Vehicle**. By adding a method to **Vehicle** that computes the range, you are enhancing its object-oriented structure.

To add a method to **Vehicle**, specify it within **Vehicle**'s declaration. For example, the following version of **Vehicle** contains a method called **range( )** that displays the range of the vehicle:

4

```
// Add range to Vehicle.

using System;

class Vehicle {
  public int passengers; // number of passengers
  public int fuelcap;    // fuel capacity in gallons
  public int mpg;        // fuel consumption in miles per gallon

  // Display the range.
  public void range() {
    Console.WriteLine("Range is " + fuelcap * mpg);
  }
}

class AddMeth {
  public static void Main() {
    Vehicle minivan = new Vehicle();
    Vehicle sportscar = new Vehicle();

    // assign values to fields in minivan
    minivan.passengers = 7;
    minivan.fuelcap = 16;
    minivan.mpg = 21;

    // assign values to fields in sportscar
    sportscar.passengers = 2;
    sportscar.fuelcap = 14;
    sportscar.mpg = 12;
```

The **range( )** method is contained within the **Vehicle** class.

Notice that **fuelcap** and **mpg** are used directly, without the dot operator.

```
   Console.Write("Minivan can carry " + minivan.passengers +
                 ". ");

   minivan.range(); // display range of minivan

   Console.Write("Sportscar can carry " + sportscar.passengers +
                 ". ");

   sportscar.range(); // display range of sportscar.
  }
}
```

This program generates the following output:

```
Minivan can carry 7. Range is 336
Sportscar can carry 2. Range is 168
```

Let's look at the key elements of this program, beginning with the **range( )** method, itself. The first line of **range( )** is

```
public void range() {
```

This line declares a method called **range** that has no parameters. It is specified as **public**, so it can be used by all other parts of the program. Its return type is **void**. Thus, **range( )** does not return a value to the caller. The line ends with the opening curly brace of the method body.

The body of **range( )** consists solely of this line:

```
Console.WriteLine("Range is " + fuelcap * mpg);
```

This statement displays the range of the vehicle by multiplying **fuelcap** by **mpg**. Since each object of type **Vehicle** has its own copy of **fuelcap** and **mpg**, when **range( )** is called, the range computation uses the calling object's copies of those variables.

The **range( )** method ends when its closing curly brace is encountered. This causes program control to transfer back to the caller.

Next, look closely at this line of code from inside **Main( )**:

```
minivan.range();
```

This statement invokes the **range( )** method on **minivan**. That is, it calls **range( )** relative to the **minivan** object, using the object's name followed by the dot operator. When a method is called, program control is transferred to the method. When the method terminates, control is transferred back to the caller, and execution resumes with the line of code following the call.

In this case, the call to **minivan.range( )** displays the range of the vehicle defined by **minivan**. In similar fashion, the call to **sportscar.range( )** displays the range of the vehicle defined by **sportscar**. Each time **range( )** is invoked, it displays the range for the specified object.

There is something very important to notice inside the **range( )** method: the instance variables **fuelcap** and **mpg** are referred to directly, without preceding them with an object name or the dot operator. When a method uses an instance variable that is defined by its class, it does so directly, without explicit reference to an object and without use of the dot operator. This is easy to understand if you think about it. A method is always invoked relative to some object of its class. Once this invocation has occurred, the object is known. Thus, within a method, there is no need to specify the object a second time. This means that **fuelcap** and **mpg** inside **range( )** implicitly refer to the copies of those variables found in the object that invokes **range( )**.

Returning from a Method

In general, there are two conditions that cause a method to return. The first, as the **range( )** method in the preceding example shows, occurs when the method's closing curly brace is encountered. The second is when a **return** statement is executed. There are two forms of **return**: one for use in **void** methods (those that do not return a value) and one for returning values. The first form is examined here. The next section explains how to return values.

In a **void** method, you can cause the immediate termination of a method by using this form of **return**:

```
return ;
```

When this statement executes, program control returns to the caller, skipping any remaining code in the method. For example, consider this method:

```
public void myMeth() {
  int i;
```

```
for(i=0; i<10; i++) {
  if(i == 5) return; // stop at 5
  Console.WriteLine();
}
}
```

Here, the **for** loop will only run from 0 to 5, because once **i** equals 5, the method returns.

It is permissible to have multiple return statements in a method, especially when there are two or more routes out of it. For example,

```
public void myMeth() {
  // ...
  if(done) return;
  // ...
  if(error) return;
}
```

Here, the method returns if it is done or if an error occurs. Be careful, however. Having too many exit points in a method can destructure your code, so avoid using them casually.

To review: A **void** method can return in one of two ways: its closing curly brace is reached, or a **return** statement is executed.

Returning a Value

Although methods with a return type of **void** are not rare, most methods will return a value. In fact, the ability to return a value is one of the most useful features of a method. You have already seen an example of a return value: when we used the **Math.Sqrt( )** function to obtain a square root.

Return values are used for a variety of purposes in programming. In some cases, such as with **Math.Sqrt( )**, the return value contains the outcome of some calculation. In other cases, the return value may simply indicate success or failure. In still others, it may contain a status code. Whatever the purpose, using method return values is an integral part of C# programming.

Methods return a value to the calling routine using this form of **return**:

return *value*;

Here, *value* is the value returned.

You can use a return value to improve the implementation of **range( )**. Instead of displaying the range, a better approach is to have **range( )** compute the range and return this value. Among the advantages to this approach is that you can use the value for other calculations. The following example modifies **range( )** to return the range rather than displaying it:

```
// Use a return value.

using System;

class Vehicle {
  public int passengers; // number of passengers
  public int fuelcap;    // fuel capacity in gallons
  public int mpg;        // fuel consumption in miles per gallon

  // Return the range.
  public int range() {
    return mpg * fuelcap;        ←——— Now range() returns a value.
  }
}

class RetMeth {
  public static void Main() {
    Vehicle minivan = new Vehicle();
    Vehicle sportscar = new Vehicle();

    int range1, range2;

    // assign values to fields in minivan
    minivan.passengers = 7;
    minivan.fuelcap = 16;
    minivan.mpg = 21;

    // assign values to fields in sportscar
    sportscar.passengers = 2;
    sportscar.fuelcap = 14;
    sportscar.mpg = 12;

    // get the ranges
    range1 = minivan.range();      ←——— Assign the value returned
    range2 = sportscar.range();          to a variable.
```

```
    Console.WriteLine("Minivan can carry " + minivan.passengers +
                   " with range of " + range1 + " miles.");

    Console.WriteLine("Sportscar can carry " + sportscar.passengers +
                   " with range of " + range2 + " miles.");
  }
}
```

The output is shown here:

```
Minivan can carry 7 with range of 336 miles.
Sportscar can carry 2 with range of 168 miles.
```

In the program, notice that when **range( )** is called, it is put on the right side of an assignment statement. On the left is a variable that will receive the value returned by **range( )**. Thus, after this line executes,

```
range1 = minivan.range();
```

the range of the **minivan** object is stored in **range1**.

Notice that **range( )** now has a return type of **int**. This means that it will return an integer value to the caller. The return type of a method is important because the type of data returned by a method must be compatible with the return type specified by the method. Thus, if you want a method to return data of type **double**, then its return type must be type **double**.

Although the preceding program is correct, it is not written as efficiently as it could be. Specifically, there is no need for the **range1** or **range2** variables. A call to **range( )** can be used in the **WriteLine( )** statement directly, as shown here:

```
Console.WriteLine("Minivan can carry " + minivan.passengers +
                   " with range of " + minivan.range() + " Miles");
```

In this case, when **WriteLine( )** is executed, **minivan.range( )** is called automatically and its value will be passed to **WriteLine( )**. Furthermore, you can use a call to **range( )** whenever the range of a **Vehicle** object is needed. For example, this statement compares the ranges of two vehicles:

```
if(v1.range() > v2.range()) Console.WriteLine("v1 has greater range");
```

Ask the Expert

Question: I have heard that C# detects "unreachable code." What does this mean?

Answer: You heard correctly. The C# compiler will issue a warning message if you create a method that contains code that cannot be executed. Consider this example:

```
public void m() {
  char a, b;

  // ...

  if(a==b) {
    Console.WriteLine("equal");
    return;
  } else {
    Console.WriteLine("not equal");
    return;
  }
  Console.WriteLine("this is unreachable");
}
```

Here, the method **m( )** will always return before the final **WriteLine( )** statement is executed. If you try to compile this method, you will receive a warning. In general, unreachable code constitutes a mistake on your part, so it is a good idea to take unreachable code warnings seriously!

Using Parameters

It is possible to pass one or more values to a method when the method is called. As explained, a value passed to a method is called an *argument*. Inside the method, the variable that receives the argument is called a *parameter*. Parameters are declared inside the parentheses that follow the method's name. The parameter declaration syntax is the same as that used for variables. A parameter is within the scope of its method and aside from its special task of receiving an argument, it acts like any other local variable.

Here is a simple example that uses a parameter. Inside the **ChkNum** class, the method **isEven( )** returns **true** if the value that it is passed is even. It returns **false** otherwise. Therefore, **isEven( )** has a return type of **bool**.

```
// A simple example that uses a parameter.

using System;

class ChkNum {
  // return true if x is even
  public bool isEven(int x) {        ◄——  Here, x is an integer
    if((x%2) == 0) return true;             parameter of isEven( ).
    else return false;
  }
}

class ParmDemo {
  public static void Main() {
    ChkNum e = new ChkNum();

    if(e.isEven(10)) Console.WriteLine("10 is even.");

    if(e.isEven(9)) Console.WriteLine("9 is even.");

    if(e.isEven(8)) Console.WriteLine("8 is even.");

  }
}
```

Here is the output produced by the program:

```
10 is even.
8 is even.
```

In the program, **isEven( )** is called three times, and each time a different value is passed. Let's look at this process closely. First, notice how **isEven( )** is called. The argument is specified between the parentheses. When **isEven( )** is called the first time, it is passed value 10. Thus, when **isEven( )** begins executing, the parameter **x** receives the value 10. In the second call, 9 is the argument, and **x**, then, has the value 9. In the third call, the argument is 8, which is the value that **x** receives. The point is that the value passed as an argument when **isEven( )** is called is the value received by its parameter, **x**.

A method can have more than one parameter. Simply declare each parameter, separating one from the next with a comma. For example, the **Factor** class defines a method called **isFactor( )** that determines if the first parameter is a factor of the second.

```
using System;

class Factor {
  public bool isFactor(int a, int b) {  ◄─ This method has two parameters.
    if( (b % a) == 0) return true;
    else return false;
  }
}

class IsFact {
  public static void Main() {
    Factor x = new Factor();

    if(x.isFactor(2, 20)) Console.WriteLine("2 is factor");
    if(x.isFactor(3, 20)) Console.WriteLine("this won't be displayed");

  }
}
```

Notice that when **isFactor( )** is called, the arguments are also separated by commas.

When using multiple parameters, each parameter specifies its own type, which can differ from the others. For example, this is perfectly valid:

```
int myMeth(int a, double b, float c) {
  // ...
```

Adding a Parameterized Method to Vehicle

You can use a parameterized method to add a new feature to the **Vehicle** class: the ability to compute the amount of fuel needed for a given distance. This new method is called **fuelneeded( )**. This method takes the number of miles that you want to drive and returns the number of gallons of gas required. The **fuelneeded( )** method is defined like this:

```
public double fuelneeded(int miles) {
  return (double) miles / mpg;
}
```

Notice that this method returns a value of type **double**. This is useful since the amount of fuel needed for a given distance might not be an even number.

The entire **Vehicle** class that includes **fuelneeded( )** is shown here:

```
/*
   Add a parameterized method that computes the
   fuel required for a given distance.
*/

using System;

class Vehicle {
  public int passengers; // number of passengers
  public int fuelcap;    // fuel capacity in gallons
  public int mpg;        // fuel consumption in miles per gallon

  // Return the range.
  public int range() {
    return mpg * fuelcap;
  }

  // Compute fuel needed for a given distance.
  public double fuelneeded(int miles) {
    return (double) miles / mpg;
  }
}

class CompFuel {
  public static void Main() {
    Vehicle minivan = new Vehicle();
    Vehicle sportscar = new Vehicle();
    double gallons;
    int dist = 252;

     // assign values to fields in minivan
    minivan.passengers = 7;
    minivan.fuelcap = 16;
    minivan.mpg = 21;

    // assign values to fields in sportscar
    sportscar.passengers = 2;
    sportscar.fuelcap = 14;
    sportscar.mpg = 12;
```

```
    gallons = minivan.fuelneeded(dist);

    Console.WriteLine("To go " + dist + " miles minivan needs " +
                      gallons + " gallons of fuel.");

    gallons = sportscar.fuelneeded(dist);

    Console.WriteLine("To go " + dist + " miles sportscar needs " +
                      gallons + " gallons of fuel.");
  }
}
```

The output from the program is shown here:

```
To go 252 miles minivan needs 12.0 gallons of fuel.
To go 252 miles sportscar needs 21.0 gallons of fuel.
```

1-Minute Drill

● When must an instance variable or method be accessed through an object reference using the dot operator? When can a variable or method be used directly?

● Explain the difference between an argument and a parameter.

● Explain the two ways that a method can return to its caller.

Project 4-1: Creating a Help Class

If you were to try to summarize the essence of the class in one sentence, it might be this: A class encapsulates functionality. Of course, sometimes the trick

HelpClassDemo.cs

● When an instance variable is accessed by code that is not part of the class in which that instance variable is defined, it must be done through an object, by use of the dot operator. When an instance variable is accessed by code that is part of the same class as the instance variable, that variable can be referred to directly. The same thing applies to methods.

● An *argument* is a value that is passed to a method when it is invoked. A *parameter* is a variable defined by a method that receives the value of the argument.

● A method can be made to return through the use of the **return** statement. If the method has a **void** return type, then it will also return when its closing curly brace is reached. Non-**void** methods must return a value, so returning by reaching the closing curly brace is not an option.

is knowing where one "functionality" ends and another begins. As a general rule, you will want your classes to be the building blocks of your larger application. To do this, each class must represent a single functional unit that performs clearly delineated actions. Thus, you will want your classes to be as small as possible—but no smaller! That is, classes that contain extraneous functionality confuse and destructure code, but classes that contain too little functionality are fragmented. What is the balance? It is at this point that the *science* of programming becomes the *art* of programming. Fortunately, most programmers find that this balancing act becomes easier with experience.

To begin gaining that experience, you will convert the help system from Project 3-3 in the preceding module into a Help class. Let's examine why this is a good idea. First, the help system defines one logical unit. It simply displays the syntax for C#'s control statements. Thus, its functionality is compact and well defined. Second, putting help in a class is an esthetically pleasing approach. Whenever you want to offer the help system to a user, simply instantiate a help-system object. Finally, because help is encapsulated, it can be upgraded or changed without causing unwanted side-effects in the programs that use it.

Step-by-Step

1. Create a new file called **HelpClassDemo.cs**. To save you some typing, you might want to copy the file from Project 3-3, **Help3.cs**, into **HelpClassDemo.cs**.

2. To convert the help system into a class, you must first determine precisely what constitutes the help system. For example, in **Help3.cs**, there is code to display a menu, input the user's choice, check for a valid response, and display information about the item selected. The program also loops until a *q* is pressed. If you think about it, it is clear that the menu, the check for a valid response, and the display of the information are integral to the help system. How user input is obtained and whether repeated requests should be processed, are not integral. Thus, you will create a class that displays the help information and the help menu, and that checks for a valid selection. These methods will be called **helpon( )**, **showmenu( )**, and **isvalid( )**, respectively.

3. Create the **helpon( )** method as shown here:

```
public void helpon(char what) {
  switch(what) {
    case '1':
      Console.WriteLine("The if:\n");
      Console.WriteLine("if(condition) statement;");
      Console.WriteLine("else statement;");
```

```
          break;
        case '2':
          Console.WriteLine("The switch:\n");
          Console.WriteLine("switch(expression) {");
          Console.WriteLine("  case constant:");
          Console.WriteLine("    statement sequence");
          Console.WriteLine("    break;");
          Console.WriteLine("  // ...");
          Console.WriteLine("}");
          break;
        case '3':
          Console.WriteLine("The for:\n");
          Console.Write("for(init; condition; iteration)");
          Console.WriteLine(" statement;");
          break;
        case '4':
          Console.WriteLine("The while:\n");
          Console.WriteLine("while(condition) statement;");
          break;
        case '5':
          Console.WriteLine("The do-while:\n");
          Console.WriteLine("do {");
          Console.WriteLine("  statement;");
          Console.WriteLine("} while (condition);");
          break;
        case '6':
          Console.WriteLine("The break:\n");
          Console.WriteLine("break; or break label;");
          break;
        case '7':
          Console.WriteLine("The continue:\n");
          Console.WriteLine("continue; or continue label;");
          break;
        case '8':
          Console.WriteLine("The goto:\n");
          Console.WriteLine("goto label;");
          break;
      }
    Console.WriteLine();
}
```

4. Create the **showmenu( )** method:

```
public void showmenu() {
  Console.WriteLine("Help on:");
```

```
  Console.WriteLine("  1. if");
  Console.WriteLine("  2. switch");
  Console.WriteLine("  3. for");
  Console.WriteLine("  4. while");
  Console.WriteLine("  5. do-while");
  Console.WriteLine("  6. break");
  Console.WriteLine("  7. continue");
  Console.WriteLine("  8. goto\n");
  Console.Write("Choose one (q to quit): ");
}
```

5. Create the **isvalid( )** method, shown here:

```
public bool isvalid(char ch) {
  if(ch < '1' | ch > '8' & ch != 'q') return false;
  else return true;
}
```

6. Assemble the foregoing methods into the **Help** class, shown here:

```
class Help {
  public void helpon(char what) {
    switch(what) {
      case '1':
        Console.WriteLine("The if:\n");
        Console.WriteLine("if(condition) statement;");
        Console.WriteLine("else statement;");
        break;
      case '2':
        Console.WriteLine("The switch:\n");
        Console.WriteLine("switch(expression) {");
        Console.WriteLine("  case constant:");
        Console.WriteLine("    statement sequence");
        Console.WriteLine("    break;");
        Console.WriteLine("  // ...");
        Console.WriteLine("}");
        break;
      case '3':
        Console.WriteLine("The for:\n");
        Console.Write("for(init; condition; iteration)");
        Console.WriteLine(" statement;");
        break;
      case '4':
        Console.WriteLine("The while:\n");
```

```csharp
      Console.WriteLine("while(condition) statement;");
      break;
    case '5':
      Console.WriteLine("The do-while:\n");
      Console.WriteLine("do {");
      Console.WriteLine("  statement;");
      Console.WriteLine("} while (condition);");
      break;
    case '6':
      Console.WriteLine("The break:\n");
      Console.WriteLine("break; or break label;");
      break;
    case '7':
      Console.WriteLine("The continue:\n");
      Console.WriteLine("continue; or continue label;");
      break;
    case '8':
      Console.WriteLine("The goto:\n");
      Console.WriteLine("goto label;");
      break;
  }
  Console.WriteLine();
}

public void showmenu() {
  Console.WriteLine("Help on:");
  Console.WriteLine("  1. if");
  Console.WriteLine("  2. switch");
  Console.WriteLine("  3. for");
  Console.WriteLine("  4. while");
  Console.WriteLine("  5. do-while");
  Console.WriteLine("  6. break");
  Console.WriteLine("  7. continue");
  Console.WriteLine("  8. goto\n");
  Console.Write("Choose one (q to quit): ");
}

public bool isvalid(char ch) {
  if(ch < '1' | ch > '8' & ch != 'q') return false;
  else return true;
}

}
```

7. Finally, rewrite the **Main( )** method from Project 3-3 so that it uses the new **Help** class. Call this class **HelpClassDemo.cs**. The entire listing for **HelpClassDemo.cs** is shown here:

```
/*
   Project 4-1

   Convert the help system from Project 3-3 into
   a Help class.
*/

using System;

class Help {
  public void helpon(char what) {
    switch(what) {
      case '1':
        Console.WriteLine("The if:\n");
        Console.WriteLine("if(condition) statement;");
        Console.WriteLine("else statement;");
        break;
      case '2':
        Console.WriteLine("The switch:\n");
        Console.WriteLine("switch(expression) {");
        Console.WriteLine("  case constant:");
        Console.WriteLine("    statement sequence");
        Console.WriteLine("    break;");
        Console.WriteLine("  // ...");
        Console.WriteLine("}");
        break;
      case '3':
        Console.WriteLine("The for:\n");
        Console.Write("for(init; condition; iteration)");
        Console.WriteLine(" statement;");
        break;
      case '4':
        Console.WriteLine("The while:\n");
        Console.WriteLine("while(condition) statement;");
        break;
      case '5':
        Console.WriteLine("The do-while:\n");
        Console.WriteLine("do {");
        Console.WriteLine("  statement;");
        Console.WriteLine("} while (condition);");
```

```
          break;
        case '6':
          Console.WriteLine("The break:\n");
          Console.WriteLine("break; or break label;");
          break;
        case '7':
          Console.WriteLine("The continue:\n");
          Console.WriteLine("continue; or continue label;");
          break;
        case '8':
          Console.WriteLine("The goto:\n");
          Console.WriteLine("goto label;");
          break;
      }
      Console.WriteLine();
  }

  public void showmenu() {
    Console.WriteLine("Help on:");
    Console.WriteLine("  1. if");
    Console.WriteLine("  2. switch");
    Console.WriteLine("  3. for");
    Console.WriteLine("  4. while");
    Console.WriteLine("  5. do-while");
    Console.WriteLine("  6. break");
    Console.WriteLine("  7. continue");
    Console.WriteLine("  8. goto\n");
    Console.Write("Choose one (q to quit): ");
  }

  public bool isvalid(char ch) {
    if(ch < '1' | ch > '8' & ch != 'q') return false;
    else return true;
  }

}

class HelpClassDemo {
  public static void Main() {
    char choice;
    Help hlpobj = new Help();

    for(;;) {
      do {
```

4

```
        hlpobj.showmenu();
        do {
          choice = (char) Console.Read();
        } while(choice == '\n' | choice == '\r');

      } while( !hlpobj.isvalid(choice) );

      if(choice == 'q') break;

      Console.WriteLine("\n");


      hlpobj.helpon(choice);
    }
  }
}
```

When you try the program, you will find that it is functionally the same as before. The advantage to this approach is that you now have a help system component that can be reused whenever it is needed.

Constructors

In the preceding examples, the instance variables of each **Vehicle** object had to be set manually using a sequence of statements, such as:

```
minivan.passengers = 7;
minivan.fuelcap = 16;
minivan.mpg = 21;
```

An approach like this would never be used in professionally written C# code. Aside from being error prone (you might forget to set one of the fields), there is simply a better way to accomplish this task: the constructor.

A *constructor* initializes an object when it is created. It has the same name as its class and is syntactically similar to a method. However, constructors have no explicit return type. The general form of a constructor is shown here:

class-name( ) {
  // constructor code
}

Typically, you will use a constructor to give initial values to the instance variables defined by the class, or to perform any other startup procedures required to create a fully formed object.

All classes have constructors, whether you define one or not, because C# automatically provides a default constructor that initializes all member variables to zero (for value types) or null (for reference types). However, once you define your own constructor, the default constructor is no longer used.

Here is a simple example that uses a constructor:

```
// A simple constructor.

using System;

class MyClass {
  public int x;

  public MyClass() {          ◄─────────  The constructor for MyClass
    x = 10;
  }
}

class ConsDemo {
  public static void Main() {
    MyClass t1 = new MyClass();
    MyClass t2 = new MyClass();

    Console.WriteLine(t1.x + " " | t2.x);
  }
}
```

In this example, the constructor for **MyClass** is

```
public MyClass() {
  x = 10;
}
```

Notice that the constructor is specified as **public**. This is because the constructor will be called from code defined outside of its class. This constructor assigns the instance variable **x** of **MyClass** the value 10. This constructor is called by **new** when an object is created. For example, in the line

```
MyClass t1 = new MyClass();
```

the constructor **MyClass( )** is called on the **t1** object, giving **t1.x** the value 10. The same is true for **t2**. After construction, **t2.x** has the value 10. Thus, the output from the program is

```
10 10
```

Parameterized Constructors

In the preceding example, a parameterless constructor was used. While this is fine for some situations, most often you will need a constructor that accepts one or more parameters. Parameters are added to a constructor in the same way that they are added to a method: just declare them inside the parentheses after the constructor's name. For example, here **MyClass** is given a parameterized constructor:

```csharp
// A parameterized constructor.

using System;

class MyClass {
  public int x;

  public MyClass(int i) {
    x = i;
  }
}

class ParmConsDemo {
  public static void Main() {
    MyClass t1 = new MyClass(10);
    MyClass t2 = new MyClass(88);

    Console.WriteLine(t1.x + " " + t2.x);
  }
}
```

The output from this program is shown here:

```
10 88
```

In this version of the program, the **MyClass( )** constructor defines one parameter called **i**, which is used to initialize the instance variable, **x**. Thus, when this line executes,

```
MyClass t1 = new MyClass(10);
```

the value 10 is passed to **i**, which is then assigned to **x**.

Adding a Constructor to the Vehicle Class

We can improve the **Vehicle** class by adding a constructor that automatically initializes the **passengers**, **fuelcap**, and **mpg** fields when an object is constructed. Pay special attention to how Vehicle objects are created.

```
// Add a constructor.

using System;

class Vehicle {
  public int passengers; // number of passengers
  public int fuelcap;    // fuel capacity in gallons
  public int mpg;        // fuel consumption in miles per gallon

  // This is a constructor for Vehicle.
  public Vehicle(int p, int f, int m) {    ◄──── Constructor for Vehicle
    passengers = p;
    fuelcap = f;
    mpg = m;
  }

  // Return the range.
  public int range() {
    return mpg * fuelcap;
  }

  // Compute fuel needed for a given distance.
  public double fuelneeded(int miles) {
    return (double) miles / mpg;
  }
}

class VehConsDemo {
```

```
public static void Main() {

    // construct complete vehicles
    Vehicle minivan = new Vehicle(7, 16, 21);
    Vehicle sportscar = new Vehicle(2, 14, 12);
    double gallons;
    int dist = 252;

    gallons = minivan.fuelneeded(dist);

    Console.WriteLine("To go " + dist + " miles minivan needs " +
                    gallons + " gallons of fuel.");

    gallons = sportscar.fuelneeded(dist);

    Console.WriteLine("To go " + dist + " miles sportscar needs " +

                    gallons + " gallons of fuel.");

    }
}
```

> Pass the vehicle information to **Vehicle** using its constructor.

Both **minivan** and **sportscar** were initialized by the **Vehicle( )** constructor when they were created. Each object is initialized as specified in the parameters to its constructor. For example, in the following line:

```
Vehicle minivan = new Vehicle(7, 16, 21);
```

the values 7, 16, and 21 are passed to the **Vehicle( )** constructor when **new** creates the object. Thus, **minivan**'s copy of **passengers**, **fuelcap**, and **mpg** will contain the values 7, 16, and 21, respectively, and the output from this program is the same as the previous version.

1-Minute Drill

- What is a constructor and when is it executed?
- Does a constructor have a return type?

- A constructor is a method that is executed when an object of its class is instantiated. A constructor is used to initialize the object being created.
- No.

The new Operator Revisited

Now that you know more about classes and their constructors, let's take a closer look at the **new** operator. The **new** operator has this general form:

class-var = new *class-name*( );

Here, *class-var* is a variable of the class type being created. The *class-name* is the name of the class that is being instantiated. The class name followed by parentheses specifies the constructor for the class. If a class does not define its own constructor, **new** will use the default constructor supplied by C#. Thus, **new** can be used to create an object of any class type.

Since memory is finite, it is possible that **new** will not be able to allocate memory for an object because insufficient memory exists. If this happens, a runtime exception will occur. (You will learn how to handle this and other exceptions in Module 9.) For the sample programs in this book, you won't need to worry about running out of memory, but you will need to consider this possibility in real-world programs that you write.

Ask the Expert

Question: Why don't I need to use new for variables of the value types, such as int or float?

Answer: In C#, a variable of a value type contains its own value. Memory to hold this value is automatically allocated by the compiler when a program is compiled. Thus, there is no need to explicitly allocate this memory using **new**. Conversely, a reference variable stores a reference to an object. The memory to hold this object is allocated dynamically, during execution.

Not making the fundamental types, such **int** or **char**, into reference types greatly improves the performance of your program. When using a reference type, there is a layer of indirection that adds overhead to each object access that is avoided by a value type.

As a point of interest, it is permitted to use **new** with the value types, as shown here.

```
int i = new int();
```

Doing so invokes the default constructor for type **int**, which initializes **i** to zero. In general, invoking **new** for a value type invokes the default constructor for that type. It does not, however, dynamically allocate memory. Frankly, most programmers do not use **new** with the value types.

Garbage Collection and Destructors

As you have seen, objects are dynamically allocated from a pool of free memory by using the **new** operator. Of course, memory is not infinite, and the free memory can be exhausted. Thus, it is possible for **new** to fail because there is insufficient free memory to create the desired object. For this reason, one of the key components of any dynamic allocation scheme is the recovery of free memory from unused objects, making that memory available for subsequent reallocation. In many programming languages, the release of previously allocated memory is handled manually. For example, in C++, you use the **delete** operator to free memory. However, C# uses a different, more trouble-free approach: *garbage collection*.

C#'s garbage collection system reclaims objects automatically—occurring transparently, behind the scenes, without any programmer intervention. It works like this: When no references to an object exist, that object is assumed to be no longer needed, and the memory occupied by the object is released. This recycled memory can then be used for a subsequent allocation.

Garbage collection occurs only sporadically during the execution of your program. It will not occur simply because one or more objects exist that are no longer used. For efficiency concerns, the garbage collector will usually run only when two conditions are met: there are objects to recycle, and there is a need to recycle them. Remember, garbage collection takes time, so the C# runtime system does it only when necessary. Thus, you can't know precisely when garbage collection will take place.

Destructors

It is possible to define a method that will be called just prior to an object's final destruction by the garbage collector. This method is called a *destructor*, and it can be used to ensure that an object terminates cleanly. For example, you might use a destructor to make sure that an open file owned by that object is closed.

Destructors have this general form:

```
~class-name( ) {
   // destruction code
}
```

Here, *class-name* is the name of the class. Thus, a destructor is declared like a constructor except that it is preceded with a ~ (tilde). Notice, it has no return type.

To add a destructor to a class, you simply include it as a member. It is called whenever an object of its class is about to be recycled. Inside the destructor you will specify those actions that must be performed before an object is destroyed.

It is important to understand that the destructor is called just prior to garbage collection. It is not called when an object goes out of scope, for example. (This differs from destructors in C++, which *are* called when an object goes out of scope.) This means that you cannot know precisely when a destructor will be executed. Furthermore, it is possible for your program to end before garbage collection occurs, so a destructor might not get called at all.

DestructDemo.cs

Project 4-2: Demonstrate Destructors

As explained, objects are not necessarily recycled as soon as they are no longer needed. Instead, the garbage collector waits until it can perform its collection efficiently, usually after there are several unused objects. Thus, to demonstrate a destructor, you often need to create and destroy a large number of objects—and this is precisely what you will do in this project.

Step-by-Step

1. Create a new file called **Destruct.cs**.

2. First, create the **Destruct** class shown here:

```
class Destruct {
  int x;
```

```
public Destruct(int i) {
  x = i;
}

// called when object is recycled
~Destruct() {
  Console.WriteLine("Destructing " + x);
}

// generates an object that is immediately destroyed
public void generator(int i) {
  Destruct o = new Destruct(i);
}

}
```

The constructor sets the instance variable **x** to a known value. In this example, **x** is used as an object ID. The destructor displays the value of **x** when an object is recycled. Of special interest is **generator( )**. This method creates and then promptly destroys a **Destruct** object. You will see how this is used in the next step.

3. Create the **DestructDemo** class, shown here:

```
class DestructDemo {
  public static void Main() {
    int count;

    Destruct ob = new Destruct(0);

    /* Now, generate a large number of objects.  At
       some point, garbage collection will occur.
       Note: you might need to increase the number
       of objects generated in order to force
       garbage collection. */

    for(count=1; count < 100000; count++)
      ob.generator(count);
  }
}
```

This class creates an initial **Destruct** object called **ob**. Then, using **ob**, it creates 100,000 objects by calling **generator( )** on **ob**. This has the net effect of creating and destroying 100,000 objects. At various points in the middle of this process, garbage collection will take place. Precisely how often or when is dependent upon several factors, such as the initial amount of free memory, the operating system, and so on. However, at some point, you will start to see the messages generated by the destructor. If you don't see the messages, try increasing the number of objects being generated by upping the count in the **for** loop.

4. Here is the entire **DestructDemo.cs** program:

```
/*
   Project 4-2
   Demonstrate a destructor.
*/

using System;

class Destruct {
  public int x;

  public Destruct(int i) {
    x = i;
  }

  // called when object is recycled
  ~Destruct() {
    Console.WriteLine("Destructing " + x);
  }

  // generates an object that is immediately destroyed
  public void generator(int i) {
    Destruct o = new Destruct(i);
  }

}

class DestructDemo {
  public static void Main() {
    int count;

    Destruct ob = new Destruct(0);

    /* Now, generate a large number of objects.  At
       some point, garbage collection will occur.
```

```
          Note: you might need to increase the number
          of objects generated in order to force
          garbage collection. */

      for(count=1; count < 100000; count++)
        ob.generator(count);
  }
}
```

The this Keyword

Before concluding this module, it is necessary to introduce **this**. When a method is called, it is automatically passed an implicit argument that is a reference to the invoking object (that is, the object on which the method is called). This reference is called **this**. To understand **this**, first consider a program that creates a class called **Pwr** that computes the result of a number raised to some integer power:

```
using System;

class Pwr {
  public double b;
  public int e;
  public double val;

  public Pwr(double num, int exp) {
    b = num;
    e = exp;

    val = 1;
    if(exp==0) return;
    for( ; exp>0; exp--) val = val * b;
  }

  public double get_pwr() {
    return val;
  }
}

class DemoPwr {
  public static void Main() {
    Pwr x = new Pwr(4.0, 2);
    Pwr y = new Pwr(2.5, 1);
    Pwr z = new Pwr(5.7, 0);
```

```
    Console.WriteLine(x.b + " raised to the " + x.e +
                        " power is " + x.get_pwr());
    Console.WriteLine(y.b + " raised to the " + y.e +
                        " power is " + y.get_pwr());
    Console.WriteLine(z.b + " raised to the " + z.e +
                        " power is " + z.get_pwr());
  }
}
```

As you know, within a method, the other members of a class can be accessed directly, without any object or class qualification. Thus, inside **get_pwr( )**, the statement

```
return val;
```

means that the copy of **val** associated with the invoking object will be returned. However, the same statement can also be written like this:

```
return this.val;
```

Here, **this** refers to the object on which **get_pwr( )** was called. Thus, **this.val** refers to that object's copy of **val**. For example, if **get_pwr( )** had been invoked on **x**, then **this** in the preceding statement would have been referring to **x**. Writing the statement without using **this** is really just shorthand.

Here is the entire **Pwr** class written using the **this** reference:

```
using System;

class Pwr {
  public double b;
  public int e;
  public double val;

  public Pwr(double num, int exp) {
    this.b = num;
    this.e = exp;

    this.val = 1;
    if(exp==0) return;
    for( ; exp>0; exp--) this.val = this.val * this.b;
```

```
  }

  public double get_pwr() {
    return this.val;
  }
}
```

Actually, no C# programmer would write **Pwr** as just shown because nothing is gained, and the standard form is easier. However, **this** has some important uses. For example, the C# syntax permits the name of a parameter or a local variable to be the same as the name of an instance variable. When this happens, the local name *hides* the instance variable. You can gain access to the hidden instance variable by referring to it through **this**. For example, while not recommended style, the following is a syntactically valid way to write the **Pwr( )** constructor:

```
public Pwr(double b, int e) {
  this.b = b;
  this.e = e;

  val = 1;
  if(e==0) return;
  for( ; e>0; e--) val = val * b;
}
```

This refers to the **b** instance variable, not the parameter.

In this version, the names of the parameters are the same as the names of the instance variables, thus hiding them. However, **this** is used to "uncover" the instance variables.

☑ Mastery Check

1. What is the difference between a class and an object?

2. How is a class defined?

3. What does each object have its own copy of?

4. Using two separate statements, show how to declare an object called **counter** of a class called **MyCounter**.

5. Show how a method called **myMeth( )** is declared if it has a return type of **double** and has two **int** parameters called **a** and **b**.

6. How must a method return if it returns a value?

7. What name does a constructor have?

8. What does **new** do?

9. What is garbage collection and how does it work? What is a destructor?

10. What is **this**?

4

Module 5

More Data Types and Operators

The Goals of This Module

- Understand arrays
- Explore string objects
- Begin working with the foreach loop
- Examine the bitwise operators
- Learn about the ? operator

This module returns to the subject of C#'s data types and operators. It discusses arrays, the **string** type, the bitwise operators, and the ? ternary operator. Along the way, the **foreach** loop is introduced.

Arrays

An array is a collection of variables of the same type that are referred to by a common name. In C#, arrays can have one or more dimensions, although the one-dimensional array is the most common. Arrays are used for a variety of purposes because they offer a convenient means of grouping together related variables. For example, you might use an array to hold a record of the daily high temperature for a month, a list of stock price averages, or your collection of programming books.

The principal advantage of an array is that it organizes data in such a way that it can be easily manipulated. For example, if you have an array containing the incomes for a selected group of households, it is easy to compute the average income by cycling through the array. Also, arrays organize data in such a way that it can be easily sorted.

Although arrays in C# can be used just like arrays in other programming languages, they have one special attribute: they are implemented as objects. This fact is one reason that a discussion of arrays was deferred until objects had been introduced. By implementing arrays as objects, several important advantages are gained, not the least of which is that unused arrays can be garbage-collected.

One-Dimensional Arrays

A one-dimensional array is a list of related variables. Such lists are common in programming. For example, you might use a one-dimensional array to store the account numbers of the active users on a network. Another array might be used to store the current batting averages for a baseball team.

To declare a one-dimensional array, you will use this general form:

type[ ] *array-name* = new *type*[*size*];

Here, *type* declares the base type of the array. The base type determines the data type of each element that comprises the array. Notice the square brackets that follow *type*. They indicate that a one-dimensional array is being declared. The number of elements that the array will hold is determined by *size*. Since arrays are implemented as objects, the creation of an array is a two-step process. First, you declare an array reference variable. Second, you allocate memory for the array, assigning a reference to that memory to the array variable. Thus, arrays in C# are dynamically allocated using the **new** operator.

Note

If you come from a C or C++ background, pay special attention to the way arrays are declared. Specifically, the square brackets follow the *type* name, not the array name.

5

Here is an example. The following creates an **int** array of ten elements and links it to an array reference variable named **sample**:

```
int[] sample = new int[10];
```

This declaration works just like an object declaration. The **sample** variable holds a reference to the memory allocated by **new**. This memory is large enough to hold ten elements of type **int**.

As with objects, it is possible to break the preceding declaration in two. For example:

```
int[] sample;
sample = new int[10];
```

In this case, when **sample** is first created, it refers to no physical object. It is only after the second statement executes that **sample** is linked with an array.

An individual element within an array is accessed by use of an index. An *index* describes the position of an element within an array. In C#, all arrays have zero as the index of their first element. Because **sample** has ten elements, it has index values of 0 through 9. To index an array, specify the number of the element you want, surrounded by square brackets. Thus, the first element in **sample** is **sample[0]**, and the last element is **sample[9]**. For example, the following program loads **sample** with the numbers 0 through 9:

```
// Demonstrate a one-dimensional array.
using System;
```

```
class ArrayDemo {
  public static void Main() {
    int[] sample = new int[10];
    int i;

    for(i = 0; i < 10; i = i+1)  ◄────── Arrays are indexed from zero.
      sample[i] = i;

    for(i = 0; i < 10; i = i+1)  ◄──────┘
      Console.WriteLine("This is sample[" + i + "]: " +
                              sample[i]);
  }
}
```

The output from the program is shown here:

```
This is sample[0]: 0
This is sample[1]: 1
This is sample[2]: 2
This is sample[3]: 3
This is sample[4]: 4
This is sample[5]: 5
This is sample[6]: 6
This is sample[7]: 7
This is sample[8]: 8
This is sample[9]: 9
```

Conceptually, the **sample** array looks like this:

0	1	2	3	4	5	6	7	8	9
sample [0]	sample [1]	sample [2]	sample [3]	sample [4]	sample [5]	sample [6]	sample [7]	sample [8]	sample [9]

Arrays are common in programming because they let you deal easily with large numbers of related variables. For example, the following program finds the minimum and maximum values stored in the **nums** array by cycling through the array using a **for** loop:

```
// Find the minimum and maximum values in an array.
using System;

class MinMax {
  public static void Main() {
    int[] nums = new int[10];
    int min, max;

    nums[0] = 99;
    nums[1] = -10;
    nums[2] = 100123;
    nums[3] = 18;
    nums[4] = -978;
    nums[5] = 5623;
    nums[6] = 463;
    nums[7] = -9;
    nums[8] = 287;
    nums[9] = 49;

    min = max = nums[0];
    for(int i=1; i < 10; i++) {
      if(nums[i] < min) min = nums[i];
      if(nums[i] > max) max = nums[i];
    }
    Console.WriteLine("min and max: " + min + " " + max);
  }
}
```

The output from the program is shown here:

```
min and max: -978 100123
```

Initializing an Array

In the preceding program, the **nums** array was given values by hand, using ten separate assignment statements. While perfectly correct, there is an easier way to accomplish this. Arrays can be initialized when they are created. The general form for initializing a one-dimensional array is shown here:

type[ ] *array-name* = { *val1, val2, val3, ... , valN* };

Here, the initial values are specified by *val1* through *valN*. They are assigned in sequence, left to right, in index order. C# automatically allocates an array large enough to hold the initializers that you specify. There is no need to explicitly use the **new** operator. For example, here is a better way to write the **MinMax** program:

```
// Use array initializers.
using System;

class MinMax {
  public static void Main() {
    int[] nums = { 99, -10, 100123, 18, -978,
                   5623, 463, -9, 287, 49 };        ◄──────  Array initializers
    int min, max;

    min = max = nums[0];
    for(int i=1; i < 10; i++) {
      if(nums[i] < min) min = nums[i];
      if(nums[i] > max) max = nums[i];
    }
    Console.WriteLine("Min and max: " + min + " " + max);
  }
}
```

As a point of interest, although not needed, you can use **new** when initializing an array. For example, this is a proper, but redundant, way to initialize **nums** in the foregoing program.

```
int[] nums = new int[] { 99, -10, 100123, 18, -978,
                         5623, 463, -9, 287, 49 };
```

While redundant here, the **new** form of array initialization is useful when you are assigning a new array to an already existent array reference variable. For example,

```
int[] nums;
nums = new int[] { 99, -10, 100123, 18, -978,
                   5623, 463, -9, 287, 49 };
```

In this case, **nums** is declared in the first statement and initialized by the second.

Boundaries Are Enforced

Array boundaries are strictly enforced in C#; it is a runtime error to overrun or underrun the end of an array. If you want to confirm this for yourself, try the following program that purposely overruns an array:

```
// Demonstrate an array overrun.
using System;

class ArrayErr {
  public static void Main() {
    int[] sample = new int[10];
    int i;

    // generate an array overrun
    for(i = 0; i < 100; i = i+1)
      sample[i] = i;                    Overrun the end of sample.
  }
}
```

As soon as i reaches 10, an **IndexOutOfRangeException** is generated and the program is terminated.

1-Minute Drill

● Arrays are accessed via an _____ .

● How is a 10-element **char** array declared?

● C# does not check for array overruns at runtime. True or False?

● Arrays are accessed via an index.
● A 10-element **char** array is declared as follows:
   char[ ] a = new char[10];
● False; C# does not allow array overruns at runtime.

Project 5-1: Sorting an Array

Because a one-dimensional array organizes data into an indexable linear list, it is the perfect data structure for sorting. In this project you will learn a simple way to sort an array. As you may know, there are a number of different sorting algorithms. There are the quick sort, the shaker sort, and the shell sort, to name just three. However, the best known, simplest, and easiest to understand sorting algorithm is called the *bubble sort*. While the bubble sort is not very efficient—in fact, its performance is unacceptable for sorting large arrays— it may be used effectively for sorting small arrays.

Step-by-Step

1. Create a file called **Bubble.cs**.

2. The bubble sort gets its name from the way it performs the sorting operation. It uses the repeated comparison and, if necessary, exchange of adjacent elements in the array. In this process, small values move toward one end and large ones toward the other end. The process is conceptually similar to bubbles finding their own level in a tank of water. The bubble sort operates by making several passes through the array, exchanging out-of-place elements when necessary. The number of passes required to ensure that the array is sorted is equal to one less than the number of elements in the array.

   Here is the code that forms the core of the bubble sort. The array being sorted here is called **nums**.

   ```
   // This is the bubble sort.
   for(a=1; a < size; a++)
     for(b=size-1; b >= a; b--) {
       if(nums[b-1] > nums[b]) { // if out of order
         // exchange elements
         t = nums[b-1];
         nums[b-1] = nums[b];
         nums[b] = t;
       }
     }
   ```

   Notice that the sort relies on two **for** loops. The inner loop checks adjacent elements in the array, looking for out-of-order elements. When an out-of-order element pair is found, the two elements are exchanged. With each pass, the smallest element of those remaining moves into its proper location. The outer loop causes this process to repeat until the entire array has been sorted.

3. Here is the entire **Bubble** program:

```
/*
   Project 5-1
   Demonstrate the Bubble sort.
*/
using System;

class Bubble {
  public static void Main() {
    int[] nums = { 99, -10, 100123, 18, -978,
                   5623, 463,  9, 287, 49 };
    Int a, b, t;
    int size;

    size = 10; // number of elements to sort

    // display original array
    Console.Write("Original array is:");
    for(int i=0; i < size; i++)
      Console.Write(" " + nums[i]);
    Console.WriteLine();

    // This is the bubble sort.
    for(a=1; a < size; a++)
      for(b=size-1; b >= a; b--) {
        if(nums[b-1] > nums[b]) { // if out of order
          // exchange elements
          t = nums[b-1];
          nums[b-1] = nums[b];
          nums[b] = t;
        }
      }

    // display sorted array
    Console.Write("Sorted array is:");
    for(int i=0; i < size; i++)
      Console.Write(" " + nums[i]);
    Console.WriteLine();
  }
}
```

The output from the program is shown here:

```
Original array is: 99 -10 100123 18 -978 5623 463 -9 287 49
Sorted array is: -978 -10 -9 18 49 99 287 463 5623 100123
```

4. Although the bubble sort is good for small arrays, it is not efficient when used on larger ones. The best general-purpose sorting algorithm is the Quicksort. The Quicksort, however, relies on features of C# that you have not yet learned about.

Multidimensional Arrays

Although the one-dimensional array is the most commonly used array in programming, multidimensional arrays are certainly not rare. A multidimensional array is an array that has two or more dimensions, and an individual element is accessed through the combination of two or more indices.

Two-Dimensional Arrays

The simplest form of the multidimensional array is the two-dimensional array. In a two-dimensional array, the location of any specific element is specified by two indices. Think of a two-dimensional array as a table of information; one index indicates the row, the other indicates the column.

To declare a two-dimensional integer array **table** of size 10, 20, you would write

```
int[,] table = new int[10, 20];
```

Pay careful attention to the declaration. Notice that the two dimensions are separated by a comma. In the first part of the declaration, the syntax

```
[,]
```

indicates that a two-dimensional array reference variable is being created. When memory is actually allocated for the array using **new**, this syntax is used:

```
int[10, 20]
```

This creates a 10×20 array, and again, the comma separates the dimensions.

To access a point in a two-dimensional array, you must specify both indices, separating the two with a comma. For example, to assign location 3, 5 of array **table** the value 10, you would use

```
table[3, 5] = 10;
```

Here is a complete example. It loads a two-dimensional array with the numbers 1 through 12 and then displays the contents of the array.

```
// Demonstrate a two-dimensional array.
using System;

class TwoD {
  public static void Main() {
    int t, i;
    int[,] table = new int[3, 4];   ◄————————  Declare a 3 by 4,
                                                two-dimensional array.
    for(t=0; t < 3; ++t) {
      for(i=0; i < 4; ++i) {
        table[t,i] = (t*4)+i+1;
        Console.Write(table[t,i] + " ");
      }
      Console.WriteLine();
    }
  }
}
```

In this example, **table**[0, 0] will have the value 1, **table**[0, 1] the value 2, **table**[0, 2] the value 3, and so on. The value of **table**[2, 3] will be 12. Conceptually, the array will look like that shown in Figure 5-1.

Note

If you come from a C, C++, or Java background, be careful when declaring or accessing multidimensional arrays. In these other languages, array dimensions and indices are specified within their own set of brackets. C# separates dimensions using commas.

5

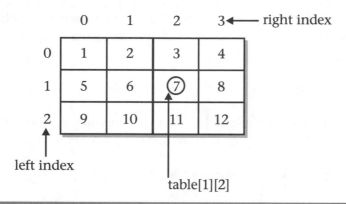

Figure 5-1 A conceptual view of the table array created by the TwoD program

Arrays of Three or More Dimensions

C# allows arrays with more than two dimensions. Here is the general form of a multidimensional array declaration:

type[,...,] name = new *type[size1,size2,...,sizeN]*;

For example, the following declaration creates a 4×10×3 three-dimensional integer array:

```
int[,,] multidim = new int[4, 10, 3];
```

To assign element 2, 4, 1 of **multidim** the value 100, use this statement:

```
multidim[2, 4, 1] = 100;
```

Initializing Multidimensional Arrays

A multidimensional array can be initialized by enclosing each dimension's initializer list within its own set of curly braces. For example, the general form of array initialization for a two-dimensional array is shown here:

type[,] array_name = {
    { *val, val, val, ..., val* },

```
{ val, val, val, ..., val },
    .
    .
    .
  { val, val, val, ..., val }
};
```

Here, *val* indicates an initialization value. Each inner block designates a row. Within each row, the first value will be stored in the first position of the array, the second value in the second position, and so on. Notice that commas separate the initializer blocks and that a semicolon follows the closing }.

For example, the following program initializes an array called **sqrs** with the numbers 1 through 10 and their squares:

```
// Initialize a two-dimensional array.
using System;

class Squares {
  public static void Main() {
    int[,] sqrs = {
      { 1, 1 },
      { 2, 4 },
      { 3, 9 },
      { 4, 16 },
      { 5, 25 },
      { 6, 36 },
      { 7, 49 },
      { 8, 64 },
      { 9, 81 },
      { 10, 100 }
    };
    int i, j;

    for(i=0; i < 10; i++) {
      for(j=0; j < 2; j++)
        Console.Write(sqrs[i,j] + " ");
      Console.WriteLine();
    }
  }
}
```

Notice how each row has its own set of initializers.

Here is the output from the program:

```
1  1
2  4
3  9
4  16
5  25
6  36
7  49
8  64
9  81
10 100
```

Jagged Arrays

In the preceding examples, when you created a two-dimensional array, you were creating what C# calls a *rectangular array*. Thinking of two-dimensional arrays as tables, a rectangular array is a two-dimensional array in which the length of each row is the same for the entire array. However, C# also allows you to create a special type of two-dimensional array called a *jagged array*. A jagged array is an *array of arrays* in which the length of each array can differ. Thus, a jagged array can be used to create a table in which the row lengths are not the same.

Jagged arrays are declared by using sets of square brackets to indicate each dimension. For example, to declare a two-dimensional jagged array, you will use this general form:

type[ ] [ ] *array-name* = new *type*[*size*][ ];

Here, *size* indicates the number of rows in the array. The rows, themselves, have not been allocated. Instead, the rows are allocated individually. This allows for the length of each row to vary. For example, the following code allocates memory for the first dimension of **jagged** when it is declared. It then allocates the second dimensions manually.

```
int[][] jagged = new int[3][];
jagged[0] = new int[2];
jagged[1] = new int[3];
jagged[2] = new int[4];
```

After this sequence executes, jagged looks like this:

| jagged [0][0] | | jagged [0][1] |

| jagged [1][0] | | jagged [1][1] | | jagged [1][2] |

| jagged [2][0] | | jagged [2][1] | | jagged [2][2] | | jagged [2][3] |

It is easy to see how jagged arrays got their name!

Once a jagged array has been created, an element is accessed by specifying each index within its own set of brackets. For example, to assign the value 10 to element 2, 1 of **jagged**, you would use this statement:

```
jagged[2][1] = 10;
```

Note that this differs from the syntax that is used to access an element of a rectangular array.

Here is an example that uses a jagged two-dimensional array. Assume that you are writing a program that stores the number of passengers that ride an airport shuttle. If the shuttle runs ten times a day during the week and twice a day on Saturday and Sunday, you could use the **riders** array shown in the following program to store the information. Notice that the length of the second dimension for the first five dimensions is 10 and that the length of the second dimension for the last two dimensions is 2.

```
// Demonstrate jagged arrays.
using System;

class Ragged {
  public static void Main() {
    int[][] riders = new int[7][];
    riders[0] = new int[10];
    riders[1] = new int[10];
    riders[2] = new int[10];
    riders[3] = new int[10];
    riders[4] = new int[10];

    riders[5] = new int[2];
    riders[6] = new int[2];

    int i, j;
```

Here, the second dimensions are 10 elements long.

But here, they are 2 elements long.

5

```
   // fabricate some fake data
   for(i=0; i < 5; i++)
     for(j=0; j < 10; j++)
       riders[i][j] = i + j + 10;
   for(i=5; i < 7; i++)
     for(j=0; j < 2; j++)
       riders[i][j] = i + j + 10;

   Console.WriteLine("Riders per trip during the week:");
   for(i=0; i < 5; i++) {
     for(j=0; j < 10; j++)
       Console.Write(riders[i][j] + " ");
     Console.WriteLine();
   }
   Console.WriteLine();

   Console.WriteLine("Riders per trip on the weekend:");
   for(i=5; i < 7; i++) {
     for(j=0; j < 2; j++)
       Console.Write(riders[i][j] + " ");
     Console.WriteLine();
   }
 }
}
```

Jagged arrays are not used by most applications, but they can be used effectively in some situations. For example, if you need a very large two-dimensional array that is sparsely populated (that is, one in which not all of the elements will be used), then an irregular array might be a perfect solution.

1-Minute Drill

● For rectangular multidimensional arrays, each dimension is specified how?

● In a jagged array, can the length of each array differ?

● How are multidimensional arrays initialized?

● The dimensions are specified within square brackets, with each dimension separated by a comma.
● Yes.
● Multidimensional arrays are initialized by putting each subarray's initializers inside its own set of curly braces.

Assigning Array References

As with other objects, when you assign one array reference variable to another, you are simply changing what object that variable refers to. You are not causing a copy of the array to be made, nor are you causing the contents of one array to be copied to the other. For example, consider this program:

```
// Assigning array reference variables.
using System;

class AssignARef {
  public static void Main() {
    int i;

    int[] nums1 = new int[10];
    int[] nums2 = new int[10];

    for(i=0; i < 10; i++) nums1[i] = i;

    for(i=0; i < 10; i++) nums2[i] = -i;

    Console.Write("Here is nums1: ");
    for(i=0; i < 10; i++)
      Console.Write(nums1[i] + " ");
    Console.WriteLine();

    Console.Write("Here is nums2: ");
    for(i=0; i < 10; i++)
      Console.Write(nums2[i] + " ");
    Console.WriteLine();

    nums2 = nums1; // now nums2 refers to nums1

    Console.Write("Here is nums2 after assignment: ");
    for(i=0; i < 10; i++)
      Console.Write(nums2[i] + " ");
    Console.WriteLine();

    // now operate on nums1 array through nums2
    nums2[3] = 99;

    Console.Write("Here is nums1 after change through nums2: ");
```

```
    for(i=0; i < 10; i++)
      Console.Write(nums1[i] + " ");
    Console.WriteLine();
  }
}
```

The output from the program is shown here:

```
Here is nums1: 0 1 2 3 4 5 6 7 8 9
Here is nums2: 0 -1 -2 -3 -4 -5 -6 -7 -8 -9
Here is nums2 after assignment: 0 1 2 3 4 5 6 7 8 9
Here is nums1 after change through nums2: 0 1 2 99 4 5 6 7 8 9
```

As the output shows, after the assignment of **nums1** to **nums2**, both array reference variables refer to the same object.

Using the Length Property

A number of benefits result because C# implements arrays as objects. One comes from the fact that each array has associated with it a **Length** property that contains the number of elements that an array can hold. Thus, each array carries with it a field that contains the array's length. Here is a program that demonstrates this property:

```
// Use the Length array property.
using System;

class LengthDemo {
  public static void Main() {
    int[] list = new int[10];
    int[] nums = { 1, 2, 3 };

    int[][] table = new int[3][]; // a variable-length table
    // add second dimensions
    table[0] = new int[] {1, 2, 3};
    table[1] = new int[] {4, 5};
    table[2] = new int[] {6, 7, 8, 9};

    Console.WriteLine("length of list is " + list.Length);
    Console.WriteLine("length of nums is " + nums.Length);
```

```
    Console.WriteLine("length of table is " + table.Length);
    Console.WriteLine("length of table[0] is " + table[0].Length);
    Console.WriteLine("length of table[1] is " + table[1].Length);
    Console.WriteLine("length of table[2] is " + table[2].Length);
    Console.WriteLine();

    // use length to initialize list
    for(int i=0; i < list.Length; i++)
      list[i] = i * i;

    Console.Write("Here is list: ");
    // now use length to display list
    for(int i=0; i < list.Length; i++)
      Console.Write(list[i] + " ");
    Console.WriteLine();
  }
}
```

This program displays the following output:

```
length of list is 10
length of nums is 3
length of table is 3
length of table[0] is 3
length of table[1] is 2
length of table[2] is 4

Here is list: 0 1 4 9 16 25 36 49 64 81
```

Pay special attention to the way **Length** is used with the two-dimensional jagged array **table**. As explained, a two-dimensional jagged array is an array of arrays. Thus, when the expression

```
table.Length
```

is used, it obtains the number of *arrays* stored in **table**, which is 3 in this case. To obtain the length of any individual array in **table**, you will use an expression such as this:

```
table[0].Length
```

which, in this case, obtains the length of the first array.

One other thing to notice in **LengthDemo** is the way that **list.Length** is used by the **for** loops to govern the number of iterations that take place. Since each array carries with it its own length, you can use this information rather than manually keeping track of an array's size. Keep in mind that the value of **Length** has nothing to do with the number of elements that are actually in use. It contains the number of elements that the array is capable of holding.

The inclusion of the **Length** property simplifies many algorithms by making certain types of array operations easier—and safer—to perform. For example, the following program uses **Length** to copy one array to another while preventing an array overrun and its attendant runtime exception:

```
// Use Length property to help copy an array.
using System;

class ACopy {
  public static void Main() {
    int i;
    int[] nums1 = new int[10];
    int[] nums2 = new int[10];

    for(i=0; i < nums1.Length; i++) nums1[i] = i;

    // copy nums1 to nums2
    if(nums2.Length >= nums1.Length)
      for(i = 0; i < nums2.Length; i++)
        nums2[i] = nums1[i];

    for(i=0; i < nums2.Length; i++)
      Console.Write(nums2[i] + " ");
  }
}
```

Here, **Length** helps perform two important functions. First, it is used to confirm that the target array is large enough to hold the contents of the source array. Second, it provides the termination condition of the **for** loop that performs the copy. Of course, in this simple example, the size of the arrays is easily known, but this same approach can be applied to a wide range of more challenging situations.

1-Minute Drill

● When one array reference is assigned to another, the elements of the first array are copied to the second. True or False?

● As it pertains to arrays, what is **Length**?

QDemo.cs

Project 5-2: A Queue Class

As you may know, a *data structure* is a means of organizing data. The simplest data structure is the array, which is a linear list that supports random access to its elements. Arrays are often used as the underpinning for more sophisticated data structures, such as stacks and queues. A *stack* is a list in which elements can be accessed in first-in, last-out (FILO) order only. A *queue* is a list in which elements can be accessed in first-in, first-out (FIFO) order only. Thus, a stack is like a stack of plates on a table; the first down is the last to be used. A queue is like a line at a bank; the first in line is the first served.

What makes data structures such as stacks and queues interesting is that they combine storage for information with the methods that access that information. Thus, stacks and queues are *data engines* in which storage and retrieval is provided by the data structure itself, and not manually by your program. Such a combination is, obviously, an excellent choice for a class, and in this project you will create a simple queue class.

In general, queues support two basic operations: *put* and *get*. Each *put* operation places a new element on the end of the queue. Each *get* operation retrieves the next element from the front of the queue. Queue operations are consumptive. Once an element has been retrieved, it cannot be retrieved again. The queue can also become full if there is no space available to store an item, and it can become empty if all of the elements have been removed.

One last point: There are two basic types of queues—circular and noncircular. A *circular* queue reuses locations in the underlying array when elements are removed. A *noncircular* queue does not and eventually becomes exhausted. For the sake of simplicity, this example creates a noncircular queue, but with a little thought and effort, you can easily transform it into a circular queue.

● False. Only the reference is changed.
● **Length** is a property that all arrays have. It contains the number of elements that the array can hold.

Step-by-Step

1. Create a file called **QDemo.cs**.

2. Although there are other ways to support a queue, the method we will use is based upon an array. That is, an array will provide the storage for the items put into the queue. This array will be accessed through two indices. The *put* index determines where the next element of data will be stored. The *get* index indicates at what location the next element of data will be obtained. Keep in mind that the *get* operation is consumptive, and it is not possible to retrieve the same element twice. Although the queue that we will be creating stores characters, the same logic can be used to store any type of object. Begin creating the **Queue** class with these lines:

```
class Queue {
  public char[] q; // this array holds the queue
  public int putloc, getloc; // the put and get indices
```

3. The constructor for the **Queue** class creates a queue of a given size. Here is the **Queue** constructor:

```
public Queue(int size) {
  q = new char[size+1]; // allocate memory for queue
  putloc = getloc = 0;
}
```

Notice that the queue is created one larger than the size specified in **size**. Because of the way the queue algorithm will be implemented, one array location will be unused, so the array must be created one larger than the requested queue size. The *put* and *get* indices are initially set to zero.

4. The **put( )** method, which stores elements, is shown next:

```
// put a character into the queue
public void put(char ch) {
  if(putloc==q.Length-1) {
    Console.WriteLine(" -- Queue is full.");
    return;
  }

  putloc++;
  q[putloc] = ch;
}
```

The method begins by checking for a queue-full condition. If **putloc** is equal to the last location in the **q** array, then there is no more room in which to store elements. Otherwise, **putloc** is incremented and the new element is stored at that location. Thus, **putloc** is always the index of the last element stored.

5. To retrieve elements, use the **get( )** method, shown next:

```
// get a character from the queue
public char get() {
  if(getloc == putloc) {
    Console.WriteLine(" -- Queue is empty.");
    return (char) 0;
  }

  getloc++;
  return q[getloc];
}
```

Notice first the check for queue-empty. If **getloc** and **putloc** both index the same element, then the queue is assumed to be empty. This is why **getloc** and **putloc** were both initialized to zero by the **Queue** constructor. Next, **getloc** is incremented and the next element is returned. Thus, **getloc** always indicates the location of the last element retrieved.

6. Here is the entire **QDemo.cs** program:

```
/*
   Project 5-2

   A queue class for characters.
*/
using System;

class Queue {
  public char[] q; // this array holds the queue
  public int putloc, getloc; // the put and get indices

  public Queue(int size) {
    q = new char[size+1]; // allocate memory for queue
    putloc = getloc = 0;
  }

  // put a character into the queue
```

```
  public void put(char ch) {
    if(putloc==q.Length-1) {
      Console.WriteLine(" -- Queue is full.");
      return;
    }

    putloc++;
    q[putloc] = ch;
  }

  // get a character from the queue
  public char get() {
    if(getloc == putloc) {
      Console.WriteLine(" -- Queue is empty.");
      return (char) 0;
    }

    getloc++;
    return q[getloc];
  }
}

// Demonstrate the Queue class.
class QDemo {
  public static void Main() {
    Queue bigQ = new Queue(100);
    Queue smallQ = new Queue(4);
    char ch;
    int i;

    Console.WriteLine("Using bigQ to store the alphabet.");
    // put some numbers into bigQ
    for(i=0; i < 26; i++)
      bigQ.put((char) ('A' + i));

    // retrieve and display elements from bigQ
    Console.Write("Contents of bigQ: ");
    for(i=0; i < 26; i++) {
      ch = bigQ.get();
      if(ch != (char) 0) Console.Write(ch);
    }
```

```
       Console.WriteLine("\n");


       Console.WriteLine("Using smallQ to generate errors.");
       // Now, use smallQ to generate some errors
       for(i=0; i < 5; i++) {
         Console.Write("Attempting to store " +
                       (char) ('Z' - i));

         smallQ.put((char) ('Z' - i));

         Console.WriteLine();
       }
       Console.WriteLine();

       // more errors on smallQ
       Console.Write("Contents of smallQ: ");
       for(i=0; i < 5; i++) {
         ch = smallQ.get();

         if(ch != (char) 0) Console.Write(ch);
       }
     }
   }
}
```

7. The output produced by the program is shown here:

```
Using bigQ to store the alphabet.
Contents of bigQ: ABCDEFGHIJKLMNOPQRSTUVWXYZ

Using smallQ to generate errors.
Attempting to store Z
Attempting to store Y
Attempting to store X
Attempting to store W
Attempting to store V -- Queue is full.


Contents of smallQ: ZYXW -- Queue is empty.
```

8. On your own, try modifying **Queue** so that it stores other types of objects. For example, have it store **int**s or **double**s.

The foreach Loop

In Module 3 it was mentioned that C# defines a loop called **foreach**, but a discussion of that statement was deferred until now.

The **foreach** loop is used to cycle through the elements of a *collection*. A collection is a group of objects. C# defines several types of collections, of which one is an array. The general form of **foreach** is shown here:

foreach(*type var-name* in *collection*) *statement;*

Here, *type var-name* specifies the type and name of an *iteration variable* that will receive the values of the elements from the collection as the **foreach** iterates. The collection being cycled through is specified by *collection*, which, for this discussion, is an array. Thus, *type* must be the same as (or compatible with) the base type of the array. One important point to remember is that the iteration variable is read-only as far as the array is concerned. Thus, you can't change the contents of the array by assigning the iteration variable a new value.

Here is a simple example that uses **foreach**. It creates an array of integers and gives it some initial values. It then displays those values, computing the summation in the process.

```
// Use foreach
using System;

class ForeachDemo {
  public static void Main() {
    int sum = 0;
    int[] nums = new int[10];

    // give nums some values
    for(int i = 0; i < 10; i++)
      nums[i] = i;

    // use foreach to display and sum the values
    foreach(int x in nums) {
      Console.WriteLine("Value is: " + x);
      sum += x;
    }
    Console.WriteLine("Summation: " + sum);
  }
}
```

Cycle through **nums** using a **foreach** loop.

The output from the program is shown here:

```
Value is: 0
Value is: 1
Value is: 2
Value is: 3
Value is: 4
Value is: 5
Value is: 6
Value is: 7
Value is: 8
Value is: 9
Summation: 45
```

As this output shows, the **foreach** cycles through an array in sequence from the lowest index to the highest.

The **foreach** also works on multidimensional arrays. It returns those elements in row order, from first to last.

```csharp
// Use foreach on a two-dimensional array.
using System;

class ForeachDemo2 {
  public static void Main() {
    int sum = 0;
    int[,] nums = new int[3,5];

    // give nums some values
    for(int i = 0; i < 3; i++)
      for(int j=0; j < 5; j++)
        nums[i,j] = (i+1)*(j+1);

    // use foreach to display and sum the values
    foreach(int x in nums) {
      Console.WriteLine("Value is: " + x);
      sum += x;
    }
    Console.WriteLine("Summation: " + sum);
  }
}
```

The output from this program is shown here:

```
Value is: 1
Value is: 2
Value is: 3
Value is: 4
Value is: 5
Value is: 2
Value is: 4
Value is: 6
Value is: 8
Value is: 10
Value is: 3
Value is: 6
Value is: 9
Value is: 12
Value is: 15
Summation: 90
```

Since the **foreach** can only cycle through an array from start to finish, you might think that its use is limited. However, this is not true. A large number of algorithms require exactly this mechanism. For example, here is another way to write the **MinMax** class shown earlier in this module that obtains the minimum and maximum from a set of values:

```
/* Find the minimum and maximum values in an array
   by using a foreach loop. */

using System;

class MinMax {
  public static void Main() {
    int[] nums = { 99, -10, 100123, 18, -978,
                   5623, 463, -9, 287, 49 };
    int min, max;

    min = max = nums[0];
    foreach(int val in nums) {
      if(val < min) min = val;
      if(val > max) max = val;
    }
    Console.WriteLine("Min and max: " + min + " " + max);
  }
}
```

The **foreach** is an excellent choice in this application because the finding of a minimum or maximum value requires examining each element. Other types of **foreach** applications include such things as computing an average, searching a list, and copying an array.

1-Minute Drill

● What does the **foreach** loop do?

● Is it possible to make the **foreach** access the elements in an array in reverse order?

● Can you use **foreach** to assign a value to an array element?

Strings

From a day-to-day programming standpoint, one of the most important of C#'s data types is **string**. **string** defines and supports character strings. In many other programming languages, a string is an array of characters. This is not the case with C#. In C#, strings are objects. Thus, **string** is a reference type.

Actually, you have been using the **string** class since Module 1, but you did not know it. When you create a string literal, you are actually creating a **string** object. For example, in the statement

```
Console.WriteLine("In C#, strings are objects.");
```

the string "In C#, strings are objects." is automatically made into a **string** object by C#. Thus, the use of the **string** class has been "below the surface" in the preceding programs. In this section you will learn to handle them explicitly. Be aware, however, that the **string** class is quite large, and we will only scratch its surface here. It is a class that you will want to explore more fully on your own.

● The **foreach** cycles through the elements in an array.
● No.
● No.

Constructing Strings

The easiest way to construct a **string** is to use a string literal. For example, here **str** is a **string** reference variable that is assigned a reference to a string literal:

```
string str = "C# strings are powerful.";
```

In this case, **str** is initialized to the character sequence "C# strings are powerful."

You can also create a **string** from a **char** array. For example:

```
char[] str = {'t', 'e', 's', 't'};
string str = new string(charray);
```

Once you have created a **string** object, you can use it anywhere that a quoted string is allowed. For example, you can use a **string** object as an argument to **WriteLine( )**, as shown in this example:

```
// Introduce string.
using System;

class StringDemo {
  public static void Main() {

    char[] charray = {'A', ' ', 's', 't', 'r', 'i', 'n', 'g', '.' };
    string str1 = new string(charray);
    string str2 = "Another string.";

    Console.WriteLine(str1);
    Console.WriteLine(str2);
  }
}
```

Construct **string** objects from a **char** array and from a string literal.

The output from the program is shown here:

```
A string.
Another string.
```

Operating on Strings

The **string** class contains several methods that operate on strings. Here are a few:

static string Copy(string *str*)	Returns a copy of *str*.
int CompareTo(string *str*)	Returns less than zero if the invoking string is less than *str*, greater than zero if the invoking string is greater than *str*, and zero if the strings are equal.
int IndexOf(string *str*)	Searches the invoking string for the substring specified by *str*. Returns the index of the first match, or –1 on failure.
int LastIndexOf(string *str*)	Searches the invoking string for the substring specified by *str*. Returns the index of the last match, or –1 on failure.

The **string** type also includes the **Length** property, which contains the length of the string.

To obtain the value of an individual character of a string, you simply use an index. For example:

```
string str = "test";
Console.WriteLine(str[0]);
```

This displays t. Like arrays, string indices begin at zero. One important point, however, is that you cannot assign a new value to a character within a string using an index. An index can only be used to obtain a character.

To test two strings for equality, you can use the = = operator. Normally, when the = = operator is applied to object references, it determines if both references refer to the same object. This differs for objects of type **string**. When the = = is applied to two **string** references, the contents of the strings, themselves, are compared for equality. The same is true for the != operator: when comparing **string** objects, the contents of the strings are compared. However, the other relational operators, such as < or >=, compare the references, just like they do for other types of objects.

Here is a program that demonstrates several string operations:

```
// Some string operations.
using System;

class StrOps {
  public static void Main() {
    string str1 =
      "When it comes to .NET programming, C# is #1.";
    string str2 = string.Copy(str1);
    string str3 = "C# strings are powerful.";
    int result, idx;
```

```
Console.WriteLine("Length of str1: " +
                  str1.Length);

// display str1, one char at a time.
for(int i=0; i < str1.Length; i++)
  Console.Write(str1[i]);
Console.WriteLine();

if(str1 == str2)
  Console.WriteLine("str1 == str2");
else
  Console.WriteLine("str1 != str2");

if(str1 == str3)
  Console.WriteLine("str1 == str3");
else
  Console.WriteLine("str1 != str3");

result = str1.CompareTo(str3);
if(result == 0)
  Console.WriteLine("str1 and str3 are equal");
else if(result < 0)
  Console.WriteLine("str1 is less than str3");
else
  Console.WriteLine("str1 is greater than str3");

// assign a new string to str2
str2 = "One Two Three One";

idx = str2.IndexOf("One");
Console.WriteLine("Index of first occurrence of One: " + idx);
idx = str2.LastIndexOf("One");
Console.WriteLine("Index of last occurrence of One: " + idx);

  }
}
```

This program generates the following output:

```
Length of str1: 44
When it comes to .NET programming, C# is #1.
str1 == str2
str1 != str3
str1 is greater than str3
Index of first occurrence of One: 0
Index of last occurrence of One: 14
```

You can *concatenate* (join together) two strings using the + operator. For example, this statement:

```
string str1 = "One";
string str2 = "Two";
string str3 = "Three";
string str4 = str1 + str2 + str3;
```

initializes **str4** with the string "OneTwoThree".

Arrays of Strings

Like any other data type, strings can be assembled into arrays. For example:

5

```
// Demonstrate string arrays.
using System;
                                          ┌──────────────────┐
                                          │ An array of strings │
                                          └──────────────────┘
class StringArrays {
  public static void Main() {
    string[] str = { "This", "is", "a", "test." };

    Console.WriteLine("Original array: ");
    for(int i=0; i < str.Length; i++)
      Console.Write(str[i] + " ");
    Console.WriteLine("\n");

    // change a string
    str[1] = "was";
    str[3] = "test, too!";

    Console.WriteLine("Modified array: ");
    for(int i=0; i < str.Length; i++)
      Console.Write(str[i] + " ");
  }
}
```

Here is the output from this program:

```
Original array:
This is a test.

Modified array:
This was a test, too!
```

Strings Are Immutable

Here is something that might surprise you: the contents of a **string** object are immutable. That is, once created, the character sequence comprising that string cannot be altered. This restriction allows C# to implement strings more efficiently. Even though this probably sounds like a serious drawback, it isn't. When you need a string that is a variation on one that already exists, simply create a new string that contains the desired changes. Since unused string objects are automatically garbage-collected, you don't even need to worry about what happens to the discarded strings.

It must be made clear, however, that **string** reference variables may, of course, change the object to which they refer. It is just that the contents of a specific **string** object cannot be changed after it is created.

To fully understand why immutable strings are not a hindrance, we will use another of **string**'s methods: **Substring( )**. The **Substring( )** method returns a new string that contains a specified portion of the invoking string. Because a new **string** object is manufactured that contains the substring, the original string is unaltered, and the rule of immutability is still intact. The form of **Substring( )** that we will be using is shown here:

string Substring(int *startIndex*, int *len*)

Here, *startIndex* specifies the beginning index, and *len* specifies the length of the substring.

Here is a program that demonstrates **Substring( )** and the principle of immutable strings:

```
// Use Substring().
using System;

class SubStr {
  public static void Main() {
    string orgstr = "C# makes strings easy.";

    // construct a substring
    string substr = orgstr.Substring(5, 12);

    Console.WriteLine("orgstr: " + orgstr);
    Console.WriteLine("substr: " + substr);
```

This creates a new string that contains the desired substring.

```
    }
}
```

Here is the output from the program:

```
orgstr: C# makes strings easy.
substr: kes strings
```

As you can see, the original string **orgstr** is unchanged and **substr** contains the substring.

1-Minute Drill

- In C#, all strings are objects. True or False?
- How can you obtain the length of a string?
- What does **Substring( )** do?

Ask the Expert

Question: You say that once created, string objects are immutable. I understand that, from a practical point of view, this is not a serious restriction. However, what if I want to create a string that *can* be changed?

Answer: You're in luck. C# offers a class called **StringBuilder** that is in the **System.Text** namespace. It creates string objects that can be changed. However, for most purposes, you will want to use **string**, not **StringBuilder**.

- True.
- The length of a string can be obtained by using the **Length** property.
- **Substring( )** constructs a new string that is a substring of the one on which it is called. The new string is returned.

The Bitwise Operators

In Module 2 you learned about C#'s arithmetic, relational, and logical operators. While these are the most commonly used, C# provides additional operators that expand the set of problems to which C# can be applied: the bitwise operators. The bitwise operators act directly upon the bits of their operands. They are defined only for integer operands. They cannot be used on **bool**, **float**, or **double**, or class types.

They are called the *bitwise* operators because they are used to test, set, or shift the bits that comprise an integer value. Bitwise operations are important to a wide variety of systems-level programming tasks, such as when status information from a device must be interrogated or constructed. Table 5-1 lists the bitwise operators.

The Bitwise AND, OR, XOR, and NOT Operators

The bitwise operators AND, OR, XOR, and NOT are, respectively, &, |, ^, and ~. They perform the same operations as their Boolean logic equivalents described in Module 2. The difference is that the bitwise operators work on a bit-by-bit basis. The following table shows the outcome of each operation using 1's and 0's:

p	q	p & q	p | q	p ^ q	~p
0	0	0	0	0	1
1	0	0	1	1	0
0	1	0	1	1	1
1	1	1	1	0	0

In terms of its most common usage, you can think of the bitwise AND as a way to turn bits off. That is, any bit that is 0 in either operand will cause the corresponding bit in the outcome to be set to 0. For example:

```
  1 1 0 1 0 0 1 1
  1 0 1 0 1 0 1 0
& --------------------
  1 0 0 0 0 0 1 0
```

Operator	Result
&	Bitwise AND
|	Bitwise OR
^	Bitwise exclusive OR (XOR)
>>	Shift right
<<	Shift left
~	One's complement (unary NOT)

Table 5-1 The Bitwise Operators

The following program demonstrates the & by turning any lowercase letter into uppercase by resetting the sixth bit to 0. As the Unicode/ASCII character set is defined, the lowercase letters are the same as the uppercase ones, except that the lowercase ones are greater in value by exactly 32. Therefore, to transform a lowercase letter to uppercase, just turn off the sixth bit, as this program illustrates:

```
// Uppercase letters.
using System;

class UpCase {
  public static void Main() {
    char ch;

    for(int i=0; i < 10; i++) {
      ch = (char) ('a' + i);
      Console.Write(ch);

      // This statement turns off the 6th bit.
      ch = (char) (ch & 65503); // ch is now uppercase

      Console.Write(ch + " ");
    }
  }
}
```

The output from this program is shown here:

```
aA bB cC dD eE fF gG hH iI jJ
```

The value 65,503 used in the AND statement is the decimal representation of 1111 1111 1101 1111. Thus, the AND operation leaves all bits in **ch** unchanged except for the sixth one, which is set to zero.

The AND operator is also useful when you want to determine whether a bit is on or off. For example, this statement determines if bit 4 in **status** is set:

```
if(status & 8) Console.WriteLine("bit 4 is on");
```

The reason 8 is used is that it translates into a binary value that has only the fourth bit set. Therefore, the **if** statement can succeed only when bit 4 of **status** is also on. An interesting use of this concept is to show the bits of a **byte** value in binary format:

```
// Display the bits within a byte.
using System;

class ShowBits {
  public static void Main() {
    int t;
    byte val;

    val = 123;
    for(t=128; t > 0; t = t/2) {
      if((val & t) != 0) Console.Write("1 ");
      else Console.Write("0 ");
    }
  }
}
```

Display the bits within a byte.

The output is shown here:

```
0 1 1 1 1 0 1 1
```

The **for** loop successively tests each bit in **val**, using the bitwise AND, to determine if it is on or off. If the bit is on, the digit **1** is displayed; otherwise 0 is displayed. In Project 5-3, you will see how this basic concept can be expanded to create a class that will display the bits in any type of integer.

The bitwise OR, as the reverse of AND, can be used to turn bits on. Any bit that is set to 1 in either operand will cause the corresponding bit in the variable to be set to 1. For example:

```
11010011
10101010
| --------------------
11111011
```

We can make use of the OR to change the uppercasing program into a lowercasing program, as shown here:

```
// Lowercase letters.
using System;

class LowCase {
  public static void Main() {
    char ch;

    for(int i=0; i < 10; i++) {
      ch = (char) ('A' + i);
      Console.Write(ch);

      // This statement turns on the 6th bit.
      ch = (char) (ch | 32); // ch is now lowercase

      Console.Write(ch + " ");
    }
  }
}
```

The output from this program is shown here:

```
Aa Bb Cc Dd Ee Ff Gg Hh Ii Jj
```

The program works by ORing each character with the value 32, which is 0000 0000 0010 0000 in binary. Thus, 32 is the value that produces a value in binary in which only the sixth bit is set. When this value is ORed with any other value, it produces a result in which the sixth bit is set and all other bits remain unchanged. As explained, for characters this means that each uppercase letter is transformed into its lowercase equivalent.

An exclusive OR, usually abbreviated XOR, will set a bit on if, and only if, the bits being compared are different, as illustrated here:

```
01111111
10111001
^ ------------------------
11000110
```

The XOR operator has an interesting property that makes it a simple way to encode a message. When some value X is XORed with another value Y, and then that result is XORed with Y again, X is produced. That is, given the sequence

R1 = X ^ Y;

R2 = R1 ^ Y;

R2 is the same value as X. Thus, the outcome of a sequence of two XORs using the same value produces the original value. You can use this principle to create a simple cipher program in which some integer is the key that is used to both encode and decode a message by XORing the characters in that message. To encode, the XOR operation is applied the first time, yielding the ciphertext. To decode, the XOR is applied a second time, yielding the plaintext. Here is a simple example that uses this approach to encode and decode a short message:

```
// Use XOR to encode and decode a message.
using System;

class Encode {
  public static void Main() {
    string msg = "This is a test";
    string encmsg = "";
    string decmsg = "";
    int key = 88;

    Console.Write("Original message: ");
    Console.WriteLine(msg);

    // encode the message
    for(int i=0; i < msg.Length; i++)
      encmsg = encmsg + (char) (msg[i] ^ key);

    Console.Write("Encoded message: ");
    Console.WriteLine(encmsg);

    // decode the message
    for(int i=0; i < msg.Length; i++)
      decmsg = decmsg + (char) (encmsg[i] ^ key);

    Console.Write("Decoded message: ");
    Console.WriteLine(decmsg);
  }
}
```

This constructs the encoded string.

This constructs the decoded string.

Here is the output:

```
Original message: This is a test
Encoded message: 01+x1+x9x,=+,
Decoded message: This is a test
```

As you can see, the result of two XORs using the same key produces the decoded message.

The unary 1's complement (NOT) operator reverses the state of all the bits of the operand. For example, if some integer called **A** has the bit pattern 1001 0110, then **~A** produces a result with the bit pattern 0110 1001.

The following program demonstrates the NOT operator by displaying a number and its complement in binary:

```
// Demonstrate the bitwise NOT.
using System;

class NotDemo {
  public static void Main() {
    sbyte b = -34;

    for(int t=128; t > 0; t = t/2) {
      if((b & t) != 0) Console.Write("1 ");
      else Console.Write("0 ");
    }
    Console.WriteLine();

    // reverse all bits
    b = (sbyte) ~b;

    for(int t=128; t > 0; t = t/2) {
      if((b & t) != 0) Console.Write("1 ");
      else Console.Write("0 ");
    }
  }
}
```

Here is the output:

```
1 1 0 1 1 1 1 0
0 0 1 0 0 0 0 1
```

The Shift Operators

In C# it is possible to shift the bits that comprise a value to the left or to the right by a specified amount. C# defines the two bit-shift operators shown here:

  <<   Left shift

  >>   Right shift

The general forms for these operators are shown here:

    value << *num-bits*

    value >> *num-bits*

Here, *value* is the value being shifted by the number of bit positions specified by *num-bits*.

A left-shift causes all bits within the specified value to be shifted left one position, and a zero bit to be brought in on the right. A right-shift causes all bits to be shifted right one position. In the case of a right shift on an unsigned value, a zero is brought in on the left. In the case of a right shift on a signed value, the sign bit is preserved. Recall that negative numbers are represented by setting the high-order bit of an integer value to 1. Thus, if the value being shifted is negative, each right-shift brings in a 1 on the left. If the value is positive, each right shift brings in a 0 on the left.

For both left and right shifts, the bits shifted out are lost. Thus, a shift is not a rotate, and there is no way to retrieve a bit that has been shifted out.

Here is a program that graphically illustrates the effect of a left and right shift. An integer is given an initial value of 1, which means that its low-order bit is set. Then, a series of eight shifts is performed on the integer. After each shift, the lower eight bits of the value are shown. The process is then repeated, except that a 1 is put in the eighth bit position, and right shifts are performed.

```
// Demonstrate the shift << and >> operators.
using System;

class ShiftDemo {
  public static void Main() {
    int val = 1;

    for(int i = 0; i < 8; i++) {
```

```
      for(int t=128; t > 0; t = t/2) {
        if((val & t) != 0) Console.Write("1 ");
        else Console.Write("0 ");
      }
      Console.WriteLine();
      val = val << 1; // left shift
    }
    Console.WriteLine();

    val = 128;
    for(int i = 0; i < 8; i++) {
      for(int t=128; t > 0; t = t/2) {
        if((val & t) != 0) Console.Write("1 ");
        else Console.Write("0 ");
      }
      Console.WriteLine();
      val = val >> 1; // right shift
    }
  }
}
```

The output from the program is shown here:

```
0 0 0 0 0 0 0 1
0 0 0 0 0 0 1 0
0 0 0 0 0 1 0 0
0 0 0 0 1 0 0 0
0 0 0 1 0 0 0 0
0 0 1 0 0 0 0 0
0 1 0 0 0 0 0 0
1 0 0 0 0 0 0 0

1 0 0 0 0 0 0 0
0 1 0 0 0 0 0 0
0 0 1 0 0 0 0 0
0 0 0 1 0 0 0 0
0 0 0 0 1 0 0 0
0 0 0 0 0 1 0 0
0 0 0 0 0 0 1 0
0 0 0 0 0 0 0 1
```

Ask the Expert

Question: Since binary is based on powers of 2, can the shift operators be used as a shortcut for multiplying or dividing an integer by 2?

Answer: Yes. The bitwise shift operators can be used to perform very fast multiplication or division by 2. A shift left doubles a value. A shift right halves it. Of course, this only works as long as you are not shifting bits off one end or the other.

Bitwise Compound Assignments

All of the binary bitwise operators can be used in compound assignments. For example, the following two statements both assign to **x** the outcome of an XOR of **x** with the value 127:

```
x = x ^ 127;
x ^= 127;
```

ShowBitsDemo.cs

Project 5-3: A ShowBits Class

This project creates a class called **ShowBits** that enables you to display in binary the bit pattern for any integer value. Such a class can be quite useful in programming. For example, if you are debugging device-driver code, then being able to monitor the data stream in binary is often a benefit.

Step-by-Step

1. Create a file called **ShowBitsDemo.cs**.

2. Begin the **ShowBits** class as shown here:

```
class ShowBits {
  public int numbits;

  public ShowBits(int n) {
    numbits = n;
  }
```

ShowBits creates objects that display a specified number of bits. For example, to create an object that will display the low-order eight bits of some value, use

```
ShowBits b = new ShowBits(8);
```

The number of bits to display is stored in **numbits**.

3. To actually display the bit pattern, **ShowBits** provides the method **show( )**, which is shown here:

```
public void show(ulong val) {
  ulong mask = 1;

  // left-shift a 1 into the proper position
  mask <<= numbits-1;

  int spacer = 0;
  for(; mask != 0; mask >>= 1) {
    if((val & mask) != 0) Console.Write("1");
    else Console.Write("0");
    spacer++;
    if((spacer % 8) == 0) {
      Console.Write(" ");
      spacer = 0;
    }
  }
  Console.WriteLine();
}
```

Notice that **show( )** specifies one **ulong** parameter. This does not mean that you have to always pass **show( )** a **ulong** value, however. Because of C#'s automatic type promotions, any integer type can be passed to **show( )**. The number of bits displayed is determined by the value stored in **numbits**. After each group of eight bits, **show( )** outputs a space. This makes it easier to read the binary values of long bit patterns.

4. The **ShowBitsDemo** program is shown here:

```
/*
   Project 5-3

   A class that displays the binary representation of a value.
```

```
*/
using System;

class ShowBits {
  public int numbits;

  public ShowBits(int n) {
    numbits = n;
  }

  public void show(ulong val) {
    ulong mask = 1;

    // left-shift a 1 into the proper position
    mask <<= numbits-1;

    int spacer = 0;
    for(; mask != 0; mask >>= 1) {
      if((val & mask) != 0) Console.Write("1");
      else Console.Write("0");
      spacer++;
      if((spacer % 8) == 0) {
        Console.Write(" ");
        spacer = 0;
      }
    }
    Console.WriteLine();
  }
}

// Demonstrate ShowBits.
class ShowBitsDemo {
  public static void Main() {
    ShowBits b = new ShowBits(8);
    ShowBits i = new ShowBits(32);
    ShowBits li = new ShowBits(64);

    Console.WriteLine("123 in binary: ");
    b.show(123);

    Console.WriteLine("\n87987 in binary: ");
    i.show(87987);
```

```
Console.WriteLine("\n237658768 in binary: ");
li.show(237658768);


// you can also show low-order bits of any integer
Console.WriteLine("\nLow order 8 bits of 87987 in binary:
");
b.show(87987);
  }
}
```

5. The output from **ShowBitsDemo** is shown here:

```
123 in binary:
01111011

87987 in binary:
00000000 00000001 01010111 10110011

237658768 in binary:
00000000 00000000 00000000 00000000 00001110 00101010 01100010
10010000

Low order 8 bits of 87987 in binary:
10110011
```

1-Minute Drill

● To what types can the bitwise operators be applied?

● What effect do >> and << have?

● What is wrong with this fragment?

```
byte val = 10;
val = val << 2;
```

● The bitwise operators can be applied to the integer types.
● >> performs a right shift and << performs a left shift.
● When the left shift is performed, **val** is promoted to **int** and the result is **int**. To assign this **int** value back to a **byte**, you must use a cast.

The ? Operator

One of C#'s most fascinating operators is the ?. The ? operator is often used to replace **if-else** statements of this general form:

```
if (condition)
 var = expression1;
else
 var = expression2;
```

Here, the value assigned to *var* depends upon the outcome of the *condition* controlling the **if**.

The ? is called a *ternary operator* because it requires three operands. It takes the general form

```
Exp1 ? Exp2 : Exp3;
```

where *Exp1* is a **bool** expression, and *Exp2* and *Exp3* are expressions. The type of *Exp2* and *Exp3* must be the same. Notice the use and placement of the colon.

The value of a ? expression is determined like this: *Exp1* is evaluated. If it is true, then *Exp2* is evaluated and becomes the value of the entire ? expression. If *Exp1* is false, then *Exp3* is evaluated and its value becomes the value of the expression. Consider this example, which assigns **absval** the absolute value of **val**:

```
absval = val < 0 ? -val : val; // get absolute value of val
```

Here, **absval** will be assigned the value of **val** if **val** is zero or greater. If **val** is negative, then **absval** will be assigned the negative of that value (which yields a positive value). The same code written using the **if-else** structure would look like this:

```
if(val < 0) absval  = -val;
else absval = val;
```

Here is another example of the ? operator. This program divides two numbers, but will not allow a division by zero:

```
// Prevent a division by zero using the ?.
using System;

class NoZeroDiv {
  public static void Main() {
    int result;

    for(int i = -5; i < 6; i++) {
      result = i != 0 ? 100 / i : 0;
      if(i != 0)
        Console.WriteLine("100 / " + i + " is " + result);
    }
  }
}
```

This prevents a divide-by-zero.

The output from the program is shown here:

```
100 / -5 is -20
100 / -4 is -25
100 / -3 is -33
100 / -2 is -50
100 / -1 is -100
100 / 1 is 100
100 / 2 is 50
100 / 3 is 33
100 / 4 is 25
100 / 5 is 20
```

Pay special attention to this line from the program:

```
result = i != 0 ? 100 / i : 0;
```

Here, **result** is assigned the outcome of the division of 100 by i. However, this division takes place only if i is not zero. When i is zero, a placeholder value of zero is assigned to **result**.

You don't actually have to assign the value produced by the ? to some variable. For example, you could use the value as an argument in a call to a method. Or, if the expressions are all of type **bool**, the ? can be used as the conditional expression in a loop or **if** statement. For example, here is the preceding program rewritten a bit more efficiently. It produces the same output as before.

```
// Prevent a division by zero using the ?.
using System;

class NoZeroDiv2 {
  public static void Main() {

    for(int i = -5; i < 6; i++)
      if(i != 0 ? true : false)
        Console.WriteLine("100 / " + i +
                          " is " + 100 / i);
  }
}
```

Notice the **if** statement. If **i** is zero, then the outcome of the **if** is false, the division by zero is prevented, and no result is displayed. Otherwise the division takes place.

✓ *Mastery Check*

1. Show how to declare a one-dimensional array of 12 **doubles**.

2. Show how to declare a 4×5, two-dimensional array of **ints**.

3. Show how to declare a jagged two-dimensional **int** array in which the first dimension is 5.

4. Show how to initialize a one-dimensional **int** array with the values 1 through 5.

5. Explain **foreach**. Show its general form.

6. Write a program that uses an array to find the average of ten **double** values. Use any ten values you like.

7. Change the sort in Project 5-1 so that it sorts an array of strings. Demonstrate that it works.

8. What is the difference between the **string** methods **IndexOf( )** and **LastIndexOf( )**?

9. Expanding on the **Encode** cipher class, modify it so that it uses an 8-character string as the key.

10. Can the bitwise operators be applied to the **double** type?

11. Show how this sequence can be rewritten using the ? operator.

```
if(x < 0) y = 10;
else y = 20;
```

12. In the following fragment, is the **&** a bitwise or logical operator? Why?

```
bool a, b;
// ...
if(a & b) ...
```

5

Module 6

A Closer Look at
Methods and Classes

The Goals of This Module

- Control access to members
- Pass objects to a method
- Return objects from a method
- Use ref and out parameters
- Overload methods
- Overload constructors
- Return values from Main( )
- Pass arguments to Main( )
- Use recursion
- Apply static

This module resumes our examination of classes and methods. It begins by explaining how to control access to the members of a class. It then discusses the passing and returning of objects, method overloading, the various forms of **Main( )**, recursion, and the use of the keyword **static**.

Controlling Access to Class Members

In its support for encapsulation, the class provides two major benefits. First, it links data with the code that manipulates it. You have been taking advantage of this aspect of the class since Module 4. Second, it provides the means by which access to members can be controlled. This feature is examined here.

Although C#'s approach is a bit more sophisticated, in essence, there are two basic types of class members: public and private. A *public* member can be freely accessed by code defined outside of its class. This is the type of class member that we have been using up to this point. A *private* member can be accessed only by other methods defined by its class. It is through the use of private members that access is controlled.

Restricting access to a class' members is a fundamental part of object-oriented programming because it helps prevent the misuse of an object. By allowing access to private data only through a well-defined set of methods, you can prevent improper values from being assigned to that data—by performing a range-check, for example. It is not possible for code outside the class to set the value of a private member directly. You can also control precisely how and when the data within an object is used. Thus, when correctly implemented, a class creates a "black box" that can be used, but the inner workings of which are not open to tampering.

C#'s Access Specifiers

Member access control is achieved through the use of four *access specifiers:* **public**, **private**, **protected**, and **internal**. In this module we will be concerned with **public** and **private**. The **protected** modifier applies only when inheritance is involved and is described in Module 7. The **internal** modifier applies mostly to the use of an *assembly*, which in the case of C# means a program, project, or component. The **internal** modifier is briefly described in Module 12.

When a member of a class is modified by the **public** specifier, that member can be accessed by any other code in your program. This includes methods defined inside other classes.

When a member of a class is specified as **private**, then that member can be accessed only by other members of its class. Thus, methods in other classes are not able to access a **private** member of another class. As explained in Module 4, if no access specifier is used, a class member is private to its class by default. Thus, the **private** specifier is optional when creating private class members.

An access specifier precedes the rest of a member's type specification. That is, it must begin a member's declaration statement. Here are some examples:

```
public string errMsg;
private double bal,
private bool isError(byte status) { // ...
```

To understand the difference between **public** and **private**, consider the following program:

```
// Public vs private access.

using System;

class MyClass {
  private int alpha; // private access explicitly specified
  int beta;          // private access by default
  public int gamma;  // public access

  /* Methods to access alpha and beta.  It is OK for a
     member of a class to access a private member
     of the same class.
  */
  public void setAlpha(int a) {
    alpha = a;
  }

  public int getAlpha() {
    return alpha;
  }

  public void setBeta(int a) {
    beta = a;
```

6

```
  }

  public int getBeta() {
    return beta;
  }
}

class AccessDemo {
  public static void Main() {
    MyClass ob = new MyClass();

    /* Access to alpha and beta is allowed only
       through methods. */
    ob.setAlpha(-99);
    ob.setBeta(19);
    Console.WriteLine("ob.alpha is " + ob.getAlpha());
    Console.WriteLine("ob.beta is " + ob.getBeta());

    // You cannot access alpha or beta like this:
//  ob.alpha = 10; // Wrong! alpha is private!          Wrong, alpha and
//  ob.beta = 9;   // Wrong! beta is private!           beta are private!

    // It is OK to directly access gamma because it is public.
    ob.gamma = 99;         OK because gamma is public.
  }
}
```

As you can see, inside the **MyClass** class, **alpha** is specified as **private**, **beta** is private by default, and **gamma** is specified as **public**. Because **alpha** and **beta** are private, they cannot be accessed by code outside of their class. Therefore, inside the **AccessDemo** class, neither can be used directly. Each must be accessed through public methods, such as **setAlpha( )** and **getAlpha( )**. For example, if you were to remove the comment symbol from the beginning of the following line:

```
//  ob.alpha = 10; // Wrong! alpha is private!
```

then you would not be able to compile this program because of the access violation. Although access to **alpha** by code outside of **MyClass** is not allowed, methods defined within **MyClass** can freely access it, as the **setAlpha( )** and **getAlpha( )** methods show. The same is true for **beta**.

The key point is this: a private member can be used freely by other members of its class, but it cannot be accessed by code outside its class.

To see how access control can be applied to a more practical example, consider the following program that implements a "fail-soft" **int** array, in which boundary errors are prevented, thus avoiding a runtime exception. This is accomplished by encapsulating the array as a private member of a class, allowing access to the array only through member methods. With this approach, any attempt to access the array beyond its boundaries can be prevented, with such an attempt failing gracefully (resulting in a "soft" landing rather than a "crash"). The fail-soft array is implemented by the **FailSoftArray** class, shown here:

```
/* This class implements a "fail-soft" array that prevents
   runtime errors.
 */

using System;
                                                        Private instance
                                                        variables
class FailSoftArray {
  private int[] a;    // reference to array
  private int errval; // value to return if get() fails

  public int Length; // Length is public

  /* Construct array given its size and the value to
     return if get() fails. */
  public FailSoftArray(int size, int errv) {
    a = new int[size];
    errval = errv;
    Length = size;
  }

  // Return value at given index.
  public int get(int index) {
    if(ok(index)) return a[index];
    return errval;
  }
                                                        Trap an
                                                        out-of-bounds
  // Put a value at an index. Return false on failure.   index.
  public bool put(int index, int val) {
    if(ok(index)) {
      a[index] = val;
      return true;
    }
    return false;
  }
```

6

```
  // Return true if index is within bounds.
  private bool ok(int index) {                        A private method
    if(index >= 0 & index < Length) return true;
    return false;
  }
}


// Demonstrate the fail-soft array.
class FSDemo {
  public static void Main() {
    FailSoftArray fs = new FailSoftArray(5, -1);
    int x;

    // show quiet failures
    Console.WriteLine("Fail quietly.");
    for(int i=0; i < (fs.Length * 2); i++)
      fs.put(i, i*10);

    for(int i=0; i < (fs.Length * 2); i++) {
      x = fs.get(i);
      if(x != -1) Console.Write(x + " ");
    }
    Console.WriteLine("");

    // now, handle failures
    Console.WriteLine("\nFail with error reports.");
    for(int i=0; i < (fs.Length * 2); i++)
      if(!fs.put(i, i*10))
        Console.WriteLine("Index " + i + " out-of-bounds");

    for(int i=0; i < (fs.Length * 2); i++) {
      x = fs.get(i);
      if(x != -1) Console.Write(x + " ");
      else
        Console.WriteLine("Index " + i + " out-of-bounds");
    }
  }
}
```

The output from the program is shown here:

```
Fail quietly.
0 10 20 30 40

Fail with error reports.
```

```
Index 5 out-of-bounds
Index 6 out-of-bounds
Index 7 out-of-bounds
Index 8 out-of-bounds
Index 9 out-of-bounds
0 10 20 30 40 Index 5 out-of-bounds
Index 6 out-of-bounds
Index 7 out-of-bounds
Index 8 out-of-bounds
Index 9 out-of-bounds
```

Let's look closely at this example. Inside **FailSoftArray** are defined three private members. The first is **a**, which stores a reference to the array that will actually hold information. The second is **errval**, which is the value that will be returned when a call to **get( )** fails. The third is the private method **ok( )**, which determines if an index is within bounds. Thus, these three members can be used only by other members of the **FailSoftArray** class. Specifically, **a** and **errval** can be used only by other methods in the class, and **ok( )** can be called only by other members of **FailSoftArray**. The rest of the class members are **public** and can be used by any other code in a program that uses **FailSoftArray**.

When a **FailSoftArray** object is constructed, you must specify the size of the array and the value that you want to return if a call to **get( )** fails. The error value must be a value that would otherwise not be stored in the array. Once constructed, the actual array referred to by **a** and the error value stored in **errval** cannot be accessed by users of the **FailSoftArray** object. Thus, they are not open to misuse. For example, the user cannot try to index **a** directly, possibly exceeding its bounds. Access is available only through the **get( )** and **put( )** methods.

The **ok( )** method is **private** mostly for the sake of illustration. It would be harmless to make it **public** because it does not modify the object. However, since it is used internally by the **FailSoftArray** class, it can be **private**.

Notice that the **Length** instance variable is **public**. This is in keeping with the way that C# implements arrays. To obtain the length of a **FailSoftArray**, simply use its **Length** member.

To use a **FailSoftArray** array, call **put( )** to store a value at the specified index. Call **get( )** to retrieve a value from a specified index. If the index is out of bounds, **put( )** returns **false** and **get( )** returns **errval**.

Since class members are private by default, there is no reason to explicitly declare them using **private**. Therefore, from this point forward, this book will not redundantly declare class members as **private**. Just remember that if a class member is not preceded by an access modifier, then its access is private.

6

Ask the Expert

Question: While it is true that the "fail-soft" array example prevents an array overrun, it does so at the expense of the normal array-indexing syntax. Is there a better way to create a "fail-soft" array?

Answer: Yes. As you will see in Module 7, C# includes a special type of class member called an *indexer*, which allows you to index a class object like an array. There is also a better way to handle the **Length** field by making it into a *property*. This is also described in Module 7.

1-Minute Drill

● Name C#'s access specifiers.

● Explain **private** and **public**.

● What is the default access setting for a class member?

Queue.cs

Project 6-1: Improving the Queue Class

You can use private access to make a rather important improvement to the **Queue** class developed in Module 5, Project 5-2. In that version, all members of the **Queue** class were public. This means that it would be possible for a program that uses a **Queue** to directly access the underlying array, possibly accessing its elements out of turn. Since the entire point of a queue is to provide a first-in, first-out list, allowing out-of-order access is not desirable. It would also be possible for a malicious programmer to alter the values stored in the **putloc** and

---

● C#'s access specifiers are **private**, **public**, **protected**, and **internal**.
● A **private** member can be accessed only by other members of its class. A **public** member is available to all code.
● The default access for a class member is private.

getloc indices, thus corrupting the queue. Fortunately, these types of problems are easy to prevent by making parts of **Queue** private.

Step-by-Step

1. Copy the original **Queue** class in Project 5-2 to a new file called **Queue.cs**.

2. In the **Queue** class, remove the **public** specifier to the **q** array, and the indices **putloc** and **getloc**, as shown here:

```
// An improved queue class for characters.
class Queue {
  // these are now private
  char[] q; // this array holds the queue
  int putloc, getloc; // the put and get indices

  public Queue(int size) {
    q = new char[size+1]; // allocate memory for queue
    putloc = getloc = 0;
  }

  // put a character into the queue
  public void put(char ch) {
    if(putloc==q.Length-1) {
      Console.WriteLine(" -- Queue is full.");
      return;
    }

    putloc++;
    q[putloc] = ch;
  }

  // get a character from the queue
  public char get() {
    if(getloc == putloc) {
      Console.WriteLine(" -- Queue is empty.");
      return (char) 0;
    }

    getloc++;
    return q[getloc];
  }
}
```

6

3. Changing **q**, **putloc**, and **getloc** from public access to private access has no effect on a program that properly uses **Queue**. For example, it still works fine with the **QDemo** class from Project 5-2. However, it prevents the improper use of a **Queue**. For example, the following types of statements are illegal:

```
Queue test = new Queue(10);

test.q[0] = 'X'; // wrong!
test.putloc = -100; // won't work!
```

4. Now that **q**, **putloc**, and **getloc** are private, the **Queue** class strictly enforces the first-in, first-out attribute of a queue.

Pass Objects to Methods

Up to this point, the examples in this book have been using value types, such as **int** or **double**, as parameters to methods. However, it is both correct and common to pass objects to methods. For example, consider the following simple program that stores the dimensions of a three-dimensional block:

```
// Objects can be passed to methods.

using System;

class Block {
  int a, b, c;
  int volume;

  public Block(int i, int j, int k) {
    a = i;
    b = j;
    c = k;
    volume = a * b * c;
  }
```

```
   // Return true if ob defines same block.
   public bool sameBlock(Block ob) {
     if((ob.a == a) & (ob.b == b) & (ob.c == c)) return true;
     else return false;
   }

   // Return true if ob has same volume.
   public bool sameVolume(Block ob) {
     if(ob.volume == volume) return true;
     else return false;
   }
}

class PassOb {
  public static void Main() {
    Block ob1 = new Block(10, 2, 5);
    Block ob2 = new Block(10, 2, 5);
    Block ob3 = new Block(4, 5, 5);

    Console.WriteLine("ob1 same dimensions as ob2: " +
                      ob1.sameBlock(ob2));
    Console.WriteLine("ob1 same dimensions as ob3: " +
                      ob1.sameBlock(ob3));
    Console.WriteLine("ob1 same volume as ob3: " +
                      ob1.sameVolume(ob3));
  }
}
```

Use object type as a parameter.

Pass an object.

This program generates the following output:

```
ob1 same dimensions as ob2: true
ob1 same dimensions as ob3: false
ob1 same volume as ob3: true
```

   The **sameBlock( )** and **sameVolume( )** methods compare the invoking object with the object passed as an argument. For **sameBlock( )**, the dimensions of the objects are compared, and **true** is returned only if the two blocks are identical.

6

For **sameVolume( )**, the two blocks are compared only to determine if they have the same volume. In both cases, notice that the parameter **ob** specifies **Block** as its type. As this example shows, syntactically, object types are passed to methods in the same way as are the value types.

How Arguments Are Passed

As the preceding example demonstrated, passing an object to a method is a straightforward task. However, there are some nuances that the example did not show. In certain cases, the effects of passing an object will be different than those experienced when passing non-object arguments. To see why, you need to understand the two ways in which an argument can be passed to a subroutine.

The first way is *call-by-value*. This method copies the *value* of an argument into the formal parameter of the subroutine. Therefore, changes made to the parameter of the subroutine have no effect on the argument used to call it. The second way an argument can be passed is *call-by-reference*. In this method, a *reference* to an argument (not the value of the argument) is passed to the parameter. Inside the subroutine, this reference is used to access the actual argument specified in the call. This means that changes made to the parameter will affect the argument used to call the subroutine. As you will see, C# can use both methods.

In C#, when you pass a value type, such as **int** or **double**, to a method, it is passed by value. Thus, what occurs to the parameter that receives the argument has no effect outside the method. For example, consider the following program:

```
// Simple types are passed by value.

using System;

class Test {
  /* This method causes no change to the arguments
     used in the call. */
  public void noChange(int i, int j) {
    i = i + j;
    j = -j;
  }
}

class CallByValue {
  public static void Main() {
    Test ob = new Test();
```

```
    int a = 15, b = 20;

    Console.WriteLine("a and b before call: " +
                       a + " " + b);

    ob.noChange(a, b);

    Console.WriteLine("a and b after call: " +
                       a + " " + b);
  }
}
```

The output from this program is shown here:

```
a and b before call: 15 20
a and b after call: 15 20
```

As you can see, the operations that occur inside **noChange( )** have no effect on the values of **a** and **b** used in the call.

When you pass an object reference to a method, the situation is a bit more complicated. Technically, the object reference, itself, is passed by value. Thus, a copy of the reference is made and changes to the parameter will not affect the argument. (For example, making the parameter refer to a new object will not change the object to which the argument refers.) However,—and this is a big however—changes *made to the object* being referred to by the parameter *will* affect the object referred to by the argument. Let's see why.

Recall that when you create a variable of a class type, you are creating a reference to an object, not the object itself. The object is allocated via **new** and a reference to it is assigned to the reference variable. When you use a reference variable as an argument to a method, the parameter receives a reference to the same object as that referred to by the argument. Thus, the argument and parameter will both refer to the same object. This effectively means that objects are passed to methods by use of call-by-reference. Changes to the object inside the method *do* affect the object used as an argument. For example, consider the following program:

```
// Objects are implicitly passed by reference.

using System;

class Test {
```

```
  public int a, b;

  public Test(int i, int j) {
    a = i;
    b = j;
  }

  /* Pass an object. Now, ob.a and ob.b in object
     used in the call will be changed. */
  public void change(Test ob) {
    ob.a = ob.a + ob.b;
    ob.b = -ob.b;
  }
}

class CallByRef {
  public static void Main() {
    Test ob = new Test(15, 20);

    Console.WriteLine("ob.a and ob.b before call: " +
                       ob.a + " " + ob.b);

    ob.change(ob);

    Console.WriteLine("ob.a and ob.b after call: " +
                       ob.a + " " + ob.b);
  }
}
```

This program generates the following output:

```
ob.a and ob.b before call: 15 20
ob.a and ob.b after call: 35 -20
```

As you can see, in this case, the actions inside **change( )** have affected the object used as an argument.

To review: When an object reference is passed to a method, the reference itself is passed by use of call-by-value. Thus, a copy of that reference is made. However, since the value being passed refers to an object, the copy of that value will still refer to the same object that its corresponding argument does.

Using ref and out Parameters

As just explained, by default, value types, such as **int** or **char**, are passed by value to a method. This means that changes to the parameter that receives a value type will not affect the actual argument used in the call. You can, however, alter this behavior. Through the use of the **ref** and **out** keywords, it is possible to pass any of the value types by reference. Doing so allows a method to alter the argument used in the call.

Before going into the mechanics of using **ref** and **out**, it is useful to understand why you might want to pass a value type by reference. In general, there are two reasons: to allow a method to alter the contents of its arguments or to allow a method to return more than one value. Let's look at each reason in detail.

Often you will want a method to be able to operate on the actual arguments that are passed to it. The quintessential example of this is a **swap( )** method that exchanges the values of its two arguments. Since value types are passed by value, it is not possible to write such a method that swaps the value of two **int**s, for example, using C#'s default call-by-value parameter passing mechanism. The **ref** modifier solves this problem.

As you know, a **return** statement enables a method to return a value to its caller. However, a method can return *only one* value each time it is called. What if you need to return two or more pieces of information? For example, what if you want to create a method that computes the area of a rectangle and also determines if that rectangle is a square? To do this requires that two pieces of information be returned: the area and a value indicating square-ness. This method cannot be written using only a single return value. The **out** modifier solves this problem.

Using ref

The **ref** parameter modifier causes C# to create a call-by-reference, rather than a call-by-value. The **ref** modifier is used when the method is declared and when it is called. Let's begin with a simple example. The following program creates a method called **sqr( )** that returns in-place the square of its integer argument. Notice the use and placement of **ref**.

6

```
// Use ref to pass a value type by reference.

using System;

class RefTest {
  // This method now changes its arguments.
  public void sqr(ref int i) {
    i = i * i;
  }
}

class RefDemo {
  public static void Main() {
    RefTest ob = new RefTest();

    int a = 10;

    Console.WriteLine("a before call: " + a);

    ob.sqr(ref a);

    Console.WriteLine("a after call: " + a);
  }
}
```

Here, **ref** precedes the parameter declaration.

Here, **ref** precedes the argument.

Notice that **ref** precedes the entire parameter declaration in the method and that it precedes the name of the argument when the method is called. The output from this program, shown here, confirms that the value of the argument, **a**, was indeed modified by **sqr( )**:

```
a before call: 10
a after call: 100
```

Using **ref**, it is now possible to write a method that exchanges the values of its two value-type arguments. For example, here is a program that contains a method called **swap( )** that exchanges the values of the two integer arguments with which it is called:

```
// Swap two values.

using System;
```

```
class Swap {
  // This method now changes its arguments.
  public void swap(ref int a, ref int b) {
    int t;

    t = a;
    a = b;
    b = t;
  }
}

class SwapDemo {
  public static void Main() {
    Swap ob = new Swap();

    int x = 10, y = 20;

    Console.WriteLine("x and y before call: " + x + " " + y);

    ob.swap(ref x, ref y);

    Console.WriteLine("x and y after call: " + x + " " + y);
  }
}
```

The output from this program is shown here:

```
x and y before call: 10 20
x and y after call: 20 10
```

Here is one important point to understand about **ref**: An argument passed by **ref** must be assigned a value prior to the call. The reason for this is that the method that receives such an argument assumes that the parameter refers to a valid value. Thus, using **ref**, you cannot use a method to give an argument an initial value.

Using out

Sometimes you will want to use a reference parameter to receive a value from a method but not pass in a value. For example, you might have a method that performs some function, such as opening a network socket, that returns a

6

success/fail code in a reference parameter. In this case, there is no information to pass into the method, but there is information to pass back out. The problem with this scenario is that a **ref** parameter must be initialized to a value prior to the call. Thus, to use a **ref** parameter would require giving the argument a dummy value just to satisfy this constraint. Fortunately, C# provides a better alternative: the **out** parameter.

An **out** parameter is similar to **ref** parameter with this one exception: it can only be used to pass a value out of a method. It is not necessary (or useful) to give the variable used as an **out** parameter an initial value prior to calling the method. The method will give the variable a value. Furthermore, inside the method, an **out** parameter is always considered *unassigned*, that is, it is assumed to have no initial value. The method *must* assign the parameter a value prior to the method's termination. Thus, after the call to the method, an **out** parameter will always contain a value.

Here is an example that uses an **out** parameter. The method **rectInfo( )** returns the area of a rectangle given the lengths of its sides. In the parameter **isSquare**, it returns **true** if the rectangle is a square, and **false** otherwise. Thus, **rectInfo( )** returns two pieces of information to the caller.

```csharp
// Use an out parameter.

using System;

class Rectangle {
  int side1;
  int side2;

  public Rectangle(int i, int j) {
    side1 = i;
    side2 = j;
  }

  // Return area and determine if square.
  public int rectInfo(out bool isSquare) {
    if(side1==side2) isSquare = true;
    else isSquare = false;
```

Pass information out using an **out** parameter.

```
      return side1 * side2;
  }
}

class SwapDemo {
  public static void Main() {
    Rectangle rect = new Rectangle(10, 23);
    int area;
    bool isSqr;

    area = rect.rectInfo(out isSqr);

    if(isSqr) Console.WriteLine("rect is a square.");
    else Console.WriteLine("rect is not a square.");

    Console.WriteLine("Its area is  " + area + ".");
  }
}
```

Notice that **isSqr** is not assigned a value prior to the call to **rectInfo( )**. This would not be allowed if the parameter to **rectInfo( )** had been a **ref** rather than an **out** parameter. After the method returns, **isSqr** contains either **true** or **false**, depending upon whether the rectangle is square or not. The area is returned via the **return** statement. The output from this program is shown here:

```
rect is not a square.
Its area is  230.
```

1-Minute Drill

● What is the difference between call-by-value and call-by-reference?

● How does C# pass value types? How does it pass objects?

● What does **ref** do? How does it differ from **out**?

● In call-by-value, a copy of the argument is passed to a subroutine. In call-by-reference, a reference to the argument is passed.

● C# passes value types by value and object types by reference.

● The **ref** modifier creates a call-by-reference for value-type parameters. The **out** modifier also creates a call-by-reference, but it cannot be used to pass information into a method.

Ask the Expert

Question: Can ref and out be used on reference-type parameters, such as when passing a reference to an object?

Answer: Yes. When **ref** or **out** modifies a reference-type parameter, it causes the reference, itself, to be passed by reference. This allows a method to change what the reference is referring to. Consider the following program:

```
// Use ref on an object parameter.
using System;

class Test {
  public int a;

  public Test(int i) {
    a = i;
  }
  // This will not change the argument.
  public void noChange(Test o) {
    Test newob = new Test(0);
    o = newob; // this has no effect outside of noChange()
  }

  // This will change what the argument refers to.
  public void change(ref Test o) {
    Test newob = new Test(0);
    o = newob; // this affects the calling argument.
  }
}

class CallObjByRef {
  public static void Main() {
    Test ob = new Test(100);

    Console.WriteLine("ob.a before call: " + ob.a);

    ob.noChange(ob);
    Console.WriteLine("ob.a after call to noChange(): " + ob.a);

    ob.change(ref ob);
    Console.WriteLine("ob.a after call to change(): " + ob.a);
  }
}
```

The output from this program is shown here:

```
ob.a before call: 100
ob.a after call to noChange(): 100
ob.a after call to change(): 0
```

As you can see, when **o** is assigned a reference to a new object inside **noChange( )**, there is no effect on the argument **ob** inside **Main( )**. However, inside **change( )**, which uses a **ref** parameter, assigning a new object to **o** does change the object referred to by **ob** inside **Main( )**.

Using a Variable Number of Arguments

When you create a method, you usually know in advance the number of arguments that you will be passing to it, but this is not always the case. Sometimes you will want to create a method that can be passed an arbitrary number of arguments. For example, consider a method that finds the smallest of a set of values. Such a method might be passed as few as two values, or three, or four, and so on. In all cases, you want that method to return the smallest value. Such a method cannot be created using normal parameters. Instead, you must use a special type of parameter that stands for an arbitrary number of parameters. This is done by creating a **params** parameter.

The **params** modifier is used to declare an array parameter that will be able to receive zero or more arguments. The number of elements in the array will be equal to the number of arguments passed to the method. Your program then accesses the array to obtain the arguments.

Here is an example that uses **params** to create a method called **minVal( )**, which returns the minimum value from a set of values:

```
// Demonstrate params.

using System;
```

```
class Min {
  public int minVal(params int[] nums) {        Create a variable-length
    int m;                                        parameter using params.

    if(nums.Length == 0) {
      Console.WriteLine("Error: no arguments.");
      return 0;
    }

    m = nums[0];
    for(int i=1; i < nums.Length; i++)
      if(nums[i] < m) m = nums[i];

    return m;
  }
}

class ParamsDemo {
  public static void Main() {
    Min ob = new Min();
    int min;
    int a = 10, b = 20;

    // call with two values
    min = ob.minVal(a, b);
    Console.WriteLine("Minimum is " + min);

    // call with 3 values
    min = ob.minVal(a, b, -1);
    Console.WriteLine("Minimum is " + min);

    // call with 5 values
    min = ob.minVal(18, 23, 3, 14, 25);
    Console.WriteLine("Minimum is " + min);

    // can call with an int array, too
    int[] args = { 45, 67, 34, 9, 112, 8 };
    min = ob.minVal(args);
    Console.WriteLine("Minimum is " + min);
  }
}
```

The output from the program is shown here:

```
Minimum is 10
Minimum is -1
Minimum is 3
Minimum is 8
```

Each time **minVal( )** is called, the arguments are passed to it via the **nums** array. The length of the array equals the number of elements. Thus, you can use **minVal( )** to find the minimum of any number of values.

Although you can pass a **params** parameter any number of arguments, they all must be of a type compatible with the array type specified by the parameter. For example, calling **minVal( )** like this:

```
    min = ob.minVal(1, 2.2);
```

is illegal because there is no automatic conversion from **double** (2.2) to **int**, which is the type of **nums** in **minVal( )**.

When using **params**, you need to be careful about boundary conditions because a **params** parameter can accept any number of arguments—*even zero*! For example, it is syntactically valid to call **minVal( )** as shown here:

```
min = ob.minVal(); // no arguments
min = ob.minVal(3); // 1 argument
```

This is why there is a check in **minVal( )** to confirm that at least one element is in the **nums** array before there is an attempt to access that element. If the check were not there, then a runtime exception would result if **minVal( )** were called with no arguments. (Later in this book when exceptions are discussed, you will see a better way to handle these types of errors.) Furthermore, the code in **minVal( )** was written in such a way as to permit the degenerate case of calling **minVal( )** with one argument. In that situation, the lone argument is returned.

A method can have normal parameters and a variable-length parameter. For example, in the following program, the method **showArgs( )** takes one **string** parameter and then a **params** integer array:

```
// Use regular parameter with a params parameter.

using System;
```

6

```
class MyClass {
  public void showArgs(string msg, params int[] nums) {
    Console.Write(msg + ": ");

    foreach(int i in nums)
      Console.Write(i + " ");

    Console.WriteLine();
  }
}

class ParamsDemo2 {
  public static void Main() {
    MyClass ob = new MyClass();

    ob.showArgs("Here are some integers",
            1, 2, 3, 4, 5);

    ob.showArgs("Here are two more",
            17, 20);

  }
}
```

This method has one normal parameter and one **params** parameter.

This program displays the following output:

```
Here are some integers: 1 2 3 4 5
Here are two more: 17 20
```

In cases where a method has regular parameters and a **params** parameter, the **params** parameter must be the last one in the parameter list. Furthermore, in all situations, there must be only one **params** parameter.

1-Minute Drill

● How do you create a parameter that accepts a variable number of arguments?

● Can there be more than one **params** parameter in a single method?

● A **params** parameter can go anywhere in the parameter list. True or false?

● To create a parameter that accepts a variable number of arguments, use the **params** modifier.
● No.
● False, it must go at the end.

Returning Objects

A method can return any type of data, including class types. For example, in the following program, the class **ErrorMsg** is used to report errors. Its method, **getErrorMsg( )**, returns a **string** object that contains a description of an error based upon the error code that it is passed.

```
// Return a string object.

using System;

class ErrorMsg {
  string[] msgs = {
    "Output Error",
    "Input Error",
    "Disk Full",
    "Index Out-Of-Bounds"
  };

  // Return the error message.
  public string getErrorMsg(int i) {
    if(i >=0 & i < msgs.Length)
      return msgs[i];
    else
      return "Invalid Error Code";
  }
}

class ErrMsg {
  public static void Main() {
    ErrorMsg err = new ErrorMsg();

    Console.WriteLine(err.getErrorMsg(2));
    Console.WriteLine(err.getErrorMsg(19));
  }
}
```

Return an object of type **string**.

Its output is shown here:

```
Disk Full
Invalid Error Code
```

You can, of course, also return objects of classes that you create. For example, here is a reworked version of the preceding program that creates two error classes. One is called **Err**, and it encapsulates an error message along with a severity code. The second is called **ErrorInfo**. It defines a method called **getErrorInfo( )** that returns an **Err** object.

```csharp
// Return a programmer-defined object.

using System;

class Err {
  public string msg; // error message
  public int severity; // code indicating severity of error

  public Err(string m, int s) {
    msg = m;
    severity  = s;
  }
}

class ErrorInfo {
  string[] msgs = {
    "Output Error",
    "Input Error",
    "Disk Full",
    "Index Out-Of-Bounds"
  };
  int[] howbad = { 3, 3, 2, 4 };

  public Err getErrorInfo(int i) {
    if(i >=0 & i < msgs.Length)
      return new Err(msgs[i], howbad[i]);
    else
      return new Err("Invalid Error Code", 0);
  }
}

class ErrInfo {
  public static void Main() {
    ErrorInfo err = new ErrorInfo();
    Err e;

    e = err.getErrorInfo(2);
    Console.WriteLine(e.msg + " severity: " + e.severity);
```

Return an object of type **Err.**

```
    e = err.getErrorInfo(19);
    Console.WriteLine(e.msg + " severity: " + e.severity);
  }
}
```

Here is the output:

```
Disk Full severity: 2
Invalid Error Code severity: 0
```

Each time **getErrorInfo( )** is invoked, a new **Err** object is created, and a reference to it is returned to the calling routine. This object is then used within **Main( )** to display the error message and severity code.

When an object is returned by a method, it remains in existence until there are no more references to it. At that point it is subject to garbage collection. Thus, an object won't be destroyed just because the method that created it terminates.

6

Method Overloading

In this section, you will learn about one of C#'s most exciting features: method overloading. In C#, two or more methods within the same class can share the same name, as long as their parameter declarations are different. When this is the case, the methods are said to be *overloaded*, and the process is referred to as *method overloading*. Method overloading is one of the ways that C# implements polymorphism.

In general, to overload a method, simply declare different versions of it. The compiler takes care of the rest. You must observe one important restriction: the type and/or number of the parameters of each overloaded method must differ. It is not sufficient for two methods to differ only in their return types. They must differ in the types or number of their parameters. (Return types by themselves do not provide sufficient information in all cases for C# to decide which method to use.) Of course, overloaded methods *may* differ in their return types, too. When an overloaded method is called, the version of the method whose parameters match the arguments is executed.

Here is a simple example that illustrates method overloading:

```
// Demonstrate method overloading.
```

```
using System;

class Overload {
  public void ovlDemo() {                          ◄──────  First version
    Console.WriteLine("No parameters");
  }

  // Overload ovlDemo for one integer parameter.
  public void ovlDemo(int a) {                     ◄──────  Second version
    Console.WriteLine("One parameter: " + a);
  }

  // Overload ovlDemo for two integer parameters.
  public int ovlDemo(int a, int b) {               ◄──────  Third version
    Console.WriteLine("Two parameters: " + a + " " + b);
    return a + b;
  }

  // Overload ovlDemo for two double parameters.
  public double ovlDemo(double a, double b) {      ◄──────  Fourth version
    Console.WriteLine("Two double parameters: " +
                      a + " "+ b);
    return a + b;
  }
}

class OverloadDemo {
  public static void Main() {
    Overload ob = new Overload();
    int resI;
    double resD;

    // call all versions of ovlDemo()
    ob.ovlDemo();
    Console.WriteLine();

    ob.ovlDemo(2);
    Console.WriteLine();

    resI = ob.ovlDemo(4, 6);
    Console.WriteLine("Result of ob.ovlDemo(4, 6): " +
                      resI);
    Console.WriteLine();
```

```
    resD = ob.ovlDemo(1.1, 2.32);
    Console.WriteLine("Result of ob.ovlDemo(1.1, 2.2): " +
                     resD);
  }
}
```

This program generates the following output:

```
No parameters

One parameter: 2

Two parameters: 4 6
Result of ob.ovlDemo(4, 6): 10

Two double parameters: 1.1 2.32
Result of ob.ovlDemo(1.1, 2.2): 3.42
```

As you can see, **ovlDemo( )** is overloaded four times. The first version takes no parameters, the second takes one integer parameter, the third takes two integer parameters, and the fourth takes two **double** parameters. Notice that the first two versions of **ovlDemo( )** return **void** and the second two return a value. This is perfectly valid, but as explained, overloading is not affected one way or the other by the return type of a method. Thus, attempting to use the following two versions of **ovlDemo( )** will cause an error.

```
// One ovlDemo(int) is OK.
public void ovlDemo(int a) {           ◄─────────────┐
  Console.WriteLine("One parameter: " + a);          │
}                                                     │
                                      ┌───────────────────────────┐
/* Error! Two ovlDemo(int)s are not OK even though   │ Return types cannot
    return types differ.                              │ be used to differentiate
*/                                                    │ overloaded methods.
public int ovlDemo(int a) {  ◄────────────────────────┘
  Console.WriteLine("One parameter: " + a);
  return a * a;
}
```

As the comments suggest, the difference in their return types is an insufficient difference for the purposes of overloading.

As you will recall from Module 2, C# provides certain automatic type conversions. These conversions also apply to parameters of overloaded methods. For example, consider the following:

```
/* Automatic type conversions can affect
   overloaded method resolution.
*/

using System;

class Overload2 {
  public void f(int x) {
    Console.WriteLine("Inside f(int): " + x);
  }

  public void f(double x) {
    Console.WriteLine("Inside f(double): " + x);
  }
}

class TypeConv {
  public static void Main() {
    Overload2 ob = new Overload2();

    int i = 10;
    double d = 10.1;

    byte b = 99;
    short s = 10;
    float f = 11.5F;


    ob.f(i); // calls ob.f(int)
    ob.f(d); // calls ob.f(double)

    ob.f(b); // calls ob.f(int) -- type conversion
    ob.f(s); // calls ob.f(int) -- type conversion
    ob.f(f); // calls ob.f(double) -- type conversion
  }
}
```

The output from the program is shown here:

```
Inside f(int): 10
Inside f(double): 10.1
Inside f(int): 99
Inside f(int): 10
Inside f(double): 11.5
```

In this example, only two versions of f( ) are defined: one that has an **int** parameter and one that has a **double** parameter. However, it is possible to pass f ( ) a **byte**, **short**, or **float** value. In the case of **byte** and **short**, C# automatically converts them to **int**. Thus, f(int) is invoked. In the case of **float**, the value is converted to **double** and f(double) is called.

It is important to understand, however, that the automatic conversions apply only if there is no direct match between a parameter and an argument. For example, here is the preceding program with the addition of a version of f( ) that specifies a **byte** parameter:

6

```
// Add f(byte).

using System;

class Overload2 {
  public void f(byte x) {
    Console.WriteLine("Inside f(byte): " + x);
  }

  public void f(int x) {
    Console.WriteLine("Inside f(int): " + x);
  }

  public void f(double x) {
    Console.WriteLine("Inside f(double): " + x);
  }
}

class TypeConv {
  public static void Main() {
    Overload2 ob = new Overload2();
```

```
    int i = 10;
    double d = 10.1;

    byte b = 99;
    short s = 10;
    float f = 11.5F;


    ob.f(i); // calls ob.f(int)
    ob.f(d); // calls ob.f(double)

    ob.f(b); // calls ob.f(byte) -- now, no type conversion

    ob.f(s); // calls ob.f(int) -- type conversion
    ob.f(f); // calls ob.f(double) -- type conversion
  }
}
```

Now when the program is run, the following output is produced:

```
Inside f(int): 10
Inside f(double): 10.1
Inside f(byte): 99
Inside f(int): 10
Inside f(double): 11.5
```

In this version, since there is a version of f( ) that takes a **byte** argument, when f( ) is called with a **byte** argument, **f(byte)** is invoked and the automatic conversion to **int** does not occur.

Both **ref** and **out** participate in overload resolution. For example, the following define two distinct and separate methods:

```
public void f(int x) {
  Console.WriteLine("Inside f(int): " + x);
}

public void f(ref int x) {
  Console.WriteLine("Inside f(ref int): " + x);
}
```

Thus,

```
ob.f(i)
```

invokes **f(int x)**, but

```
ob.f(ref i)
```

invokes **f(ref int x)**.

Method overloading supports polymorphism because it is one way that C# implements the "one interface, multiple methods" paradigm. To understand how, consider the following. In languages that do not support method overloading, each method must be given a unique name. However, frequently you will want to implement essentially the same method for different types of data. Consider the absolute value function. In languages that do not support overloading, there are usually three or more versions of this function, each with a slightly different name. For instance, in C, the function **abs( )** returns the absolute value of an integer, **labs( )** returns the absolute value of a long integer, and **fabs( )** returns the absolute value of a floating-point value. Since C does not support overloading, each function has to have its own name, even though all three functions do essentially the same thing. This makes the situation more complex, conceptually, than it actually is. Although the underlying concept of each function is the same, you still have three names to remember. This situation does not occur in C#, because each absolute value method can use the same name. Indeed, C#'s standard class library includes an absolute value method, called **Abs( )**. This method is overloaded by C#'s **System.Math** class to handle all the numeric types. C# determines which version of **Abs( )** to call based upon the type of argument.

The value of overloading is that it allows related methods to be accessed by use of a common name. Thus, the name **Abs** represents the *general action* that is being performed. It is left to the compiler to choose the right *specific* version for a particular circumstance. You, the programmer, need only remember the general operation. Through the application of polymorphism, several names have been reduced to one. Although this example is fairly simple, if you expand the concept, you can see how overloading can help manage greater complexity.

6

Ask the Expert

Question: I've heard the term *signature* used by C# programmers. What is it?

Answer: As it applies to C#, a signature is the name of a method plus its parameter list. Thus, for the purposes of overloading, no two methods within the same class can have the same signature. Notice that a signature does not include the return type since it is not used by C# for overload resolution.

When you overload a method, each version of that method can perform any activity you desire. There is no rule stating that overloaded methods must relate to one another. However, from a stylistic point of view, method overloading implies a relationship. Thus, while you can use the same name to overload unrelated methods, you should not. For example, you could use the name **sqr** to create methods that return the *square* of an integer and the *square root* of a floating-point value. But these two operations are fundamentally different. Applying method overloading in this manner defeats its original purpose. In practice, you should only overload closely related operations.

1-Minute Drill

● In order for a method to be overloaded, what condition must be met?

● Does the return type play a role in method overloading?

● How does C#'s automatic type conversion affect overloading?

● For one method to overload another, the type and/or number of parameters must differ.
● No. The return type can differ between overloaded methods, but it does not affect method overloading one way or another.
● When there is no direct match between a set of arguments and a set of parameters, then the method with the closest matching set of parameters is used if the arguments can be automatically converted to the type of the parameters.

Overloading Constructors

Like methods, constructors can also be overloaded. Doing so allows you to construct objects in a variety of ways. For example, consider the following program:

```
// Demonstrate an overloaded constructor.

using System;

class MyClass {
  public int x;

  public MyClass() {
    Console.WriteLine("Inside MyClass().");
    x = 0;
  }

  public MyClass(int i) {
    Console.WriteLine("Inside MyClass(int).");
    x = i;
  }

  public MyClass(double d) {
    Console.WriteLine("Inside MyClass(double).");
    x = (int) d;
  }

  public MyClass(int i, int j) {
    Console.WriteLine("Inside MyClass(int, int).");
    x = i * j;
  }
}

class OverloadConsDemo {
  public static void Main() {
    MyClass t1 = new MyClass();
    MyClass t2 = new MyClass(88);
```

Construct objects in a variety of ways.

6

```
    MyClass t3 = new MyClass(17.23);
    MyClass t4 = new MyClass(2, 4);

    Console.WriteLine("t1.x: " + t1.x);
    Console.WriteLine("t2.x: " + t2.x);
    Console.WriteLine("t3.x: " + t3.x);
    Console.WriteLine("t4.x: " + t4.x);
  }
}
```

The output from the program is shown here:

```
Inside MyClass().
Inside MyClass(int).
Inside MyClass(double).
Inside MyClass(int, int).
t1.x: 0
t2.x: 88
t3.x: 17
t4.x: 8
```

MyClass( ) is overloaded four ways, each constructing an object differently.
The proper constructor is called based upon the parameters specified when **new**
is executed. By overloading a class' constructor, you give the user of your class
flexibility in the way objects are constructed.

One of the most common reasons that constructors are overloaded is to
allow one object to initialize another. For example, consider this program that
uses the **Summation** class to compute the summation of an integer value:

```
// Initialize one object with another.

using System;

class Summation {
  public int sum;

  // Construct from an int.
  public Summation(int num) {
    sum = 0;
    for(int i=1; i <= num; i++)
      sum += i;
  }
```

```
  // Construct from another object.
  public Summation(Summation ob) {        Construct one object
    sum = ob.sum;                         from another.
  }
}

class SumDemo {
  public static void Main() {
    Summation s1 = new Summation(5);
    Summation s2 = new Summation(s1);

    Console.WriteLine("s1.sum: " + s1.sum);
    Console.WriteLine("s2.sum: " + s2.sum);
  }
}
```

The output is shown here:

```
s1.sum: 15
s2.sum: 15
```

Often, as this example shows, an advantage of providing a constructor that uses one object to initialize another is efficiency. In this case, when **s2** is constructed, it is not necessary to recompute the summation. Of course, even in cases when efficiency is not an issue, it is often useful to provide a constructor that makes a copy of an object.

Invoking an Overloaded Constructor Through this

When working with overloaded construtors it is sometimes useful for one constructor to invoke another. In C#, this is accomplished by using another form of the **this** keyword. The general form is shown here.

```
constructor-name(parameter-list) : this(argument-list) {
  // ... body of constructor, which may be empty
}
```

When the constructor is executed, the overloaded constructor that matches the parameter list specified by *argument-list* is first executed. Then, if there are any statements inside the original constructor, they are executed. Here is an example.

```
// Demonstrate invoking a constructor through this.

using System;

class XYCoord {
  public int x, y;

  public XYCoord() : this(0, 0) {
    Console.WriteLine("Inside XYCoord()");
  }

  public XYCoord(XYCoord obj) : this(obj.x, obj.y) {
    Console.WriteLine("Inside XYCoord(XYCoord obj)");
  }

  public XYCoord(int i, int j) {
    Console.WriteLine("Inside XYCoord(XYCoord(int, int)");
    x = i;
    y = j;
  }
}

class OverloadConsDemo {
  public static void Main() {
    XYCoord t1 = new XYCoord();
    XYCoord t2 = new XYCoord(8, 9);
    XYCoord t3 = new XYCoord(t2);

    Console.WriteLine("t1.x, t1.y: " + t1.x + ", " + t1.y);
    Console.WriteLine("t2.x, t2.y: " + t2.x + ", " + t2.y);
    Console.WriteLine("t3.x, t3.y: " + t3.x + ", " + t3.y);
  }
}
```

The output from the program is shown here.

```
Inside XYCoord(XYCoord(int, int)
Inside XYCoord()
Inside XYCoord(XYCoord(int, int)
Inside XYCoord(XYCoord(int, int)
Inside XYCoord(XYCoord obj)
t1.x, t1.y: 0, 0
t2.x, t2.y: 8, 9
t3.x, t3.y: 8, 9
```

Here is how the program works. In the **XYCoord** class, the only constructor that actually initializes the **x** and **y** fields is **XYCoord(int, int)**. The other two constructors simply invoke **XYCoord(int, int)** through **this**. For example, when object **t1** is created, its constructor, **XYCoord( )**, is called. This causes **this**(0, 0) to be executed, which in this case translates into a call to **XYCoord**(0, 0). The creation of **t2** works in similar fashion.

One reason why invoking overloaded constructors through **this** can be useful is that it can prevent the unnecessary duplication of code. In the foregoing example, there is no reason for all three constructors to duplicate the same initialization sequence, which the use of **this** voids. Another advantage is that you can create constructors with implied "default arguments," which are used when these arguments are not explicitly specfied. For example, you could create another **XYCoord** constructor as shown here.

```
public XYCoord(int x) : this(x, x) { }
```

This constructor automatically defaults the **y** coordinate to same value as the **x** coordinate. Of course, it is wise to use such "default arguments" carefully because their misuse could easily confuse users of your classes.

QDemo2.cs

Project 6-2: Overloading the Queue Constructor

In this project you will enhance the **Queue** class by giving it two additional constructors. The first will construct a new queue from another queue. The second will construct a queue, giving it initial values. As you will see, adding these constructors enhances the usability of **Queue** substantially.

Step-by-Step

1. Create a file called **QDemo2.cs**, and copy the updated **Queue** class from Project 6-1 into it.

2. Add the following constructor, which constructs a queue from a queue:

```
// Construct a Queue from a Queue.
public Queue(Queue ob) {
   putloc = ob.putloc;
   getloc = ob.getloc;
   q = new char[ob.q.Length];

   // copy elements
   for(int i=getloc+1; i <= putloc; i++)
```

6

```
    q[i] = ob.q[i];
}
```

Look closely at this constructor. It initializes **putloc** and **getloc** to the values contained in the **ob** parameter. It then allocates a new array to hold the queue and copies the elements from **ob** into that array. Once constructed, the new queue will be an identical copy of the original, but both will be completely separate objects.

3. Add the constructor that initializes the queue from a character array, as shown here:

```
// Construct a Queue with initial values.
public Queue(char[] a) {
  putloc = 0;
  getloc = 0;
  q = new char[a.Length+1];

  for(int i = 0; i < a.Length; i++) put(a[i]);
}
```

This constructor creates a queue large enough to hold the characters in **a** and then stores those characters in the queue. Because of the way the queue algorithm works, the length of the queue must be 1 greater than the array.

4. Here is the complete updated **Queue** class along with the **QDemo2** class, which demonstrates it:

```
// A queue class for characters.

using System;

class Queue {
  // these are now private
  char[] q; // this array holds the queue
  int putloc, getloc; // the put and get indices

  // Construct an empty Queue given its size.
  public Queue(int size) {
    q = new char[size+1]; // allocate memory for queue
    putloc = getloc = 0;
  }
```

```
    // Construct a Queue from a Queue.
    public Queue(Queue ob) {
      putloc = ob.putloc;
      getloc = ob.getloc;
      q = new char[ob.q.Length];

      // copy elements
      for(int i=getloc+1; i <= putloc; i++)
        q[i] = ob.q[i];
    }

    // Construct a Queue with initial values.
    public Queue(char[] a) {
      putloc = 0;
      getloc = 0;
      q = new char[a.Length+1];

      for(int i = 0; i < a.Length; i++) put(a[i]);
    }

    // Put a character into the queue.
    public void put(char ch) {
      if(putloc==q.Length-1) {
        Console.WriteLine(" -- Queue is full.");
        return;
      }

      putloc++;
      q[putloc] = ch;
    }

    // Get a character from the queue.
    public char get() {
      if(getloc == putloc) {
        Console.WriteLine(" -- Queue is empty.");
        return (char) 0;
      }

      getloc++;
      return q[getloc];
    }
}

// Demonstrate the Queue class.
```

6

```
class QDemo2 {
  public static void Main() {
    // construct 10-element empty queue
    Queue q1 = new Queue(10);

    char[] name = {'T', 'o', 'm'};
    // construct queue from array
    Queue q2 = new Queue(name);

    char ch;
    int i;

    // put some characters into q1
    for(i=0; i < 10; i++)
      q1.put((char) ('A' + i));

    // construct queue from another queue
    Queue q3 = new Queue(q1);

    // Show the queues.
    Console.Write("Contents of q1: ");
    for(i=0; i < 10; i++) {
      ch = q1.get();
      Console.Write(ch);
    }

    Console.WriteLine("\n");

    Console.Write("Contents of q2: ");
    for(i=0; i < 3; i++) {
      ch = q2.get();
      Console.Write(ch);
    }

    Console.WriteLine("\n");

    Console.Write("Contents of q3: ");
    for(i=0; i < 10; i++) {
      ch = q3.get();
      Console.Write(ch);
    }
  }
}
```

5. The output from the program is shown here:

```
Contents of q1: ABCDEFGHIJ

Contents of q2: Tom

Contents of q3: ABCDEFGHIJ
```

The Main( ) Method

Up to this point, you have been using one form of **Main( )**. However, there are several overloaded forms of **Main( )**. Some can be used to return a value, and some can receive arguments. Each is examined here.

Returning Values from Main( )

When a program ends, you can return a value to the calling process (often the operating system) by returning a value from **Main( )**. To do so, you can use this form of **Main( )**.

```
public static int Main( )
```

Notice that instead of being declared **void**, this version of **Main( )** has a return type of **int**.

Usually, the return value from **Main( )** indicates whether the program ended normally or due to some abnormal condition. By convention, a return value of 0 usually indicates normal termination. All other values indicate that some type of error occurred.

Passing Arguments to Main( )

Many programs accept what are called *command-line* arguments. A command-line argument is the information that directly follows the program's name on the command line when it is executed. For C# programs, these arguments are then passed to the **Main( )** method. To receive the arguments, you must use one of these forms of **Main( )**:

```
public static void Main(string[ ] args)
```

```
public static int Main(string[ ] args)
```

The first form returns **void**; the second can be used to return an integer value, as described in the preceding section. For both, the command-line arguments are stored as strings in the **string** array passed to **Main( )**.

For example, the following program displays all of the command-line arguments that it is called with:

```
// Display all command-line information.
using System;

class CLDemo {
  public static void Main(string[] args) {
    Console.WriteLine("There are " + args.Length +
                        " command-line arguments.");

    Console.WriteLine("They are: ");
    for(int i=0; i<args.Length; i++)
      Console.WriteLine(args[i]);
  }
}
```

If **CLDemo** is executed like this:

```
CLDemo one two three
```

you will see the following output:

```
There are 3 command-line arguments.
They are:
one
two
three
```

To get a taste of the way that command-line arguments can be used, consider the next program. It takes one command-line argument that specifies a person's name. It then searches through a two-dimensional array of strings for that name. If it finds a match, it displays that person's telephone number.

```
// A simple automated telephone directory.
using System;
```

```
class Phone {
  public static int Main(string[] args) {
    string[,] numbers = {
      { "Tom", "555-3322" },
      { "Mary", "555-8976" },
      { "Jon", "555-1037" },
      { "Rachel", "555-1400" },
      { "", "" } // terminate with null-strings
    };
    int i;

    if(args.Length != 1) {
      Console.WriteLine("Usage: Phone <name>");
      return 1; // indicate improper usage terminated program
    }
    else {
      for(i=0; numbers[i, 0] != ""; i++) {
        if(numbers[i, 0] == args[0]) {
          Console.WriteLine(numbers[i, 0] + ": " +
                                  numbers[i, 1]);
          break;
        }
      }
      if(numbers[i, 0] == "")
        Console.WriteLine("Name not found.");
    }
    return 0;
  }
}
```

Here is a sample run:

```
C>Phone Mary
Mary: 555-8976
```

There are two interesting things in this program. First, notice how the program checks that a command-line argument is present before it continues execution. This is very important and can be generalized. When a program relies on there being one or more command-line arguments, it must always confirm that the proper arguments have been supplied. Failure to do this will often lead to a program crash!

Second, notice how the program returns a termination code. If the required command-line is not present, then 1 is returned, indicating abnormal termination. Otherwise, 0 is returned when the program ends.

1-Minute Drill

● Can a constructor take an object of its own class as a parameter?

● Why might you want to provide overloaded constructors?

● Show the form of **Main( )** that can receive command-line arguments, but does not return a value.

Recursion

In C#, a method can call itself. This process is called *recursion,* and a method that calls itself is said to be *recursive.* In general, recursion is the process of defining something in terms of itself and is somewhat similar to a circular definition. The key component of a recursive method is that it contains a statement that executes a call to itself. Recursion is a powerful control mechanism.

The classic example of recursion is the computation of the factorial of a number. The factorial of a number *N* is the product of all the whole numbers between 1 and *N*. For example, 3 factorial is $1 \times 2 \times 3$, or 6. The following program shows a recursive way to compute the factorial of a number. For comparison purposes, a nonrecursive equivalent is also included.

● Yes.
● You might want to provide overloaded constructors to provide convenience and flexibility to the user of your class.
● The form of **Main( )** that can receive command-line arguments, but does not return a value is

   public static void Main(string [ ] *args*)

```
// A simple example of recursion.

using System;

class Factorial {
  // This is a recursive function.
  public int factR(int n) {
    int result;

    if(n==1) return 1;
    result = factR(n-1) * n;         Execute a recursive
    return result;                   call to factR( ).
  }

  // This is an iterative equivalent.
  public int factI(int n) {
    int t, result;

    result = 1;
    for(t=1; t <= n; t++) result *= t;
    return result;
  }
}

class Recursion {
  public static void Main() {
    Factorial f = new Factorial();

    Console.WriteLine("Factorials using recursive method.");
    Console.WriteLine("Factorial of 3 is " + f.factR(3));
    Console.WriteLine("Factorial of 4 is " + f.factR(4));
    Console.WriteLine("Factorial of 5 is " + f.factR(5));
    Console.WriteLine();

    Console.WriteLine("Factorials using iterative method.");
    Console.WriteLine("Factorial of 3 is " + f.factI(3));
    Console.WriteLine("Factorial of 4 is " + f.factI(4));
    Console.WriteLine("Factorial of 5 is " + f.factI(5));
  }
}
```

6

The output from this program is shown here:

```
Factorials using recursive method.
Factorial of 3 is 6
Factorial of 4 is 24
Factorial of 5 is 120

Factorials using iterative method.
Factorial of 3 is 6
Factorial of 4 is 24
Factorial of 5 is 120
```

The operation of the nonrecursive method **factI( )** should be clear. It uses a loop starting at 1 and progressively multiplies each number by the moving product.

The operation of the recursive **factR( )** is a bit more complex. When **factR( )** is called with an argument of 1, the method returns 1; otherwise it returns the product of **factR(n–1)*n**. To evaluate this expression, **factR( )** is called with **n–1**. This process repeats until **n** equals 1 and the calls to the method begin returning. For example, when the factorial of 2 is calculated, the first call to **factR( )** will cause a second call to be made with an argument of 1. This call will return 1, which is then multiplied by 2 (the original value of **n**). The answer is then 2. You might find it interesting to insert **WriteLine( )** statements into **factR( )** that show at what level each call is, and what the intermediate results are.

When a method calls itself, new local variables and parameters are allocated storage on the stack, and the method code is executed with these new variables from the start. A recursive call does not make a new copy of the method. Only the arguments are new. As each recursive call returns, the old local variables and parameters are removed from the stack, and execution resumes at the point of the call inside the method. Recursive methods could be said to "telescope" out and back.

Recursive versions of many routines may execute a bit more slowly than the iterative equivalent because of the added overhead of the additional method calls. Too many recursive calls to a method could cause a stack overrun. Because storage for parameters and local variables is on the stack and each new call creates a new copy of these variables, it is possible that the stack could be exhausted. If this occurs, the C# runtime system will cause an exception. However, you probably will not have to worry about this unless a recursive routine runs wild.

The main advantage to recursion is that some types of algorithms can be implemented more clearly and simply recursively than they can be iteratively. For example, the Quicksort sorting algorithm is quite difficult to implement in an iterative way. Also, some problems, especially AI-related ones, seem to lend themselves to recursive solutions.

When writing recursive methods, you must have a conditional statement, such as an **if**, somewhere to force the method to return without the recursive call being executed. If you don't do this, once you call the method, it will never return. This type of error is a very common when working with recursion. Use **WriteLine( )** statements liberally so that you can watch what is going on and abort execution if you see that you have made a mistake.

Understanding static

There will be times when you will want to define a class member that will be used independently of any object of that class. Normally a class member must be accessed through an object of its class, but it is possible to create a member that can be used by itself, without reference to a specific instance. To create such a member, precede its declaration with the keyword **static**. When a member is declared **static**, it can be accessed before any objects of its class are created, and without reference to any object. You can declare both methods and variables to be **static**. The most common example of a **static** member is **Main( )**, which is declared **static** because it must be called by the operating system when your program begins.

Outside the class, to use a **static** member, you must specify the name of its class followed by the dot operator. No object needs to be created. In fact, a **static** member cannot be accessed through an object instance. It must be accessed through its class name. For example, if you want to assign the value 10 to a **static** variable called **count** that is part of the **Timer** class, use this line:

```
Timer.count = 10;
```

This format is similar to that used to access normal instance variables through an object, except that the class name is used. A **static** method can be called in the same way—by use of the dot operator on the name of the class.

Variables declared as **static** are, essentially, global variables. When objects of its class are declared, no copy of a **static** variable is made. Instead, all instances of the class share the same **static** variable. A **static** variable is initialized when its class is loaded. If no explicit initializer is specified, it is initialized to zero for numeric values, null in the case of object references, or **false** for variables of type **bool**. Thus, a **static** variable always has a value.

The difference between a **static** method and a normal method is that the **static** method can be called through its class name, without any object of that method being created. You have seen an example of this already: the **Sqrt( )** method, which is a **static** method within C#'s **System.Math** class.

Here is an example that creates a **static** variable and a **static** method:

```
// Use static.

using System;

class StaticDemo {
  // a static variable
  public static int val = 100;

  // a static method
  public static int valDiv2() {
    return val/2;
  }
}

class SDemo {
  public static void Main() {
```

```
    Console.WriteLine("Initial value of StaticDemo.val is "
                      + StaticDemo.val);

    StaticDemo.val = 8;
    Console.WriteLine("StaticDemo.val is " + StaticDemo.val);
    Console.WriteLine("StaticDemo.valDiv2(): " +
                      StaticDemo.valDiv2());
  }
}
```

The output is shown here:

```
Initial value of StaticDemo.val is 100
StaticDemo.val is 8
StaticDemo.valDiv2(): 4
```

As the output shows, a **static** variable is initialized when the program begins, before any object of its class is created.

There are several restrictions that apply to **static** methods:

● A **static** method does not have a **this** reference.

● A **static** method can directly call only other **static** methods. It cannot call an instance method of its class. The reason is that instance methods operate on specific instances of a class, but a **static** method does not.

● A **static** method must directly access only **static** data. It cannot use an instance variable because it is not operating on an instance of its class.

For example, in the following class, the **static** method **valDivDenom( )** is illegal:

```
class StaticError {
  int denom = 3; // a normal instance variable
  static int val = 1024; // a static variable

  /* Error! Can't directly access a non-static variable
     from within a static method. */
```

```
   static int valDivDenom() {
     return val/denom; // won't compile!
   }
}
```

Here, **denom** is a normal instance variable that cannot be accessed within a **static** method. However, the use of **val** is okay since it is a **static** variable.

The same problem occurs when trying to call a non-**static** method from within a **static** method of the same class. For example:

```
using System;

class AnotherStaticError {
  // non-static method.
  void nonStaticMeth() {
    Console.WriteLine("Inside nonStaticMeth().");
  }

  /* Error! Can't directly call a non-static method
     from within a static method. */
  static void staticMeth() {
    nonStaticMeth(); // won't compile
  }
}
```

In this case, the attempt to call a non-**static** (that is, instance method) from a **static** method causes a compile-time error.

It is important to understand that a **static** method *can* call instance methods and access instance variables of it class, but it must do so through an object of that class. It is just that it cannot use one without an object qualification. For example, this fragment is perfectly valid:

```
class MyClass {
  // non-static method.
  void nonStaticMeth() {
```

```
    Console.WriteLine("Inside nonStaticMeth().");
  }

  /* Can call a non-static method through an
     object reference from within a static method. */
  public static void staticMeth(MyClass ob) {
    ob.nonStaticMeth(); // this is OK
  }
}
```

1-Minute Drill

● Define recursion.

● Explain the difference between **static** variables and instance variables.

● Can a **static** method call a non-**static** method in its own class without
the use of an object reference?

6

QSDemo.cs

Project 6-3: The Quicksort

In Module 5 you were shown a simple sorting method called the bubble sort.
It was mentioned that substantially better sorts exist. Here you will develop a
version of one of the best: the Quicksort. The Quicksort, invented and named
by C.A.R. Hoare, is the best general-purpose sorting algorithm currently available.
The reason it could not be shown in Module 5 is that the best implementations
of the Quicksort rely on recursion. The version we will develop sorts a character
array, but the logic can be adapted to sort any type of object you like.

The Quicksort is built on the idea of *partitions.* The general procedure is
to select a value, called the *comparand,* and then to partition the array into
two sections. All elements greater than or equal to the partition value are put

---

● Recursion is the process of a method calling itself.
● Each object of a class has its own copy of the instance variables defined by the class.
Each object of a class shares one copy of a **static** variable.
● No.

on one side, and those less than the value are put on the other. This process is then repeated for each remaining section until the array is sorted. For example, given the array **fedacb** and using the value **d** as the comparand, the first pass of the Quicksort would rearrange the array as follows:

Initial	f e d a c b
Pass1	b c a d e f

This process is then repeated for each section—that is, **bca** and **def**. As you can see, the process is essentially recursive in nature and, indeed, the cleanest implementation of Quicksort is as a recursive method.

You can select the comparand value in two ways. You can either choose it at random, or you can select it by averaging a small set of values taken from the array. For optimal sorting, you should select a value that is precisely in the middle of the range of values. However, this is not easy to do for most sets of data. In the worst case, the value chosen is at one extremity. Even in this case, however, Quicksort still performs correctly. The version of Quicksort that we will develop selects the middle element of the array as the comparand.

Step-By-Step

1. Create a file called **QSDemo.cs**.

2. Create the **Quicksort** class shown here:

```
// A simple version of the Quicksort.

using System;

class Quicksort {

  // Set up a call to the actual Quicksort method.
  public static void qsort(char[] items) {
    qs(items, 0, items.Length-1);
  }

  // A recursive version of Quicksort for characters.
  static void qs(char[] items, int left, int right)
  {
    int i, j;
    char x, y;

    i = left; j = right;
    x = items[(left+right)/2];
```

```
    do {
      while((items[i] < x) && (i < right)) i++;
      while((x < items[j]) && (j > left)) j--;

      if(i <= j) {
        y = items[i];
        items[i] = items[j];
        items[j] = y;
        i++; j--;
      }
    } while(i <= j);

    if(left < j) qs(items, left, j);
    if(i < right) qs(items, i, right);
  }
}
```

To keep the interface to the Quicksort simple, the **Quicksort** class provides the **qsort( )** method, which sets up a call to the actual Quicksort method, **qs( )**. This enables the Quicksort to be called with just the name of the array to be sorted, without having to provide an initial partition. Since **qs( )** is only used internally, it is private by default.

3. To use the **Quicksort**, simply call **Quicksort.qsort( )**. Since **qsort( )** is specified as **static**, it can be called through its class rather than on an object. Thus, there is no need to create a **Quicksort** object. After the call returns, the array will be sorted. Remember, this version works only for character arrays, but you can adapt the logic to sort any type of arrays you want.

4. Here is a program that demonstrates **Quicksort**:

```
// A simple version of the Quicksort.

using System;

class Quicksort {

  // Set up a call to the actual Quicksort method.
  public static void qsort(char[] items) {
    qs(items, 0, items.Length-1);
  }

  // A recursive version of Quicksort for characters.
  static void qs(char[] items, int left, int right)
  {
```

```
    int i, j;
    char x, y;

    i = left; j = right;
    x = items[(left+right)/2];

    do {
      while((items[i] < x) && (i < right)) i++;
      while((x < items[j]) && (j > left)) j--;

      if(i <= j) {
        y = items[i];
        items[i] = items[j];
        items[j] = y;
        i++; j--;
      }
    } while(i <= j);

    if(left < j) qs(items, left, j);
    if(i < right) qs(items, i, right);
  }
}

class QSDemo {
  public static void Main() {
    char[] a = { 'd', 'x', 'a', 'r', 'p', 'j', 'i' };
    int i;

    Console.Write("Original array: ");
    for(i=0; i < a.Length; i++)
      Console.Write(a[i]);

    Console.WriteLine();

    // now, sort the array
    Quicksort.qsort(a);

    Console.Write("Sorted array: ");
    for(i=0; i < a.Length; i++)
      Console.Write(a[i]);
  }
}
```

☑ *Mastery Check*

1. Given this fragment:

```
class X {
  int count;
```

is the following fragment correct?

```
class Y {
  public static void Main() {
    X ob = new X();

    ob.count = 10;
```

2. An access specifier must _____ a member's declaration.

3. The complement of a queue is a stack. It uses first-in, last-out accessing and is often likened to a stack of plates. The first plate put on the table is the last plate used. Create a stack class called **Stack** that can hold characters. Call the methods that access the stack **push( )** and **pop( )**. Allow the user to specify the size of the stack when it is created. Keep all other members of the **Stack** class private. Hint: You can use the **Queue** class as a model; just change the way that the data is accessed.

4. Given this class:

```
class Test {
  int a;
  Test(int i) { a = i; }
}
```

write a method called **swap( )** that exchanges the contents of the objects referred to by two **Test** object references.

5. Is the following fragment correct?

```
class X {
  int meth(int a, int b) { ... }
  string meth(int a, int b) { ... }
```

6

☑ *Mastery Check*

6. Write a recursive method that displays the contents of a string backwards.

7. If all objects of a class need to share the same variable, how must you declare that variable?

8. What do **ref** and **out** do? How do they differ?

9. Show the four forms of **Main( )**.

10. Given this fragment, which of the following calls are legal?

```
void meth(int i, int j, params int [] args) { // ...
```

A. meth(10, 12, 19);

B. meth(10, 12, 19, 100);

C. meth(10, 12, 19, 100, 200);

D. meth(10, 12);

Module 7

Operator Overloading, Indexers, and Properties

The Goals of This Module

- Understand the fundamentals of operator overloading
- Overload binary operators
- Overload unary operators
- Overload relational operators
- Use indexers
- Create properties

This module examines three special types of class members: overloaded operators, indexers, and properties. Each of these expands the power of a class by improving its usability, its integration into C#'s type system, and its resiliency. Using these members it is possible to create class types that look and feel like the built-in types. This *type extensibility* is an important part of the power of an object-oriented language such as C#.

Operator Overloading

C# allows you to define the meaning of an operator relative to a class that you create. This process is called *operator overloading*. By overloading an operator, you expand its usage to your class. The effects of the operator are completely under your control and may differ from class to class. For example, a class that defines a linked list might use the + operator to add an object to the list. A class that implements a stack might use the + to push an object onto the stack. Another class might use the + operator in an entirely different way.

When an operator is overloaded, none of its original meaning is lost. It is simply that a new operation, relative to a specific class, is added. Therefore, overloading the + to handle a linked list, for example, does not cause its meaning relative to integers (that is, addition) to be changed.

A principal advantage of operator overloading is that it allows you to seamlessly integrate a new class type into your programming environment. Once operators are defined for a class, you can operate on objects of that class using the normal C# expression syntax. You can even use an object in expressions involving other types of data.

Operator overloading is closely related to method overloading. To overload an operator, you use the **operator** keyword to define an *operator method,* which defines the action of the operator.

The General Forms of an Operator Method

There are two forms of **operator** methods: one for unary operators and one for binary operators. The general form for each is shown here:

```
// General form for overloading a unary operator.
public static ret-type operator op(param-type operand)
{
  // operations
```

```
}

// General form for overloading a binary operator.
public static ret-type operator op(param-type1 operand1, param-type1 operand2)
{
  // operations
}
```

The operator that you are overloading, such as + or /, is substituted for the *op*. The *ret-type* is the type of value returned by the specified operation. Although it can be of any type you choose, the return value is often of the same type as the class for which the operator is being overloaded. This correlation facilitates the use of the overloaded operator in expressions. For unary operators, the operand is passed in *operand*. For binary operators, the operands are passed in *operand1* and *operand2*.

For unary operators, the operand must be of the same type as the class for which the operator is being defined. For binary operators, at least one of the operands must be of the same type as its class. Thus, you cannot overload any C# operators for objects that you have not created. For example, you can't redefine + for **int** or **string**.

One other point: operator parameters must not use the **ref** or **out** modifier.

Overloading Binary Operators

To see how operator overloading works, let's start with an example that overloads two binary operators, the + and the –. The following program creates a class called **ThreeD**, which maintains the coordinates of an object in three-dimensional space. The overloaded + adds the individual coordinates of one **ThreeD** object to another. The overloaded – subtracts the coordinates of one object from the other.

```
// An example of operator overloading.
using System;

// A three-dimensional coordinate class.
class ThreeD {
  int x, y, z; // 3-D coordinates

  public ThreeD() { x = y = z = 0; }
  public ThreeD(int i, int j, int k) { x = i; y = j; z = k; }
```

```
// Overload binary +.
public static ThreeD operator +(ThreeD op1, ThreeD op2)
{
  ThreeD result = new ThreeD();
```
> Overload + for objects of type **ThreeD**.

```
  /* This adds together the coordinates of the two points
     and returns the result. */
  result.x = op1.x + op2.x; // These are integer additions
  result.y = op1.y + op2.y; // and the + retains its original
  result.z = op1.z + op2.z; // meaning relative to them.

  return result;
}

// Overload binary -.
public static ThreeD operator -(ThreeD op1, ThreeD op2)
{
  ThreeD result = new ThreeD();
```
> Overload – for objects of type **ThreeD**.

```
  /* Notice the order of the operands. op1 is the left
     operand and op2 is the right. */
  result.x = op1.x - op2.x; // these are integer subtractions
  result.y = op1.y - op2.y;
  result.z = op1.z - op2.z;

  return result;
}

// Show X, Y, Z coordinates.
public void show()
{
  Console.WriteLine(x + ", " + y + ", " + z);
}
}

class ThreeDDemo {
  public static void Main() {
    ThreeD a = new ThreeD(1, 2, 3);
    ThreeD b = new ThreeD(10, 10, 10);
    ThreeD c = new ThreeD();

    Console.Write("Here is a: ");
    a.show();
    Console.WriteLine();
```

```
     Console.Write("Here is b: ");
     b.show();
     Console.WriteLine();

     c = a + b; // add a and b together
     Console.Write("Result of a + b: ");
     c.show();
     Console.WriteLine();

     c = a + b + c; // add a, b and c together
     Console.Write("Result of a + b + c: ");
     c.show();
     Console.WriteLine();

     c = c - a; // subtract a
     Console.Write("Result of c - a: ");
     c.show();
     Console.WriteLine();

     c = c - b; // subtract b
     Console.Write("Result of c - b: ");
     c.show();
     Console.WriteLine();
  }
}
```

Use **ThreeD** objects and the + and − in expressions.

This program produces the following output:

```
Here is a: 1, 2, 3

Here is b: 10, 10, 10

Result of a + b: 11, 12, 13

Result of a + b + c: 22, 24, 26

Result of c - a: 21, 22, 23

Result of c - b: 11, 12, 13
```

Let's examine the preceding program carefully, beginning with the overloaded operator **+**. When two objects of type **ThreeD** are operated on by the **+** operator, the magnitudes of their respective coordinates are added together, as shown in

operator+( ). Notice, however, that this method does not modify the value of either operand. Instead, a new object of type **ThreeD**, which contains the result of the operation, is returned by the method. To understand why the + operation does not change the contents of either object, think about the standard arithmetic + operation as applied like this: 10 + 12. The outcome of this operation is 22, but neither 10 nor 12 is changed by it. Although there is no rule that prevents an overloaded operator from altering the value of one of its operands, it is best for the actions of an overloaded operator to be consistent with its usual meaning.

As mentioned, **operator+( )** returns an object of type **ThreeD**. Although the method could have returned any valid C# type, the fact that it returns a **ThreeD** object allows the + operator to be used in compound expressions, such as **a+b+c**. Here, **a+b** generates a result that is of type **ThreeD**. This value can then be added to **c**. Had any other type of value been generated by **a+b**, such an expression would not work.

Here is another important point: when the coordinates are added together inside **operator+( )**, the addition of the individual coordinates results in an integer addition. This is because the individual coordinates, **x**, **y**, and **z**, are integer quantities. The fact that the + operator is overloaded for objects of type **ThreeD** has no effect on the + as it is applied to integer values.

Now, look at **operator–( )**. The – operator works just like the + operator except that the order of the parameters is important. Recall that addition is commutative, but subtraction is not. (That is, A – B is not the same as B – A!) For all binary operators, the first parameter to an operator method will contain the left operand. The second parameter will contain the operand on the right. When implementing overloaded versions of the non-commutative operators, you must remember which operand is on the left and which is on the right.

Overloading Unary Operators

The unary operators are overloaded just like the binary operators. The main difference, of course, is that there is only one operand. For example, here is a method that overloads the unary minus for the **ThreeD** class:

```
// Overload unary -.
public static ThreeD operator -(ThreeD op)
{
  ThreeD result = new ThreeD();
```

```
  result.x = -op.x;
  result.y = -op.y;
  result.z = -op.z;

  return result;
}
```

Here, a new object is created that contains the negated fields of the operand.
This object is then returned. Notice that the operand is unchanged. Again,
this is in keeping with the usual meaning of the unary minus. For example,
in an expression such as

```
a = -b
```

a receives the negation of **b**, but **b** is not changed.

There are, however, two cases in which an operator method will need to change
the contents of an operand: ++ and − −. Since the usual meaning of these operators
is increment and decrement, an overloaded ++ or − − should usually increment
or decrement the operand. Thus, when overloading these two operators, the
operand will usually be modified. For example, here is an **operator++( )** method
for the **ThreeD** class:

```
// Overload unary ++.
public static ThreeD operator ++(ThreeD op)
{
  // for ++, modify argument
  op.x++;
  op.y++;          The ++ operator modifies
  op.z++;          its operand.

  return op; // operand is returned
}
```

Here is an expanded version of the previous example program that
demonstrates the unary − and the ++ operator:

```
// More operator overloading.
using System;

// A three-dimensional coordinate class.
class ThreeD {
```

7

```csharp
int x, y, z; // 3-D coordinates

public ThreeD() { x = y = z = 0; }
public ThreeD(int i, int j, int k) { x = i; y = j; z = k; }

// Overload binary +.
public static ThreeD operator +(ThreeD op1, ThreeD op2)
{
  ThreeD result = new ThreeD();

  /* This adds together the coordinates of the two points
     and returns the result. */
  result.x = op1.x + op2.x; // These are integer additions
  result.y = op1.y + op2.y; // and the + retains its original
  result.z = op1.z + op2.z; // meaning relative to them.

  return result;
}

// Overload binary -.
public static ThreeD operator -(ThreeD op1, ThreeD op2)
{
  ThreeD result = new ThreeD();

  /* Notice the order of the operands. op1 is the left
     operand and op2 is the right. */
  result.x = op1.x - op2.x; // these are integer subtractions
  result.y = op1.y - op2.y;
  result.z = op1.z - op2.z;

  return result;
}

// Overload unary -.
public static ThreeD operator -(ThreeD op)
{
  ThreeD result = new ThreeD();

  result.x = -op.x;
  result.y = -op.y;
  result.z = -op.z;

  return result;
}
```

```
    // Overload unary ++.
    public static ThreeD operator ++(ThreeD op)
    {
      // for ++, modify argument
      op.x++;
      op.y++;
      op.z++;

      return op;
    }

    // Show X, Y, Z coordinates.
    public void show()
    {
      Console.WriteLine(x + ", " + y + ", " + z);
    }
}

class ThreeDDemo {
  public static void Main() {
    ThreeD a = new ThreeD(1, 2, 3);
    ThreeD b = new ThreeD(10, 10, 10);
    ThreeD c = new ThreeD();

    Console.Write("Here is a: ");
    a.show();
    Console.WriteLine();
    Console.Write("Here is b: ");
    b.show();
    Console.WriteLine();

    c = a + b; // add a and b together
    Console.Write("Result of a + b: ");
    c.show();
    Console.WriteLine();

    c = a + b + c; // add a, b and c together
    Console.Write("Result of a + b + c: ");
    c.show();
    Console.WriteLine();

    c = c - a; // subtract a
    Console.Write("Result of c - a: ");
    c.show();
    Console.WriteLine();
```

7

```
    c = c - b; // subtract b
    Console.Write("Result of c - b: ");
    c.show();
    Console.WriteLine();

    c = -a; // assign -a to c
    Console.Write("Result of -a: ");
    c.show();
    Console.WriteLine();

    a++; // increment a
    Console.Write("Result of a++: ");
    a.show();
  }
}
```

The output from the program is shown here:

```
Here is a: 1, 2, 3

Here is b: 10, 10, 10

Result of a + b: 11, 12, 13

Result of a + b + c: 22, 24, 26

Result of c - a: 21, 22, 23

Result of c - b: 11, 12, 13

Result of -a: -1, -2, -3

Result of a++: 2, 3, 4
```

As you know, the ++ and − − have both a prefix and a postfix form. For example, both

```
++0;
```

and

```
O++;
```

are valid uses of the increment operator. However, when overloading the **++** or **– –**, both forms call the same method. Thus, when overloading, there is no way to distinguish between a prefix or postfix form of **++** or **– –**.

1-Minute Drill

- What is operator overloading? What keyword is used?
- What is the general form of an overloaded binary operator?
- What makes overloading the **++** or **– –** unique?

Adding Flexibility

For any given class and operator, an operator method can, itself, be overloaded. For example, once again consider the **ThreeD** class. To this point, you have seen how to overload the **+** so that it adds the coordinates of one **ThreeD** object to another. However, this is not the only way in which we might want to define addition for **ThreeD**. For example, it might be useful to add an integer value to each coordinate of a **ThreeD** object. Such an operation could be used to

---

- Operator overloading defines the meaning of an operator relative to a class that you create. The keyword **operator** is used.
- The general form of an overloaded binary operator is as follows:

      public static *ret-type* operator *op(param-type1 operand1, param-type1 operand2)*

      {

      // operations

      }

- When the **++** or **– –** is overloaded, the operator method will usually alter the value of the operand. This is not the case with the other operators.

translate the axes. To perform such an operation, you will need to overload + a second time, as shown here:

```
// Overload binary + for object + int.
public static ThreeD operator +(ThreeD op1, int op2)
{
  ThreeD result = new ThreeD();                    This defines addition for
                                                   an object + an integer.
  result.x = op1.x + op2;
  result.y = op1.y + op2;
  result.z = op1.z + op2;

  return result;
}
```

Notice that the second parameter is of type **int**. Thus, the preceding method allows an integer value to be added to each field of a **ThreeD** object. This is permissible because, as explained earlier, when overloading a binary operator, one of the operands must be of the same type as the class for which the operator is being overloaded. However, the other operand can be of any other type.

Here is a version of **ThreeD** that has two overloaded + methods:

```
/* Overload addition for object + object, and
   for object + int. */
using System;

// A three-dimensional coordinate class.
class ThreeD {
  int x, y, z; // 3-D coordinates

  public ThreeD() { x = y = z = 0; }
  public ThreeD(int i, int j, int k) { x = i; y = j; z = k; }

  // Overload binary + for object + object.
  public static ThreeD operator +(ThreeD op1, ThreeD op2)
  {
    ThreeD result = new ThreeD();

    /* This adds together the coordinates of the two points
       and returns the result. */
    result.x = op1.x + op2.x; // These are integer additions
    result.y = op1.y + op2.y; // and the + retains its original
    result.z = op1.z + op2.z; // meaning relative to them.
```

```
      return result;
  }

  // Overload binary + for object + int.
  public static ThreeD operator +(ThreeD op1, int op2)
  {
    ThreeD result = new ThreeD();

    result.x = op1.x + op2;
    result.y = op1.y + op2;
    result.z = op1.z + op2;

    return result;
  }

  // Show X, Y, Z coordinates.
  public void show()
  {
    Console.WriteLine(x + ", " + y + ", " + z);
  }
}

class ThreeDDemo {
  public static void Main() {
    ThreeD a = new ThreeD(1, 2, 3);
    ThreeD b = new ThreeD(10, 10, 10);
    ThreeD c = new ThreeD();

    Console.Write("Here is a: ");
    a.show();
    Console.WriteLine();
    Console.Write("Here is b: ");
    b.show();
    Console.WriteLine();

    c = a + b; // object + object
    Console.Write("Result of a + b: ");
    c.show();
    Console.WriteLine();

    c = b + 10; // object + int
    Console.Write("Result of b + 10: ");
    c.show();
  }
}
```

7

The output from this program is shown here:

```
Here is a: 1, 2, 3

Here is b: 10, 10, 10

Result of a + b: 11, 12, 13

Result of b + 10: 20, 20, 20
```

As the output confirms, when the + is applied to two objects, their coordinates are added together. When the + is applied to an object and an integer, the coordinates are increased by the integer value.

While the overloading of + just shown certainly adds a useful capability to the **ThreeD** class, it does not quite finish the job. Here is why. The **operator+(ThreeD, int)** method allows statements like this:

```
ob1 = ob2 + 10;
```

It does not, unfortunately, allow ones like this:

```
ob1 = 10 + ob2;
```

The trouble is that the preceding statement puts the integer argument on the left, but the **operator+( )** method expects it on the right. To allow both forms of statements, you will need to overload the + yet another time. This version must have its first parameter as type **int** and its second parameter as type **ThreeD**. One version of the **operator+( )** method handles *object + integer,* and the other handles *integer + object*. Overloading the + (or any other binary operator) this way allows a built-in type to occur on the left or right side of the operator. Here is a version of **ThreeD** that overloads the + operator as just described:

```
/* Overload the + for object + object,
   object + int, and int + object. */
using System;

// A three-dimensional coordinate class.
class ThreeD {
  int x, y, z; // 3-D coordinates

  public ThreeD() { x = y = z = 0; }
```

```
public ThreeD(int i, int j, int k) { x = i; y = j; z = k; }

// Overload binary + for object + object.
public static ThreeD operator +(ThreeD op1, ThreeD op2)
{
  ThreeD result = new ThreeD();

  /* This adds together the coordinates of the two points
     and returns the result. */
  result.x = op1.x + op2.x; // These are integer additions
  result.y = op1.y + op2.y; // and the + retains its original
  result.z = op1.z + op2.z; // meaning relative to them.

  return result;
}

// Overload binary + for object + int.
public static ThreeD operator +(ThreeD op1, int op2)
{
  ThreeD result = new ThreeD();

  result.x = op1.x + op2;
  result.y = op1.y + op2;
  result.z = op1.z + op2;

  return result;
}

// Overload binary + for int + object.
public static ThreeD operator +(int op1, ThreeD op2)
{
  ThreeD result = new ThreeD();

  result.x = op2.x + op1;
  result.y = op2.y + op1;
  result.z = op2.z + op1;

  return result;
}

// Show X, Y, Z coordinates.
public void show()
{
  Console.WriteLine(x + ", " + y + ", " + z);
}
```

Addition of object + integer

Addition of integer + object

7

```
}

class ThreeDDemo {
  public static void Main() {
    ThreeD a = new ThreeD(1, 2, 3);
    ThreeD b = new ThreeD(10, 10, 10);
    ThreeD c = new ThreeD();

    Console.Write("Here is a: ");
    a.show();
    Console.WriteLine();
    Console.Write("Here is b: ");
    b.show();
    Console.WriteLine();

    c = a + b; // object + object
    Console.Write("Result of a + b: ");
    c.show();
    Console.WriteLine();

    c = b + 10; // object + int
    Console.Write("Result of b + 10: ");
    c.show();
    Console.WriteLine();

    c = 15 + b; // int + object
    Console.Write("Result of 15 + b: ");
    c.show();
  }
}
```

The output from this program is shown here:

```
Here is a: 1, 2, 3

Here is b: 10, 10, 10

Result of a + b: 11, 12, 13

Result of b + 10: 20, 20, 20

Result of 15 + b: 25, 25, 25
```

Overloading the Relational Operators

The relational operators, such as = = or <, can also be overloaded and the process is straightforward. Usually, an overloaded relational operator returns a **true** or **false** value. This is in keeping with the normal usage of these operators and allows the overloaded relational operators to be used in conditional expressions. If you return a different type result, then you are greatly restricting the operator's utility.

Here is a version of the **ThreeD** class that overloads the < and > operators. As implemented, one object is greater than another if all three of its coordinates are greater than those in the other object, and one object is less than another if all three of its coordinates are less than those in the other object.

```
// Overload < and >.
using System;

// A three-dimensional coordinate class.
class ThreeD {
  int x, y, z; // 3-D coordinates

  public ThreeD() { x = y = z = 0; }
  public ThreeD(int i, int j, int k) { x = i; y = j; z = k; }

  // Overload <.
  public static bool operator <(ThreeD op1, ThreeD op2)
  {
    if((op1.x < op2.x) && (op1.y < op2.y) && (op1.z < op2.z))
      return true;
    else
      return false;
  }
```

Return true if **op1** is less than **op2**.

```
  // Overload >.
  public static bool operator >(ThreeD op1, ThreeD op2)
  {
    if((op1.x > op2.x) && (op1.y > op2.y) && (op1.z > op2.z))
      return true;
    else
      return false;
  }
```

Return true if **op1** is greater than **op2**.

```
  // Show X, Y, Z coordinates.
  public void show()
```

7

```
    {
      Console.WriteLine(x + ", " + y + ", " + z);
    }
}

class ThreeDDemo {
  public static void Main() {
    ThreeD a = new ThreeD(5, 6, 7);
    ThreeD b = new ThreeD(10, 10, 10);
    ThreeD c = new ThreeD(1, 2, 3);

    Console.Write("Here is a: ");
    a.show();
    Console.Write("Here is b: ");
    b.show();
    Console.Write("Here is c: ");
    c.show();
    Console.WriteLine();

    if(a > c) Console.WriteLine("a > c is true");
    if(a < c) Console.WriteLine("a < c is true");
    if(a > b) Console.WriteLine("a > b is true");
    if(a < b) Console.WriteLine("a < b is true");
  }
}
```

The output from this program is shown here:

```
Here is a: 5, 6, 7
Here is b: 10, 10, 10
Here is c: 1, 2, 3

a > c is true
a < b is true
```

There is an important restriction that applies to overloading the relational operators: you must overload them in pairs. For example, if you overload <, you must also overload >, and vice versa. The operator pairs are

```
==          !=
<           >
<=          >=
```

Note

If you overload the = = and **!=** operators, then you will usually need to override **Object.Equals( )** and **Object.GetHashCode( )**. These methods and the technique of overriding are discussed in Module 8.

Operator Overloading Tips and Restrictions

The action of an overloaded operator as applied to the class for which it is defined need not bear any relationship to that operator's default usage, as applied to C#'s built-in types. However, for the purposes of the structure and readability of your code, an overloaded operator should reflect, when possible, the spirit of the operator's original use. For example, the + relative to **ThreeD** is conceptually similar to the + relative to integer types. There would be little benefit in defining the + operator relative to some class in such a way that it acts more the way you would expect the / operator to perform, for instance. The central concept is that while you can give an overloaded operator any meaning you like, for clarity it is best when its new meaning is related to its original meaning.

There are some restrictions to overloading operators. You cannot alter the precedence of any operator. You cannot alter the number of operands required by the operator, although your operator method could choose to ignore an operand. There are several operators that you cannot overload. Perhaps most significantly, you cannot overload any assignment operator, including the compound assignments, such as **+=**. Here are the other operators that cannot be overloaded.

&&	||	[ ]	( )	new	is
sizeof	typeof	?	->	.	=

One last point: The keywords **true** and **false** can also be used as unary operators for the purposes of overloading. Overloaded versions of these operators can provide custom determinations of true and false, or be used to implement tri-state boolean logic: true, false, or neither. You might find it interesting to explore these operators on your own.

1-Minute Drill

● To allow both integer / obj and obj / integer, what must you do?

● What type of data do overloaded relational operators usually return?

● Can the assignment operator be overloaded?

Ask the Expert

Question: Since I can't overload operators such as +=, what happens if I try to use += with an object of a class for which I have defined +, for example? More generally, what happens when I use any compound assignment on an object for which I have defined the operational part of that assignment?

Answer: In general, if you have defined an operator, then if that operator is used in a compound assignment, your overloaded operator method is invoked. Thus, += automatically uses your version of **operator+( )**. For example, assuming the **ThreeD** class, if you use a sequence like this:

```
ThreeD a = new ThreeD(1, 2, 3);
ThreeD b = new ThreeD(10, 10, 10);

b += a; // add a and b together
```

ThreeD's **operator+( )** is automatically invoked, and **b** will contain the coordinates 11, 12, 13.

● You must overload the / operator two ways, once with the object as the first parameter and once with the object as the second parameter.
● The relational operators typically return **bool**.
● No.

Indexers

As you know, array indexing is performed using the [ ] operator. It is possible to overload the [ ] operator for classes that you create, but you don't use an **operator** method. Instead, you create an *indexer*. An indexer allows an object to be indexed like an array. The main use of indexers is to support the creation of specialized arrays that are subject to one or more constraints. However, you can use an indexer for any purpose for which an array-like syntax is beneficial. Indexers can have one or more dimensions.

We will begin with one-dimensional indexers. One-dimensional indexers have this general form:

```
element-type this[int index] {
  // The get accessor.
  get {
     // return the value specified by index
  }

  // The set accessor.
  set {
     // set the value specified by index
  }
}
```

Here, *element-type* is the base type of the indexer. Thus, each element accessed by the indexer will be of type *element-type*. It corresponds to the base type of an array. The parameter *index* receives the index of the element being accessed. Technically, this parameter does not have to be of type **int**, but since indexers are typically used to provide array indexing, an integer type is customary.

Inside the body of the indexer are defined two *accessors* called **get** and **set**. An accessor is similar to a method except that it does not have a return type or parameter declarations. The accessors are automatically called when the indexer is used, and both accessors receive *index* as a parameter. If the indexer is on the left side of an assignment statement, then the **set** accessor is called and the element specified by *index* must be set. Otherwise, the **get** accessor is called and the value associated with *index* must be returned. The **set** method also receives a value called **value**, which contains the value being assigned to the specified index.

One of the benefits of an indexer is that you can control precisely how an array is accessed, heading off improper accesses. For example, here is a better way to implement the "fail-soft" array created in Module 6. It uses an indexer, thus allowing the array to be accessed using the normal array notation.

```csharp
// Improve the fail-soft array by adding an indexer.
using System;

class FailSoftArray {
  int[] a;     // reference to array

  public int Length; // Length is public

  public bool errflag; // indicates outcome of last operation

  // Construct array given its size.
  public FailSoftArray(int size) {
    a = new int[size];
    Length = size;
  }

  // This is the indexer for FailSoftArray.
  public int this[int index] {          ← An indexer for FailSoftArray
    // This is the get accessor.
    get {
      if(ok(index)) {
        errflag = false;
        return a[index];
      } else {
        errflag = true;
        return 0;
      }
    }

    // This is the set accessor
    set {
      if(ok(index)) {
        a[index] = value;
```

```
        errflag = false;
      }
      else errflag = true;
    }
  }

  // Return true if index is within bounds.
  private bool ok(int index) {
   if(index >= 0 & index < Length) return true;
   return false;
  }
}

// Demonstrate the improved fail-soft array.
class ImprovedFSDemo {
  public static void Main() {
    FailSoftArray fs = new FailSoftArray(5);
    int x;

    // show quiet failures
    Console.WriteLine("Fail quietly.");
    for(int i=0; i < (fs.Length * 2); i++)
      fs[i] = i*10;
```

Invoke the indexer's set accessor.

```
    for(int i=0; i < (fs.Length * 2); i++) {
      x = fs[i];
```

Invoke the indexer's get accessor.

```
      if(x != -1) Console.Write(x + " ");
    }
    Console.WriteLine();

    // now, generate failures
    Console.WriteLine("\nFail with error reports.");
    for(int i=0; i < (fs.Length * 2); i++) {
      fs[i] = i*10;
      if(fs.errflag)
        Console.WriteLine("fs[" + i + "] out-of-bounds");
    }

    for(int i=0; i < (fs.Length * 2); i++) {
      x = fs[i];
      if(!fs.errflag) Console.Write(x + " ");
      else
        Console.WriteLine("fs[" + i + "] out-of-bounds");
    }
```

7

```
    }
}
```

The output from the program is shown here:

```
Fail quietly.
0 10 20 30 40 0 0 0 0 0

Fail with error reports.
fs[5] out-of-bounds
fs[6] out-of-bounds
fs[7] out-of-bounds
fs[8] out-of-bounds
fs[9] out-of-bounds
0 10 20 30 40 fs[5] out-of-bounds
fs[6] out-of-bounds
fs[7] out-of-bounds
fs[8] out-of-bounds
fs[9] out-of-bounds
```

This output is similar to that produced by the previous version of the program shown in Module 6. In this version, the indexer prevents the array boundaries from being overrun. Let's look closely at each part of the indexer. It begins with this line:

```
public int this[int index] {
```

This declares an indexer that operates on **int** elements. The index is passed in *index*. The indexer is public, allowing it to be used by code outside of its class. The **get** accessor is shown here:

```
get {
  if(ok(index)) {
    errflag = false;
    return a[index];
  } else {
    errflag = true;
    return 0;
  }
}
```

The **get** accessor prevents array boundary errors. If the specified index is within bounds, the element corresponding to the index is returned. If it is out of bounds, no operation takes place and no overrun occurs. In this version of **FailSoftArray**, a variable called **errflag** contains the outcome of each operation. This field can be examined after each operation to assess the success or failure of the operation. (In Module 10 you will see a better way to handle errors by using C#'s exception subsystem, but for now, using an error flag is an acceptable approach.)

The **set** accessor is shown here. It, too, prevents a boundary error.

```
set {
  if(ok(index)) {
    a[index] = value;
    errflag = false;
  }
  else errflag = true;
}
```

Here, if **index** is within bounds, the value passed in **value** is assigned to the corresponding element. Otherwise, **errflag** is set to **true**. Recall that in an accessor method, **value** is an automatic parameter that contains the value being assigned. You do not need to (nor can you) declare it.

Indexers do not have to support both **get** and **set**. You can create a read-only indexer by implementing only the **get** accessor. You can create a write-only indexer by implementing only **set**.

It is important to understand that there is no requirement that an indexer actually operate on an array. It simply must provide functionality that appears "array-like" to the user of the indexer. For example, the following program has an indexer that acts like a read-only array that contains the powers of 2 from 0 to 15. Notice, however, that no actual array exists. Instead, the indexer simply computes the proper value for a given index.

```
// Indexers don't have to operate on actual arrays.
using System;

class PwrOfTwo {

  /* Access a logical array that contains
     the powers of 2 from 0 to 15. */
```

7

```
  public int this[int index] {
    // Compute and return power of 2.
    get {
      if((index >= 0) && (index < 16)) return pwr(index);
      else return -1;
    }

    // there is no set accessor
  }

  int pwr(int p) {
    int result = 1;

    for(int i=0; i<p; i++)
      result *= 2;

    return result;
  }
}

class UsePwrOfTwo {
  public static void Main() {
    PwrOfTwo pwr = new PwrOfTwo();

    Console.Write("First 8 powers of 2: ");
    for(int i=0; i < 8; i++)
      Console.Write(pwr[i] + " ");
    Console.WriteLine();

    Console.Write("Here are some errors: ");
    Console.Write(pwr[-1] + " " + pwr[17]);
  }
}
```

Here, no underlying array is indexed.

The output from the program is shown here:

```
First 8 powers of 2: 1 2 4 8 16 32 64 128
Here are some errors: -1 -1
```

Notice that the indexer for **PwrOfTwo** includes a **get** accessor, but no **set** accessor. As explained, this means that the indexer is read-only. Thus, a **PwrOfTwo** object can be used on the right side of an assignment statement, but not on the left. For example, attempting to add this statement to the preceding program won't work:

```
pwr[0] = 11; // won't compile
```

This statement will cause a compilation error because there is no **set** accessor defined for the indexer.

There is one important restriction to using indexers: because an indexer does not define a storage location, a value produced by an indexer cannot be passed as a **ref** or **out** parameter to a method.

Multidimensional Indexers

You can create indexers for multidimensional arrays, too. For example, here is a two-dimensional fail-soft array. Pay close attention to the way that the indexer is declared.

```
// A two-dimensional fail-soft array.
using System;

class FailSoftArray2D {
  int[,] a; // reference to 2D array
  int rows, cols; // dimensions
  public int Length; // Length is public

  public bool errflag; // indicates outcome of last operation

  // Construct array given its dimensions.
  public FailSoftArray2D(int r, int c) {
    rows = r;
    cols = c;
    a = new int[rows, cols];
    Length = rows * cols;
  }

  // This is the indexer for FailSoftArray2D.
  public int this[int index1, int index2] {        ◄─── A two-dimensional
    // This is the get accessor.                          indexer
    get {
      if(ok(index1, index2)) {
        errflag = false;
```

7

```
          return a[index1, index2];
        } else {
          errflag = true;
          return 0;
        }
    }

    // This is the set accessor.
    set {
      if(ok(index1, index2)) {
        a[index1, index2] = value;
        errflag = false;
      }
      else errflag = true;
    }
  }

  // Return true if indexes are within bounds.
  private bool ok(int index1, int index2) {
   if(index1 >= 0 & index1 < rows &
      index2 >= 0 & index2 < cols)
          return true;

   return false;
  }
}

// Demonstrate a 2D indexer.
class TwoDIndexerDemo {
  public static void Main() {
    FailSoftArray2D fs = new FailSoftArray2D(3, 5);
    int x;

    // show quiet failures
    Console.WriteLine("Fail quietly.");
    for(int i=0; i < 6; i++)
      fs[i, i] = i*10;

    for(int i=0; i < 6; i++) {
      x = fs[i,i];
      if(x != -1) Console.Write(x + " ");
    }
    Console.WriteLine();
```

```
    // now, generate failures
    Console.WriteLine("\nFail with error reports.");
    for(int i=0; i < 6; i++) {
      fs[i,i] = i*10;
      if(fs.errflag)
        Console.WriteLine("fs[" + i + ", " + i + "] out-of-bounds");
    }

    for(int i=0; i < 6; i++) {
      x = fs[i,i];
      if(!fs.errflag) Console.Write(x + " ");
      else
        Console.WriteLine("fs[" + i + ", " + i + "] out-of-bounds");
    }
  }
}
```

The output from this program is shown here:

```
Fail quietly.
0 10 20 0 0 0

Fail with error reports.
fs[3, 3] out-of-bounds
fs[4, 4] out-of-bounds
fs[5, 5] out-of-bounds
0 10 20 fs[3, 3] out-of-bounds
fs[4, 4] out-of-bounds
fs[5, 5] out-of-bounds
```

1-Minute Drill

● In an indexer, what are the accessors called and what do they do?

● Can an indexer be read-only?

● Can you create an indexer for a two-dimensional array?

● The accessors are called **get** and **set**, and they set or get the element being indexed.
● Yes.
● Yes.

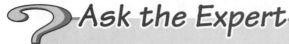

Properties

Another type of class member is the *property*. A property combines a field with the methods that access it. As some examples earlier in this book have shown, often you will want to create a field that is available to users of an object, but you want to maintain control over what operations are allowed on that field. For instance, you might want to limit the range of values that can be assigned to that field. While it is possible to accomplish this goal through the use of a private variable along with methods to access its value, a property offers a better, more streamlined approach.

Properties are similar to indexers. A property consists of a name along with **get** and **set** accessors. The accessors are used to get and set the value of a variable. The key benefit of a property is that its name can be used in expressions and assignments like a normal variable, but in actuality the **get** and **set** accessors are automatically invoked. This is similar to the way that an indexer's **get** and **set** methods are automatically used.

The general form of a property is shown here:

```
type name {
   get {
      // get accessor code
   }

   set {
      // set accessor code
   }
}
```

Here, *type* specifies the type of the property, such as **int**, and *name* is the name of the property. Once the property has been defined, any use of *name* results in a call to its appropriate accessor. The **set** accessor automatically receives a parameter called **value** that contains the value being assigned to the property.

It is important to understand that properties do not define storage locations. Thus, a property manages access to a field. It does not, itself, provide that field. The field must be specified independently of the property.

Here is a simple example that defines a property called **myprop**, which is used to access the field **prop**. In this case, the property allows only positive values to be assigned.

```
// A simple property example.
using System;

class SimpProp {
  int prop; // field being managed by myprop

  public SimpProp() { prop = 0; }

  /* This is the property that supports access to
     the private instance variable prop.  It
     allows only positive values. */
  public int myprop {
    get {
      return prop;
    }
    set {
      if(value >= 0) prop = value;
    }
  }
}

// Demonstrate a property.
class PropertyDemo {
  public static void Main() {
    SimpProp ob = new SimpProp();

    Console.WriteLine("Original value of ob.myprop: " +
```

A property called **myprop** that controls access to **prop**

7

```
      ob.myprop);
```
Use **myprop** just like a variable.

```
   ob.myprop = 100; // assign value
   Console.WriteLine("Value of ob.myprop: " + ob.myprop);

   // Can't assign negative value to prop
   Console.WriteLine("Attempt to assign -10 to ob.myprop");
   ob.myprop = -10;
   Console.WriteLine("Value of ob.myprop: " + ob.myprop);
  }
}
```

Output from this program is shown here:

```
Original value of ob.myprop: 0
Value of ob.myprop: 100
Attempt to assign -10 to ob.myprop
Value of ob.myprop: 100
```

Let's examine this program carefully. The program defines one private field, called **prop**, and a property called **myprop** that manages access to **prop**. As explained, a property by itself does not define a storage location. A property simply manages access to a field. Thus, there is no concept of a property without an underlying field. Furthermore, because **prop** is private, it can be accessed *only* through **myprop**.

The property **myprop** is specified as **public** so that it can be accessed by code outside of its class. This makes sense because it provides access to **prop**, which is private. The **get** accessor simply returns the value of **prop**. The **set** accessor sets the value of **prop** if and only if that value is positive. Thus, the **myprop** property controls what values **prop** can have. This is the essence of why properties are important.

The type of property defined by **myprop** is called a read-write property because it allows its underlying field to be read and written. It is possible, however, to create read-only and write-only properties. To create a read-only property, define only a **get** accessor. To define a write-only property, define only a **set** accessor.

You can use a property to further improve the fail-soft array class. As you know, all arrays have a **Length** property associated with them. Up to now, the **FailSoftArray** class simply used a public integer field called **Length** for this purpose. This is not good practice, though, because it allows **Length** to be set to some value other than the length of the fail-soft array. (For example, a malicious programmer could intentionally corrupt its value.) We can remedy this situation by transforming **Length** into a read-only property, as shown in this version of **FailSoftArray**.

```
// Add Length property to FailSoftArray.
using System;

class FailSoftArray {
  int[] a; // reference to array
  int len; // length of array

  public bool errflag; // indicates outcome of last operation

  // Construct array given its size.
  public FailSoftArray(int size) {
    a = new int[size];
    len = size;
  }

  // Read-only Length property.
  public int Length {
    get {
      return len;
    }
  }

  // This is the indexer for FailSoftArray.
  public int this[int index] {
    // This is the get accessor.
    get {
      if(ok(index)) {
        errflag = false;
        return a[index];
      } else {
        errflag = true;
        return 0;
      }
    }

    // This is the set accessor
    set {
      if(ok(index)) {
        a[index] = value;
```

Length is now a property rather than a field.

7

```
            errflag = false;
        }
        else errflag = true;
    }
}


    // Return true if index is within bounds.
    private bool ok(int index) {
      if(index >= 0 & index < Length) return true;
      return false;
    }
}

// Demonstrate the improved fail-soft array.
class ImprovedFSDemo {
  public static void Main() {
    FailSoftArray fs = new FailSoftArray(5);
    int x;

    // can read Length
    for(int i=0; i < (fs.Length); i++)
      fs[i] = i*10;

    for(int i=0; i < (fs.Length); i++) {
      x = fs[i];
      if(x != -1) Console.Write(x + " ");
    }
    Console.WriteLine();

    // fs.Length = 10; // Error, illegal!

  }
}
```

Now, **Length** is a read-only property that can be read but not assigned. To prove this to yourself, try removing the comment symbol preceding this line in the program:

```
// fs.Length = 10; // Error, illegal!
```

When you try to compile, you will receive an error message stating that **Length** is read-only.

Property Restrictions

Properties have some important restrictions. First, because a property does not define a storage location, it cannot be passed as a **ref** or **out** parameter to a method. Second, you cannot overload a property. (You *can* have two different properties that both access the same variable, but this would be unusual.) Finally, a property should not alter the state of the underlying variable when the **get** accessor is called. Although this rule is not enforced by the compiler, it is semantically wrong. A **get** operation should be nonintrusive.

1-Minute Drill

● Does a property define a storage location?

● What is a primary benefit of a property?

● Can a property be passed as a **ref** parameter?

SetDemo.cs

Project 7-1: Creating a Set Class

As mentioned at the start of this module, operator overloading, indexers, and properties help you create classes that can be fully integrated into C#'s programming environment. Consider this point: by defining the necessary operators, indexers, and properties, you enable a class type to be used in a program in just the same way as you would use a built-in type. You can act on objects of that class through operators and indexers, and use objects of that class in expressions. Adding properties enables the class to provide an interface consistent with C#'s built-in objects. To illustrate the creation and integration of a new class into the C# environment, this project creates a class called **Set** that defines a set type.

● No, a separate variable must underlie the property.
● A property allows a variable-like syntax to be used to call accessor methods.
● No.

7

Before we begin, it is important to understand precisely what we mean by a set. For the purposes of this project, a *set* is a collection of unique elements. That is, no two elements in any given set can be the same. The ordering of a set's members is irrelevant. Thus, the set

{ A, B, C }

is the same as the set

{ A, C, B }

A set can also be empty.

Sets support a number of operations. The ones that we will implement are

● Adding an element to a set

● Removing an element from a set

● Set union

● Set difference

Adding an element to a set and removing an element from a set are self-explanatory operations. The other two warrant some explanation.

The *union* of two sets is a set that contains all of the elements from both sets. (Of course, no duplicate elements are allowed.) We will use the + operator to perform a set union.

The *difference* between two sets is a set that contains those elements in the first set that are not part of the second set. We will use the – operator to perform a set difference. For example, given two sets S1 and S2, this statement removes the elements of S2 from S1, putting the result in S3:

S3 = S1 – S2

If S1 and S2 are the same, then S3 will be the null set.

Of course, there are several other operations that can be performed on sets. Some are developed in the Mastery Check. Others you might find fun to try adding on your own.

For the sake of simplicity, the **Set** class stores sets of characters, but the same basic principles could be used to create a **Set** class capable of storing other types of elements.

Step-by-Step

1. Create a new file called **SetDemo.cs**.

2. Begin creating **Set** with the following lines:

```
class Set {
  char[] members; // this array holds the set
  int len; // number of members
```

Each set is stored in a **char** array referred to by **members**. The number of members actually in the set is stored in **len**.

3. Add the following **Set** constructors:

```
// Construct a null set.
public Set() {
  len = 0;
}

// Construct an empty set of a given size.
public Set(int size) {
  members = new char[size]; // allocate memory for set
  len = 0; // no members when constructed
}

// Construct a set from another set.
public Set(Set s) {
  members = new char[s.len]; // allocate memory for set
  for(int i=0; i < s.len; i++) members[i] = s[i];
  len = s.len; // number of members
}
```

Sets can be constructed three ways. First, a null set can be created. A null set contains no members, nor does it allocate an array for members. Thus, a null set is simply a placeholder. Second, an empty set can be created of a given size. Finally, a set can be constructed from another set. In this case, the two sets contain the same members, but refer to separate objects.

4. Add the read-only **Length** property and the read-only indexer, as shown here:

```
// Implement read-only Length property.
public int Length {
  get{
    return len;
  }
}

// Implement read-only indexer.
```

7

```
public char this[int idx]{
  get {
    if(idx >= 0 & idx < len) return members[idx];
    else return (char)0;
  }
}
```

The operation of the **Length** property is self-evident. The indexer returns a member of a set given its index. A bounds check is performed to prevent an array overrun. If the index is invalid, the null character is returned.

5. Add the **find( )** method shown here. This method determines if the element passed in **ch** is a member of the set. It returns the index of the element if it is found and –1 if the element is not part of the set.

```
/* See if an element is in the set.
   Return the index of the element
   or -1 if not found. */
int find(char ch) {
  int i;

  for(i=0; i < len; i++)
    if(members[i] == ch) return i;

  return -1;
}
```

6. Begin adding the set operators, starting with set addition. To do this, overload + for objects of type **Set**, as shown here. This version adds an element to a set.

```
// Add a unique element to a set.
public static Set operator +(Set ob, char ch) {
  Set newset = new Set(ob.len + 1); // make a new set one element larger

  // copy elements
  for(int i=0; i < ob.len; i++)
    newset.members[i] = ob.members[i];

  // set len
  newset.len = ob.len;

  // see if element already exists
  if(ob.find(ch) == -1) { // if not found, then add
```

```
    // add new element to new set
    newset.members[newset.len] = ch;
    newset.len++;
  }
  return newset; // return updated set
}
```

This method bears some close examination. First, a new set is created that will hold the contents of the original set referred to by **ob**, plus the new element, **ch**. Notice that it is created one element larger than **ob** to accommodate the new element. Next, the original elements are copied into the new set, and the length of the new set is set to that of the original set. The reason is that **ch** will be added to the set only if it is not already part of the set. Thus, **len** is set to the original length to begin with. It will be increased by 1 if the new element is added. Next, the **find( )** method is called to determine if **ch** is already part of the set. If it is not, then **ch** is added and **len** is updated. In either case, **newset** is returned. Thus, the original set is untouched by this operation.

7. Next, overload – so that it removes an element from the set, as shown here:

```
// Remove an element from the set.
public static Set operator -(Set ob, char ch) {
  Set newset = new Set();
  int i = ob.find(ch); // i will be -1 if element not found

  // copy and compress the remaining elements
  for(int j=0; j < ob.len; j++)
    if(j != i) newset = newset + ob.members[j];

  return newset;
}
```

First, a new null set is created. Second, **find( )** is called to determine whether **ch** is a member of the original set. Recall that **find( )** returns –1 if **ch** is not a member. Next, the elements of the original set are added to the new set, except for the element whose index matches that returned by **find( )**. Thus, the resulting set contains all of the elements of the original set except for **ch**. If **ch** was not part of the original set to begin with, then the two sets are equivalent.

8. Overload the + and – again, as shown here. These versions implement set union and set difference.

```
// Set union.
public static Set operator +(Set ob1, Set ob2) {
  Set newset = new Set(ob1); // copy the first set

  // add unique elements from second set
  for(int i=0; i < ob2.len; i++)
    newset = newset + ob2[i];

  return newset; // return updated set
}

// Set difference.
public static Set operator -(Set ob1, Set ob2) {
  Set newset = new Set(ob1); // copy the first set

  // subtract elements from second set
  for(int i=0; i < ob2.len; i++)
    newset = newset - ob2[i];

  return newset; // return updated set
}
```

As you can see, these methods utilize the previously defined versions of
the + and – operators to help perform their operations. In the case of set
union, a new set is created that contains the elements of the first set. Then,
the elements of the second set are added. Because the + operation adds an
element only if it is not already part of the set, the resulting set is the union
(without duplication) of the two sets. The set difference operator subtracts
matching elements.

9. Here is the complete code for the **Set** class along with the **SetDemo** class
that demonstrates it:

```
/*
   Project 7-1

   A set class for characters.
*/
using System;

class Set {
  char[] members; // this array holds the set
  int len; // number of members

  // Construct a null set.
```

```
public Set() {
  len = 0;
}

// Construct an empty set of a given size.
public Set(int size) {
  members = new char[size]; // allocate memory for set
  len = 0; // no members when constructed
}

// Construct a set from another set.
public Set(Set s) {
  members = new char[s.len]; // allocate memory for set
  for(int i=0; i < s.len; i++) members[i] = s[i];
  len = s.len; // number of members
}

// Implement read-only Length property.
public int Length {
  get{
    return len;
  }
}

// Implement read-only indexer.
public char this[int idx]{
  get {
    if(idx >= 0 & idx < len) return members[idx];
    else return (char)0;
  }
}

/* See if an element is in the set.
   Return the index of the element
   or -1 if not found. */
int find(char ch) {
  int i;

  for(i=0; i < len; i++)
    if(members[i] == ch) return i;

  return -1;
}

// Add a unique element to a set.
public static Set operator +(Set ob, char ch) {
  Set newset = new Set(ob.len + 1); // make a new set one element larger

  // copy elements
```

```
      for(int i=0; i < ob.len; i++)
        newset.members[i] = ob.members[i];

      // set len
      newset.len = ob.len;

      // see if element already exists
      if(ob.find(ch) == -1) { // if not found, then add
        // add new element to new set
        newset.members[newset.len] = ch;
        newset.len++;
      }
      return newset; // return updated set
    }

    // Remove an element from the set.
    public static Set operator -(Set ob, char ch) {
      Set newset = new Set();
      int i = ob.find(ch); // i will be -1 if element not found

      // copy and compress the remaining elements
      for(int j=0; j < ob.len; j++)
        if(j != i) newset = newset + ob.members[j];

      return newset;
    }

    // Set union.
    public static Set operator +(Set ob1, Set ob2) {
      Set newset = new Set(ob1); // copy the first set

      // add unique elements from second set
      for(int i=0; i < ob2.len; i++)
          newset = newset + ob2[i];

      return newset; // return updated set
    }

    // Set difference.
    public static Set operator -(Set ob1, Set ob2) {
      Set newset = new Set(ob1); // copy the first set

      // subtract elements from second set
      for(int i=0; i < ob2.len; i++)
          newset = newset - ob2[i];

      return newset; // return updated set
    }
```

```
}

// Demonstrate the Set class.
class SetDemo {
  public static void Main() {
    // construct 10-element empty Set
    Set s1 = new Set();
    Set s2 = new Set();
    Set s3 = new Set();

    s1 = s1 + 'A';
    s1 = s1 + 'B';
    s1 = s1 + 'C';

    Console.Write("s1 after adding A B C: ");
    for(int i=0; i<s1.Length; i++)
      Console.Write(s1[i] + " ");
    Console.WriteLine();

    s1 = s1 - 'B';
    Console.Write("s1 after s1 = s1 - 'B': ");
    for(int i=0; i<s1.Length; i++)
      Console.Write(s1[i] + " ");
    Console.WriteLine();

    s1 = s1 - 'A';
    Console.Write("s1 after s1 = s1 - 'A': ");
    for(int i=0; i<s1.Length; i++)
      Console.Write(s1[i] + " ");
    Console.WriteLine();

    s1 = s1 - 'C';
    Console.Write("s1 after s1 = s1 - 'C': ");
    for(int i=0; i<s1.Length; i++)
      Console.Write(s1[i] + " ");
    Console.WriteLine("\n");

    s1 = s1 + 'A';
    s1 = s1 + 'B';
    s1 = s1 + 'C';
    Console.Write("s1 after adding A B C: ");
    for(int i=0; i<s1.Length; i++)
      Console.Write(s1[i] + " ");
    Console.WriteLine();

    s2 = s2 + 'A';
    s2 = s2 + 'X';
    s2 = s2 + 'W';
```

```
Console.Write("s2 after adding A X W: ");
for(int i=0; i<s2.Length; i++)
  Console.Write(s2[i] + " ");
Console.WriteLine();

s3 = s1 + s2;
Console.Write("s3 after s3 = s1 + s2: ");
for(int i=0; i<s3.Length; i++)
  Console.Write(s3[i] + " ");
Console.WriteLine();

s3 = s3 - s1;
Console.Write("s3 after s3 - s1: ");
for(int i=0; i<s3.Length; i++)
  Console.Write(s3[i] + " ");
Console.WriteLine("\n");

s2 = s2 - s2; // clear s2
s2 = s2 + 'C'; // add ABC in reverse order
s2 = s2 + 'B';
s2 = s2 + 'A';

Console.Write("s1 is now: ");
for(int i=0; i<s1.Length; i++)
  Console.Write(s1[i] + " ");
Console.WriteLine();

Console.Write("s2 is now: ");
for(int i=0; i<s2.Length; i++)
  Console.Write(s2[i] + " ");
Console.WriteLine();

Console.Write("s3 is now: ");
for(int i=0; i<s3.Length; i++)
  Console.Write(s3[i] + " ");
Console.WriteLine();
  }
}
```

The output from this program is shown here:

```
s1 after adding A B C: A B C
s1 after s1 = s1 - 'B': A C
s1 after s1 = s1 - 'A': C
s1 after s1 = s1 - 'C':

s1 after adding A B C: A B C
```

```
s2 after adding A X W: A X W
s3 after s3 = s1 + s2: A B C X W
s3 after s3 - s1: X W

s1 is now: A B C
s2 is now: C B A
s3 is now: X W
```

✓ Mastery Check

1. Show the general form used for overloading a unary operator. Of what type must the parameter to the operator method be?

2. To allow operations involving a class type and a built-in type, what must you do?

3. Can the ? be overloaded? Can you change the precedence of an operator?

4. What is an indexer? Show its general form.

5. In an indexer, what functions must its **get** and **set** accessors perform?

6. What is a property? Show its general form.

7. Does a property define a storage location? If not, where does a property store its value?

8. Can a property be passed as a **ref** or **out** argument?

9. For the **Set** class developed in Project 7-1, define < and > such that they determine if one set is a subset or a superset of another set. Have < return **true** if the left set is a subset of the set on the right, and **false** otherwise. Have > return **true** if the left set is a superset of the set on the right, and **false** otherwise.

10. For the **Set** class, define the & so that it yields the intersection of two sets.

11. On your own, try adding other **Set** operators. For example, try defining | so that it yields the *symmetric difference* between two sets. (The symmetric difference consists of those elements that the two sets do not have in common.)

Module 8

Inheritance

The Goals of This Module

- Learn inheritance fundamentals
- Use protected access
- Call base class constructors
- Use base
- Create a multilevel class hierarchy
- Understand base class references to derived class objects
- Create virtual methods
- Use abstract classes
- Utilize sealed
- Examine the object class

Inheritance is one of the three foundational principles of object-oriented programming because it allows the creation of hierarchical classifications. Using inheritance, you can create a general class that defines traits common to a set of related items. This class can then be inherited by other, more specific classes, each adding those things that are unique to it.

In the language of C#, a class that is inherited is called a *base class*. The class that does the inheriting is called a *derived class*. Therefore, a derived class is a specialized version of a base class. It inherits all of the variables, methods, properties, and indexers defined by the base class and adds its own, unique elements.

Inheritance Basics

C# supports inheritance by allowing one class to incorporate another class into its declaration. This is done by specifying a base class when a derived class is declared. Let's begin with a short example that illustrates several of the key features of inheritance. The following program creates a base class called **TwoDShape** that stores the width and height of a two-dimensional object, and creates a derived class called **Triangle**. Pay close attention to the way that **Triangle** is declared.

```
// A simple class hierarchy.
using System;

// A class for two-dimensional objects.
class TwoDShape {
  public double width;
  public double height;

  public void showDim() {
    Console.WriteLine("Width and height are " +
                      width + " and " + height);
  }
}

// Triangle is derived from TwoDShape.
class Triangle : TwoDShape {  ←——————————
  public string style;
```

Triangle inherits **TwoDShape**.
Notice the syntax.

```
  public double area() {
    return width * height / 2;  ◄──────
  }

  public void showStyle() {
    Console.WriteLine("Triangle is " + style);
  }
}

class Shapes {
  public static void Main() {
    Triangle t1 = new Triangle();
    Triangle t2 = new Triangle();

    t1.width = 4.0;
    t1.height = 4.0;  ◄──────
    t1.style = "isosceles";

    t2.width = 8.0;
    t2.height = 12.0;
    t2.style = "right";

    Console.WriteLine("Info for t1: ");
    t1.showStyle();
    t1.showDim();
    Console.WriteLine("Area is " + t1.area());

    Console.WriteLine();

    Console.WriteLine("Info for t2: ");
    t2.showStyle();
    t2.showDim();
    Console.WriteLine("Area is " + t2.area());
  }
}
```

Triangle can refer to the members of **TwoDShape** as if they were part of **Triangle**.

All members of **Triangle** are available to **Triangle** objects, even those inherited from **TwoDShape**.

8

The output from this program is shown here:

```
Info for t1:
Triangle is isosceles
Width and height are 4 and 4
Area is 8
```

```
Info for t2:
Triangle is right
Width and height are 8 and 12
Area is 48
```

Here, **TwoDShape** defines the attributes of a "generic" two-dimensional shape, such as a square, rectangle, triangle, and so on. The **Triangle** class creates a specific type of **TwoDShape**, in this case, a triangle. The **Triangle** class includes all of **TwoDShape** and adds the field **style**, the method **area( )**, and the method **showStyle( )**. A description of the type of triangle is stored in **style**, **area( )** computes and returns the area of the triangle, and **showStyle( )** displays the triangle style.

Notice the syntax that is used to inherit a base class. The base class name follows the name of the derived class, and they are separated by a colon. The syntax for inheriting a class is remarkably simple and easy to use.

Because **Triangle** includes all of the members of its base class, **TwoDShape**, it can access **width** and **height** inside **area( )**. Also, inside **Main( )**, objects **t1** and **t2** can refer to **width** and **height** directly, as if they were part of **Triangle**. Figure 8-1 depicts conceptually how **TwoDShape** is incorporated into **Triangle**.

Even though **TwoDShape** is a base for **Triangle**, it is also a completely independent, stand-alone class. Being a base class for a derived class does not mean that the base class cannot be used by itself. For example, the following is perfectly valid:

```
TwoDShape shape = new TwoDShape();

shape.width = 10;
shape.height = 20;

shape.showDim();
```

Of course, an object of **TwoDShape** has no knowledge of or access to any derived classes of **TwoDShape**.

The general form of a **class** declaration that inherits a base class is shown here:

```
class derived-class-name : base-class-name {
  // body of class
}
```

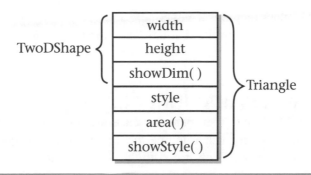

Figure 8-1   A conceptual depiction of the Triangle class

You can specify only one base class for any derived class that you create. C# does not support the inheritance of multiple base classes into a single derived class. (This differs from C++, in which you can inherit multiple base classes. Be aware of this when converting C++ code to C#.) You can, however, create a hierarchy of inheritance in which a derived class becomes a base class of another derived class. Of course, no class can be a base class of itself.

A major advantage of inheritance is that once you have created a base class that defines the attributes common to a set of objects, it can be used to create any number of more specific derived classes. Each derived class can precisely tailor its own classification. For example, here is another class derived from **TwoDShape** that encapsulates rectangles:

```
// A derived class of TwoDShape for rectangles.
class Rectangle : TwoDShape {
  public bool isSquare() {
    if(width == height) return true;
    return false;
  }

  public double area() {
    return width * height;
  }
}
```

8

The **Rectangle** class includes **TwoDShape** and adds the methods **isSquare( )**, which determines if the rectangle is square, and **area( )**, which computes the area of a rectangle.

Member Access and Inheritance

As you learned in Module 6, members of a class are often declared as private to prevent their unauthorized use or tampering. Inheriting a class *does not* overrule the private access restriction. Thus, even though a derived class includes all of the members of its base class, it cannot access those members of the base class that are private. For example, if, as shown here, **width** and **height** are made private in **TwoDShape**, then **Triangle** will not be able to access them.

```
// Private members are not inherited.

// This example will not compile.
using System;

// A class for two-dimensional objects.
class TwoDShape {
  double width;  // now private
  double height; // now private

  public void showDim() {
    Console.WriteLine("Width and height are " +
                      width + " and " + height);
  }
}

// Triangle is derived from TwoDShape.
class Triangle : TwoDShape {
  public string style;

  public double area() {
    return width * height / 2; // error, can't access
  }

  public void showStyle() {
    Console.WriteLine("Triangle is " + style);
  }
}
```

Can't access private members of a base class.

The **Triangle** class will not compile because the reference to **width** and **height** inside the **area( )** method causes an access violation. Since **width** and **height** are now private, they are accessible only by other members of their own class. Derived classes have no access to them.

Remember: A private class member will remain private to its class. It is not accessible by any code outside its class, including derived classes.

At first, you might think that it is a serious restriction that derived classes do not have access to the private members of base classes because it would prevent the use of private members in many situations. However, this is not true; C# provides various solutions. One is to use **protected** members, which is described in the next section. A second is to use public properties to provide access to private data. As you have seen in the preceding modules, C# programmers typically grant access to the private members of a class through methods or by making them into properties. Here is a rewrite of the **TwoDShape** classes that makes **width** and **height** into properties:

```
// Use properties to set and get private members.
using System;

// A class for two-dimensional objects.
class TwoDShape {
  double pri_width;  // now private
  double pri_height; // now private

  // Properties for width and height.
  public double width {              ◄──────────   Here are the **width** and
     get { return pri_width; }                      **height** properties.
     set { pri_width = value; }
  }

  public double height {  ◄──
     get { return pri_height; }
     set { pri_height = value; }
  }

  public void showDim() {
    Console.WriteLine("Width and height are " +
                      width + " and " + height);
  }
}
```

8

```
// A derived class of TwoDShape for triangles.
class Triangle : TwoDShape {
  public string style;

  public double area() {
    return width * height / 2;
  }

  public void showStyle() {
    Console.WriteLine("Triangle is " + style);
  }
}

class Shapes2 {
  public static void Main() {
    Triangle t1 = new Triangle();
    Triangle t2 = new Triangle();

    t1.width = 4.0;
    t1.height = 4.0;
    t1.style = "isosceles";

    t2.width = 8.0;
    t2.height = 12.0;
    t2.style = "right";

    Console.WriteLine("Info for t1: ");
    t1.showStyle();
    t1.showDim();
    Console.WriteLine("Area is " + t1.area());

    Console.WriteLine();

    Console.WriteLine("Info for t2: ");
    t2.showStyle();
    t2.showDim();
    Console.WriteLine("Area is " + t2.area());
  }
}
```

Use of **width** and **height** now OK because access is through properties.

Ask the Expert

Question: I have heard the terms "superclass" and "subclass" used in discussions of Java programming. Do these terms have meaning in C#?

Answer: What Java calls a superclass, C# calls a base class. What Java calls a subclass, C# calls a derived class. You will commonly hear both sets of terms applied to a class of either language, but this book will continue to use the standard C# terms. By the way, C++ also uses the base class, derived class terminology.

1-Minute Drill

- How is a base class inherited by a derived class?
- Does a derived class include the members of its base class?
- Does a derived class have access to the private members of its base class?

Using Protected Access

8

As explained in the preceding section, a private member of a base class is not accessible by a derived class. This would seem to imply that if you wanted a derived class to have access to some member in the base class, it would need to be public. Of course, making the member public also makes it available to all other code, which may not be desirable. Fortunately, this implication is wrong because C# allows you to create a *protected member*. A protected member is public within a class hierarchy, but private outside that hierarchy.

A protected member is created by using the **protected** access modifier. When a member of a class is declared as **protected**, that member is, with one important exception, private. The exception occurs when a protected member is inherited. In this case, a protected member of the base class becomes a protected member

---

- A base class is specified after the derived class' name and is separated from it by a colon.
- Yes.
- No.

of the derived class and is, therefore, accessible by the derived class. Therefore, by using **protected**, you can create class members that are private to their class but that can still be inherited and accessed by a derived class.

Here is a simple example that uses **protected**:

```
// Demonstrate protected.
using System;

class B {                          The fields i and j
  protected int i, j; // private to B, but accessible by D

  public void set(int a, int b) {
    i = a;
    j = b;
  }

  public void show() {
    Console.WriteLine(i + " " + j);
  }
}

class D : B {
  int k; // private

  // D can access B's i and j
  public void setk() {
    k = i * j;              D can access i and j
  }                         because they are protected,
                            not private.
  public void showk() {
    Console.WriteLine(k);
  }
}

class ProtectedDemo {
  public static void Main() {
    D ob = new D();

    ob.set(2, 3); // OK, known to D
    ob.show();    // OK, known to D

    ob.setk();  // OK, part of D
    ob.showk(); // OK, part of D
  }
}
```

In this example, because **B** is inherited by **D** and because **i** and **j** are declared as **protected** in **B**, the **setk( )** method can access them. If **i** and **j** had been declared as private by **B**, then **D** would not have access to them, and the program would not compile.

Like **public** and **private**, **protected** status stays with a member no matter how many layers of inheritance are involved. Therefore, when a derived class is used as a base class for another derived class, any protected member of the initial base class that is inherited by the first derived class is also inherited as protected by a second derived class.

Constructors and Inheritance

In a hierarchy, it is possible for both base classes and derived classes to have their own constructors. This raises an important question: what constructor is responsible for building an object of the derived class? The one in the base class, the one in the derived class, or both? The answer is this: the constructor for the base class constructs the base class portion of the object, and the constructor for the derived class constructs the derived class part. This makes sense because the base class has no knowledge of or access to any element in a derived class. Thus, their construction must be separate. The preceding examples have relied upon the default constructors created automatically by C#, so this was not an issue. However, in practice, most classes will have constructors. Here, you will see how to handle this situation.

When only the derived class defines a constructor, the process is straight-forward: simply construct the derived class object. The base class portion of the object is constructed automatically using its default constructor. For example, here is a reworked version of **Triangle** that defines a constructor. It also makes **style** private since it is now set by the constructor.

```
// Add a constructor to Triangle.
using System;

// A class for two-dimensional objects.
class TwoDShape {
  double pri_width;  // private
  double pri_height; // private

  // properties for width and height.
```

8

```
   public double width {
      get { return pri_width; }
      set { pri_width = value; }
   }

   public double height {
      get { return pri_height; }
      set { pri_height = value; }
   }

   public void showDim() {
     Console.WriteLine("Width and height are " +
                        width + " and " + height);
   }
}

// A derived class of TwoDShape for triangles.
class Triangle : TwoDShape {
  string style; // private

  // Constructor
  public Triangle(string s, double w, double h) {
    width = w;  // init the base class
    height = h; // init the base class

    style = s;  // init the derived class
  }

  public double area() {
    return width * height / 2;
  }

  public void showStyle() {
    Console.WriteLine("Triangle is " + style);
  }
}

class Shapes3 {
  public static void Main() {
    Triangle t1 = new Triangle("isosceles", 4.0, 4.0);
    Triangle t2 = new Triangle("right", 8.0, 12.0);

    Console.WriteLine("Info for t1: ");
    t1.showStyle();
```

Construct **TwoDShape** portion of object.

```
   t1.showDim();
   Console.WriteLine("Area is " + t1.area());

   Console.WriteLine();

   Console.WriteLine("Info for t2: ");
   t2.showStyle();
   t2.showDim();
   Console.WriteLine("Area is " + t2.area());
   }
}
```

Here, **Triangle**'s constructor initializes the members of **TwoDShape** that it inherits along with its own **style** field.

When both the base class and the derived class define constructors, the process is a bit more complicated because both the base class and derived class constructors must be executed. In this case you must use another of C#'s keywords: **base**, which has two uses. The first calls a base class constructor. The second is used to access a member of the base class that has been hidden by a member of a derived class. Here, we will look at its first use.

Calling Base Class Constructors

A derived class can call a constructor defined in its base class by using an expanded form of the derived class' constructor declaration and the **base** keyword. The general form of this expanded declaration is shown here:

```
derived-constructor(parameter-list) : base(arg-list) {
   // body of constructor
}
```

Here, *arg-list* specifies any arguments needed by the constructor in the base class. Notice the placement of the colon.

To see how **base** is used, consider the version of **TwoDShape** in the following program. It defines a constructor that initializes the **width** and **height** properties.

```
// Add constructors to TwoDShape.
using System;

// A class for two-dimensional objects.
```

```csharp
class TwoDShape {
  double pri_width;  // private
  double pri_height; // private

  // Constructor for TwoDShape.
  public TwoDShape(double w, double h) {
    width = w;
    height = h;
  }

  // properties for width and height.
  public double width {
    get { return pri_width; }
    set { pri_width = value; }
  }

  public double height {
    get { return pri_height; }
    set { pri_height = value; }
  }

  public void showDim() {
    Console.WriteLine("Width and height are " +
                      width + " and " + height);
  }
}

// A derived class of TwoDShape for triangles.
class Triangle : TwoDShape {
  string style; // private

  // Call the base class constructor.
  public Triangle(string s, double w, double h) : base(w, h) {
    style = s;
  }

  public double area() {
    return width * height / 2;
  }

  public void showStyle() {
    Console.WriteLine("Triangle is " + style);
  }
}
```

Use **base** to execute the **TwoDShape** constructor.

```
class Shapes4 {
  public static void Main() {
    Triangle t1 = new Triangle("isosceles", 4.0, 4.0);
    Triangle t2 = new Triangle("right", 8.0, 12.0);

    Console.WriteLine("Info for t1: ");
    t1.showStyle();
    t1.showDim();
    Console.WriteLine("Area is " + t1.area());

    Console.WriteLine();

    Console.WriteLine("Info for t2: ");
    t2.showStyle();
    t2.showDim();
    Console.WriteLine("Area is " + t2.area());
  }
}
```

Here, **Triangle( )** calls **base** with the parameters w and h. This causes the
TwoDShape( ) constructor to be called, which initializes **width** and **height**
using these values. **Triangle** no longer initializes these values itself. It need
only initialize the value unique to it: **style**. This leaves **TwoDShape** free to
construct its subobject in any manner that it chooses. Furthermore, **TwoDShape**
can add functionality about which existing derived classes have no knowledge,
thus preventing existing code from breaking.

Any form of constructor defined by the base class can be called by **base**.
The constructor executed will be the one that matches the arguments. For
example, here are expanded versions of both **TwoDShape** and **Triangle** that
include default constructors and constructors that take one argument.

```
// Add more constructors to TwoDShape.
using System;

class TwoDShape {
  double pri_width;  // private
  double pri_height; // private

  // Default constructor.
  public TwoDShape() {
    width = height = 0.0;
```

8

```
    }

    // Constructor for TwoDShape.
    public TwoDShape(double w, double h) {
      width = w;
      height = h;
    }

    // Construct object with equal width and height.
    public TwoDShape(double x) {
      width = height = x;
    }

    // Properties for width and height.
    public double width {
      get { return pri_width; }
      set { pri_width = value; }
    }

    public double height {
      get { return pri_height; }
      set { pri_height = value; }
    }

    public void showDim() {
      Console.WriteLine("Width and height are " +
                        width + " and " + height);
    }
  }

  // A derived class of TwoDShape for triangles.
  class Triangle : TwoDShape {
    string style; // private

    /* A default constructor. This automatically invokes
       the default constructor of TwoDShape. */
    public Triangle() {
      style = "null";
    }

    // Constructor
    public Triangle(string s, double w, double h) : base(w, h) {
      style = s;
    }
```

Use **base** to call the various forms of the **TwoDShape** constructor.

```
  // Construct an isosceles triangle.
  public Triangle(double x) : base(x) {
    style = "isosceles";
  }

  public double area() {
    return width * height / 2;
  }

  public void showStyle() {
    Console.WriteLine("Triangle is " + style);
  }
}

class Shapes5 {
  public static void Main() {
    Triangle t1 = new Triangle();
    Triangle t2 = new Triangle("right", 8.0, 12.0);
    Triangle t3 = new Triangle(4.0);

    t1 = t2;

    Console.WriteLine("Info for t1: ");
    t1.showStyle();
    t1.showDim();
    Console.WriteLine("Area is " + t1.area());

    Console.WriteLine();

    Console.WriteLine("Info for t2: ");
    t2.showStyle();
    t2.showDim();
    Console.WriteLine("Area is " + t2.area());

    Console.WriteLine();

    Console.WriteLine("Info for t3: ");
    t3.showStyle();
    t3.showDim();
    Console.WriteLine("Area is " + t3.area());

    Console.WriteLine();
  }
}
```

8

Here is the output from this version:

```
Info for t1:
Triangle is right
Width and height are 8 and 12
Area is 48

Info for t2:
Triangle is right
Width and height are 8 and 12
Area is 48

Info for t3:
Triangle is isosceles
Width and height are 4 and 4
Area is 8
```

Let's review the key concepts behind **base**. When a derived class specifies a **base** clause, it is calling the constructor of its immediate base class. Thus, **base** always refers to the base class immediately above the calling class. This is true even in a multileveled hierarchy. You pass arguments to the base constructor by specifying them as arguments to **base**. If no **base** clause is present, then the base class' default constructor is called automatically.

1-Minute Drill

- How does a derived class execute its base class' constructor?
- Can parameters be passed via **base**?
- Does **base** always refer to the immediate base class' constructor?

- It specifies a **base** clause.
- Yes.
- Yes.

Inheritance and Name Hiding

It is possible for a derived class to define a member that has the same name as a member in its base class. When this happens, the member in the base class is hidden within the derived class. While this is not technically an error in C#, the compiler will issue a warning message. This warning alerts you to the fact that a name is being hidden. If your intent is to hide a base class member, then to prevent this warning, the derived class member must be preceded by the **new** keyword. Understand that this use of **new** is separate and distinct from its use when creating an object instance.

Here is an example of name hiding:

```
// An example of inheritance-related name hiding.
using System;

class A {
  public int i = 0;
}

// Create a derived class.
class B : A {
  new int i; // this i hides the i in A

  public B(int b) {
    i = b; // i in B
  }

  public void show() {
    Console.WriteLine("i in derived class: " + i);
  }
}

class NameHiding {
  public static void Main() {
    B ob = new B(2);

    ob.show();
  }
}
```

The i in **A** is hidden by the i in **B**. Notice the use of **new**.

8

First, notice the use of **new**. In essence, it tells the compiler that you know that a new variable called **i** is being created that hides the **i** in the base class **A**. If you leave **new** out, a warning is generated.

The output produced by this program is shown here:

```
i in derived class: 2
```

Since **B** defines its own instance variable called **i**, it hides the **i** in **A**. Therefore, when **show( )** is invoked on an object of type **B**, the value of **i** as defined by **B** is displayed—not the one defined in **A**.

Using base to Access a Hidden Name

There is a second form of **base** that acts somewhat like **this**, except that it always refers to the base class of the derived class in which it is used. This usage has the following general form:

base.*member*

Here, *member* can be either a method or an instance variable. This form of **base** is most applicable to situations in which member names of a derived class hide members by the same name in the base class. Consider this version of the class hierarchy from the preceding example:

```
// Using base to overcome name hiding.
using System;

class A {
  public int i = 0;
}

// Create a derived class.
class B : A {
  new int i; // this i hides the i in A

  public B(int a, int b) {
    base.i = a; // this uncovers the i in A
    i = b; // i in B
  }

  public void show() {
    // this displays the i in A.
```

Here, **base.i** refers to the **i** in **A**.

```
      Console.WriteLine("i in base class: " + base.i);

      // this displays the i in B
      Console.WriteLine("i in derived class: " + i);
  }
}

class UncoverName {
  public static void Main() {
    B ob = new B(1, 2);

    ob.show();
  }
}
```

This program displays the following:

```
i in base class: 1
i in derived class: 2
```

Although the instance variable **i** in **B** hides the **i** in **A**, **base** allows access to the **i** defined in the base class.

Hidden methods can also be called through the use of **base**. For example:

8

```
// Call a hidden method.
using System;

class A {
  public int i = 0;

  // show() in A
  public void show() {
    Console.WriteLine("i in base class: " + i);
  }
}

// Create a derived class.
class B : A {
  new int i; // this i hides the i in A

  public B(int a, int b) {
    base.i = a; // this uncovers the i in A
    i = b; // i in B
  }
```

```
  // This hides show() in A.
  new public void show() {
    base.show(); // this calls show() in A

    // this displays the i in B
    Console.WriteLine("i in derived class: " + i);
  }
}

class UncoverName {
  public static void Main() {
    B ob = new B(1, 2);

    ob.show();
  }
}
```

This **show( )** hides the one in **A**.

This calls the hidden **show( )**.

The output from the program is shown here:

```
i in base class: 1
i in derived class: 2
```

As you can see, **base.show( )** calls the base class version of **show( )**.

One other point: notice that **new** is used in this program to tell the compiler that you know that a new method called **show( )** is being created that hides the **show( )** in A.

1-Minute Drill

- When a base-class name is hidden by a derived class, what keyword should precede that name in the derived class?

- To uncover a name in a base class, a derived class uses what keyword?

- Can a derived class call a method in a base class that has been hidden by the derived class?

- **new**.
- **base**.
- Yes.

TruckDemo.cs

Project 8-1: Extending the Vehicle Class

To illustrate the power of inheritance, we will extend the **Vehicle** class first developed in Module 4. As you should recall, **Vehicle** encapsulates information about vehicles, including the number of passengers they can carry, their fuel capacity, and their fuel consumption rate. We can use the **Vehicle** class as a starting point from which more specialized classes are developed. For example, one type of vehicle is a truck. An important attribute of a truck is its cargo capacity. Thus, to create a **Truck** class, you can inherit **Vehicle**, adding an instance variable that stores the carrying capacity. In this project, you will create the **Truck** class. In the process, the instance variables in **Vehicle** will be made private, and properties are provided to get and set their values.

Step-by-Step

1. Create a file called **TruckDemo.cs**, and copy the last implementation of **Vehicle** from Module 4 into the file.

2. Create the **Truck** class as shown here:

```
// Use Vehicle to create a Truck specialization.
class Truck : Vehicle {
  int pri_cargocap; // cargo capacity in pounds

  // This is a constructor for Truck.
  public Truck(int p, int f, int m, int c) : base(p, f, m)
  {
    cargocap = c;
  }

  // Property for cargocap.
  public int cargocap {
    get { return pri_cargocap; }
    set { pri_cargocap = value; }
  }
}
```

Here, **Truck** inherits **Vehicle**, adding the **cargocap** property. Thus, **Truck** includes all of the general vehicle attributes defined by **Vehicle**. It need add only those items that are unique to its own class.

3. Make the instance variables of **Vehicle** private, and rename them as shown next.

8

```
int pri_passengers; // number of passengers
int pri_fuelcap;    // fuel capacity in gallons
int pri_mpg;        // fuel consumption in miles per gallon
```

4. Add the properties that access these variables, as shown here:

```
// Properties
public int passengers {
  get { return pri_passengers; }
  set { pri_passengers = value; }
}

public int fuelcap {
  get { return pri_fuelcap; }
  set { pri_fuelcap = value; }
}

public int mpg {
  get { return pri_mpg; }
  set { pri_mpg = value; }
}
```

5. Here is an entire program that demonstrates the **Truck** class:

```
/*
  Project 8-1

  Build a derived class of Vehicle for trucks.
*/
using System;

class Vehicle {
  int pri_passengers; // number of passengers
  int pri_fuelcap;    // fuel capacity in gallons
  int pri_mpg;        // fuel consumption in miles per gallon

  // This is a constructor for Vehicle.
  public Vehicle(int p, int f, int m) {
    passengers = p;
    fuelcap = f;
    mpg = m;
  }

  // Return the range.
  public int range() {
```

```
      return mpg * fuelcap;
    }

    // Compute fuel needed for a given distance.
    public double fuelneeded(int miles) {
      return (double) miles / mpg;
    }

    // Properties
    public int passengers {
      get { return pri_passengers; }
      set { pri_passengers = value; }
    }

    public int fuelcap {
      get { return pri_fuelcap; }
      set { pri_fuelcap = value; }
    }

    public int mpg {
      get { return pri_mpg; }
      set { pri_mpg = value; }
    }
}

// Use Vehicle to create a Truck specialization.
class Truck : Vehicle {
  int pri_cargocap; // cargo capacity in pounds

    // This is a constructor for Truck.
    public Truck(int p, int f, int m, int c) : base(p, f, m)
    {
      cargocap = c;
    }

    // Property for cargocap.
    public int cargocap {
      get { return pri_cargocap; }
      set { pri_cargocap = value; }
    }
}

class TruckDemo {
  public static void Main() {
```

```
// construct some trucks
Truck semi = new Truck(2, 200, 7, 44000);
Truck pickup = new Truck(3, 28, 15, 2000);
double gallons;
int dist = 252;

gallons = semi.fuelneeded(dist);

Console.WriteLine("Semi can carry " + semi.cargocap +
                  " pounds.");
Console.WriteLine("To go " + dist + " miles semi needs " +
                  gallons + " gallons of fuel.\n");

gallons = pickup.fuelneeded(dist);

Console.WriteLine("Pickup can carry " + pickup.cargocap +
                  " pounds.");
Console.WriteLine("To go " + dist + " miles pickup needs " +
                  gallons + " gallons of fuel.");
  }
}
```

6. The output from this program is shown here:

```
Semi can carry 44000 pounds.
To go 252 miles semi needs 36 gallons of fuel.

Pickup can carry 2000 pounds.
To go 252 miles pickup needs 16.8 gallons of fuel.
```

7. Many other types of classes can be derived from **Vehicle**. For example, the following skeleton creates an off-road class that stores the ground clearance of the vehicle:

```
// Create an off-road vehicle class
class OffRoad : Vehicle {
  int groundClearance; // ground clearance in inches

  // ...
}
```

The key point is that once you have created a base class that defines the general aspects of an object, that base class can be inherited to form specialized classes. Each derived class simply adds its own, unique attributes. This is the essence of inheritance.

Creating a Multilevel Hierarchy

Up to this point, we have been using simple class hierarchies consisting of only a base class and a derived class. However, you can build hierarchies that contain as many layers of inheritance as you like. As mentioned, it is perfectly acceptable to use a derived class as a base class of another. For example, given three classes called **A**, **B**, and **C**, **C** can be derived from **B**, which can be derived from **A**. When this type of situation occurs, each derived class inherits all of the traits found in all of its base classes. In this case, **C** inherits all aspects of **B** and **A**.

To see how a multilevel hierarchy can be useful, consider the following program. In it, the derived class **Triangle** is used as a base class to create the derived class called **ColorTriangle**. **ColorTriangle** inherits all of the traits of **Triangle** and **TwoDShape**, and adds a field called **color**, which holds the color of the triangle.

```
// A multilevel hierarchy.
using System;

class TwoDShape {
  double pri_width;  // private
  double pri_height; // private

  // Default constructor.
  public TwoDShape() {
    width = height = 0.0;
  }

  // Constructor for TwoDShape.
  public TwoDShape(double w, double h) {
    width = w;
    height = h;
  }

  // Construct object with equal width and height.
  public TwoDShape(double x) {
    width = height = x;
  }
```

8

```csharp
  // Properties for width and height.
  public double width {
    get { return pri_width; }
    set { pri_width = value; }
  }

  public double height {
    get { return pri_height; }
    set { pri_height = value; }
  }

  public void showDim() {
    Console.WriteLine("Width and height are " +
                      width + " and " + height);
  }
}

// A derived class of TwoDShape for triangles.
class Triangle : TwoDShape {
  string style; // private

  /* A default constructor. This invokes the default
     constructor of TwoDShape. */
  public Triangle() {
    style = "null";
  }

  // Constructor
  public Triangle(string s, double w, double h) : base(w, h) {
    style = s;
  }

  // Construct an isosceles triangle.
  public Triangle(double x) : base(x) {
    style = "isosceles";
  }

  public double area() {
    return width * height / 2;
  }
```

```
   public void showStyle() {
     Console.WriteLine("Triangle is " + style);
   }
}

// Extend Triangle.
class ColorTriangle : Triangle {
  string color;

  public ColorTriangle(string c, string s,
            double w, double h) : base(s, w, h) {
    color = c;
  }

  // Display the color.
  public void showColor() {
    Console.WriteLine("Color is " + color);
  }
}

class Shapes6 {
  public static void Main() {
    ColorTriangle t1 =
        new ColorTriangle("Blue", "right", 8.0, 12.0);
    ColorTriangle t2 =
        new ColorTriangle("Red", "isosceles", 2.0, 2.0);

    Console.WriteLine("Info for t1: ");
    t1.showStyle();
    t1.showDim();
    t1.showColor();
    Console.WriteLine("Area is " + t1.area());

    Console.WriteLine();

    Console.WriteLine("Info for t2: ");
    t2.showStyle();
    t2.showDim();
    t2.showColor();
    Console.WriteLine("Area is " + t2.area());
  }
}
```

ColorTriangle inherits **Triangle**, which is descended from **TwoDShape**, so **ColorTriangle** includes all members of **Triangle** and **TwoDShape**.

A **ColorTriangle** object can call methods defined by itself and its base classes.

8

The output of this program is shown here:

```
Info for t1:
Triangle is right
Width and height are 8 and 12
Color is Blue
Area is 48

Info for t2:
Triangle is isosceles
Width and height are 2 and 2
Color is Red
Area is 2
```

Because of inheritance, **ColorTriangle** can make use of the previously defined classes of **Triangle** and **TwoDShape**, adding only the extra information it needs for its own, specific application. This is part of the value of inheritance— it allows the reuse of code.

This example illustrates one other important point: **base** always refers to the constructor in the closest base class. The **base** in **ColorTriangle** calls the constructor in **Triangle**. The **base** in **Triangle** calls the constructor in **TwoDShape**. In a class hierarchy, if a base class constructor requires parameters, then all derived classes must pass those parameters "up the line." This is true whether or not a derived class needs parameters of its own.

When Are Constructors Called?

In the foregoing discussion of inheritance and class hierarchies, an important question may have occurred to you: when a derived class object is created, whose constructor is executed first? The one in the derived class or the one defined by the base class? For example, given a derived class called **B** and a base class called **A**, is A's constructor called before B's, or vice versa? The answer is that in a class hierarchy, constructors are called in order of derivation, from base class to derived class. Furthermore, this order is the same whether or not **base** is used. If **base** is not used, then the default (parameterless) constructor of each base class will be executed. The following program illustrates when constructors are executed:

```
// Demonstrate when constructors are called.
using System;

// Create a base class.
class A {
  public A() {
    Console.WriteLine("Constructing A.");
  }
}

// Create a class derived from A.
class B : A {
  public B() {
    Console.WriteLine("Constructing B.");
  }
}

// Create a class derived from B.
class C : B {
  public C() {
    Console.WriteLine("Constructing C.");
  }
}

class OrderOfConstruction {
  public static void Main() {

    C c = new C();
  }
}
```

The output from this program is shown here:

```
Constructing A
Constructing B
Constructing C
```

As you can see, the constructors are called in order of derivation.

It makes sense that constructor functions are executed in order of derivation. Because a base class has no knowledge of any derived class, any initialization it needs to perform is separate from and possibly prerequisite to any initialization performed by the derived class. Therefore, it must be executed first.

Base Class References and Derived Objects

As you know, C# is a strongly typed language. Aside from the standard conversions and automatic promotions that apply to its simple types, type compatibility is strictly enforced. Therefore, a reference variable for one class type cannot normally refer to an object of another class type. For example, consider the following program:

```
// This will not compile.
class X {
  int a;

  public X(int i) { a = i; }
}

class Y {
  int a;

  public Y(int i) { a = i; }
}

class IncompatibleRef {
  public static void Main() {
    X x = new X(10);
    X x2;
    Y y = new Y(5);

    x2 = x; // OK, both of same type

    x2 = y; // Error, not of same type        ◄─── These references
  }                                                are not compatible.
}
```

Here, even though class **X** and class **Y** are physically the same, it is not possible to assign an **X** reference to a **Y** object, because they have different types. In general, an object reference variable can refer only to objects of its type.

There is, however, an important exception to C#'s strict type enforcement. A reference variable of a base class can be assigned a reference to an object of any class derived from that base class. Here is an example:

```
// A base class reference can refer to a derived class object.
using System;

class X {
  public int a;

  public X(int i) {
    a = i;
  }
}

class Y : X {
  public int b;

  public Y(int i, int j) : base(j) {
    b = i;
  }
}

class BaseRef {
  public static void Main() {
    X x = new X(10);
    X x2;
    Y y = new Y(5, 6);

    x2 = x; // OK, both of same type
    Console.WriteLine("x2.a: " + x2.a);

    x2 = y; // still OK because Y is derived from X
    Console.WriteLine("x2.a: " + x2.a);

    // X references know only about X members
    x2.a = 19; // OK
//    x2.b = 27; // Error, X doesn't have a b member
  }
}
```

> OK because **Y** is derived from **X**, thus **x2** can refer to **y**.

Here, **Y** is now derived from **X**; thus it is permissible for **x2** to be assigned a reference to a **Y** object.

It is important to understand that it is the type of the reference variable—not the type of the object that it refers to—that determines what members can be accessed. That is, when a reference to a derived class object is assigned to a base class reference variable, you will have access only to those parts of the object defined by the base class. This is why **x2** can't access **b** even when it refers to a **Y** object. This makes sense, because the base class has no knowledge of what a derived class adds to it. This is why the last line of code in the program is commented out.

Although the preceding discussion may seem a bit esoteric, it has some important practical applications. One is described here. The other is discussed later in this module, when virtual methods are covered.

An important place where derived class references are assigned to base class variables is when constructors are called in a class hierarchy. As you know, it is common for a class to define a constructor that takes an object of its class as a parameter. This allows the class to construct a copy of an object. Classes derived from such a class can take advantage of this feature. For example, consider the following versions of **TwoDShape** and **Triangle**. Both add constructors that take an object as a parameter.

```csharp
// Pass a derived class reference to a base class reference.
using System;

class TwoDShape {
  double pri_width;  // private
  double pri_height; // private

  // Default constructor.
  public TwoDShape() {
    width = height = 0.0;
  }

  // Constructor for TwoDShape.
  public TwoDShape(double w, double h) {
    width = w;
    height = h;
  }

  // Construct object with equal width and height.
  public TwoDShape(double x) {
    width = height = x;
  }
```

```
    // Construct object from an object.
    public TwoDShape(TwoDShape ob) {          ← Construct object
      width = ob.width;                            from an object.
      height = ob.height;
    }

    // Properties for width and height.
    public double width {
       get { return pri_width; }
       set { pri_width = value; }
    }

    public double height {
       get { return pri_height; }
       set { pri_height = value; }
    }

    public void showDim() {
      Console.WriteLine("Width and height are " +
                        width + " and " + height);
    }
}

// A derived class of TwoDShape for triangles.
class Triangle : TwoDShape {
  string style; // private

  // A default constructor.
  public Triangle() {
    style = "null";
  }

  // Constructor for Triangle.
  public Triangle(string s, double w, double h) : base(w, h) {
    style = s;
  }

  // Construct an isosceles triangle.
  public Triangle(double x) : base(x) {
    style = "isosceles";
  }

  // Construct an object from an object.
  public Triangle(Triangle ob) : base(ob) {
    style = ob.style;
```

Pass a **Triangle** reference to **TwoDShape**'s constructor.

8

```
  }

  public double area() {
    return width * height / 2;
  }

  public void showStyle() {
    Console.WriteLine("Triangle is " + style);
  }
}

class Shapes7 {
  public static void Main() {
    Triangle t1 = new Triangle("right", 8.0, 12.0);

    // make a copy of t1
    Triangle t2 = new Triangle(t1);

    Console.WriteLine("Info for t1: ");
    t1.showStyle();
    t1.showDim();
    Console.WriteLine("Area is " + t1.area());

    Console.WriteLine();

    Console.WriteLine("Info for t2: ");
    t2.showStyle();
    t2.showDim();
    Console.WriteLine("Area is " + t2.area());
  }
}
```

In this program, **t2** is constructed from **t1** and is, thus, identical. The output is shown here:

```
Info for t1:
Triangle is right
Width and height are 8 and 12
Area is 48

Info for t2:
Triangle is right
Width and height are 8 and 12
Area is 48
```

Pay special attention to this **Triangle** constructor:

```
// Construct an object from an object.
public Triangle(Triangle ob) : base(ob) {
  style = ob.style;
}
```

It receives an object of type **Triangle**, and it passes that object (through **base**) to this **TwoDShape** constructor:

```
// Construct object from an object.
public TwoDShape(TwoDShape ob) {
  width = ob.width;
  height = ob.height;
}
```

The key point is that **TwoDShape( )** is expecting a **TwoDShape** object. However, **Triangle( )** passes it a **Triangle** object. As explained, the reason this works is because a base class reference can refer to a derived class object. Thus, it is perfectly acceptable to pass **TwoDShape( )** a reference to an object of a class derived from **TwoDShape**. Because the **TwoDShape( )** constructor is initializing only those portions of the derived class object that are members of **TwoDShape**, it doesn't matter that the object might also contain other members added by derived classes.

1-Minute Drill

- Can a derived class be used as a base class for another derived class?
- In a class hierarchy, in what order are the constructors called?
- Given that **Jet** is derived from **Airplane**, can an **Airplane** reference refer to a **Jet** object?

8

- Yes.
- Constructors are called in order of derivation.
- Yes. In all cases, a base class reference can refer to a derived class object, but not vice versa.

Virtual Methods and Overriding

A *virtual method* is a method that is declared as **virtual** in a base class and redefined in one or more derived classes. Thus, each derived class can have its own version of a virtual method. Virtual methods are interesting because of what happens when one is called through a base class reference. In this situation, C# determines which version of the method to call based upon the *type* of the object *referred to* by the reference—and this determination is made *at runtime*. Thus, when different objects are referred to, different versions of the virtual method are executed. In other words, it is the type of the object being referred to (not the type of the reference) that determines which version of the virtual method will be executed. Therefore, if a base class contains a virtual method and classes are derived from that base class, then when different types of objects are referred to through a base class reference, different versions of the virtual method are executed.

You declare a method as virtual inside a base class by preceding its declaration with the keyword **virtual**. When a virtual method is redefined by a derived class, the **override** modifier is used. Thus, the process of redefining a virtual method inside a derived class is called *method overriding*. When overriding a method, the names and the type signatures of the override method must be the same as the virtual method that is being overridden. Also, a virtual method cannot be specified as **static** or **abstract** (discussed later in this module).

Method overriding forms the basis for one of C#'s most powerful concepts: *dynamic method dispatch*. Dynamic method dispatch is the mechanism by which a call to an overridden function is resolved at runtime, rather than at compile time. Dynamic method dispatch is important because this is how C# implements runtime polymorphism.

Here is an example that illustrates virtual methods and overriding:

```
// Demonstrate a virtual method.
using System;

class Base {
  // Create virtual method in the base class.
  public virtual void who() {          ◄——————  Declare a virtual method.
    Console.WriteLine("who() in Base");
  }
}
```

```
class Derived1 : Base {
  // Override who() in a derived class.
  public override void who() {
    Console.WriteLine("who() in Derived1");
  }
}

class Derived2 : Base {
  // Override who() again in another derived class.
  public override void who() {
    Console.WriteLine("who() in Derived2");
  }
}

class OverrideDemo {
  public static void Main() {
    Base baseOb = new Base();
    Derived1 dOb1 = new Derived1();
    Derived2 dOb2 = new Derived2();

    Base baseRef; // a base-class reference

    baseRef = baseOb;
    baseRef.who();

    baseRef = dOb1;
    baseRef.who();

    baseRef = dOb2;
    baseRef.who();
  }
}
```

Override the
virtual method.

In each case, the version
of **who( )** to call is
determined at runtime
by the type of object
being referred to.

The output from the program is shown here:

```
who() in Base
who() in Derived1
who() in Derived2
```

This program creates a base class called **Base** and two derived classes of it,
called **Derived1** and **Derived2**. **Base** declares a method called **who( )**, and the
derived classes override it. Inside the **Main( )** method, objects of type **Base**,

Derived1, and **Derived2** are declared. Also, a reference of type **Base**, called **baseRef**, is declared. The program then assigns a reference to each type of object to **baseRef** and uses that reference to call **who( )**. As the output shows, the version of **who( )** executed is determined by the type of object being referred to at the time of the call, not by the class type of **baseRef**.

It is not necessary to override a virtual method. If a derived class does not provide its own version of a virtual method, then the one in the base class is used. For example:

```
/* When a virtual method is not overridden,
   the base class method is used. */
using System;

class Base {
  // Create virtual method in the base class.
  public virtual void who() {
    Console.WriteLine("who() in Base");
  }
}

class Derived1 : Base {
  // Override who() in a derived class.
  public override void who() {
    Console.WriteLine("who() in Derived1");
  }
}

class Derived2 : Base {        ◄──────────  No override of who( ) here
  // This class does not override who().
}

class NoOverrideDemo {
  public static void Main() {
    Base baseOb = new Base();
    Derived1 dOb1 = new Derived1();
    Derived2 dOb2 = new Derived2();

    Base baseRef; // a base-class reference

    baseRef = baseOb;
    baseRef.who();
```

```
    baseRef = dOb1;
    baseRef.who();

    baseRef = dOb2;
    baseRef.who(); // calls Base's who()
  }
}
```

Call **Base**'s **who( )**.

The output from this program is shown here:

```
who() in Base
who() in Derived1
who() in Base
```

Here, **Derived2** does not override **who( )**. Thus, when **who( )** is called on a **Derived2** object, the **who( )** in **Base** is executed.

Why Overridden Methods?

Overridden methods allow C# to support runtime polymorphism. Polymorphism is essential to object-oriented programming for one reason: it allows a general class to specify methods that will be common to all of its derivatives, while allowing derived classes to define the specific implementation of some or all of those methods. Overridden methods are another way that C# implements the "one interface, multiple methods" aspect of polymorphism.

Part of the key to successfully applying polymorphism is understanding that the base classes and derived classes form a hierarchy that moves from lesser to greater specialization. Used correctly, the base class provides all elements that a derived class can use directly. It also defines those methods that the derived class must implement on its own. This allows the derived class the flexibility

8

Ask the Expert

Question: Can properties be virtual?

Answer: Yes. Properties can be modified by the **virtual** keyword and overridden using **override**. The same is true for indexers.

to define its own methods, yet still enforces a consistent interface. Thus, by combining inheritance with overridden methods, a base class can define the general form of the methods that will be used by all of its derived classes.

Applying Virtual Methods

To better understand the power of virtual methods, we will apply it to the **TwoDShape** class. In the preceding examples, each class derived from **TwoDShape** defines a method called **area( )**. This suggests that it might be better to make **area( )** a virtual method of the **TwoDShape** class, allowing each derived class to override it, defining how the area is calculated for the type of shape that the class encapsulates. The following program does this. For convenience, it also adds a name field to **TwoDShape**. (This makes it easier to demonstrate the classes.)

```
// Use virtual methods and polymorphism.
using System;

class TwoDShape {
  double pri_width;  // private
  double pri_height; // private
  string pri_name;   // private

  // A default constructor.
  public TwoDShape() {
    width = height = 0.0;
    name = "null";
  }

  // Parameterized constructor.
  public TwoDShape(double w, double h, string n) {
    width = w;
    height = h;
    name = n;
  }

  // Construct object with equal width and height.
  public TwoDShape(double x, string n) {
    width = height = x;
    name = n;
  }

  // Construct an object from an object.
```

```
  public TwoDShape(TwoDShape ob) {
    width = ob.width;
    height = ob.height;
    name = ob.name;
  }

  // Properties for width, height, and name
  public double width {
    get { return pri_width; }
    set { pri_width = value; }
  }

  public double height {
    get { return pri_height; }
    set { pri_height = value; }
  }

  public string name {
    get { return pri_name; }
    set { pri_name = value; }
  }

  public void showDim() {
    Console.WriteLine("Width and height are " +
                      width + " and " + height);
  }

  public virtual double area() {
    Console.WriteLine("area() must be overridden");
    return 0.0;
  }
}

// A derived class of TwoDShape for triangles.
class Triangle : TwoDShape {
  string style; // private

  // A default constructor.
  public Triangle() {
    style = "null";
  }

  // Constructor for Triangle.
  public Triangle(string s, double w, double h) :
```

The **area( )** method defined by **TwoDShape** is now virtual.

8

```
      base(w, h, "triangle") {
        style = s;
    }

    // Construct an isosceles triangle.
    public Triangle(double x) : base(x, "triangle") {
      style = "isosceles";
    }

    // Construct an object from an object.
    public Triangle(Triangle ob) : base(ob) {
      style = ob.style;
    }

    // Override area() for Triangle.
    public override double area() {        ◄——— Override **area( )** for **Triangle**.
      return width * height / 2;
    }

    public void showStyle() {
      Console.WriteLine("Triangle is " + style);
    }
}

// A derived class of TwoDShape for rectangles.
class Rectangle : TwoDShape {
  // Constructor for Rectangle.
  public Rectangle(double w, double h) :
    base(w, h, "rectangle"){ }

  // Construct a square.
  public Rectangle(double x) :
    base(x, "rectangle") { }

  // Construct an object from an object.
  public Rectangle(Rectangle ob) : base(ob) { }

  public bool isSquare() {
    if(width == height) return true;
    return false;
  }
```

```
  // Override area() for Rectangle.
  public override double area() {          ← Override area( ) for Rectangle.
    return width * height;
  }
}

class DynShapes {
  public static void Main() {
    TwoDShape[] shapes = new TwoDShape[5];

    shapes[0] = new Triangle("right", 8.0, 12.0);
    shapes[1] = new Rectangle(10);
    shapes[2] = new Rectangle(10, 4);
    shapes[3] = new Triangle(7.0);
    shapes[4] = new TwoDShape(10, 20, "generic");

    for(int i=0; i < shapes.Length; i++) {
      Console.WriteLine("object is " + shapes[i].name);
      Console.WriteLine("Area is " + shapes[i].area());   ←

      Console.WriteLine();                     The proper version
    }                                          of area( ) is called
  }                                            for each shape.
}
```

The output from the program is shown here:

```
object is triangle
Area is 48

object is rectangle
Area is 100

object is rectangle
Area is 40

object is triangle
Area is 24.5

object is generic
area() must be overridden
Area is 0
```

8

Let's examine this program closely. First, as explained, **area( )** is declared as **virtual** in the **TwoDShape** class and is overridden by Triangle and **Rectangle**. Inside **TwoDShape**, **area( )** is given a placeholder implementation that simply informs the user that this method must be overridden by a derived class. Each override of **area( )** supplies an implementation that is suitable for the type of object encapsulated by the derived class. Thus, if you were to implement a ellipse class, for example, then **area( )** would need to compute the **area( )** of an ellipse.

There is one other important feature in the preceding program. Notice in **Main( )** that **shapes** is declared as an array of **TwoDShape** objects. However, the elements of this array are assigned **Triangle**, **Rectangle**, and **TwoDShape** references. This is valid because a base class reference can refer to a derived class object. The program then cycles through the array, displaying information about each object. Although quite simple, this illustrates the power of both inheritance and method overriding. The type of object stored in a base class reference variable is determined at runtime and acted on accordingly. If an object is derived from **TwoDShape**, then its area can be obtained by calling **area( )**. The interface to this operation is the same no matter what type of shape is being used.

1-Minute Drill

- What is a virtual method? How is one overridden?
- Why are virtual methods important?
- When an overridden method is called through a base class reference, which version of the method is executed?

- A virtual method is a method that is declared **virtual** in a base class, and overridden in a derived class. A virtual method is overridden using the **override** modifier.
- Virtual methods are one way that C# supports polymorphism.
- The version of an overridden method that is executed is determined by the type of the object being referred to at the time of the call. Thus, this determination is made at runtime.

Using Abstract Classes

Sometimes you will want to create a base class that defines only a generalized form that will be shared by all of its derived classes, leaving it to each derived class to fill in the details. Such a class determines the nature of the methods that the derived classes must implement, but does not, itself, provide an implementation of one or more of these methods. One way this situation can occur is when a base class is unable to create a meaningful implementation for a method. This is the case with the version of **TwoDShape** used in the preceding example. The definition of **area( )** is simply a placeholder. It will not compute and display the area of any type of object.

As you will see as you create your own class libraries, it is not uncommon for a method to have no meaningful definition in the context of its base class. You can handle this situation two ways. One way, as shown in the previous example, is to simply have it report a warning message. While this approach can be useful in certain situations—such as debugging—it is not usually appropriate. You may have methods that *must* be overridden by the derived class in order for the derived class to have any meaning. Consider the class **Triangle**. It has no meaning if **area( )** is not defined. In this case, you want some way to ensure that a derived class does, indeed, override all necessary methods. C#'s solution to this problem is the *abstract method*.

An abstract method is created by specifying the **abstract** type modifier. An abstract method contains no body and is, therefore, not implemented by the base class. Thus, a derived class must override it—it cannot simply use the version defined in the base class. As you can probably guess, an abstract method is automatically virtual, and there is no need to use the **virtual** modifier. In fact, it is an error to use **virtual** and **abstract** together.

To declare an abstract method, use this general form:

abstract *type name*(*parameter-list*);

As you can see, no method body is present. The **abstract** modifier can be used only on normal methods. It cannot be applied to **static** methods.

8

A class that contains one or more abstract methods must also be declared as abstract by preceding its **class** declaration with the **abstract** specifier. Since an abstract class does not define a complete implementation, there can be no objects of an abstract class. Thus, attempting to create an object of an abstract class by using **new** will result in a compile-time error.

When a derived class inherits an abstract class, it must implement all of the abstract methods in the base class. If it doesn't, then the derived class must also be specified as **abstract**. Thus, the **abstract** attribute is inherited until such time as a complete implementation is achieved.

Using an abstract class, you can improve the **TwoDShape** class. Since there is no meaningful concept of area for an undefined two-dimensional figure, the following version of the preceding program declares **area( )** as **abstract** inside **TwoDShape**, and **TwoDShape** as **abstract**. This, of course, means that all classes derived from **TwoDShape** must override **area( )**.

```
// Create an abstract class.
using System;

abstract class TwoDShape {          ←  TwoDShape is now abstract.
  double pri_width;  // private
  double pri_height; // private
  string pri_name;   // private

  // A default constructor.
  public TwoDShape() {
    width = height = 0.0;
    name = "null";
  }

  // Parameterized constructor.
  public TwoDShape(double w, double h, string n) {
    width = w;
    height = h;
    name = n;
  }

  // Construct object with equal width and height.
  public TwoDShape(double x, string n) {
    width = height = x;
    name = n;
  }
```

```
    // Construct an object from an object.
    public TwoDShape(TwoDShape ob) {
      width = ob.width;
      height = ob.height;
      name = ob.name;
    }

    // Properties for width, height, and name
    public double width {
      get { return pri_width; }
      set { pri_width = value; }
    }

    public double height {
      get { return pri_height; }
      set { pri_height = value; }
    }

    public string name {
      get { return pri_name; }
      set { pri_name = value; }
    }

    public void showDim() {
      Console.WriteLine("Width and height are " +
                        width + " and " + height);
    }

    // Now, area() is abstract.
    public abstract double area();  ◄─── The area() method defined by
}                                        TwoDShape is now abstract.

// A derived class of TwoDShape for triangles.
class Triangle : TwoDShape {
    string style; // private

    // A default constructor.
    public Triangle() {
      style = "null";
    }

    // Constructor for Triangle.
    public Triangle(string s, double w, double h) :
      base(w, h, "triangle") {
        style = s;
    }
```

```
  // Construct an isosceles triangle.
  public Triangle(double x) : base(x, "triangle") {
    style = "isosceles";
  }

  // Construct an object from an object.
  public Triangle(Triangle ob) : base(ob) {
    style = ob.style;
  }

  // Override area() for Triangle.
  public override double area() {          Override area( ) for Triangle.
    return width * height / 2;
  }

  public void showStyle() {
    Console.WriteLine("Triangle is " + style);
  }
}

// A derived class of TwoDShape for rectangles.
class Rectangle : TwoDShape {
  // Constructor for Rectangle.
  public Rectangle(double w, double h) :
    base(w, h, "rectangle"){ }

  // Construct a square.
  public Rectangle(double x) :
    base(x, "rectangle") { }

  // Construct an object from an object.
  public Rectangle(Rectangle ob) : base(ob) { }

  public bool isSquare() {
    if(width == height) return true;
    return false;
  }

  // Override area() for Rectangle.
  public override double area() {          Override area( ) for Rectangle.
    return width * height;
  }
}
```

```
class AbsShape {
  public static void Main() {
    TwoDShape[] shapes = new TwoDShape[4];

    shapes[0] = new Triangle("right", 8.0, 12.0);
    shapes[1] = new Rectangle(10);
    shapes[2] = new Rectangle(10, 4);
    shapes[3] = new Triangle(7.0);

    for(int i=0; i < shapes.Length; i++) {
      Console.WriteLine("object is " + shapes[i].name);
      Console.WriteLine("Area is " + shapes[i].area());

      Console.WriteLine();
    }
  }
}
```

As the program illustrates, all derived classes *must* override **area( )** (or also be declared **abstract**). To prove this to yourself, try creating a derived class that does not override **area( )**. You will receive a compile-time error. Of course, it is still possible to create an object reference of type **TwoDShape**, which the program does. However, it is no longer possible to declare objects of type **TwoDShape**. Because of this, in **Main( )** the **shapes** array has been shortened to 4 and a generic **TwoDShape** object is no longer created.

One last point: notice that **TwoDShape** still includes the **showDim( )** method and that it is not modified by **abstract**. It is perfectly acceptable—indeed, quite common—for an abstract class to contain concrete methods that a derived class is free to use as-is. Only those methods declared as **abstract** must be overridden by derived classes.

1-Minute Drill

● What is an abstract method? How is one created?

● What is an abstract class?

● Can an object of an abstract class be instantiated?

● An abstract method is a method without a body. Thus, it consists of a return type, name, and parameter list, and is preceded by the keyword **abstract**.
● An abstract class contains at least one abstract method.
● No.

Using sealed to Prevent Inheritance

As powerful and useful as inheritance is, sometimes you will want to prevent it. For example, you might have a class that encapsulates the initialization sequence of some specialized hardware device, such as a medical monitor. In this case, you don't want users of your class to be able to change the way the monitor is initialized, possibly setting the device incorrectly. Whatever the reason, in C# it is easy to prevent a class from being inherited by using the keyword **sealed**.

To prevent a class from being inherited, precede its declaration with **sealed**. As you might expect, it is illegal to declare a class as both **abstract** and **sealed** since an abstract class is incomplete by itself and relies upon its derived classes to provide complete implementations.

Here is an example of a **sealed** class:

```
sealed class A {        ◄—— This class can't be inherited.
  // ...
}

// The following class is illegal.
class B : A { // ERROR! Can't derive class A
  // ...
}
```

As the comments imply, it is illegal for **B** to inherit **A** since **A** is declared as **sealed**.

The object Class

C# defines one special class called **object** that is an implicit base class of all other classes, and for all other types (including the value types). In other words, all other types are derived from **object**. This means that a reference variable of type **object** can refer to an object of any other type. Also, since arrays are implemented as classes, a variable of type **object** can also refer to any array. Technically, the C# name **object** is just another name for **System.Object**, which is part of the .NET Framework class library.

The **object** class defines the following methods, which means that they are available in every object:

Method	Purpose
public virtual bool Equals(object *object*)	Determines whether the invoking object is the same as the one referred to by *object*.
public static bool Equals(object *ob1*, object *ob2*)	Determines whether *ob1* and *ob2* refer to the same object.
protected Finalize	Performs shutdown actions prior to garbage collection. In C#, **Finalize** is accessed through a destructor.
public virtual int GetHashCode( )	Returns the hash code associated with the invoking object.
public Type GetType( )	Obtains the type of an object at runtime.
protected object MemberwiseClone( )	Makes a "shallow copy" of the object. This is one in which the members are copied, but objects referred to by members are not.
public static bool ReferenceEquals(object *ob1*, object *ob2*)	Determines whether *ob1* and *ob2* refer to the same object.
public virtual string ToString( )	Returns a string that describes the object.

8

A few of these methods warrant some additional explanation. By default, the **Equals(object)** method determines if the invoking object refers to the same object as the one referred to by the argument. (That is, it determines if the two references are the same.) It returns **true** if the objects are the same, and **false** otherwise. You can override this method in classes that you create. Doing so allows you to define what equality means relative to a class. For example, you could define **Equals(object)** so that it compares the contents of two objects for equality. The **Equals(object, object)** method invokes **Equals(object)** to compute its result.

The **GetHashCode( )** method returns a hash code associated with the invoking object. This hash code can be used with any algorithm that employs hashing as a means of accessing stored objects.

As mentioned in Module 7, if you overload the = = operator, then you will usually need to override **Equals(object)** and **GetHashCode( )** because most of the time you will want the = = operator and the **Equals(object)** methods to function the same way. When **Equals( )** is overridden, you should also override **GetHashCode( )** so that the two methods are compatible.

The **ToString( )** method returns a string that contains a description of the object on which it is called. Also, this method is automatically called when an object is output using **WriteLine( )**. Many classes override this method. Doing so allows them to tailor a description specifically for the types of objects that they create. For example:

```
// Demonstrate ToString()
using System;

class MyClass {
  static int count = 0;
  int id;

  public MyClass() {
    id = count;
    count++;
  }

  public override string ToString() {          Override ToString( ).
    return "MyClass object #" + id;
  }
}

class Test {
  public static void Main() {
    MyClass ob1 = new MyClass();
    MyClass ob2 = new MyClass();
    MyClass ob3 = new MyClass();

    Console.WriteLine(ob1);
    Console.WriteLine(ob2);
    Console.WriteLine(ob3);

  }
}
```

The output from the program is shown here:

```
MyClass object #0
MyClass object #1
MyClass object #2
```

Boxing and Unboxing

As explained, all C# types, including the value types, are derived from **object**. Thus, a reference of type **object** can be used to refer to any other type, including value types. When an **object** reference refers to a value type, a process known as *boxing* occurs. Boxing causes the value of a value type to be stored in an object instance. Thus, a value type is "boxed" inside an object. This object can then be used like any other object. In all cases, boxing occurs automatically. You simply assign a value to an **object** reference. C# handles the rest.

Unboxing is the process of retrieving a value from an object. This action is performed using a cast from the **object** reference to the desired value type.

Here is a simple example that illustrates boxing and unboxing:

```
// A simple boxing/unboxing example.
using System;

class BoxingDemo {
  public static void Main() {
    int x;
    object obj;

    x = 10;
    obj = x; // box x into an object          Here, the value of x is boxed.

    int y = (int)obj; // unbox obj into an int
    Console.WriteLine(y);
  }                                            Here, the value is unboxed.
}
```

This program displays the value 10. Notice that the value in **x** is boxed simply by assigning it to **obj**, which is an **object** reference. The integer value in **obj** is retrieved by casting **obj** to **int**.

Here is another, more interesting example of boxing. In this case, an **int** is passed as an argument to the **sqr( )** method, which uses an **object** parameter.

```
// Boxing also occurs when passing values.
using System;

class BoxingDemo {
  public static void Main() {
```

8

```
    int x;

    x = 10;
    Console.WriteLine("Here is x: " + x);

    // x is automatically boxed when passed to sqr()
    x = BoxingDemo.sqr(x);
    Console.WriteLine("Here is x squared: " + x);
  }

  static int sqr(object o) {
    return (int)o * (int)o;
  }
}
```

The value in **x** is boxed when **sqr( )** is called.

The output from the program is shown here:

```
Here is x: 10
Here is x squared: 100
```

Here, the value of **x** is automatically boxed when it is passed to **sqr( )**.

Boxing and unboxing allows C#'s type system to be fully unified. All types derive from **object**. A reference to any type can be assigned to an object reference. Boxing/unboxing automatically handles the details for the value types. Furthermore, because all types are derived from **object**, they all have access to **object**'s methods. For example, consider the following rather surprising program:

```
// Boxing makes it possible to call methods on a value!
using System;

class MethOnValue {
  public static void Main() {

    Console.WriteLine(10.ToString());

  }
}
```

This is perfectly legal in C#!

This program displays 10. The reason is that the **ToString( )** method returns a string representation of the object on which it is called. In this case, the string representation of 10 is 10!

1-Minute Drill

● If a class is declared as **sealed**, can it be inherited?

● What is **object**?

● How do you prevent a class from being inherited?

8

● No.
● The **object** class is the base class for all types defined by C#.
● To prevent inheritance, declare the class **sealed**.

✓ Mastery Check

1. Does a base class have access to the members of a derived class? Does a derived class have access to the members of a base class?

2. Create a derived class of **TwoDShape** called **Circle**. Include an **area( )** method that computes the area of the circle and a constructor that uses **base** to initialize the **TwoDShape** portion.

3. How do you prevent a derived class from having access to a member of a base class?

4. Describe the purpose of **base**.

5. Given the following hierarchy, in what order are the constructors for these classes called when a **Gamma** object is instantiated?

   ```
   class Alpha { ...

   class Beta : Alpha { ...

   Class Gamma : Beta { ...
   ```

6. A base class reference can refer to a derived class object. Explain why this is important as it relates to method overriding.

7. What is an abstract class?

8. How do you prevent a class from being inherited?

9. Explain how inheritance, method overriding, and abstract classes are used to support polymorphism.

10. What class is a base class of every other class?

11. Explain boxing.

12. How can **protected** members be accessed?

Module 9

Interfaces, Structures, and Enumerations

The Goals of This Module

- Use interfaces
- Apply interface references
- Add properties and indexers to interfaces
- Inherit interfaces
- Use explicit implementations
- Explore the structure
- Apply enumerations

This module discusses one of C#'s most important features: the interface. An *interface* defines a set of methods that will be implemented by a class. An interface does not, itself, implement any method. It is a purely logical construct that describes a set of methods that a class will provide without dictating the specifics of the implementation.

Also discussed in this module are two more C# data types: *structures* and *enumerations*. Structures are similar to classes except that they are handled as value types rather than reference types. Enumerations are lists of named integer constants. Structures and enumerations contribute to the richness of the C# programming environment.

Interfaces

In object-oriented programming it is sometimes helpful to define what a class must do, but not how it will do it. You have already seen an example of this: the abstract method. An abstract method defines the signature for a method, but provides no implementation. A derived class must provide its own implementation of each abstract method defined by its base class. Thus, an abstract method specifies the *interface* to the method, but not the *implementation*. While abstract classes and methods are useful, it is possible to take this concept a step further. In C#, you can fully separate a class' interface from its implementation by using the keyword **interface**.

Interfaces are syntactically similar to abstract classes. However, in an interface, no method can include a body. That is, an interface provides no implementation whatsoever. It specifies what must be done, but not how. Once an interface is defined, any number of classes can implement it. Also, one class can implement any number of interfaces.

To implement an interface, a class must provide bodies (implementations) for the methods described by the interface. Each class is free to determine the details of its own implementation. Thus, two classes might implement the same interface in different ways, but each class still supports the same set of methods. Therefore, code that has knowledge of the interface can use objects of either class since the interface to those objects is the same. By providing the interface, C# allows you to fully utilize the "one interface, multiple methods" aspect of polymorphism.

Interfaces are declared by using the **interface** keyword. Here is a simplified form of an interface declaration:

```
interface name {
  ret-type method-name1(param-list);
  ret-type method-name2(param-list);
  // ...
  ret-type method-nameN(param-list);
}
```

The name of the interface is specified by *name*. Methods are declared using only their return type and signature. They are, essentially, abstract methods. As explained, in an **interface**, no method can have an implementation. Thus, each class that includes an **interface** must implement all of the methods. In an interface, methods are implicitly **public**, and no explicit access specifier is allowed.

Here is an example of an **interface**. It specifies the interface to a class that generates a series of numbers.

```
public interface Series {
  int getNext(); // return next number in series
  void reset(); // restart
  void setStart(int x); // set starting value
}
```

This interface is declared **public** so that it can be implemented by any class in any program.

In addition to method signatures, interfaces can declare the signatures for properties, indexers, and events. Events are described in Module 10, and we will be concerned with only methods, properties, and indexers here. Interfaces cannot have data members. They cannot define constructors, destructors, or operator methods. Also, no member can be declared as **static**.

Implementing Interfaces

Once an **interface** has been defined, one or more classes can implement that interface. To implement an interface, the name of the interface is specified after the class name in just the same way that a base class is specified. The general form of a class that implements an interface is shown here:

```
class class-name : interface-name {
  // class-body
}
```

9

The name of the interface being implemented is specified in *interface-name.*

When a class implements an interface, the class must implement the entire interface. It cannot pick and choose which parts to implement, for example.

Classes can implement more than one interface. To implement more than one interface, the interfaces are separated with a comma. A class can inherit a base class and implement one or more interfaces. In this case, the name of the base class must come first in the comma-separated list.

The methods that implement an interface must be declared **public**. The reason is that methods are implicitly public within an interface, so their implementations must also be public. Also, the type signature of the implementing method must match exactly the type signature specified in the **interface** definition.

Here is an example that implements the **Series** interface shown earlier. It creates a class called **ByTwos**, which generates a series of numbers, each 2 greater than the previous one.

```
// Implement Series.
class ByTwos : Series {          ◄———— Implement the Series interface.
  int start;
  int val;

  public ByTwos() {
    start = 0;
    val = 0;
  }

  public int getNext() {
    val += 2;
    return val;
  }

  public void reset() {
    start = 0;
    val = 0;
  }

  public void setStart(int x) {
    start = x;
    val = x;
  }
}
```

As you can see, **ByTwos** implements all three methods defined by **Series**. As explained, this is necessary since a class cannot create a partial implementation of an interface.

Here is a class that demonstrates **ByTwos**:

```
// Demonstrate the ByTwos interface.
using System;

class SeriesDemo {
  public static void Main() {
    ByTwos ob = new ByTwos();

    for(int i=0; i < 5; i++)
      Console.WriteLine("Next value is " +
                        ob.getNext());

    Console.WriteLine("\nResetting");
    ob.reset();
    for(int i=0; i < 5; i++)
      Console.WriteLine("Next value is " +
                        ob.getNext());   .

    Console.WriteLine("\nStarting at 100");
    ob.setStart(100);
    for(int i=0; i < 5; i++)
      Console.WriteLine("Next value is " +
                        ob.getNext());
  }
}
```

To compile **SeriesDemo**, you must include the classes **Series**, **ByTwos**, and **SeriesDemo** in the compilation. The compiler will automatically compile all three files to create the final executable. For example, if you called these files **Series.cs**, **ByTwos.cs**, and **SeriesDemo.cs**, then the following command line will compile the program:

```
>csc Series.cs ByTwos.cs SeriesDemo.cs
```

If you are using the Visual C++ IDE, then simply add all three files to your C# project. One other point: it is perfectly valid to put all three of these classes in the same file, too.

The output from this program is shown here:

```
Next value is 2
Next value is 4
Next value is 6
Next value is 8
Next value is 10

Resetting
Next value is 2
Next value is 4
Next value is 6
Next value is 8
Next value is 10

Starting at 100
Next value is 102
Next value is 104
Next value is 106
Next value is 108
Next value is 110
```

It is both permissible and common for classes that implement interfaces to define additional members of their own. For example, the following version of **ByTwos** adds the method **getPrevious( )**, which returns the previous value:

```
// Implement Series and add getPrevious().
class ByTwos : Series {
  int start;
  int val;
  int prev;

  public ByTwos() {
    start = 0;
    val = 0;
    prev = -2;
  }
```

```
  public int getNext() {
    prev = val;
    val += 2;
    return val;
  }

  public void reset() {
    start = 0;
    val = 0;
    prev = -2;
  }

  public void setStart(int x) {
    start = x;
    val = x;
    prev = x - 2;
  }

  // A method not specified by Series.
  int getPrevious() {   ◄─────    Add a method not defined by Series.
    return prev;
  }
}
```

Notice that the addition of **getPrevious( )** required a change to implementations of the methods defined by **Series**. However, since the interface to those methods stays the same, the change is seamless and does not break preexisting code. This is one of the advantages of interfaces.

As explained, any number of classes can implement an **interface**. For example, here is a class called **ByThrees** that generates a series of multiples of three:

```
// Implement Series.
class ByThrees : Series {   ◄─────    Implement Series a different way.
  int start;
  int val;

  public ByThrees() {
    start = 0;
    val = 0;
  }
```

9

```
public int getNext() {
  val += 3;
  return val;
}

public void reset() {
  start = 0;
  val = 0;
}

public void setStart(int x) {
  start = x;
  val = x;
}
}
```

1-Minute Drill

● In general, what is the purpose of an interface?

● What elements can be members of an interface?

● How is an interface implemented by a class?

Using Interface References

You might be somewhat surprised to learn that you can declare a reference variable of an interface type. In other words, you can create an interface reference variable. Such a variable can refer to any object that implements its interface. When you call a method on an object through an interface reference, it is the version of the method implemented by the object that is executed. This process is similar to using a base class reference to access a derived class object, as described in Module 8.

● An interface defines what a class must do, but not how it will do it.
● Methods, properties, indexers, and events can be interface members.
● To implement an interface, include that interface after the class name and then provide an implementation of each member of the interface.

The following example illustrates the use of an interface reference. It uses the same interface reference variable to call methods on objects of both **ByTwos** and **ByThrees**.

```
// Demonstrate interface references.
using System;

// Define the interface
public interface Series {
  int getNext(); // return next number in series
  void reset(); // restart
  void setStart(int x); // set starting value
}

// Implement Series one way.
class ByTwos : Series {
  int start;
  int val;

  public ByTwos() {
    start = 0;
    val = 0;
  }

  public int getNext() {
    val += 2;
    return val;
  }

  public void reset() {
    start = 0;
    val = 0;
  }

  public void setStart(int x) {
    start = x;
    val = x;
  }
}
```

9

```csharp
// Implement Series another way.
class ByThrees : Series {
  int start;
  int val;

  public ByThrees() {
    start = 0;
    val = 0;
  }

  public int getNext() {
    val += 3;
    return val;
  }

  public void reset() {
    start = 0;
    val = 0;
  }

  public void setStart(int x) {
    start = x;
    val = x;
  }
}

class SeriesDemo2 {
  public static void Main() {
    ByTwos twoOb = new ByTwos();
    ByThrees threeOb = new ByThrees();
    Series ob;

    for(int i=0; i < 5; i++) {
      ob = twoOb;
      Console.WriteLine("Next ByTwos value is " +
                              ob.getNext());
      ob = threeOb;
      Console.WriteLine("Next ByThrees value is " +
                              ob.getNext());
    }
  }
}
```

Access an object via an interface reference.

In **Main( )**, **ob** is declared to be a reference to a **Series** interface. This means that it can be used to store references to any object that implements **Series**. In this case, it is used to refer to **twoOb** and **threeOb**, which are objects of type **ByTwos** and **ByThrees**, respectively, which both implement **Series**. An interface reference variable has knowledge only of the methods declared by its **interface** declaration. Thus, **ob** could not be used to access any other variables or methods that might be supported by the object.

ICharQ.cs,
IQDemo.cs

Project 9-1: Creating a Queue Interface

To see the power of interfaces in action, we will look at a practical example. In earlier modules you developed a class called **Queue** that implemented a simple fixed-size queue for characters. However, there are many ways to implement a queue. For example, the queue can be of a fixed size or it can be "growable." The queue can be *linear,* in which case it can be used up, or it can be *circular,* in which case elements can be put in as long as elements are being taken off. The queue can also be held in an array, a linked list, a binary tree, and so on. No matter how the queue is implemented, the interface to the queue remains the same, and the methods **put( )** and **get( )** define the interface to the queue independently of the details of the implementation. Because the interface to a queue is separate from its implementation, it is easy to define a queue interface, leaving it to each implementation to define the specifics.

In this project you will create an interface for a character queue, and three implementations. All three implementations will use an array to store the characters. One queue will be the fixed-size, linear queue developed earlier. Another will be a circular queue. In a circular queue, when the end of the underlying array is encountered, the get and put indices automatically loop back to the start. Thus, any number of items can be stored in a circular queue as long as items are also being taken out. The final implementation creates a dynamic queue, which grows as necessary when its size is exceeded.

Step-By-Step

1. Create a file called **ICharQ.cs**, and put into that file the following interface definition:

```
// A character queue interface.
public interface ICharQ {
  // Put a character into the queue.
  void put(char ch);
```

9

```
   // Get a character from the queue.
   char get();
}
```

As you can see, this interface is very simple, consisting of only two methods. Each class that implements **ICharQ** will need to implement these methods.

2. Create a file called **IQDemo.cs**.

3. Begin creating **IQDemo.cs** by adding the **FixedQueue** class shown here:

```
/*
   Project 9-1

   Demonstrate the ICharQ interface.
*/
using System;

// A fixed-size queue class for characters.
 class FixedQueue : ICharQ {
  char[] q; // this array holds the queue
  int putloc, getloc; // the put and get indices

  // Construct an empty queue given its size.
  public FixedQueue(int size) {
    q = new char[size+1]; // allocate memory for queue
    putloc = getloc = 0;
  }

  // Put a character into the queue.
  public void put(char ch) {
    if(putloc==q.Length-1) {
      Console.WriteLine(" -- Queue is full.");
      return;
    }

    putloc++;
    q[putloc] = ch;
  }

  // Get a character from the queue.
  public char get() {
    if(getloc == putloc) {
```

```
        Console.WriteLine(" -- Queue is empty.");
        return (char) 0;
    }

    getloc++;
    return q[getloc];
  }
}
```

This implementation of **ICharQ** is adapted from the **Queue** class shown in Module 5 and should already be familiar to you.

4. To **IQDemo.cs** add the **CircularQueue** class shown here. It implements a circular queue for characters.

```
// A circular queue.
class CircularQueue : ICharQ {
  char[] q; // this array holds the queue
  int putloc, getloc; // the put and get indices

  // Construct an empty queue given its size.
  public CircularQueue(int size) {
    q = new char[size+1]; // allocate memory for queue
    putloc = getloc = 0;
  }

  // Put a character into the queue.
  public void put(char ch) {
    /* Queue is full if either putloc is one less than
       getloc, or if putloc is at the end of the array
       and getloc is at the beginning. */
    if(putloc+1==getloc |
       ((putloc==q.Length-1) & (getloc==0))) {
      Console.WriteLine(" -- Queue is full.");
      return;
    }

    putloc++;
    if(putloc==q.Length) putloc = 0; // loop back
    q[putloc] = ch;
  }

  // Get a character from the queue.
  public char get() {
```

9

```
    if(getloc == putloc) {
      Console.WriteLine(" -- Queue is empty.");
      return (char) 0;
    }

    getloc++;
    if(getloc==q.Length) getloc = 0; // loop back
    return q[getloc];
  }
}
```

The circular queue works by reusing space in the array that is freed when elements are retrieved. Thus, it can store an unlimited number of elements as long as elements are also being removed. While conceptually simple—just reset the appropriate index to zero when the end of the array is reached—the boundary conditions are a bit confusing at first. In a circular queue, the queue is full not when the end of the underlying array is reached, but rather when storing an item would cause an unretrieved item to be overwritten. Thus, **put( )** must check several conditions in order to determine if the queue is full. As the comments suggest, the queue is full when either **putloc** is one less than **getloc**, or if **putloc** is at the end of the array and **getloc** is at the beginning. As before, the queue is empty when **getloc** and **putloc** are equal.

5. Finally, put into **IQDemo.cs** the **DynQueue** class shown next. It implements a "growable" queue that expands its size when space is exhausted.

```
// A dynamic queue.
class DynQueue : ICharQ {
  char[] q; // this array holds the queue
  int putloc, getloc; // the put and get indices

  // Construct an empty queue given its size.
  public DynQueue(int size) {
    q = new char[size+1]; // allocate memory for queue
    putloc = getloc = 0;
  }

  // Put a character into the queue.
  public void put(char ch) {
    if(putloc==q.Length-1) {
      // increase queue size
      char[] t = new char[q.Length * 2];
```

```
    // copy elements into new queue
    for(int i=0; i < q.Length; i++)
      t[i] = q[i];

    q = t;
  }

  putloc++;
  q[putloc] = ch;
}

// Get a character from the queue.
public char get() {
  if(getloc == putloc) {
    Console.WriteLine(" -- Queue is empty.");
    return (char) 0;
  }

  getloc++;
  return q[getloc];
}
}
```

In this queue implementation, when the queue is full, an attempt to store another element causes a new underlying array to be allocated that is twice as large as the original, the current contents of the queue are copied into this array, and a reference to the new array is stored in **q**.

6. To demonstrate the three **ICharQ** implementations, enter the following class into **IQDemo.cs**. It uses an **ICharQ** reference to access all three queues.

```
// Demonstrate the queues.
class IQDemo {
  public static void Main() {
    FixedQueue q1 = new FixedQueue(10);
    DynQueue q2 = new DynQueue(5);
    CircularQueue q3 = new CircularQueue(10);

    ICharQ iQ;

    char ch;
    int i;

    iQ = q1;
```

9

```csharp
    // Put some characters into fixed queue.
    for(i=0; i < 10; i++)
      iQ.put((char) ('A' + i));

    // Show the queue.
    Console.Write("Contents of fixed queue: ");
    for(i=0; i < 10; i++) {
      ch = iQ.get();
      Console.Write(ch);
    }
    Console.WriteLine();

    iQ = q2;
    // Put some characters into dynamic queue.
    for(i=0; i < 10; i++)
      iQ.put((char) ('Z' - i));

    // Show the queue.
    Console.Write("Contents of dynamic queue: ");
    for(i=0; i < 10; i++) {
      ch = iQ.get();
      Console.Write(ch);
    }

    Console.WriteLine();

    iQ = q3;
    // Put some characters into circular queue.
    for(i=0; i < 10; i++)
      iQ.put((char) ('A' + i));

    // Show the queue.
    Console.Write("Contents of circular queue: ");
    for(i=0; i < 10; i++) {
      ch = iQ.get();
      Console.Write(ch);
    }

    Console.WriteLine();

    // Put more characters into circular queue.
    for(i=10; i < 20; i++)
      iQ.put((char) ('A' + i));

    // Show the queue.
    Console.Write("Contents of circular queue: ");
```

```
    for(i=0; i < 10; i++) {
      ch = iQ.get();
      Console.Write(ch);
    }

    Console.WriteLine("\nStore and consume from" +
                      " circular queue.");

    // Use and consume from circular queue.
    for(i=0; i < 20; i++) {
      iQ.put((char) ('A' + i));
      ch = iQ.get();
      Console.Write(ch);
    }

  }
}
```

7. Compile the program by including both **ICharQ.cs** and **IQDemo.cs**.

8. The output from this program is shown here:

```
Contents of fixed queue: ABCDEFGHIJ
Contents of dynamic queue: ZYXWVUTSRQ
Contents of circular queue: ABCDEFGHIJ
Contents of circular queue: KLMNOPQRST
Store and consume from circular queue.
ABCDEFGHIJKLMNOPQRST
```

9. Here are some things to try on your own. Create a circular version of **DynQueue**. Add a **reset( )** method to **ICharQ** that resets the queue. Create a **static** method that copies the contents of one type of queue into another.

Interface Properties

Like methods, properties are specified in an interface without any body. Here is the general form of a property specification:

```
// interface property
type name {
  get;
  set;
}
```

Of course, only **get** or **set** will be present for read-only or write-only properties, respectively.

Here is a rewrite of the **Series** interface and the **ByTwos** class that uses a property to obtain and set the next element in the series:

```
// Use a property in an interface.
using System;

public interface Series {
  // an interface property
  int next {            ←————————————  Declare a property in Series interface.
    get; // return the next number in series
    set; // set next number
  }
}

// Implement Series.
class ByTwos : Series {
  int val;

  public ByTwos() {
    val = 0;
  }

  // get or set value
  public int next {      ←————————————  Implement the property.
    get {
      val += 2;
      return val;
    }
    set {
      val = value;
    }
  }
}

// Demonstrate an interface property.
class SeriesDemo3 {
  public static void Main() {
    ByTwos ob = new ByTwos();
```

```
  // access series through a property
  for(int i=0; i < 5; i++)
    Console.WriteLine("Next value is " + ob.next);

  Console.WriteLine("\nStarting at 21");
  ob.next = 21;
  for(int i=0; i < 5; i++)
    Console.WriteLine("Next value is " + ob.next);
  }
}
```

The output from this program is shown here:

```
Next value is 2
Next value is 4
Next value is 6
Next value is 8
Next value is 10

Starting at 21
Next value is 23
Next value is 25
Next value is 27
Next value is 29
Next value is 31
```

Interface Indexers

An indexer declared in an interface has this general form:

```
// interface indexer
element-type this[int index] {
  get;
  set;
}
```

As before, only **get** or **set** will be present for read-only or write-only indexers, respectively.

Here is another version of **Series** that adds a read-only indexer that returns the ith element in the series:

```
// Add an indexer in an interface.
using System;

public interface Series {
  // an interface property
  int next {
    get; // return the next number in series
    set; // set next number
  }

  // an interface indexer
  int this[int index] {          <——————  Specify a read-only indexer.
    get; // return the specified number in series
  }
}

// Implement Series.
class ByTwos : Series {
  int val;

  public ByTwos() {
    val = 0;
  }

  // get or set value using a property
  public int next {
    get {
      val += 2;
      return val;
    }
    set {
      val = value;
```

```
    }
  }

  // get a value using an index
  public int this[int index] {        ◄────────[ Implement the indexer. ]
    get {
      val = 0;
      for(int i=0; i<index; i++)
        val += 2;
      return val;
    }
  }
}

// Demonstrate an interface indexer.
class SeriesDemo4 {
  public static void Main() {
    ByTwos ob = new ByTwos();

    // access series through a property
    for(int i=0; i < 5; i++)
      Console.WriteLine("Next value is " + ob.next);

    Console.WriteLine("\nStarting at 21");
    ob.next = 21;
    for(int i=0; i < 5; i++)
      Console.WriteLine("Next value is " +
                            ob.next);

    Console.WriteLine("\nResetting to 0");
    ob.next = 0;

    // access series through an indexer
    for(int i=0; i < 5; i++)
      Console.WriteLine("Next value is " + ob[i]);
  }
}
```

9

The output from this program is shown here:

```
Next value is 2
Next value is 4
Next value is 6
Next value is 8
Next value is 10

Starting at 21
Next value is 23
Next value is 25
Next value is 27
Next value is 29
Next value is 31

Resetting to 0
Next value is 0
Next value is 2
Next value is 4
Next value is 6
Next value is 8
```

1-Minute Drill

● Can an interface reference variable refer to an object that implements that interface?

● Can an interface property be read-only?

● Do indexer and property specifications inside an interface have bodies?

Interfaces Can Be Inherited

One interface can inherit another. The syntax is the same as for inheriting classes. When a class implements an interface that inherits another interface, it

---

● Yes.
● Yes.
● No.

must provide implementations for all the members defined within the interface inheritance chain. Following is an example:

```
// One interface can inherit another.
using System;

public interface A {
  void meth1();
  void meth2();
}

// B now includes meth1() and meth2() -- it adds meth3().
public interface B : A {          ◄────────   B inherits A.
  void meth3();
}

// This class must implement all of A and B
class MyClass : B {
  public void meth1() {
    Console.WriteLine("Implement meth1().");
  }

  public void meth2() {
    Console.WriteLine("Implement meth2().");
  }

  public void meth3() {
    Console.WriteLine("Implement meth3().");
  }
}

class IFExtend {
  public static void Main() {
    MyClass ob = new MyClass();

    ob.meth1();
    ob.meth2();
    ob.meth3();
  }
}
```

9

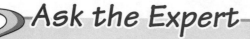

Ask the Expert

Question: When one interface inherits another, is it possible to declare a member in the derived interface that hides a member defined by the base interface?

Answer: Yes. When a member in a derived interface has the same signature as one in the base interface, the base interface name is hidden. As is the case with class inheritance, this hiding will cause a warning message unless you specify the derived interface member with **new**.

As an experiment you might want to try removing the implementation for **meth1( )** in **MyClass**. This will cause a compile-time error. As stated earlier, any class that implements an interface must implement all methods defined by that interface, including any that are inherited from other interfaces.

Explicit Implementations

When implementing a member of an interface, it is possible to *fully qualify* its name with its interface name. Doing this creates an *explicit interface member implementation*, or *explicit implementation*, for short. For example, given

```
interface IMyIF {
  int myMeth(int x);
}
```

it is legal to implement **IMyIF** as shown here:

```
class MyClass : IMyIF {
  int IMyIF.myMeth(int x) {
    return x / 3;
  }
}
```

A fully qualified name used to create an explicit implementation

As you can see, when the **myMeth( )** member of **IMyIF** is implemented, its complete name, including its interface name, is specified.

There are two reasons that you might need to create an explicit implementation of an interface member. First, it is possible for a class to implement two interfaces, both of which declare methods by the same name and type signature. Fully qualifying the names removes the ambiguity from this situation. Second, when you implement a method using its fully qualified name, you are providing what amounts to a private implementation that is not exposed to code outside the class. Let's look at an example of each.

The following program contains an interface called **IEven**, which defines two methods: **isEven( )** and **isOdd( )**, which determine if a number is even or odd. **MyClass** then implements **IEven**. When it does so, it implements **isOdd( )** explicitly.

```csharp
// Explicitly implement an interface member.
using System;

interface IEven {
  bool isOdd(int x);
  bool isEven(int x);
}

class MyClass : IEven {
  // explicit implementation
  bool IEven.isOdd(int x) {          // Explicitly implement isOdd( ).
    if((x%2) != 0) return true;      // This makes it effectively private.
    else return false;
  }

  // normal implementation
  public bool isEven(int x) {
    IEven o = this; // reference to invoking object

    return !o.isOdd(x);
  }
}

class Demo {
  public static void Main() {
    MyClass ob = new MyClass();
    bool result;

    result = ob.isEven(4);
    if(result) Console.WriteLine("4 is even.");
    else Console.WriteLine("3 is odd.");

    // result = ob.isOdd(); // Error, not exposed
  }
}
```

9

Since **isOdd( )** is implemented explicitly, it is not available outside of
MyClass. This makes its implementation effectively private. Inside **MyClass**,
isOdd( ) can be accessed only through an interface reference. This is why it is
invoked through **o** in the implementation for **isEven( )**.

Here is an example in which two interfaces are implemented and both
interfaces declare a method called **meth( )**. Explicit implementation is used
to eliminate the ambiguity inherent in this situation.

```
// Use explicit implementation to remove ambiguity.
using System;

interface IMyIF_A {
  int meth(int x);          The signatures for these two methods
}                           are the same.

interface IMyIF_B {
  int meth(int x);
}

// MyClass implements both interfaces.
class MyClass : IMyIF_A, IMyIF_B {
  IMyIF_A a_ob;
  IMyIF_B b_ob;

  // explicitly implement the two meth()s
  int IMyIF_A.meth(int x) {        Explicit implementation
    return x + x;                  removes ambiguity.
  }
  int IMyIF_B.meth(int x) {
    return x * x;
  }

  // call meth() through an interface reference.
  public int methA(int x){
    a_ob = this;
    return a_ob.meth(x); // calls IMyIF_A
  }

  public int methB(int x){
    b_ob = this;
    return b_ob.meth(x); // calls IMyIF_B
  }
```

```
}

class FQIFNames {
  public static void Main() {
    MyClass ob = new MyClass();

    Console.Write("Calling IMyIF_A.meth(): ");
    Console.WriteLine(ob.methA(3));

    Console.Write("Calling IMyIF_B.meth(): ");
    Console.WriteLine(ob.methB(3));
  }
}
```

The output from this program is shown here:

```
Calling IMyIF_A.meth(): 6
Calling IMyIF_B.meth(): 9
```

Looking at the program, first notice that **meth( )** has the same signature in both **IMyIF_A** and **IMyIF_B**. Thus, when **MyClass** implements both of these interfaces, it must explicitly implement each one separately, fully qualifying its name in the process. Since the only way that an explicitly implemented method can be called is on an interface reference, **MyClass** creates two such references, one for **IMyIF_A** and one for **IMyIF_B**. It then calls two of its own methods, which call the interface methods, thereby removing the ambiguity.

9

1-Minute Drill

● If interface A is inherited by interface B, and then B is implemented by class C, does C have to implement all of the members of A and B, or only those defined by B?

● Give the two reasons that you might want to use an explicit interface implementation.

● An implementing class must implement all members specified by an interface hierarchy.
● You will use an explicit implementation to remove ambiguity and to avoid exposing an interface member.

Structures

As you know, classes are reference types. This means that class objects are accessed through a reference. This differs from the value types, which are accessed directly. However, there can be times when it would be useful to be able to access an object directly. One reason for this is efficiency. Accessing class objects through a reference adds overhead to every access. It also consumes space. For very small objects, this extra space might be significant. To address these concerns, C# offers the structure. A *structure* is similar to a class, but is a value type, rather than a reference type.

Structures are declared using the keyword **struct** and are syntactically similar to classes. Here is the general form of a **struct**:

```
struct name : interfaces {
   // member declarations
}
```

The name of the structure is specified by *name*.

Structures cannot inherit other structures or classes, or be used as a base for other structures or classes. However, a structure can implement one or more interfaces. These are specified after the structure name using a comma-separated list.

Like classes, structure members include methods, fields, indexers, properties, operator methods, and events. Structures can also define constructors, but not destructors. However, you cannot define a default (parameterless) constructor for a structure. The reason for this is that a default constructor is automatically defined for all structures and this default constructor can't be changed.

A structure object can be created using **new** in the same way as a class object, but it is not required. When **new** is used, the specified constructor is called. When **new** is not used, the object is still created, but it is not initialized. Thus, you will need to perform any initialization manually.

Here is an example that uses a structure:

```
// Demonstrate a structure.
using System;
```

```
// Define a structure.
struct account {          ◄────────────────────   Define a structure.
  public string name;
  public double balance;

  public account(string n, double b) {
    name = n;
    balance = b;
  }
}

// Demonstrate account structure.
class StructDemo {
  public static void Main() {
    account acc1 = new account("Tom", 1232.22); // explicit
                                                 // constructor
    account acc2 = new account(); // default constructor
    account acc3; // no constructor

    Console.WriteLine(acc1.name + " has a balance of " +
                      acc1.balance);
    Console.WriteLine();

    if(acc2.name == null) Console.WriteLine("acc2.name is null.");
    Console.WriteLine("acc2.balance is " + acc2.balance);
    Console.WriteLine();

    // must initialize acc3 prior to use
    acc3.name = "Mary";
    acc3.balance = 99.33;
    Console.WriteLine(acc3.name + " has a balance of " +
                      acc3.balance);
  }
}
```

The output from this program is shown here:

```
Tom has a balance of 1232.22

acc2.name is null.
acc2.balance is 0

Mary has a balance of 99.33
```

9

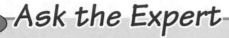

Ask the Expert

Question: I know that C++ also has structures and uses the **struct** keyword. Are C# and C++ structures the same?

Answer: No. In C++, **struct** defines a class type. Thus, in C++, **struct** and **class** are nearly equivalent. (The difference has to do with the default access of their members, which is private for **class** and public for **struct**.) In C#, a **struct** defines a value type, and a **class** defines a reference type.

As the program shows, a structure can be initialized either by using **new** to invoke a constructor, or by simply declaring an object. If **new** is used, then the fields of the structure will be initialized, either by the default constructor that initializes all fields to their default values, or by a user-defined constructor. If **new** is not used, then the object is not initialized and its fields must be set prior to using the object.

Enumerations

An *enumeration* is a set of named integer constants that specifies all the legal values a variable of that type may have. Enumerations are common in everyday life. For example, an enumeration of the coins used in the United States is

penny, nickel, dime, quarter, half-dollar, dollar

The keyword **enum** declares an enumerated type. The general form for an enumeration is

enum *name* { *enumeration list* };

Here, the type name of the enumeration is specified by *name*. The *enumeration list* is a comma-separated list of identifiers.

The following code fragment defines an enumeration called **coin**:

```
enum coin { penny, nickel, dime, quarter, half_dollar, dollar};
```

A key point to understand about an enumeration is that each of the symbols stands for an integer value. As such, they can be used anywhere that an integer may be used. Each symbol is given a value one greater than the symbol that precedes it. By default, the value of the first enumeration symbol is 0.

The members of an enumeration are accessed through their type name via the dot operator. For example, this code:

```
Console.WriteLine("penny is " + coin.penny +
                  " nickel is " + coin.nickel);
```

displays

```
penny is 0 nickel is 1
```

Here is a program that illustrates the **coin** enumeration:

```
// Demonstrate an enumeration.
using System;

class EnumDemo {
  enum coin { penny, nickel, dime, quarter,
              half_dollar, dollar };

  public static void Main() {
    string[] names = {
      "penny",
      "nickel",
      "dime",
      "quarter",
      "half_dollar",
      "dollar"
    };

    coin i; // declare an enum variable

    // use i to cycle through the enum
    for(i = coin.penny; i <= coin.dollar; i++)
      Console.WriteLine(names[(int)i] + " has value of " + i);

  }
}
```

A **coin** variable can control a **for** loop.

9

The output from the program is shown here:

```
penny has value of 0
nickel has value of 1
dime has value of 2
quarter has value of 3
half_dollar has value of 4
dollar has value of 5
```

Notice how the **for** loop is controlled by a variable of type **coin**. Since an enumeration is an integer type, an enumeration value can be used anywhere that an integer can. However, notice that a cast is required when the enumeration value is used to index the **names** array. One other point: since the enumerated values in **coin** start at zero, these values can be used to index **names** to obtain the name of the coin. This is a useful technique when human-readable strings that correspond to enumeration values are required.

Initialize an Enumeration

You can specify the value of one or more of the symbols by using an initializer. Do this by following the symbol with an equal sign and an integer value. Symbols that appear after initializers are assigned values greater than the previous initialization value. For example, the following code assigns the value of 100 to **quarter**:

```
enum coin { penny, nickel, dime, quarter=100,
            half_dollar, dollar};
```

Now, the values of these symbols are

penny	0
nickel	1
dime	2
quarter	100
half_dollar	101
dollar	102

Specifying the Base Type of an Enumeration

By default, enumerations are based on type **int**, but you can create an enumeration of any integer type, except for type **char**. To specify a type other than **int**, put the base type after the enumeration name, separated by a colon. For example, this statement makes **coin** an enumeration based on **byte**.

```
enum coin : byte { penny, nickel, dime, quarter,
        half_dollar, dollar};
```

Now, **coin.penny**, for example, is a **byte** quantity.

1-Minute Drill

● Must a **struct** be created by using **new**?

● Can a **struct** define a destructor?

● What is an enumeration?

● No, a **struct** object can be created like any other value type, without the use of **new**. However, the object will be uninitialized.
● No. Structures cannot have destructors.
● An enumeration is a list of named integer constants.

✓ Mastery Check

1. "One interface, multiple methods" is a key tenet of C#. What feature best exemplifies it?

2. How many classes can implement an interface? How many interfaces can a class implement?

3. Can interfaces be inherited?

4. Must a class implement all of the members of an interface?

5. Can an interface declare a constructor?

6. Create an interface for the **Vehicle** class from Module 7. Call the interface **IVehicle**.

7. Create an interface for safe arrays. Do this by adapting the final fail-soft array example from Module 7.

8. How does a **struct** differ from a **class**?

9. Show how to create an enumeration for the planets. Call the enumeration **Planets**.

Module 10

Exception Handling

The Goals of This Module

- Use try and catch
- Understand the effects of an uncaught exception
- Use multiple catch statements
- Nest try blocks
- Throw an exception
- Examine Exception
- Use finally
- Explore C#'s built-in exceptions
- Create custom exception classes
- Use checked and unchecked

This module discusses exception handling. An *exception* is an error that occurs at runtime. Using C#'s exception handling subsystem you can, in a structured and controlled manner, handle runtime errors. C#'s approach to exception handling is a blend of and improvement on the methods used by C++ and Java. Thus, it will be familiar territory to readers with a background in either of these languages. What makes C#'s exception handling unique, however, is its clean, straightforward implementation.

A principal advantage of exception handling is that it automates much of the error-handling code that previously had to be entered "by hand" into any large program. For example, in a computer language without exception handling, error codes must be returned when a method fails, and these values must be checked manually each time the method is called. This approach is both tedious and error-prone. Exception handling streamlines error handling by allowing your program to define a block of code, called an *exception handler,* that is executed automatically when an error occurs. It is not necessary to manually check the success or failure of each specific operation or method call. If an error occurs, it will be processed by the exception handler.

Another reason that exception handling is important is that C# defines standard exceptions for common program errors, such as divide-by-zero or index-out-of-range. To respond to these errors, your program must watch for and handle these exceptions.

In the final analysis, to be a successful C# programmer means that you are fully capable of navigating C#'s exception-handling subsystem.

The System.Exception Class

In C#, exceptions are represented by classes. All exception classes must be derived from the built-in exception class **Exception**, which is part of the **System** namespace. Thus, all exceptions are subclasses of **Exception**.

From **Exception** are derived **SystemException** and **ApplicationException**. These support the two general categories of execptions defined by C#: those generated by the C# runtime system (that is, the CLR) and those generated by application programs. Neither **SystemException** nor **ApplicationException** add anything to **Exception**. They simply define the tops of two different exception hierarchies.

C# defines several built-in exceptions that are derived from **SystemException**. For example, when a division-by-zero is attempted, a **DivideByZeroException**

exception is generated. As you will see later in this module, you can create your own exception classes by deriving them from **ApplicationException**.

Exception Handling Fundamentals

C# exception handling is managed via four keywords: **try**, **catch**, **throw**, and **finally**. They form an interrelated subsystem in which the use of one implies the use of another. Throughout the course of this module each keyword is examined in detail. However, it is useful at the outset to have a general understanding of the role each plays in exception handling. Briefly, here is how they work.

Program statements that you want to monitor for exceptions are contained within a **try** block. If an exception occurs within the **try** block, it is *thrown*. Your code can catch this exception using **catch** and handle it in some rational manner. System-generated exceptions are automatically thrown by the C# runtime system. To manually throw an exception, use the keyword **throw**. Any code that absolutely must be executed upon exiting from a **try** block is put in a **finally** block.

Using try and catch

At the core of exception handling are **try** and **catch**. These keywords work together; you can't have a **try** without a **catch**, or a **catch** without a **try**. Here is the general form of the **try/catch** exception-handling blocks:

```
try {
   // block of code to monitor for errors
}

catch (ExcepType1 exOb) {
   // handler for ExcepType1
}

catch (ExcepType2 exOb) {
   // handler for ExcepType2
}
```

Here, *ExcepType* is the type of exception that has occurred. When an exception is thrown, it is caught by its corresponding **catch** statement, which then processes the exception. As the general form shows, there can be more than one **catch**

10

statement associated with a **try**. The type of the exception determines which **catch** statement is executed. That is, if the exception type specified by a **catch** statement matches that of the exception, then that **catch** statement is executed (and all others are bypassed). When an exception is caught, *exOb* will receive its value.

Actually, specifying *exOb* is optional. If the exception handler does not need access to the exception object (as is often the case) then there is no need to specify *exOb*. For this reason, many of the examples in this module will not specify *exOb*.

Here is an important point: if no exception is thrown, then a **try** block ends normally, and all of its **catch** statements are bypassed. Execution resumes with the first statement following the last **catch**. Thus, **catch** statements are executed only if an exception is thrown.

A Simple Exception Example

Here is a simple example that illustrates how to watch for and catch an exception. As you know, it is an error to attempt to index an array beyond its boundaries. When this occurs, the C# runtime system throws an **IndexOutOfRangeException**, which is a standard exception defined by C#. The following program purposely generates such an exception and then catches it:

```
// Demonstrate exception handling.
using System;

class ExcDemo1 {
  public static void Main() {
    int[] nums = new int[4];

    try {
      Console.WriteLine("Before exception is generated.");

      // Generate an index out-of-bounds exception.
      nums[7] = 10;          ← Attempt to
      Console.WriteLine("this won't be displayed");    index past
    }                                                  nums
    catch (IndexOutOfRangeException) {                 boundary.
      // catch the exception
      Console.WriteLine("Index out-of-bounds!");
    }
    Console.WriteLine("After catch statement.");
  }
}
```

This program displays the following output:

```
Before exception is generated.
Index out-of-bounds!
After catch statement.
```

Although quite short, the preceding program illustrates several key points about exception handling. First, the code that you want to monitor for errors is contained within a **try** block. Second, when an exception occurs (in this case, because of the attempt to index **nums** beyond its bounds), the exception is thrown out of the **try** block and caught by the **catch** statement. At this point, control passes to the **catch**, and the **try** block is terminated. That is, **catch** is *not* called. Rather, program execution is transferred to it. Thus, the **WriteLine( )** statement following the out-of-bounds index will never execute. After the **catch** statement executes, program control continues with the statements following the **catch**. It is the job of your exception handler to remedy the problem that caused the exception so that program execution can continue normally.

Notice that no parameter is specified in the **catch** clause. As mentioned, a parameter is needed only when access to the exception objects is required. In some cases, the value of the exception object can be used by the exception handler to obtain additional information about the error, but in many cases it is sufficient to simply know that an exception occurred. Thus, it is not unusual for the **catch** parameter to be absent in the exception handler, as is the case in the preceeding program.

As explained, if no exception is thrown by a **try** block, then no **catch** statements will be executed and program control resumes after the **catch** statement. To confirm this, in the preceding program, change the line

```
nums[7] = 10;
```

to

```
nums[0] = 10;
```

Now, no exception is generated and the **catch** block is not executed.

A Second Exception Example

It is important to understand that all code within a **try** block is monitored for exceptions. This includes exceptions that might be generated by a method called from within the **try** block. An exception thrown by a method called from within a **try** block can be caught by that **try** block—assuming, of course, that the method, itself, did not catch the exception. For example, this is a valid program:

```
/* An exception can be generated by one
   method and caught by another. */
using System;

class ExcTest {
  // Generate an exception.
  public static void genException() {
    int[] nums = new int[4];

    Console.WriteLine("Before exception is generated.");

    // generate an index out-of-bounds exception
    nums[7] = 10;            ◄─────────────────────    Exception
    Console.WriteLine("this won't be displayed");      generated here.
  }
}

class ExcDemo2 {
  public static void Main() {

    try {
      ExcTest.genException();
    }
    catch (IndexOutOfRangeException) {  ◄──────    Exception caught here.
      // catch the exception
      Console.WriteLine("Index out-of-bounds!");
    }
    Console.WriteLine("After catch statement.");
  }
}
```

This program produces the following output, which is the same as that produced by the first version of the program shown earlier:

```
Before exception is generated.
Index out-of-bounds!
After catch statement.
```

Since **genException( )** is called from within a **try** block, the exception that it generates (and does not catch) is caught by the **catch** in **Main( )**. Understand, however, that if **genException( )** had caught the exception, then it would never had been passed back to **Main( )**.

1-Minute Drill

● What is an exception?

● Code monitored for exceptions must be part of what statement?

● What does **catch** do? After a **catch** executes, what happens to the flow of execution?

The Consequences of an Uncaught Exception

Catching one of C#'s standard exceptions, as the preceding program does, has a side benefit: it prevents abnormal program termination. When an exception is thrown, it must be caught by some piece of code, somewhere. In general, if your program does not catch an exception, then it will be caught by the C# runtime system. The trouble is that the runtime system will report an error and terminate the program. For example, in this version of the preceding example, the index out-of-bounds exception is not caught by the program:

```
// Let the C# runtime system handle the error.
using System;

class NotHandled {
  public static void Main() {
    int[] nums = new int[4];

    Console.WriteLine("Before exception is generated.");

    // generate an index out-of-bounds exception
    nums[7] = 10;
  }
}
```

10

● An exception is a runtime error.
● To monitor code for exceptions, it must be part of a **try** block.
● The **catch** statement receives exceptions. A **catch** statement is not called, thus execution *does not* return to the point at which the exception was generated. Rather, execution continues on after the **catch** block.

When the array index error occurs, execution is halted and the following error message is displayed:

```
Unhandled Exception: System.IndexOutOfRangeException:
        Exception of type System.IndexOutOfRangeException
        was thrown.
   at NotHandled.Main()
```

While such a message is useful for you while debugging, it would not be something that you would want others to see, to say the least! This is why it is important for your program to handle exceptions itself.

As mentioned earlier, the type of the exception must match the type specified in a **catch** statement. If it doesn't, the exception won't be caught. For example, the following program tries to catch an array boundary error with a **catch** statement for a **DivideByZeroException** (another of C#'s built-in exceptions). When the array boundary is overrun, an **IndexOutOfRangeException** is generated, but it won't be caught by the **catch** statement. This results in abnormal program termination.

```
// This won't work!
using System;

class ExcTypeMismatch {
  public static void Main() {
    int[] nums = new int[4];                    This throws an
                                                IndexOutOfRangeException.

    try {
      Console.WriteLine("Before exception is generated.");

      // generate an index out-of-bounds exception
      nums[7] = 10;           ◄
      Console.WriteLine("this won't be displayed");
    }

    /* Can't catch an array boundary error with a
       DivideByZeroException. */
    catch (DivideByZeroException) {  ◄    This tries to catch it with a
      // catch the exception                DivideByZeroException.
      Console.WriteLine("Index out-of-bounds!");
    }
    Console.WriteLine("After catch statement.");
  }
}
```

The output is shown here:

```
Before exception is generated.

Unhandled Exception: System.IndexOutOfRangeException:
        Exception of type System.IndexOutOfRangeException
        was thrown.
   at ExcTypeMismatch.Main()
```

As the output demonstrates, a **catch** for **DivideByZeroException** won't catch an **IndexOutOfRangeException**.

Exceptions Let You Handle Errors Gracefully

One of the key benefits of exception handling is that it enables your program to respond to an error and then continue running. For instance, consider the following example that divides the elements of one array by the elements of another. If a division by zero occurs, a **DivideByZeroException** is generated. In the program, this exception is handled by reporting the error and then continuing with execution. Thus, attempting to divide by zero does not cause an abrupt runtime error resulting in the termination of the program. Instead, it is handled gracefully, allowing program execution to continue.

```
// Handle error gracefully and continue.
using System;

class ExcDemo3 {
  public static void Main() {
    int[] numer = { 4, 8, 16, 32, 64, 128 };
    int[] denom = { 2, 0, 4, 4, 0, 8 };

    for(int i=0; i<numer.Length; i++) {
      try {
        Console.WriteLine(numer[i] + " / " +
                          denom[i] + " is " +
                          numer[i]/denom[i]);
      }
      catch (DivideByZeroException) {
```

10

```
          // catch the exception
          Console.WriteLine("Can't divide by Zero!");
      }
    }
  }
}
```

The output from the program is shown here:

```
4 / 2 is 2
Can't divide by Zero!
16 / 4 is 4
32 / 4 is 8
Can't divide by Zero!
128 / 8 is 16
```

This example makes another important point: once an exception has been handled, it is removed from the system. Therefore, in the program, each pass through the loop enters the **try** block anew—any prior exceptions have been handled. This enables your program to handle repeated errors.

1-Minute Drill

● Does the exception type in a **catch** statement matter?

● What happens if an exception is not caught?

● When an exception occurs, what should your program do?

Using Multiple catch Statements

You can associate more than one **catch** statement with a **try**. In fact, it is common to do so. However, each **catch** must catch a different type of exception. For example, the program shown next catches both array-boundary and divide-by-zero errors.

● The type of exception in a **catch** must match the type of exception that you want to catch.
● An uncaught exception ultimately leads to abnormal program termination.
● A program should handle exceptions in a rational, graceful manner, eliminating the cause of the exception if possible, and then continuing.

```
// Use multiple catch statements.
using System;

class ExcDemo4 {
  public static void Main() {
    // Here, numer is longer than denom.
    int[] numer = { 4, 8, 16, 32, 64, 128, 256, 512 };
    int[] denom = { 2, 0, 4, 4, 0, 8 };

    for(int i=0; i<numer.Length; i++) {
      try {
        Console.WriteLine(numer[i] + " / " +
                          denom[i] + " is " +
                          numer[i]/denom[i]);
      }
      catch (DivideByZeroException) {
        // catch the exception
        Console.WriteLine("Can't divide by Zero!");
      }
      catch (IndexOutOfRangeException) {
        // catch the exception
        Console.WriteLine("No matching element found.");
      }
    }
  }
}
```

Multiple **catch** statements

This program produces the following output:

```
4 / 2 is 2
Can't divide by Zero!
16 / 4 is 4
32 / 4 is 8
Can't divide by Zero!
128 / 8 is 16
No matching element found.
No matching element found.
```

As the output confirms, each **catch** statement responds only to its own type of exception.

In general, **catch** expressions are checked in the order in which they occur in a program. Only a matching statement is executed. All other **catch** blocks are ignored.

Catching All Exceptions

Sometimes you will want to catch all exceptions, no matter the type. To do this, use a **catch** statement that specifies no parameter. This creates a "catch all" handler that is useful when you want to ensure that all exceptions are handled by your program. For example, here the only **catch** is the "catch all," and it catches both the **IndexOutOfRangeException** and the **DivideByZeroException** that is generated by the program:

```
// Use the "catch all" catch statement.
using System;

class ExcDemo5 {
  public static void Main() {
    // Here, numer is longer than denom.
    int[] numer = { 4, 8, 16, 32, 64, 128, 256, 512 };
    int[] denom = { 2, 0, 4, 4, 0, 8 };

    for(int i=0; i<numer.Length; i++) {
      try {
        Console.WriteLine(numer[i] + " / " +
                          denom[i] + " is " +
                          numer[i]/denom[i]);
      }
      catch {                                          This catches all exceptions.
        Console.WriteLine("Some exception occurred.");
      }
    }
  }
}
```

The output is shown here:

```
4 / 2 is 2
Some exception occurred.
16 / 4 is 4
32 / 4 is 8
Some exception occurred.
128 / 8 is 16
Some exception occurred.
Some exception occurred.
```

try Blocks Can Be Nested

One **try** block can be nested within another. An exception generated within the inner **try** block that is not caught by a **catch** associated with that **try** is propagated to the outer **try** block. For example, here the **IndexOutOfRangeException** is not caught by the inner **try** block, but by the outer **try**:

```
// Use a nested try block.
using System;

class NestTrys {
  public static void Main() {
    // Here, numer is longer than denom.
    int[] numer = { 4, 8, 16, 32, 64, 128, 256, 512 };
    int[] denom = { 2, 0, 4, 4, 0, 8 };

    try { // outer try
      for(int i=0; i<numer.Length; i++) {
        try { // nested try
          Console.WriteLine(numer[i] + " / " +
                            denom[i] + " is " +
                            numer[i]/denom[i]);
        }
        catch (DivideByZeroException) {
          // catch the exception
          Console.WriteLine("Can't divide by Zero!");
        }
      }
    }
    catch (IndexOutOfRangeException) {
      // catch the exception
      Console.WriteLine("No matching element found.");
      Console.WriteLine("Fatal error -- program terminated.");
    }
  }
}
```

Nested **try** blocks

The output from the program is shown here:

```
4 / 2 is 2
Can't divide by Zero!
16 / 4 is 4
```

10

```
32 / 4 is 8
Can't divide by Zero!
128 / 8 is 16
No matching element found.
Fatal error -- program terminated.
```

In this example, an exception that can be handled by the inner **try**—in this case a divide-by-zero error—allows the program to continue. However, an array boundary error is caught by the outer **try**, which causes the program to terminate.

Although certainly not the only reason for nested **try** statements, the preceding program makes an important point that can be generalized. Often nested **try** blocks are used to allow different categories of errors to be handled in different ways. Some types of errors are catastrophic and cannot be fixed. Some are minor and can be handled immediately. Many programmers use an outer **try** block to catch the most severe errors, allowing inner **try** blocks to handle less serious ones. You can also use an outer **try** block as a "catch all" block for those errors that are not handled by the inner block.

1-Minute Drill

- How can you catch all exceptions?

- Can one **try** block be used to catch two or more different types of exceptions?

- In nested **try** blocks, what happens to an exception that is not caught by the inner block?

Throwing an Exception

The preceding examples have been catching exceptions generated automatically by C#. However, it is possible to manually throw an exception by using the **throw** statement. Its general form is shown here:

throw *exceptOb*;

Here, *exceptOb* must be an object of an exception class derived from **Exception**.

- To catch all exceptions, use a **catch** statement without an exception parameter.
- Yes, use a **catch** statement for each exception that you want to catch.
- An exception not caught by an inner **try/catch** block moves outward to the enclosing **try** block.

Here is an example that illustrates the **throw** statement by manually throwing a **DivideByZeroException**:

```
// Manually throw an exception.
using System;

class ThrowDemo {
  public static void Main() {
    try {
      Console.WriteLine("Before throw.");
      throw new DivideByZeroException();          ◄─────  Throw an exception.
    }
    catch (DivideByZeroException) {
      // catch the exception
      Console.WriteLine("Exception caught.");
    }
    Console.WriteLine("After try/catch block.");
  }
}
```

The output from the program is shown here:

```
Before throw.
Exception caught.
After try/catch block.
```

Notice how the **DivideByZeroException** was created using **new** in the **throw** statement. Remember, **throw** throws an object. Thus, you must create an object for it to throw. That is, you can't just throw a type. In this case, the default constructor is used to create a **DivideByZeroException** object, but other constructors are available for exceptions (as you will see later).

10

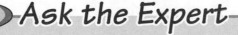

Ask the Expert

Question: Why would I want to manually throw an exception?

Answer: Most often, the exceptions that you will throw will be instances of exception classes that you created. As you will see later in this module, creating your own exception classes allows you to handle errors in your code as part of your program's overall exception handling strategy.

Rethrowing an Exception

An exception caught by one **catch** statement can be rethrown so that it can be caught by an outer **catch**. The most likely reason for rethrowing an exception is to allow multiple handlers access to the exception. For example, perhaps one exception handler manages one aspect of an exception, and a second handler copes with another aspect. To rethrow an expression, you simply specify **throw**, without specifying an exception. That is, you use this form of **throw**:

    throw ;

Remember that when you rethrow an exception, it will not be recaught by the same **catch** statement. It will propagate to the next **catch** statement.

The following program illustrates rethrowing an exception:

```
// Rethrow an exception.
using System;

class Rethrow {
  public static void genException() {
    // here, numer is longer than denom
    int[] numer = { 4, 8, 16, 32, 64, 128, 256, 512 };
    int[] denom = { 2, 0, 4, 4, 0, 8 };

    for(int i=0; i<numer.Length; i++) {
      try {
        Console.WriteLine(numer[i] + " / " +
                          denom[i] + " is " +
                          numer[i]/denom[i]);
      }
      catch (DivideByZeroException) {
        // catch the exception
        Console.WriteLine("Can't divide by Zero!");
      }
      catch (IndexOutOfRangeException) {
        // catch the exception
        Console.WriteLine("No matching element found.");
        throw; // rethrow the exception
      }
    }
  }
}

class RethrowDemo {
  public static void Main() {
```

Rethrow the exception.

```
   try {
     Rethrow.genException();
   }
   catch(IndexOutOfRangeException) {
     // recatch exception
     Console.WriteLine("Fatal error -- " +
                        "program terminated.");
   }
 }
}
```

Catch rethrown exception.

In this program, divide-by-zero errors are handled locally, by **genException( )**, but an array boundary error is rethrown. In this case, it is caught by **Main( )**.

1-Minute Drill

● What does **throw** do?

● Does **throw** throw types or objects?

● Can an exception be rethrown after it is caught? If so, what form of **throw** do you use?

Using finally

Sometimes you will want to define a block of code that will execute when a **try/catch** block is left. For example, an exception might cause an error that terminates the current method, causing its premature return. However, that method may have opened a file or a network connection that needs to be closed. Such types of circumstances are common in programming, and C# provides a convenient way to handle them: **finally**.

To specify a block of code to execute when a **try/catch** block is exited, include a **finally** block at the end of a **try/catch** sequence. The general form of a **try/catch** that includes **finally** is shown here:

```
try {
  // block of code to monitor for errors
}
```

● **throw** generates an exception.
● **throw** throws objects. These objects must be instances of valid exception classes, of course.
● Yes. Specify **throw** without any exception.

```
catch (ExcepType1 exOb) {
  // handler for ExcepType1
}

catch (ExcepType2 exOb) {
  // handler for ExcepType2
}

finally {
  // finally code
}
```

The **finally** block will be executed whenever execution leaves a **try/catch** block, no matter what conditions cause it. That is, whether the **try** block ends normally or because of an exception, the last code executed is that defined by **finally**. The **finally** block is also executed if any code within the **try** block or any of its **catch** statements returns from the method.

Here is an example of **finally**.

```
// Use finally.
using System;

class UseFinally {
  public static void genException(int what) {
    int t;
    int[] nums = new int[2];

    Console.WriteLine("Receiving " + what);
    try {
      switch(what) {
        case 0:
          t = 10 / what; // generate div-by-zero error
          break;
        case 1:
          nums[4] = 4; // generate array index error.
          break;
        case 2:
          return; // return from try block
      }
    }
    catch (DivideByZeroException) {
      // catch the exception
      Console.WriteLine("Can't divide by Zero!");
      return; // return from catch
    }
```

```
      catch (IndexOutOfRangeException) {
        // catch the exception
        Console.WriteLine("No matching element found.");
      }
      finally {  ◄——————————————  This is executed on the way
        Console.WriteLine("Leaving try.");            out of try/catch blocks.
      }
    }
}

class FinallyDemo {
  public static void Main() {

    for(int i=0; i < 3; i++) {
      UseFinally.genException(i);
      Console.WriteLine();
    }
  }
}
```

Here is the output produced by the program:

```
Receiving 0
Can't divide by Zero!
Leaving try.

Receiving 1
No matching element found.
Leaving try.

Receiving 2
Leaving try.
```

As the output shows, no matter how the **try** block is exited, the **finally** block is executed.

A Closer Look at Exception

Up to this point, we have been catching exceptions, but we haven't been doing anything with the exception object itself. As explained earlier, a **catch** clause allows you to specifiy an exception type *and* a parameter. The parameter receives the exception object. Since all exceptions are derived from **Exception**, all exceptions support the members defined by **Exception**. Here we will examine

10

several of its most useful members and constructors, and put the **catch** parameter to use.

Exception defines several properties. Three of the most interesting are **Message**, **StackTrace**, and **TargetSite**. All are read-only. **Message** contains a string that describes the nature of the error. **StackTrace** contains a string that contains the stack of calls that lead to the exception. **TargetSite** returns an object that specifies the method that generated the exception.

Exception also defines several methods. The one that you will most often use is **ToString( )**, which returns a string that describes the exception. **ToString( )** is automatically called when an exception is displayed via **WriteLine( )**, for example.

The following program demonstrates these properties and this method:

```csharp
// Using Exception members.
using System;

class ExcTest {
  public static void genException() {
    int[] nums = new int[4];

    Console.WriteLine("Before exception is generated.");

    // generate an index out-of-bounds exception
    nums[7] = 10;
    Console.WriteLine("this won't be displayed");
  }
}

class UseExcept {
  public static void Main() {

    try {
      ExcTest.genException();
    }
    catch (IndexOutOfRangeException exc) {
      // catch the exception
      Console.WriteLine("Standard message is: ");
      Console.WriteLine(exc); // calls ToString()
      Console.WriteLine("Stack trace: " + exc.StackTrace);
      Console.WriteLine("Message: " + exc.Message);
      Console.WriteLine("TargetSite: " + exc.TargetSite);
    }
    Console.WriteLine("After catch statement.");
  }
}
```

The output from this program is shown here:

```
Before exception is generated.
Standard message is:
System.IndexOutOfRangeException: Exception of type
                   System.IndexOutOfRangeException was thrown.
  at ExcTest.genException()
  at UseExcept.Main()
Stack trace:    at ExcTest.genException()
  at UseExcept.Main()
Message: Exception of type System.IndexOutOfRangeException
       was thrown.
TargetSite: Void genException()
After catch statement.
```

Exception defines four constructors. The two that we will examine are shown here:

Exception( )

Exception(string *str*)

The first is the default constructor. The second specifies the **Message** property associated with the exception. When creating your own exception classes, you should implement both of these constructors.

Commonly Used Exceptions

The **System** namespace defines several standard, built-in exceptions. All are derived from **SystemException** since they are generated by the CLR when runtime errors occur. Several of the more commonly used standard exceptions defined by C# are shown in Table 10-1.

10

Exception	Meaning
ArrayTypeMismatchException	Type of value being stored is incompatible with the type of the array.
DivideByZeroException	Division by zero attempted.
IndexOutOfRangeException	Array index is out of bounds.
InvalidCastException	A runtime cast is invalid.

Table 10-1   Commonly Used Exceptions Defined Within the System Namespace

Exception	Meaning
OutOfMemoryException	A call to **new** fails because insufficient free memory exists.
OverflowException	An arithmetic overflow occurred.
StackOverflowException	The stack was overrun.

Table 10-1 Commonly Used Exceptions Defined Within the System Namespace (*continued*)

1-Minute Drill

- What does **Message** contain?
- When is the code within a **finally** block executed?
- How can you display a stack trace of the events leading up to an exception?

Deriving Exception Classes

Although C#'s built-in exceptions handle most common errors, C#'s exception handling mechanism is not limited to these errors. In fact, part of the power of C#'s approach to exceptions is its ability to handle exceptions that you create. You can use custom exceptions to handle errors in your own code. Creating an exception is easy. Just define a class derived from **Exception**. As a general rule, exceptions defined by you should be derived from **ApplicationException** since this is the hierarchy reserved for application-related exceptions. Your derived classes don't need to actually implement anything—it is their existence in the type system that allows you to use them as exceptions.

The exception classes that you create will automatically have the properties and methods defined by **Exception** available to them. Of course, you can override one or more of these members in exception classes that you create.

Here is an example that creates an exception called **NonIntResultException**. In the program, this exception is thrown when dividing two integer values produces a result with a fractional component. **NonIntResultException** defines the two standard constructors and overrides the **ToString( )** method.

- **Message** contains a message that describes the exception.
- A **finally** block is the last thing executed when a **try** block is exited.
- To print a stack trace, display the **StackTrace** property defined by **Exception**.

```
// Use a custom exception.
using System;                                          ⟶ A custom exception

// Create an exception.
class NonIntResultException : ApplicationException {  ◄───
  // Implement the standard constructors
  public NonIntResultFxception() : base() { }
  public NonIntResultException(string str) : base(str) { }

  // Override ToString for NonIntResultException.
  public override string ToString() {  ◄───   Override ToString( ).
    return Message;
  }
}

class CustomExceptDemo {
  public static void Main() {

    // Here, numer contains some odd values.
    int[] numer = { 4, 8, 15, 32, 64, 127, 256, 512 };
    int[] denom = { 2, 0, 4, 4, 0, 8 };

    for(int i=0; i<numer.Length; i++) {
      try {
        if((numer[i]%2) != 0)                 Throw a custom exception.
          throw new   ◄───────
            NonIntResultException("Outcome of " +
                  numer[i] + " / " + denom[i] + " is not even.");

        Console.WriteLine(numer[i] + " / " +
                          denom[i] + " is " +
                          numer[i]/denom[i]);
      }
      catch (DivideByZeroException) {
        // catch the exception
        Console.WriteLine("Can't divide by Zero!");
      }
      catch (IndexOutOfRangeException) {
        // catch the exception
        Console.WriteLine("No matching element found.");
      }
      catch (NonIntResultException exc) {
        Console.WriteLine(exc);
      }
```

10

```
     }
   }
}
```

The output from the program is shown here:

```
4 / 2 is 2
Can't divide by Zero!
Outcome of 15 / 4 is not even.
32 / 4 is 8
Can't divide by Zero!
Outcome of 127 / 8 is not even.
No matching element found.
No matching element found.
```

Before moving on, you might want to experiment with this program a bit. For example, try commenting-out the override of **ToString( )** and observe the results. Also, try creating an exception using the default constructor, and observe what C# generates as its default message.

Catching Derived Class Exceptions

You need to be careful how you order **catch** statements when trying to catch exception types that involve base and derived classes, because a **catch** clause for a base class will also match any of its derived classes. For example, since the base class of all exceptions is **Exception**, catching **Exception** catches all possible exceptions. Of course, using **catch** without an argument provides a cleaner way to catch all exceptions, as described earlier. However, the issue of catching derived class exceptions is very important in other contexts, especially when you create exceptions of your own.

If you want to catch exceptions of both a base class type and a derived class type, put the derived class first in the **catch** sequence. If you don't, then the base class **catch** will also catch all derived classes. This rule is self-enforcing because putting the base class first causes unreachable code to be created, since the derived class **catch** clause can never execute. In C#, an unreachable **catch** clause is an error.

The following program creates two exception classes called **ExceptA** and **ExceptB**. **ExceptA** is derived from **ApplicationException**. **ExceptB** is derived from **ExceptA**. The program then throws an exception of each type.

```
// Derived exceptions must appear before base class exceptions.
using System;

// Create an exception.
class ExceptA : ApplicationException {          Derive an exception.
  public ExceptA() : base() { }
  public ExceptA(string str) : base(str) { }

  public override string ToString() {
    return Message;
  }
}

// Create an exception derived from ExceptA
class ExceptB : ExceptA {                        Derive an exception
  public ExceptB() : base() { }                  from ExceptA.
  public ExceptB(string str) : base(str) { }

  public override string ToString() {
    return Message;
  }
}

class OrderMatters {
  public static void Main() {
    for(int x = 0; x < 3; x++) {
      try {
        if(x==0) throw new ExceptA("Caught an ExceptA exception");
        else if(x==1) throw new ExceptB("Caught an ExceptB exception");
        else throw new Exception();
      }
      catch (ExceptB exc) {
        // catch the exception
        Console.WriteLine(exc);
      }
      catch (ExceptA exc) {              The order of these catch
        // catch the exception           statements matters.
        Console.WriteLine(exc);
      }
      catch (Exception exc) {
        Console.WriteLine(exc);
      }
    }
  }
}
```

10

Ask the Expert

Question: Since an exception usually indicates a specific error, why would I want to catch a base class exception?

Answer: A **catch** clause that catches a base class exception allows you to catch an entire category of exceptions, possibly handling them with a single catch statement and avoiding duplicated code. For example, you might create a set of exceptions that describes some sort of device error. If your exception handlers simply tell the user that a device error occurred, then you could use a common **catch** for all exceptions of this type. The handler could just display the **Message** string. Since the code that accomplishes this is the same for all exceptions, one **catch** can respond to all device exceptions.

The output from the program is shown here:

```
Caught an ExceptA exception
Caught an ExceptB exception
System.Exception: Exception of type System.Exception was thrown.
   at OrderMatters.Main()
```

Notice the order of the **catch** statements. This is the only order in which they can occur. Since **ExceptB** is derived from **ExceptA**, the **catch** statement for **ExceptB** must be before the one for **ExceptA**. Similarly, the **catch** for **Exception** (which is the base class for all exceptions) must appear last. To prove this point for yourself, try rearranging the **catch** statements. Doing so will result in a compile-time error.

QExcDemo.cs

Project 10-1: Adding Exceptions to the Queue Class

In this project you will create two exception classes that can be used by the queue classes developed by Project 9-1. They will indicate the queue-full and queue-empty error conditions. These exceptions are thrown by the **put( )** and **get( )** methods, respectively, when an error occurs. For the sake of simplicity, this project will add these exceptions to only the **FixedQueue** class, but you can easily incorporate them into the other queue classes from Project 9-1.

Step-by-Step

1. Create a file called **QExcDemo.cs**.

2. Into **QExcDemo.cs** define the following exceptions:

```
/*
    Project 10-1

    Add exception handling to the queue classes.
*/
using System;

// An exception for queue-full errors.
class QueueFullException : ApplicationException {
  public QueueFullException() : base() { }
  public QueueFullException(string str) : base(str) { }

  public override string ToString() {
    return "\n" + Message;
  }
}

// An exception for queue-empty errors.
class QueueEmptyException : ApplicationException {
  public QueueEmptyException() : base() { }
  public QueueEmptyException(string str) : base(str) { }

  public override string ToString() {
    return "\n" + Message;
  }
}
```

A **QueueFullException** is generated when an attempt is made to store an item in an already full queue. A **QueueEmptyException** is generated when an attempt is made to remove an element from an empty queue.

3. Modify the **FixedQueue** class so that it throws an exception when an error occurs, as shown here. Add it to **QExcDemo.cs**.

```
// A fixed-size queue class for characters that uses exceptions.
class FixedQueue : ICharQ {
  char[] q; // this array holds the queue
```

10

```
int putloc, getloc; // the put and get indices

// Construct an empty queue given its size.
public FixedQueue(int size) {
  q = new char[size+1]; // allocate memory for queue
  putloc = getloc = 0;
}

// Put a character into the queue.
public void put(char ch) {
  if(putloc==q.Length-1)
    throw new QueueFullException("Max length is " +
                                   (q.Length-1));

  putloc++;
  q[putloc] = ch;
}

// Get a character from the queue.
public char get() {
  if(getloc == putloc)
    throw new QueueEmptyException();

  getloc++;
  return q[getloc];
}
}
```

The addition of exceptions to **FixedQueue** allows a queue error to be handled in a rational fashion. You might recall that the previous version of **FixedQueue** simply reported the error. Throwing an exception is a much better approach because it allows the code that uses **FixedQueue** to handle the error in an appropriate manner.

4. To try the updated **FixedQueue** class, add the **QExcDemo** class shown here to **QExcDemo.cs**.

```
// Demonstrate the queue exceptions.

class QExcDemo {
  public static void Main() {
    FixedQueue q = new FixedQueue(10);
    char ch;
    int i;

    try {
```

```
      // overrun the queue
      for(i=0; i < 11; i++) {
        Console.Write("Attempting to store : " +
                         (char) ('A' + i));
        q.put((char) ('A' + i));
        Console.WriteLine(" -- OK");
      }
      Console.WriteLine();
    }
    catch (QueueFullException exc) {
      Console.WriteLine(exc);
    }
    Console.WriteLine();

    try {
      // over-empty the queue
      for(i=0; i < 11; i++) {
        Console.Write("Getting next char: ");
        ch = q.get();
        Console.WriteLine(ch);
      }
    }
    catch (QueueEmptyException exc) {
      Console.WriteLine(exc);
    }
  }
}
```

5. To create the program, you must compile **QExcDemo.cs** with the
   IQChar.cs file. Recall that **IQChar.cs** contains the queue interface.
   When you run **QExcDemo**, you will see the following output:

```
Attempting to store : A -- OK
Attempting to store : B -- OK
Attempting to store : C -- OK
Attempting to store : D -- OK
Attempting to store : E -- OK
Attempting to store : F -- OK
Attempting to store : G -- OK
Attempting to store : H -- OK
Attempting to store : I -- OK
Attempting to store : J -- OK
Attempting to store : K
Max length is 10

Getting next char: A
```

10

```
Getting next char: B
Getting next char: C
Getting next char: D
Getting next char: E
Getting next char: F
Getting next char: G
Getting next char: H
Getting next char: I
Getting next char: J
Getting next char:
An exception of type QueueEmptyException was thrown.
```

Using checked and unchecked

An arithmetic computation can cause an overflow. For example, consider the following sequence:

```
byte a, b, result;
a = 127;
b = 127;

result = (byte)(a * b);
```

Here, the product of **a** and **b** exceeds the range of a **byte** value. Thus, the result overflows the type of the result.

C# allows you to specify whether your code will raise an exception when overflow occurs using the keywords **checked** and **unchecked**. To specify that an expression be checked for overflow, use **checked**. To specify that overflow be ignored, use **unchecked**. In this case, the result is truncated to fit into the target type of the expression.

The **checked** statement has these two general forms. One checks a specific expression. The other checks a block of statements.

```
checked (expr)

checked {
    // statements to be checked
}
```

Here, *expr* is the expression being checked. If a checked expression overflows, then an **OverflowException** is thrown.

The **unchecked** statement has these two general forms. One ignores overflow for a specific expression. The other ignores overflow for a block of statements.

unchecked (*expr*)

```
unchecked {
    // statements for which overflow is ignored
}
```

Here, *expr* is the expression that is not being checked for overflow. If an unchecked expression overflows, then truncation will occur.

Here is a program that demonstrates both **checked** and **unchecked**.

```
// Using checked and unchecked.
using System;

class CheckedDemo {
  public static void Main() {
    byte a, b;
    byte result;

    a = 127;
    b = 127;

    try {
      result = unchecked((byte)(a * b));
      Console.WriteLine("Unchecked result: " + result);

      result = checked((byte)(a * b)); // this causes exception
      Console.WriteLine("Checked result: " + result); // won't execute
    }
    catch (OverflowException exc) {
      // catch the exception
      Console.WriteLine(exc);
    }
  }
}
```

> Overflow in this expression is truncated.

> Overflow here causes an exception.

The output from the program is shown here:

```
Unchecked result: 1
System.OverflowException: Exception of type
                         System.OverflowException was thrown.
                         at CheckedDemo.Main()
```

As is evident, the unchecked expression resulted in a truncation. The checked expression caused an exception.

The preceding program demonstrated the use of **checked** and **unchecked** for a single expression. The following program shows how to check and uncheck a block of statements:

```
// Using checked and unchecked with statement blocks.
using System;

class CheckedBlocks {
  public static void Main() {
    byte a, b;
    byte result;

    a = 127;
    b = 127;

    try {
      unchecked {          ◄────────────  An unchecked block
        a = 127;
        b = 127;
        result = unchecked((byte)(a * b));
        Console.WriteLine("Unchecked result: " + result);

        a = 125;
        b = 5;
        result = unchecked((byte)(a * b));
        Console.WriteLine("Unchecked result: " + result);
      }

      checked {            ◄────────────  A checked block
        a = 2;
        b = 7;
        result = checked((byte)(a * b)); // this is OK
        Console.WriteLine("Checked result: " + result);

        a = 127;
        b = 127;
        result = checked((byte)(a * b)); // this causes exception
        Console.WriteLine("Checked result: " + result); // won't execute
      }
    }
    catch (OverflowException exc) {
      // catch the exception
      Console.WriteLine(exc);
    }
  }
}
```

The output from the program is shown here:

```
Unchecked result: 1
Unchecked result: 113
Checked result: 14
System.OverflowException: Exception of type
            System.OverflowException was thrown.
  at CheckedBlocks.Main()
```

As you can see, the unchecked block results in the overflow being truncated. When overflow occurred in the checked block, an exception was raised.

One reason that you may need to use **checked** or **unchecked** is that the checked/unchecked status of overflow is determined by the setting of a compiler option, and by the execution environment itself. Thus, for some types of programs, it is best to explicitly specify the overflow check status.

Ask the Expert

Question: When should I use exception handling in a program? When should I create my own, custom exception classes?

Answer: Since C# extensively uses exceptions to report errors, nearly all real-world programs will make use of exception handling. This is the part of exception handling that most new C# programmers find easy. It is harder to decide when and how to use your own, custom-made exceptions. In general, there are two ways errors can be reported: return values and exceptions. When is one approach better than the other? Simply put, in C#, exception handling should be the norm. Certainly, returning an error code is a valid alternative in some cases, but exceptions provide a more powerful, structured way to handle errors. They are the way professional C# programmers handle errors in their code.

10

☑ *Mastery Check*

1. What class is at the top of the exception hierarchy?

2. Briefly explain how to use **try** and **catch**.

3. What is wrong with this fragment?

```
// ...
vals[18] = 10;
catch (IndexOutOfRangeException exc) {
  // handle error
}
```

4. What happens if an exception is not caught?

5. What is wrong with this fragment?

```
class A : Exception { ...

class B : A { ...

// ...

try {
  // ...
}
catch (A exc) { ... }
catch (B exc) { ... }
```

6. Can an exception caught by an inner **catch** rethrow that exception to an outer **catch**?

7. The **finally** block is the last bit of code executed before your program ends. True or false? Explain your answer.

8. In Exercise 3 of the Mastery Check in Module 6 you created a **Stack** class. Add custom exceptions to your class that report stack-full and stack-empty conditions.

9. Explain the purpose of **checked** and **unchecked**.

10. How can all exceptions be caught?

Module 11

Using I/O

The Goals of This Module

- Learn about the stream
- Explore the stream classes
- Examine console I/O
- Explore file I/O
- Read and write binary data
- Use random-access files
- Convert numeric strings

Since the beginning of this book you have been using parts of the C# I/O system, such as **Console.WriteLine( )**, but you have been doing so without much formal explanation. Because the C# I/O system is built upon a hierarchy of classes, it was not possible to present its theory and details without first discussing classes, inheritance, and exceptions. Now it is time to examine C#'s approach to I/O in detail. As explained in Module 1, C# uses the I/O system and classes defined by the .NET Framework. Thus, a discussion of I/O under C# is also a discussion of the .NET I/O system in general.

This module examines C#'s approach to both console I/O and file I/O. Be forewarned that C#'s I/O system is quite large. This module introduces the most important and commonly used features, but there will be several aspects of I/O that you will want to study on your own. Fortunately, C#'s I/O system is cohesive and consistent; once you understand its fundamentals, the rest of the I/O system is easy to master.

C#'s I/O Is Built upon Streams

C# programs perform I/O through streams. A *stream* is an abstraction that either produces or consumes information. A stream is linked to a physical device by the C# I/O system. All streams behave in the same manner, even if the actual physical devices they are linked to differ. Thus, the I/O classes and methods can be applied to many types of devices. For example, the same methods that you use to write to the console can also be used to write to a disk file.

Byte Streams and Character Streams

At the lowest level, all C# I/O operates on bytes. This makes sense because many devices are byte-oriented when it comes to I/O operations. Frequently, though, we humans prefer to communicate using characters. Recall that in C#, **char** is a 16-bit type and **byte** is an 8-bit type. If you are using the ASCII character set, then it is easy to convert between **char** and **byte**; just ignore the high-order byte of the **char** value. But this won't work for the rest of the Unicode characters, which need both bytes. Thus, byte streams are not perfectly suited to handling character-based I/O. To solve this problem, C# defines several classes that convert a byte stream into a character stream, handling the translation of **byte**-to-**char** and **char**-to-**byte** for you automatically.

The Predefined Streams

Three predefined streams, which are exposed by the propterties **Console.In**, **Console.Out**, and **Console.Error**, are available to all programs that use the **System** namespace. **Console.Out** refers to the standard output stream. By default, this is the console. When you call **Console.WriteLine( )**, for example, it automatically sends information to **Console.Out**. **Console.In** refers to standard input, which is by default the keyboard. **Console.Error** refers to the standard error stream, which is also the console by default. However, these streams can be redirected to any compatible I/O device. The standard streams are character streams. Thus, these streams read and write characters.

1-Minute Drill

● What is a stream?

● What types of streams does C# define?

● What are the predefined streams?

The Stream Classes

C# defines both byte and character stream classes. However, the character stream classes are really just wrappers that convert an underlying byte stream in a character stream, handling any conversion automatically. Thus, the character streams, while logically separate, are built upon byte streams.

All stream classes are defined within the **System.IO** namespace. To use these classes, you will usually include the following statement near the top of your program:

```
using System.IO;
```

The reason that you don't have to specify **System.IO** for console input and output is that the **Console** class is defined in the **System** namespace.

11

● A stream is an abstraction that either produces or consumes information.

● C# defines both byte and character streams.

● **Console.In**, **Console.Out**, and **Console.Error** are the predefined streams.

The Stream Class

At the core of C#'s streams is **System.IO.Stream**. **Stream** represents a byte stream and is a base class for all other stream classes. It is also abstract, which means that you cannot instantiate a **Stream** object. **Stream** defines a set of standard stream operations. Table 11-1 shows several commonly used methods defined by **Stream**.

In general, if an I/O error occurs, the methods shown in Table 11-1 will throw an **IOException**. If an invalid operation is attempted, such as attempting to write to a stream that is read-only, a **NotSupportedException** is thrown.

Notice that **Stream** defines methods that read and write data. However, not all streams will support both of these operations, because it is possible to open read-only or write-only streams. Also, not all streams will support position requests via **Seek( )**. To determine the capabilities of a stream, you will use one or more of **Stream**'s properties. They are shown in Table 11-2. Also shown are the **Length** and **Position** properties, which contain the length of the stream and its current position.

Method	Description
void Close( )	Closes the stream.
void Flush( )	Writes the contents of the stream to the physical device.
int ReadByte( )	Returns an integer representation of the next available byte of input. Returns –1 when the end of the file is encountered.
int Read(byte[ ] *buf*, int *offset*, int *numBytes*)	Attempts to read up to *numBytes* bytes into *buf* starting at *buf*[*offset*], returning the number of bytes successfully read.
long Seek(long *offset*, SeekOrigin *origin*)	Sets the current position in the stream to the specified *offset* from the specified *origin*.
void WriteByte(byte *b*)	Writes a single byte to an output stream.
int Write(byte[ ] *buf*, int *offset*, int *numBytes*)	Writes a subrange of *numBytes* bytes from the array *buf*, beginning at *buf*[*offset*]. The number of bytes written is returned.

Table 11-1   Some of the Methods Defined by Stream

Method	Description
bool CanRead	This property is true if the stream can be read. This property is read-only.
bool CanSeek	This property is true if the stream supports position requests. This property is read-only.
bool CanWrite	This property is true if the stream can be written. This property is read-only.
long Length	This property contains the length of the stream. This property is read-only.
long Position	This property represents the current position of the stream. This property is read/write.

Table 11-2   The Properties Defined by Stream

The Byte Stream Classes

From **Stream** are derived the three concrete byte stream classes shown here:

Stream Class	Description
BufferedStream	Wraps a byte stream and adds buffering. Buffering provides a performance enhancement in many cases.
FileStream	A byte stream designed for file I/O.
MemoryStream	A byte stream that uses memory for storage.

It is also possible for you to derive your own stream classes. However, for the vast majority of applications, the built-in streams will be sufficient.

The Character Stream Wrapper Classes

To create a character stream, you will wrap a byte stream inside one of C#'s character stream wrappers. At the top of the character-stream hierarchy are the abstract classes **TextReader** and **TextWriter**. The methods defined by these two abstract classes are available to all of their subclasses. Thus, they form a minimal set of I/O functions that all character streams will have.

Table 11-3 shows the input methods in **TextReader**. In general, these methods can throw an **IOException** on error. (Some can throw other types of

11

Method	Description
void Close( )	Closes the input source.
int Peek( )	Obtains the next character from the input stream, but does not remove that character. Returns –1 if no character is available.
int Read( )	Returns an integer representation of the next available character from the invoking input stream. Returns –1 when the end of the stream is encountered.
int Read(char[ ] *buf*, int *offset*, int *numChars*)	Attempts to read up to *numChars* characters into *buf* starting at *buf*[*offset*], returning the number of characters successfully read.
int ReadBlock(char[ ] *buf*, int *offset*, int *numChars*)	Attempts to read up to *numChars* characters into *buf* starting at *buf*[*offset*], returning the number of characters successfully read.
string ReadLine( )	Reads the next line of text and returns it as a string. Null is returned if an attempt is made to read at end-of-file.
string ReadToEnd( )	Reads all of the remaining characters in a stream and returns them as a string.

Table 11-3 The Input Methods Defined by TextReader

exceptions, too.) Of particular interest is the **ReadLine( )** method, which reads an entire line of text, returning it as a **string**. This method is useful when reading input that contains embedded spaces.

TextWriter defines versions of **Write( )** and **WriteLine( )** that output all of the built-in types. For example, here are just a few of their overloaded versions:

Method	Description
void Write(int *val*)	Write an **int**.
void Write(double *val*)	Write a **double**.
void Write(bool *val*)	Write a **bool**.
void WriteLine(string *val*)	Write a string followed by a new line.
void WriteLine(uint *val*)	Write a **uint** followed by a new line.
void WriteLine(char *val*)	Write a character followed by a new line.

In addition to **Write( )** and **WriteLine( )**, **TextWriter** also defines the **Close( )** and **Flush( )** methods shown here:

virtual void Close( )

virtual void Flush( )

Flush( ) causes any input remaining in the output buffer to be written to the physical medium. **Close( )** closes the stream.

The **TextReader** and **TextWriter** classes are implemented by the character-based stream classes shown here. Thus, these streams provide the methods and properties specified by **TextReader** and **TextWriter**.

Stream Class	Description
StreamReader	Read characters from a byte stream. This class wraps a byte input stream.
StreamWriter	Write characters to a byte stream. This class wraps a byte output stream.
StringReader	Read characters from a string.
StringWriter	Write characters to a string.

Binary Streams

In addition to the byte and character streams, C# defines two binary stream classes, which can be used to read and write binary data directly. These streams are called **BinaryReader** and **BinaryWriter**. We will look closely at these later in this module when binary file I/O is discussed.

Now that you understand the general layout of the C# I/O system, the rest of this module will examine its various pieces in detail, beginning with console I/O.

1-Minute Drill

● What class is at the top of the stream hierarchy?

● Name three **Stream** properties.

● What classes are at the top of the character stream classes?

● The **Stream** class is at the top of the stream hierarchy.
● The properties are **CanSeek**, **CanRead**, **CanWrite**, **Length**, and **Position.**
● **TextReader** and **TextWriter** are at the top of the character stream classes.

Console I/O

Console I/O is accomplished through the standard streams **Console.In**, **Console.Out**, and **Console.Error**. You have been using console I/O since Module 1, so you are already familiar with it. As you will see, it has some additional capabilities.

Before we begin, however, it is important to emphasize a point made earlier in this book: most real applications of C# will not be text-based, console programs. Rather, they will be graphically oriented programs or components that rely upon a windowed interface for interaction with the user. Thus, the portion of C#'s I/O system that relates to console input and output is not widely used. Although text-based programs are excellent as teaching examples, and for short utility programs, they are not suitable for most real-world applications.

Reading Console Input

Console.In is an instance of **TextReader**, and you can use the methods and properties defined by **TextReader** to access it. However, you will usually use the methods provided by **Console**, which automatically reads from **Console.In**. **Console** defines two input methods: **Read( )** and **ReadLine( )**.

To read a single character, use the **Read( )** method. It is shown here:

```
static int Read( )
```

This method was introduced in Module 3. It returns the next character read from the console. The character is returned as an **int**, which must be cast to **char**. It returns –1 on error. This method will throw an **IOException** on failure.

To read a string of characters, use the **ReadLine( )** method. It is shown here:

```
static string ReadLine( )
```

ReadLine( ) reads characters until you press ENTER and returns them in a **string** object. This method will also throw an **IOException** on failure.

Here is a program that demonstrates reading an array of characters from **Console.In**:

```
// Input from the console using ReadLine().
using System;

class ReadChars {
  public static void Main() {
    string str;

    Console.WriteLine("Enter some characters.");
    str = Console.ReadLine();   ◄——————————   Read a string from
    Console.WriteLine("You entered: " + str);                the keyboard.
  }
}
```

Here is a sample run:

```
Enter some characters.
This is a test.
You entered: This is a test.
```

Although the **Console** methods are the easiest way to read from **Console.In**, you can call methods on the underlying TextReader. For example, here is the preceding program rewritten to use the methods defined by **TextReader**:

```
/* Read an array of bytes from the keyboard, using
   Console.In directly. */
using System;

class ReadChars2 {
  public static void Main() {
    string str;

    Console.WriteLine("Enter some characters.");

    str = Console.In.ReadLine();   ◄——————————   Read from **Console.In**
                                                  explicitly.
    Console.WriteLine("You entered: " + str);
  }
}
```

11

Notice how **ReadLine( )** is now invoked directly on **Console.In**. The key point here is that if you need access to the methods defined by the **TextReader** that underlies **Console.In**, you will invoke those methods as shown in this example.

Writing Console Output

Console.Out and **Console.Error** are objects of type **TextWriter**. Console output is most easily accomplished with **Write( )** and **WriteLine( )**, with which you are already familiar. Versions of these methods exist that output for each of the built-in types. **Console** defines its own versions of **Write( )** and **WriteLine( )** so that they can be called directly on **Console**, as you have been doing throughout this book. However, you can invoke these (and other) methods on the **TextWriter** that underlies **Console.Out** and **Console.Error** if you choose.

Here is a program that demonstrates writing to **Console.Out** and **Console.Error**.

```
// Write to Console.Out and Console.Error.
using System;

class ErrOut {
  public static void Main() {
    int a=10, b=0;
    int result;

    Console.Out.WriteLine("This will generate an exception.");
    try {
      result = a / b; // generate an exception
    } catch(DivideByZeroException exc) {
      Console.Error.WriteLine(exc.Message);
    }
  }
}
```

Write to **Console.Out** and **Console.Error**.

The output from the program is shown here:

```
This will generate an exception.
Attempted to divide by zero.
```

Sometimes newcomers to programming are confused about when to use **Console.Error**. Since both **Console.Out** and **Console.Error** default to writing their output to the console, why are there two different streams? The answer lies in the fact that the standard streams can be redirected to other devices. For example, **Console.Error** can be redirected to write to a disk file, rather than the screen. Thus, it is possible to direct error output to a log file, for example, without affecting console output. Conversely, if console output is redirected and error output is not, then error messages will appear on the console, where they can be seen. We will examine redirection later, after file I/O has been described.

FileStream and Byte-Oriented File I/O

C# provides classes that allow you to read and write files. Of course, the most common type of files are disk files. At the operating system level, all files are byte oriented. As you would expect, C# provides methods to read and write bytes from and to a file. Thus, reading and writing files using byte streams is very common. C# also allows you to wrap a byte-oriented file stream within a character-based object. Character-based file operations are useful when text is being stored. Character streams are discussed later in this module. Here, byte-oriented I/O is described.

To create a byte-oriented stream attached to a file, you will use the **FileStream** class. **FileStream** is derived from **Stream** and contains all of **Stream**'s functionality.

Remember, the stream classes, including **FileStream**, are defined in **System.IO**. Thus, you will usually include

```
using System.IO;
```

near the top of any program that uses them.

Opening and Closing a File

To create a byte stream linked to a file, create a **FileStream** object. **FileStream** defines several constructors. Perhaps its most commonly used one is the one shown here:

FileStream(string *filename*, FileMode *mode*)

11

Here, *filename* specifies the name of the file to open, which can include a full path specification. The *mode* parameter specifies how the file will be opened. It must be one of the values defined by the **FileMode** enumeration. These values are shown in Table 11-4.

If a failure occurs when attempting to open the file, an exception will be thrown. If the file cannot be opened because it does not exist, **FileNotFound-**

Value	Description
FileMode.Append	Output is appended to the end of file.
FileMode.Create	Creates a new output file. Any preexisting file by the same name will be destroyed.
FileMode.CreateNew	Creates a new output file.
FileMode.Open	Opens a preexisting file.
FileMode.OpenOrCreate	Opens a file if it exists, or creates the file if it does not already exist.
FileMode.Truncate	Opens a preexisting file, but reduces its length to zero.

Table 11-4 The FileMode Values

Exception will be thrown. If the file cannot be opened because of an I/O error, **IOException** will be thrown. Other possible exceptions are **ArgumentNull-Exception** (the filename is null), **ArgumentException** (the mode parameter is invalid), **SecurityException** (user does not have access rights), and **Directory-NotFoundException** (specified directory is invalid).

The following shows one way to open the file **test.dat** for input:

```
FileStream fin;

try {
  fin = new FileStream("test.dat", FileMode.Open);
}
catch(FileNotFoundException exc) {
  Console.WriteLine(exc.Message);
  return;
}
catch {
  Console.WriteLine("Cannot open file.");
  return;
}
```

Here, the first **catch** clause catches the file-not-found error. The second **catch**, which is a "catch all" clause, handles the other possible file errors. You could also check for each error individually, reporting more specifically the problem that occurred. For the sake of simplicity, the examples in this book will catch only **FileNotFoundException**, but your real-world code may need to handle the other possible exceptions, depending upon the circumstances.

As mentioned, the **FileStream** constructor just described opens a file that has read/write access. If you want to restrict access to just reading or just writing, use this constructor instead:

FileStream(string *filename*, FileMode *mode*, FileAccess *how*)

As before, *filename* specifies the name of the file to open, and *mode* specifies how the file will be opened. The value passed in *how* determines how the file can be accessed. It must be one of the values defined by the **FileAccess** enumeration, which are shown here:

FileAccess.Read   FileAccess.Write   FileAccess.ReadWrite

For example, this opens a read-only file:

```
FileStream fin = new FileStream("test.dat", FileMode.Open,
                                FileAccess.Read);
```

When you are done with a file, you should close it by calling **Close( )**. Its general form is shown here:

void Close( )

Closing a file releases the system resources allocated to the file, allowing them to be used by another file. **Close( )** can throw an **IOException**.

Reading Bytes from a FileStream

FileStream defines two methods that read bytes from a file: **ReadByte( )** and **Read( )**. To read a single byte from a file, use **ReadByte( )**, whose general form is shown here:

int ReadByte( )

Each time it is called, it reads a single byte from the file and returns it as an integer value. It returns −1 when the end of the file is encountered. It throws an **IOException** when an error occurs.

11

To read a block of bytes, use **Read( )**, which has this general form:

int Read(byte[ ] *buf*, int *offset*, int *numBytes*)

Read( ) attempts to read up to *numBytes* bytes into *buf* starting at *buf[offset]*. It returns the number of bytes successfully read. An **IOException** is thrown if an I/O error occurs. Several other types of exceptions are possible, including **Not-SupportedException**, which is thrown if reading is not supported by the stream.

The following program uses **ReadByte( )** to input and display the contents of a text file, the name of which is specified as a command-line argument. Note the **try/catch** blocks that handle the two errors that might occur when this program is first executed: the specified file not being found or the user forgetting to include the name of the file. You can use this same approach any time you use command-line arguments.

```
/* Display a file.

   To use this program, specify the name
   of the file that you want to see.
   For example, to see a file called TEST.CS,
   use the following command line.

   ShowFile TEST.CS
*/

using System;
using System.IO;

class ShowFile {
  public static void Main(string[] args) {
    int i;
    FileStream fin;

    try {
      fin = new FileStream(args[0], FileMode.Open);
    } catch(FileNotFoundException exc) {
      Console.WriteLine(exc.Message);
      return;
    } catch(IndexOutOfRangeException exc) {
      Console.WriteLine(exc.Message + "\nUsage: ShowFile File");
      return;
    }
```

```
// read bytes until EOF is encountered
do {
  try {
    i = fin.ReadByte();  ◄──────────  Read from the file.
  } catch(IOException exc) {
    Console.WriteLine(exc.Message);
    return;
  }
  if(i != -1) Console.Write((char) i);
} while(i != -1);  ◄──────────  When i equals -1, the end
                                 of the file has been reached.

fin.Close();
}
}
```

Writing to a File

To write a byte to a file, use the **WriteByte( )** method. Its simplest form is shown here:

> void WriteByte(byte *val*)

This method writes the byte specified by *val* to the file. If an error occurs during writing, an **IOException** is thrown. If the underlying stream is not opened for output, a **NotSupportedException** is thrown.

You can write an array of bytes to a file by calling **Write( )**. It is shown here:

> int Write(byte[ ] *buf*, int *offset*, int *numBytes*)

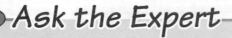

Ask the Expert

11

Question: I noticed that ReadByte( ) returns −1 when the end of the file has been reached, but that it does not have a special return value for a file error. Why not?

Answer: In C#, errors are handled by exceptions. Thus, if **ReadByte( )**, or any other I/O method, returns a value, it means that no error has occurred. This is a much cleaner way of handling I/O errors than by using special error codes.

Write( ) writes *numBytes* bytes from the array *buf,* beginning at *buf*[*offset*], to the file. The number of bytes written is returned. If an error occurs during writing, an **IOException** is thrown. If the underlying stream is not opened for output, a **NotSupportedException** is thrown. Other exceptions are also possible.

As you may know, when file output is performed, often that output is not immediately written to the actual physical device. Instead, output is buffered by the operating system until a sizable chunk of data can be written all at once. This improves the efficiency of the system. For example, disk files are organized by sectors, which might be anywhere from 128 bytes long, on up. Output is usually buffered until an entire sector can be written all at once. However, if you want to cause data to be written to the physical device whether the buffer is full or not, you can call **Flush( )**, shown here:

```
void Flush( )
```

An **IOException** is thrown on failure.

Once you are done with an output file, you must remember to close it using **Close( )**. Doing so ensures that any output remaining in a disk buffer is actually written to the disk. Thus, there is no reason to call **Flush( )** before closing a file.

The following example copies a file. The names of the source and destination files are specified on the command line.

```
/* Copy a file.

   To use this program, specify the name
   of the source file and the destination file.
   For example, to copy a file called FIRST.TXT
   to a file called SECOND.TXT, use the following
   command line.

   CopyFile FIRST.TXT SECOND.TXT
*/

using System;
using System.IO;

class CopyFile {
```

```
public static void Main(string[] args) {
  int i;
  FileStream fin;
  FileStream fout;

  try {
    // open input file
    try {
      fin = new FileStream(args[0], FileMode.Open);
    } catch(FileNotFoundException exc) {
      Console.WriteLine(exc.Message + "\nInput File Not Found");
      return;
    }

    // open output file
    try {
      fout = new FileStream(args[1], FileMode.Create);
    } catch(FileNotFoundException exc) {
      Console.WriteLine(exc.Message + "\nError Opening Output File");
      return;
    }
  } catch(IndexOutOfRangeException exc) {
    Console.WriteLine(exc.Message + "\nUsage: CopyFile From To");
    return;
  }

  // Copy File
  try {
    do {
      i = fin.ReadByte();
      if(i != -1) fout.WriteByte((byte)i);
    } while(i != -1);
  } catch(IOException exc) {
    Console.WriteLine(exc.Message + "File Error");
  }

  fin.Close();
  fout.Close();
  }
}
```

Read bytes from one file and write them to another.

11

1-Minute Drill

● What does **ReadByte( )** return when the end of the file is reached?

● What does **Flush( )** do?

● What method do you call to write a block of bytes?

Character-Based File I/O

Although byte-oriented file handling is quite common, it is possible to use character-based streams for this purpose. The advantage to the character streams is that they operate directly on Unicode characters. Thus, if you want to store Unicode text, the character streams are certainly your best option. In general, to perform character-based file operations, you will wrap a **FileStream** inside either a **StreamReader** or a **StreamWriter**. These classes automatically convert a byte stream into a character stream, and vice versa.

Remember, at the operating system level, a file consists of a set of bytes. Using a **StreamReader** or **StreamWriter** does not alter this fact.

StreamWriter is derived from **TextWriter**. **StreamReader** is derived from **TextReader**. Thus, **StreamWriter** and **StreamReader** have access to the methods and properties defined by their base classes.

Using StreamWriter

To create a character-based output stream, wrap a **Stream** object (such as a **FileStream**) inside a **StreamWriter**. **StreamWriter** defines several constructors. One of its most popular is shown here:

    StreamWriter(Stream *stream*)

Here, *stream* is the name of an open stream. This constructor throws an **Argument-Exception** if the specified stream is empty and an **ArgumentNullException** if *stream* is null. Once created, a **StreamWriter** automatically handles the conversion of characters to bytes.

● A –1 is returned by **ReadByte( )** when the end of the file is encountered.
● A call to **Flush( )** causes any buffered output to be physically written to the storage device.
● To write a block of bytes, call **Write( )**.

Here is a simple key-to-disk utility that reads lines of text entered at the keyboard and writes them to a file called **test.txt**. Text is read until the user enters the word "stop". The utility uses a **FileStream** wrapped in a **Stream-Writer** to output to the file.

```
/* A simple key-to-disk utility that
   demonstrates a StreamWriter. */

using System;
using System.IO;

class KtoD {
  public static void Main() {
    string str;
    FileStream fout;

    try {
      fout = new FileStream("test.txt", FileMode.Create);
    }
    catch(IOException exc) {
      Console.WriteLine(exc.Message + "Cannot open file.");
      return ;
    }
    StreamWriter fstr_out = new StreamWriter(fout);    ←──────┐

    Console.WriteLine("Enter text ('stop' to quit).");        │
    do {                                            ┌─────────────────────┐
      Console.Write(": ");                          │ Create a StreamWriter. │
      str = Console.ReadLine();                      └─────────────────────┘

      if(str != "stop") {
        str = str + "\r\n"; // add newline
        try {                                  ┌────────────────────────┐
          fstr_out.Write(str);    ←─────────── │ Write strings to the file. │
        } catch(IOException exc) {              └────────────────────────┘
          Console.WriteLine(exc.Message + "File Error");
          return ;
        }
      }
    } while(str != "stop");

    fstr_out.Close();
  }
}
```

11

In some cases, you can open a file directly using **StreamWriter**. To do so, use one of these constructors:

StreamWriter(string *filename*)

StreamWriter(string *filename,* bool *appendFlag*)

Here, *filename* specifies the name of the file to open, which can include a full path specifier. In the second form, if *appendFlag* is true, then output is appended to the end of an existing file. Otherwise, output overwrites the specified file. In both cases, if the file does not exist, it is created. Also, both throw an **IOException** if an I/O error occurs. Other exceptions are also possible.

Here is the key-to-disk program rewritten so that it uses **StreamWriter** to open the output file:

```
/* Open a file using StreamWriter. */

using System;
using System.IO;

class KtoD {
  public static void Main() {
    string str;
    StreamWriter fstr_out;

    try {
      fstr_out = new StreamWriter("test.txt");
    }
    catch(IOException exc) {
      Console.WriteLine(exc.Message + "Cannot open file.");
      return ;
    }

    Console.WriteLine("Enter text ('stop' to quit).");
    do {
      Console.Write(": ");
      str = Console.ReadLine();

      if(str != "stop") {
        str = str + "\r\n"; // add newline
        try {
          fstr_out.Write(str);
        } catch(IOException exc) {
```

Open a file using only **StreamWriter**.

```
        Console.WriteLine(exc.Message + "File Error");
        return ;
      }
    }
  } while(str != "stop");

  fstr_out.Close();
  }
}
```

Using a StreamReader

To create a character-based input stream, wrap a byte stream inside a **Stream-Reader**. **StreamReader** defines several constructors. A frequently used one is shown here:

StreamReader(Stream *stream*)

Here, *stream* is the name of an open stream. This constructor throws an **ArgumentNullException** if *stream* is null. Once created, a **StreamReader** will automatically handle the conversion of bytes to characters.

The following program creates a simple disk-to-screen utility that reads a text file called **test.txt** and displays its contents on the screen. Thus, it is the complement of the key-to-disk utility shown in the previous section.

```
/* A simple disk-to-screen utility that
   demonstrates a FileReader. */

using System;
using System.IO;

class DtoS {
  public static void Main() {
    FileStream fin;
    string s;

    try {
      fin = new FileStream("test.txt", FileMode.Open);
    }
    catch(IOException exc) {
      Console.WriteLine(exc.Message + "Cannot open file.");
      return ;
```

```
    }
    StreamReader fstr_in = new StreamReader(fin);

    while((s = fstr_in.ReadLine()) != null) {
      Console.WriteLine(s);
    }
    fstr_in.Close();
  }
}
```

Read lines from the file and display them on the screen.

Notice how the end of the file is determined. When the reference returned by **ReadLine( )** is null, the end of the file has been reached.

As with **StreamWriter**, in some cases you can open a file directly using **StreamReader**. To do so, use this constructor:

StreamReader(string *filename*)

Here, *filename* specifies the name of the file to open, which can include a full path specifier. The file must exist. If it doesn't, an **IOException** is thrown. If *filename* is null, then an **ArgumentNullException** is thrown. If *filename* is an empty string, **ArgumentException** is thrown.

1-Minute Drill

● What class is used to read characters from a file?

● What class is used to write characters to a file?

● Why are separate character-based I/O classes necessary?

Redirecting the Standard Streams

As mentioned earlier, the standard streams, such as **Console.In**, can be redirected. By far, the most common redirection is to a file. When a standard

---

● To read characters, use a **StreamReader**.
● To write characters, use a **StreamWriter**.
● The character-based I/O classes automate the conversion of **byte**-to-**char**, and vice versa.

Ask the Expert

Question: I have heard that I can specify a "character encoding" when opening a StreamReader or StreamWriter. What is a character encoding and when should I use one?

Answer: StreamReader and StreamWriter convert bytes to characters and vice versa based upon a *character encoding* that specifies how the translation occurs. By default, C# uses the UTF-8 encoding, which is compatible with Unicode. Since ASCII is a subset of Unicode, the default encoding properly handles both ASCII and Unicode characters. To specify another encoding, you will use overloaded versions of the **StreamReader** or **StreamWriter** constructors that include an encoding parameter. In general, you will need to specify a character encoding only under unusual circumstances.

stream is redirected, input or output is automatically directed to the new stream, bypassing the default devices. By redirecting the standard streams, your program can read commands from a disk file, create log files, or even read input from a network connection.

Redirection of the standard streams can be accomplished in two ways. First, when you execute a program on the command line, you can use the < and > operators to redirect **Console.In** and **Console.Out**, respectively. For example, given this program:

```
using System;

class Test {
  public static void Main() {
    Console.WriteLine("This is a test.");
  }
}
```

Executing the program like this:

    Test > log

will cause the line "This is a test." to be written to a file called **log**. Input can be redirected in the same way. The thing to remember when input is redirected is that you must make sure that what you specify as an input source contains sufficient input to satisfy the demands of the program. If it doesn't, the program will hang.

The < and > command-line redirection operators are not part of C#, but are provided by the operating system. Thus, if your environment supports I/O redirection (as is the case with Windows), you can redirect standard input and standard output without making any changes to your program. However, there is a second way that you can redirect the standard streams that is under program control. To do so you will use the **SetIn( )**, **SetOut( )**, and **SetError( )** methods, shown here, which are members of **Console**.

static void SetIn(TextReader *input*)

static void SetOut(TextWriter *output*)

static void SetError(TextWriter *output*)

Thus, to redirect input, call **SetIn( )**, specifying the desired stream. You can use any input stream as long as it is derived from **TextReader**. To redirect output to a file, specify a file that is wrapped in a **StreamWriter**. The following program shows an example:

```
// Redirect Console.Out.

using System;
using System.IO;

class Redirect {
  public static void Main() {
    StreamWriter log_out;

    try {
      log_out = new StreamWriter("logfile.txt");
    }
    catch(IOException exc) {
      Console.WriteLine(exc.Message + "Cannot open file.");
      return ;
```

```
        }

        Console.SetOut(log_out);  ◄──────────    Redirect Console.Out.
        Console.WriteLine("This is the start of the log file.");

        for(int i=0; i<10; i++) Console.WriteLine(i);

        Console.WriteLine("This is the end of the log file.");
        log_out.Close();
    }
}
```

When you run this program, you won't see any output on the screen. However, the file logfile.txt will contain the following:

```
This is the start of the log file.
0
1
2
3
4
5
6
7
8
9
This is the end of the log file.
```

On your own, you might want to experiment with redirecting the other built-in streams.

CompFiles.cs

Project 11-1: A File Comparison Utility

This project develops a simple, yet useful file comparison utility. It works by opening both files to be compared and then reading and comparing each corresponding set of bytes. If a mismatch is found, the files differ. If the end of each file is reached at the same time and if no mismatches have been found, then the files are the same.

Step-by-Step

1. Create a file called **CompFiles.cs**.

2. Into **CompFiles.cs**, add the following program:

```
/*
   Project 11-1

   Compare two files.

   To use this program, specify the names
   of the files to be compared on the command line.

   For example:
       CompFile FIRST.TXT SECOND.TXT
*/

using System;
using System.IO;

class CompFiles {
  public static void Main(string[] args) {
    int i=0, j=0;
    FileStream f1;
    FileStream f2;

    try {
      // open first file
      try {
        f1 = new FileStream(args[0], FileMode.Open);
      } catch(FileNotFoundException exc) {
        Console.WriteLine(exc.Message);
        return;
      }

      // open second file
      try {
        f2 = new FileStream(args[1], FileMode.Open);
      } catch(FileNotFoundException exc) {
        Console.WriteLine(exc.Message);
        return;
      }
    } catch(IndexOutOfRangeException exc) {
      Console.WriteLine(exc.Message + "\nUsage: CompFile f1 f2");
      return;
```

```
  }

  // Compare files
  try {
    do {
      i = f1.ReadByte();
      j = f2.ReadByte();
      if(i != j) break;
    } while(i != -1 && j != -1);
  } catch(IOException exc) {
    Console.WriteLine(exc.Message);
  }
  if(i != j)
    Console.WriteLine("Files differ.");
  else
    Console.WriteLine("Files are the same.");

  f1.Close();
  f2.Close();
  }
}
```

3. To try **CompFiles**, first copy **CompFiles.cs** to a file called **temp**. Then, try this command line:

   CompFiles CompFiles.cs temp

   The program will report that the files are the same.

4. Next, compare **CompFiles.cs** to **CopyFile.cs** (shown earlier) using this command line:

   CompFiles CompFiles.cs CopyFile.cs

   These files differ and **CompFiles** will report this fact.

5. On your own, try enhancing **CompFiles** with various options. For example, add an option that ignores the case of letters. Another idea is to have **CompFiles** display the position within the file where the files differ.

Reading and Writing Binary Data

So far, we have just been reading and writing bytes or characters, but it is possible—indeed, common—to read and write other types of data. For example, you might want to create a file that contains ints, **doubles**,

11

or **short**s. To read and write binary values of the C# built-in types, you will use **BinaryReader** and **BinaryWriter**. When using these streams, it is important to understand that this data is read and written using its internal, binary format, not its human-readable text form.

BinaryWriter

A **BinaryWriter** is a wrapper around a byte stream that manages the writing of binary data. Its most commonly used constructor is shown here:

BinaryWriter(Stream *outputStream*)

Here, *outputStream* is the stream to which data is written. To write output to a file, you can use the object created by **FileStream** for this parameter. If *outputStream* is null, then an **ArgumentNullException** is thrown. If *outputStream* has not been opened for writing, **ArgumentException** is thrown.

BinaryWriter defines methods that can write all of C#'s built-in types. Several are shown in Table 11-5. **BinaryWriter** also defines the standard **Close( )** and **Flush( )** methods that work as described earlier.

Method	Description
void Write(sbyte *val*)	Writes a signed byte.
void Write(byte *val*)	Writes an unsigned byte.
void Write(byte[ ] *buf*)	Writes an array of bytes.
void Write(short *val*)	Writes a short integer.
void Write(ushort *val*)	Writes an unsigned short integer.
void Write(int *val*)	Writes an integer.
void Write(uint *val*)	Writes an unsigned integer.
void Write(long *val*)	Writes a long integer.
void Write(ulong *val*)	Writes an unsigned long integer.
void Write(float *val*)	Writes a **float**.
void Write(double *val*)	Writes a **double**.
void Write(char *val*)	Writes a character.
void Write(char[ ] *buf*)	Writes an array of characters.
void Write(string *val*)	Writes a string.

Table 11-5   Commonly Used Output Methods Defined by BinaryWriter

BinaryReader

A **BinaryReader** is a wrapper around a byte stream that handles the reading of binary data. Its most commonly used constructor is shown here:

BinaryReader(Stream *inputStream*)

Here, *inputStream* is the stream from which data is read. To read from a file, you can use the object created by **FileStream** for this parameter. If *inputStream* is null, then an **ArgumentNullException** is thrown. If *inputStream* has not been opened for reading, **ArgumentException** is thrown.

BinaryReader provides methods for reading all of C#'s simple types. The most commonly used are shown in Table 11-6. **BinaryReader** also defines three versions of **Read( )**, which are shown here:

int Read( )	Returns an integer representation of the next available character from the invoking input stream. Returns –1 when the end of the file is encountered.
int Read(byte[ ] *buf*, int *offset*, int *num*)	Attempts to read up to *num* bytes into *buf* starting at *buf[offset]*, returning the number of bytes successfully read.
int Read(char[ ] *buf*, int *offset*, int *num*)	Attempts to read up to *num* characters into *buf* starting at *buf[offset]*, returning the number of characters successfully read.

These methods will throw an **IOException** on failure.

Also defined is the standard **Close( )** method.

Method	Description
bool ReadBoolean( )	Reads a **bool**.
byte ReadByte( )	Reads a **byte**.
sbyte ReadSByte( )	Reads an **sbyte.**
byte[ ] ReadBytes(int *num*)	Reads *num* bytes and returns them as an array.
char readChar( )	Reads a **char**.
char[ ] ReadChars(int *num*)	Reads *num* characters and returns them as an array.
double ReadDouble( )	Reads a **double**.

Table 11-6   Commonly Used Input Methods Defined by BinaryReader

11

Method	Description
float ReadSingle( )	Reads a **float**.
short ReadInt16( )	Reads a **short**.
int ReadInt32( )	Reads an **int**.
long ReadInt64( )	Reads a **long**.
ushort ReadUInt16( )	Reads a **ushort**.
uint ReadUInt32( )	Reads a **uint**.
ulong ReadUInt64( )	Reads a **ulong**.
string ReadString( )	Reads a string.

Table 11-6 Commonly Used Input Methods Defined by BinaryReader (*continued*)

Demonstrating Binary I/O

Here is a program that demonstrates **BinaryReader** and **BinaryWriter**. It writes and then reads back various types of data to and from a file.

```
// Write and then read back binary data.
using System;
using System.IO;

class RWData {
  public static void Main() {
    BinaryWriter dataOut;
    BinaryReader dataIn;

    int i = 10;
    double d = 1023.56;
    bool b = true;

    try {
      dataOut = new
        BinaryWriter(new FileStream("testdata", FileMode.Create));
    }
    catch(IOException exc) {
      Console.WriteLine(exc.Message + "\nCannot open file.");
      return;
    }

    try {
```

```
    Console.WriteLine("Writing " + i);
    dataOut.Write(i);            ◄─────────────────────┐

    Console.WriteLine("Writing " + d);                 │
    dataOut.Write(d);            ◄──────────┐          │   ┌─────────────────┐
                                            │          └───┤ Write binary data.│
    Console.WriteLine("Writing " + b);      │              └─────────────────┘
    dataOut.Write(b);            ◄──────────┤          │

    Console.WriteLine("Writing " + 12.2 * 7.4);        │
    dataOut.Write(12.2 * 7.4);   ◄─────────────────────┘

  }
  catch(IOException exc) {
    Console.WriteLine(exc.Message + "\nWrite error.");
  }

  dataOut.Close();

  Console.WriteLine();

  // Now, read them back.
  try {
    dataIn = new
        BinaryReader(new FileStream("testdata", FileMode.Open));
  }
  catch(IOException exc) {
    Console.WriteLine(exc.Message + "\nCannot open file.");
    return;
  }

  try {
    i = dataIn.ReadInt32();      ◄─────────────────────┐
    Console.WriteLine("Reading " + i);                 │

    d = dataIn.ReadDouble();     ◄──────────┐          │
    Console.WriteLine("Reading " + d);      │          │   ┌────────────────────┐
                                            │          └───┤ Read back binary data.│
    b = dataIn.ReadBoolean();    ◄──────────┤              └────────────────────┘
    Console.WriteLine("Reading " + b);      │

    d = dataIn.ReadDouble();     ◄─────────────────────┘
    Console.WriteLine("Reading " + d);
  }
```

11

```
    catch(IOException exc) {
      Console.WriteLine(exc.Message + "Read error.");
    }

    dataIn.Close();
  }
}
```

The output from the program is shown here:

```
Writing 10
Writing 1023.56
Writing True
Writing 90.28

Reading 10
Reading 1023.56
Reading True
Reading 90.28
```

1-Minute Drill

● To write binary data, what type of stream should you use?

● What method do you call to write a **double** in binary format?

● What method do you call to read a **short** in binary format?

Random Access Files

Up to this point, we have been using *sequential files*, which are files that are accessed in a strictly linear fashion, one byte after another. However, C# also allows you to access the contents of a file in random order. To do this, you will use the **Seek( )** method defined by **FileStream**. This method allows you to set the *file position indicator* (also called the *file pointer*) to any point within a file.

● To write binary data, use **BinaryWriter**.
● To write a **double**, call **Write( )**.
● To read a **short**, call **readInt16( )**.

The method **Seek( )** is shown here:

long Seek(long *newPos*, SeekOrigin *origin*)

Here, *newPos* specifies the new position, in bytes, of the file pointer from the location specified by *origin*. The origin will be one of these values, which are defined by the **SeekOrigin** enumeration:

Value	Meaning
Begin	Seek from the beginning of the file.
Current	Seek from the current location.
End	Seek from the end of the file.

After a call to **Seek( )**, the next read or write operation will occur at the new file position. If an error occurs while seeking, an **IOException** is thrown. If the underlying stream does not support position requests, a **NotSupportedException** is thrown.

Here is an example that demonstrates random access I/O. It writes the uppercase alphabet to a file and then reads it back in nonsequential order.

```
// Demonstrate random access.
using System;
using System.IO;

class RandomAccessDemo {
  public static void Main() {
    FileStream f;
    char ch;

    try {
      f = new FileStream("random.dat", FileMode.Create);
    }
    catch(FileNotFoundException exc) {
      Console.WriteLine(exc.Message);
      return ;
    }

    // Write the alphabet.
    for(int i=0; i < 26; i++) {
      try {
        f.WriteByte((byte)('A'+i));
```

11

```
      }
      catch(IOException exc) {
        Console.WriteLine(exc.Message);
        return ;
      }
    }

    try {
      // Now, read back specific values
      f.Seek(0, SeekOrigin.Begin); // seek to first byte
      ch = (char) f.ReadByte();
      Console.WriteLine("First value is " + ch);

      f.Seek(1, SeekOrigin.Begin); // seek to second byte
      ch = (char) f.ReadByte();
      Console.WriteLine("Second value is " + ch);

      f.Seek(4, SeekOrigin.Begin); // seek to 5th byte
      ch = (char) f.ReadByte();
      Console.WriteLine("Fifth value is " + ch);

      Console.WriteLine();

      // Now, read every other value.
      Console.WriteLine("Here is every other value: ");
      for(int i=0; i < 26; i += 2) {
        f.Seek(i, SeekOrigin.Begin); // seek to ith double
        ch = (char) f.ReadByte();
        Console.Write(ch + " ");
      }
    }
    catch(IOException exc) {
      Console.WriteLine(exc.Message);
    }

    f.Close();
  }
}
```

Use **Seek( )** to move the file pointer.

The output from the program is shown here:

```
First value is A
Second value is B
```

```
Fifth value is E

Here is every other value:
A C E G I K M O Q S U W Y
```

1-Minute Drill

● How do you position the file pointer?

● What value for *origin* seeks from the current location in the file?

● What exception is thrown if **Seek( )** is called on a stream that does not support position requests?

Converting Numeric Strings to Their Internal Representation

Before leaving the topic of I/O, we will examine a technique useful when reading numeric strings. As you know, C#'s **WriteLine( )** method provides a convenient way to output various types of data to the console, including numeric values of the built-in types, such as **int** and **double**. Thus, **WriteLine( )** automatically converts numeric values into their human-readable form. However, C# does not provide an input method that reads and converts strings containing numeric values into their internal, binary format. For example, there is no way to enter at the keyboard a string such as "100" and have it automatically converted into its corresponding binary value that can be stored in an **int** variable. To accomplish this task, you will need to use a method that is defined for all of the built-in numeric types: **Parse( )**.

Before we begin, it is necessary to state an important fact: all of C#'s built-in types, such as **int** and **double**, are actually just aliases (that is, other names) for structures defined by the .NET Framework. In fact, Microsoft explicitly states that the C# type and .NET structure type are indistinguishable. One is just another name for the other. Because C#'s value types are supported by structures, the value types have members defined for them.

11

● To position the file pointer, use **Seek( )**.
● **SeekOrigin.Current** seeks from the current location in the file.
● If **Seek( )** is not supported on a stream, **NotSupportedException** is thrown.

For the C# numeric value types, the .NET structure names and their C# keyword equivalents are shown here:

.NET Structure Name	C# Name
Double	double
Single	float
Int16	short
Int32	int
Int64	long
UInt16	ushort
UInt32	uint
UInt64	ulong
Byte	byte
Sbyte	sbyte

These structures are defined inside the **System** namespace. Thus, the fully qualified name for **Int32** is **System.Int32**. These structures offer a wide array of methods that help fully integrate the value types into C#'s object hierarchy. As a side benefit, the numeric structures also define static methods that convert a numeric string into its corresponding binary equivalent. These conversion methods are shown here. Each returns a binary value that corresponds to the string.

Structure	Conversion Method
Double	static double Parse(string *str*)
Single	static float Parse(string *str*)
Int64	static long Parse(string *str*)
Int32	static int Parse(string *str*)
Int16	static short Parse(string *str*)
UInt64	static ulong Parse(string *str*)
UInt32	static uint Parse(string *str*)
UInt16	static ushort Parse(string *str*)
Byte	static byte Parse(string *str*)
SByte	static sbyte Parse(string *str*)

The **Parse( )** methods will throw a **FormatException** if *str* does not contain a valid number as defined by the invoking type. **ArgumentNullException** is thrown if *str* is null, and **OverflowException** is thrown if the value in *str* exceeds the invoking type.

The parsing methods give you an easy way to convert a numeric value, read as a string from the keyboard or a text file, into its proper internal format. For example, the following program averages a list of numbers entered by the user. It first asks the user for the number of values to be averaged. It then reads that number using **ReadLine( )** and uses **Int32.Parse( )** to convert the string into an integer. Next, it inputs the values, using **Double.Parse( )** to convert the strings into their **double** equivalents.

```
/* This program averages a list of numbers entered
   by the user.  */

using System;
using System.IO;

class AvgNums {
  public static void Main() {
    string str;
    int n;
    double sum = 0.0;
    double avg, t;

    Console.Write("How many numbers will you enter: ");
    str = Console.ReadLine();
    try {
      n = Int32.Parse(str);  ←———————  Convert a string to an int.
    }
    catch(FormatException exc) {
      Console.WriteLine(exc.Message);
      n = 0;
    }
    catch(OverflowException exc) {
      Console.WriteLine(exc.Message);
      n = 0;
    }

    Console.WriteLine("Enter " + n + " values.");
    for(int i=0; i < n ; i++)  {
      Console.Write(": ");
      str = Console.ReadLine();
      try {
        t = Double.Parse(str);  ←———————  Convert string to double.
      } catch(FormatException exc) {
```

```
      Console.WriteLine(exc.Message);
      t = 0.0;
    }
    catch(OverflowException exc) {
      Console.WriteLine(exc.Message);
      t = 0;
    }
    sum += t;
  }
  avg = sum / n;
  Console.WriteLine("Average is " + avg);
  }
}
```

Here is a sample run:

```
How many numbers will you enter: 5
Enter 5 values.
: 1.1
: 2.2
: 3.3
: 4.4
: 5.5
Average is 3.3
```

You can put the **Parse( )** methods to good use by improving the loan payment calculator developed in Project 2-3. In that version, the loan principal, interest, and so on, were "hard-coded" into the program. The program would be much more useful if the user were prompted for these values. Here is an improved version of the loan calculator that does this:

```
/*
   Improved Project 2-3

   Compute the regular payments for a loan.
*/

using System;

class RegPay {
  public static void Main() {
    decimal Principal;    // original principal
```

```
decimal IntRate;        // interest rate as a decimal, such as 0.075
decimal PayPerYear;     // number of payments per year
decimal NumYears;       // number of years
decimal Payment;        // the regular payment
decimal numer, denom;   // temporary work variables
double b, e;            // base and exponent for call to Pow()

string str;

Console.Write("Enter principal: ");
str = Console.ReadLine();
try {
  Principal = Decimal.Parse(str);
} catch(FormatException exc) {
  Console.WriteLine(exc.Message);
  return;
}

Console.Write("Enter interest rate (such as 0.085): ");
str = Console.ReadLine();
try {
  IntRate = Decimal.Parse(str);
} catch(FormatException exc) {
  Console.WriteLine(exc.Message);
  return;
}

Console.Write("Enter number of years: ");
str = Console.ReadLine();
try {
  NumYears = Decimal.Parse(str);
} catch(FormatException exc) {
  Console.WriteLine(exc.Message);
  return;
}


Console.Write("Enter number of payments per year: ");
str = Console.ReadLine();
try {
  PayPerYear = Decimal.Parse(str);
} catch(FormatException exc) {
  Console.WriteLine(exc.Message);
  return;
```

11

```
    }

    numer = IntRate * Principal / PayPerYear;

    e = (double) -(PayPerYear * NumYears);
    b = (double) (IntRate / PayPerYear) + 1;

    denom = 1 - (decimal) Math.Pow(b, e);

    Payment = numer / denom;

    Console.WriteLine("Payment is {0:C}", Payment);
  }
}
```

A sample run is shown here:

```
Enter principal: 10000
Enter interest rate (such as 0.085): 0.075
Enter number of years: 5
Enter number of payments per year: 12
Payment is $200.38
```

Ask the Expert

Question: What else can the value-type structures, such as Int32 or Double, do?

Answer: The value-type structures provide a number of methods that help integrate the C# built-in types into the object hierarchy. For example, all of the structures have methods called **CompareTo( )**, which compare the values contained within the wrapper; **Equals( )**, which tests two values for equality; and methods that return the value of the object in various forms. The numeric structures also include the fields **MinValue** and **MaxValue**, which contain the minimum and maximum value that can be stored by an object of its type.

FileHelp.cs

Project 11-2: Creating a Disk-Based Help System

In Project 4-1 you created a **Help** class that displayed information about C#'s control statements. In that implementation, the help information was stored within the class, itself, and the user selected help from a menu of numbered options. Although this approach was fully functional, it is certainly not the ideal way of creating a Help system. For example, to add to or change the help information, the source code of the program needed to be modified. Also, the selection of the topic by number rather than by name is tedious, and not suitable for long lists of topics. Here, we will remedy this shortcoming by creating a disk-based Help system.

The disk-based Help system stores help information in a help file. The help file is a standard text file, which can be changed or expanded at will, without changing the Help program. The user obtains help about a topic by typing in its name. The Help system searches the help file for the topic. If it is found, information about the topic is displayed.

Step-by-Step

1. You must create the help file that will be used by the Help system. The help file is a standard text file that is organized like this:

```
#topic-name1
topic info

#topic-name2
topic info

        .
        .
        .

#topic-nameN
topic info
```

The name of each topic must be preceded by a #, and the topic name must be on a line of its own. By preceding each topic name with a #, it allows the program to quickly find the start of each topic. After the topic name are any number of information lines about the topic. However, there must be a blank line between the end of one topic's information and the start of the next topic. Also, there must be no trailing spaces at the end of any lines.

Here is a simple help file that that you can use to try the disk-based Help system. It stores information about C#'s control statements.

```
#if
if(condition) statement;
else statement;

#switch
switch(expression) {
  case constant:
    statement sequence
    break;
    // ...
  }

#for
for(init; condition; iteration) statement;

#while
while(condition) statement;

#do
do {
  statement;
} while (condition);

#break
break; or break label;

#continue
continue; or continue label;

#goto
goto label;
```

Call this file **helpfile.txt**.

2. Create a file called **FileHelp.cs**.

3. Begin creating the new **Help** class with these lines of code:

```
class Help {
  string helpfile; // name of help file
```

```
public Help(string fname) {
  helpfile = fname;
}
```

The name of the help file is passed to the **Help** constructor and stored in the instance variable **helpfile**. Since each instance of **Help** will have its own copy of **helpfile**, each instance can use a different file. Thus, you can create different sets of help files for different sets of topics.

4. Add the **helpon( )** method shown here to the **Help** class. This method retrieves help on the specified topic.

```
// Display help on a topic.
public bool helpon(string what) {
  StreamReader helpRdr;
  int ch;
  string topic, info;

  try {
    helpRdr = new StreamReader(helpfile);
  }
  catch(FileNotFoundException exc) {
    Console.WriteLine(exc.Message);
    return false;
  }

  try {
    do {
      // read characters until a # is found
      ch = helpRdr.Read();

      // now, see if topics match
      if(ch == '#') {
        topic = helpRdr.ReadLine();
        if(what == topic) { // found topic
          do {
            info = helpRdr.ReadLine();
            if(info != null) Console.WriteLine(info);
          } while((info != null) && (info != ""));
          helpRdr.Close();
          return true;
        }
      }
```

11

```
    } while(ch != -1);
  }
  catch(IOException exc) {
    Console.WriteLine(exc.Message);
  }
  helpRdr.Close();
  return false; // topic not found
}
```

The help file is opened using a **StreamReader**. Since the help file contains text, using a character stream allows the Help system to be more efficiently internationalized.

The **helpon( )** method works like this: A string containing the name of the topic is passed in the **what** parameter. The help file is then opened. Then, the file is searched, looking for a match between **what** and a topic in the file. Remember, in the file, each topic is preceded by a #, so the search loop scans the file for #s. When it finds one, it then checks to see if the topic following that # matches the one passed in **what**. If it does, the information associated with that topic is displayed. If a match is found, **helpon( )** returns **true**. Otherwise, it returns **false**.

5. The Help class also provides a method called **getSelection( )**, shown here:

```
// Get a Help topic.
public string getSelection() {
  string topic = "";

  Console.Write("Enter topic: ");
  try {
    topic = Console.ReadLine();
  }
  catch(IOException exc) {
    Console.WriteLine(exc.Message);
    return "";
  }
  return topic;
}
```

This method prompts for the name of a topic, reads the topic, and returns it to the caller.

6. The entire disk-based Help system is shown here:

```
/*
   Project 11-2

   A help program that uses a disk file
   to store help information.
*/

using System;
using System.IO;

/* The Help class opens a help file,
   searches for a topic, and then displays
   the information associated with that topic. */
class Help {
  string helpfile; // name of help file

  public Help(string fname) {
    helpfile = fname;
  }

  // Display help on a topic.
  public bool helpon(string what) {
    StreamReader helpRdr;
    int ch;
    string topic, info;

    try {
      helpRdr = new StreamReader(helpfile);
    }
    catch(FileNotFoundException exc) {
      Console.WriteLine(exc.Message);
      return false;
    }

    try {
      do {
        // read characters until a # is found
        ch = helpRdr.Read();

        // now, see if topics match
        if(ch == '#') {
          topic = helpRdr.ReadLine();
```

11

```csharp
        if(what == topic) { // found topic
          do {
            info = helpRdr.ReadLine();
            if(info != null) Console.WriteLine(info);
          } while((info != null) && (info != ""));
          helpRdr.Close();
          return true;
        }
      }
    } while(ch != -1);
  }
  catch(IOException exc) {
    Console.WriteLine(exc.Message);
  }
  helpRdr.Close();
  return false; // topic not found
}

// Get a Help topic.
public string getSelection() {
  string topic = "";

  Console.Write("Enter topic: ");
  try {
    topic = Console.ReadLine();
  }
  catch(IOException exc) {
    Console.WriteLine(exc.Message);
    return "";
  }
  return topic;
}
}

// Demonstrate the file-based Help system.
class FileHelp {
  public static void Main() {
    Help hlpobj = new Help("helpfile.txt");
    string topic;

    Console.WriteLine("Try the help system. " +
                      "Enter 'stop' to end.");
    do {
      topic = hlpobj.getSelection();
```

```
      if(!hlpobj.helpon(topic))
        Console.WriteLine("Topic not found.\n");

   } while(topic != "stop");
  }
}
```

Ask the Expert

Question: Earlier in this module you mentioned the stream class MemoryStream, which uses memory for storage. How can this stream be used?

Answer: MemoryStream is an implementation of Stream that uses an array of bytes for input or output. Here is one of the constructors that it defines:

    MemoryStream(byte[ ] *buf*)

Here, *buf* is an array of bytes that will be used for the source or target of I/O requests. The stream created by this constructor can be written or read, and supports Seek( ). You must remember to make *buf* large enough to hold whatever output you will be directing to it.

Memory-based streams are quite useful in programming. For example, you can construct complicated output in advance, storing it in the array until it is needed. This technique is especially useful when programming for a GUI environment, such as Windows. You can also redirect a standard stream to read from an array. This might be useful for feeding test information into a program, for example.

One last point: To create a memory-based character stream, use **StringReader** or **StringWriter**.

11

✓ Mastery Check

1. Why does C# define both byte and character streams?

2. What class is at the top of the stream hierarchy?

3. Show how to open a file for reading bytes.

4. Show how to open a file for reading characters.

5. What does **Seek( )** do?

6. What classes support binary I/O for the built-in types?

7. What methods are used to redirect the standard streams under program control?

8. How do you convert a numeric string such as "123.23" into its binary equivalent?

9. Write a program that copies a text file. In the process, have it convert all spaces into hyphens. Use the byte stream file classes.

10. Rewrite the program in question 9 so that it uses the character stream classes.

Module 12

Delegates, Events, Namespaces, and Advanced Topics

The Goals of This Module

- Understand delegates
- Use events
- Examine namespaces
- Create conversion operators
- Examine the preprocessor
- Explore attributes
- Introduce pointers and the unsafe context
- Use runtime type identification
- Examine more C# keywords

Y ou have come a long way since the start of this book. In this, the final module, you will examine several important C# topics, including delegates, events, and namespaces. Also covered are conversion operators, attributes, and the C# preprocessor. Finally, several advanced features, which apply mostly to specialized situations, are briefly described for the sake of completeness.

Delegates

Newcomers to C# are sometimes intimidated by the delegate, but there is nothing to fear. Delegates are no more difficult to understand or use than any other C# feature, as long as you bear in mind precisely what a delegate is. In straightforward terms, a *delegate* is an object that can refer to a method. Thus, when you create a delegate, you are creating an object that can hold a reference to a method. Furthermore, the method can be called through this reference. Thus, a delegate can invoke the method to which it refers.

Even though a method is not an object, it still has a physical location in memory. This address is the entry point of the method and is the address called when the method is invoked. The address of a method can be assigned to a delegate. Once a delegate refers to a method, the method can be called through that delegate. Furthermore, the same delegate can be used to call a different method by simply changing the method to which the delegate refers. The principal advantage of a delegate is that it allows you to specify a call to a method, but the method actually invoked is determined at runtime, not at compile time.

Note

If you are familiar with C/C++, then it will help to know that a delegate in C# is similar to a function pointer in C/C++.

A delegate is declared using the keyword **delegate**. The general form of a delegate declaration is shown here:

delegate *ret-type name(parameter-list);*

Here, *ret-type* is the type of value returned by the methods that the delegate will be calling. The name of the delegate is specified by *name*. The parameters required by the methods called through the delegate are specified in the *parameter-list*. Once declared, a delegate can call only methods whose return type and parameter list match those specified by the delegate.

As mentioned, the key point about delegates is that a delegate can be used to call any method that agrees with its signature. This makes it possible to determine which method to invoke at runtime. Furthermore, the method invoked can be an instance method associated with an object, or a static method associated with a class. All that matters is that the signature of the method agrees with that of the delegate.

To see delegates in action, let's begin with the simple example shown here:

```
// A simple delegate example.

using System;

// Declare a delegate.
delegate string strMod(string str);        A delegate called strMod.

class DelegateTest {
  // Replaces spaces with hyphens.
  static string replaceSpaces(string a) {
    Console.WriteLine("Replaces spaces with hyphens.");
    return a.Replace(' ', '-');
  }

  // Remove spaces.
  static string removeSpaces(string a) {
    string temp = "";
    int i;

    Console.WriteLine("Removing spaces.");
    for(i=0; i < a.Length; i++)
      if(a[i] != ' ') temp += a[i];

    return temp;
  }

  // Reverse a string.
  static string reverse(string a) {
    string temp = "";
    int i, j;

    Console.WriteLine("Reversing string.");
```

```
   for(j=0, i=a.Length-1; i >= 0; i--, j++)
     temp += a[i];

   return temp;
}

public static void Main() {
  // Construct delegates.
  strMod strOp = new strMod(replaceSpaces);      ◄—— Construct a
  string str;                                          delegate.

  // Call methods through delegates.
  str = strOp("This is a test.");◄——— Call a method through a delegate.
  Console.WriteLine("Resulting string: " + str);
  Console.WriteLine();

  strOp = new strMod(removeSpaces);
  str = strOp("This is a test.");
  Console.WriteLine("Resulting string: " + str);
  Console.WriteLine();

  strOp = new strMod(reverse);
  str = strOp("This is a test.");
  Console.WriteLine("Resulting string: " + str);
 }
}
```

The output from the program is shown here:

```
Replaces spaces with hyphens.
Resulting string: This-is-a-test.

Removing spaces.
Resulting string: Thisisatest.

Reversing string.
Resulting string: .tset a si sihT
```

Let's examine this program closely. The program declares a delegate called **strMod** that takes one **string** parameter and returns a **string**. In **DelegateTest**, three static methods are declared, each with a matching signature. These methods perform some type of string modification. Notice that **replaceSpaces( )** uses one of **string**'s methods, called **Replace( )**, to replace spaces with hyphens.

In **Main( )**, a **strMod** reference called **strOp** is created and assigned a reference to **replaceSpaces( )**. Pay close attention to this line:

```
strMod strOp = new strMod(replaceSpaces);
```

Notice how the method **replaceSpaces( )** is passed as a parameter. Only its name is used; no parameters are specified. This can be generalized. When instantiating a delegate, you specify only the name of the method that you want the delegate to refer to. Also, the method's signature must match that of the delegate's declaration. If it doesn't, a compile-time error will result.

Next, **replaceSpaces( )** is called through the delegate instance **strOp**, as shown here:

```
str = strOp("This is a test.");
```

Because **strOp** refers to **replaceSpaces( )**, it is **replaceSpaces( )** that is invoked.

Next, **strOp** is assigned a reference to **removeSpaces( )**, and then **strOp** is called again. This time, **removeSpaces( )** is invoked.

Finally, **strOp** is assigned a reference to **reverse( )** and **strOp** is called. This results in **reverse( )** being called.

The key point of the example is that the invocation of **strOp** results in a call to the method referred to by **strOp** at the time at which the invocation occurred. Thus, the method to call is resolved at runtime, not compile time.

Although the preceding example used static methods, a delegate can also refer to instance methods. It must do so, however, through an object reference. For example, here is a rewrite of the previous example, which encapsulates the string operations inside a class called **StringOps**:

```
// Delegates can refer to instance methods, too.

using System;

// Declare a delegate.
delegate string strMod(string str);

class StringOps {
  // Replaces spaces with hyphens.
  public string replaceSpaces(string a) {
    Console.WriteLine("Replaces spaces with hyphens.");
    return a.Replace(' ', '-');
```

12

```
  }

  // Remove spaces.
  public string removeSpaces(string a) {
    string temp = "";
    int i;

    Console.WriteLine("Removing spaces.");
    for(i=0; i < a.Length; i++)
      if(a[i] != ' ') temp += a[i];

    return temp;
  }

  // Reverse a string.
  public string reverse(string a) {
    string temp = "";
    int i, j;

    Console.WriteLine("Reversing string.");
    for(j=0, i=a.Length-1; i >= 0; i--, j++)
      temp += a[i];

    return temp;
  }
}

class DelegateTest {
  public static void Main() {
    StringOps so = new StringOps();

    // Construct delegates.
    strMod strOp = new strMod(so.replaceSpaces);
    string str;

    // Call methods through delegates.
    str = strOp("This is a test.");
    Console.WriteLine("Resulting string: " + str);
    Console.WriteLine();

    strOp = new strMod(so.removeSpaces);
    str = strOp("This is a test.");
    Console.WriteLine("Resulting string: " + str);
    Console.WriteLine();
```

Create a delegate using an instance method.

```
    strOp = new strMod(so.reverse);
    str = strOp("This is a test.");
    Console.WriteLine("Resulting string: " + str);
  }
}
```

This program produces the same output as the first, but in this case, the delegate refers to methods on an instance of **StringOps**.

Multicasting

One of the most exciting features of a delegate is its support for *multicasting*. In simple terms, multicasting is the ability to create a chain of methods that will be automatically called when a delegate is invoked. Such a chain is very easy to create. Simply instantiate a delegate, and then use the += operator to add methods to the chain. To remove a method, use – =. (You can also use the +, –, and = operators separately to add and subtract delegates, but += and – = are more convenient.) The only restriction is that the delegate being multicast must have a **void** return type.

Here is an example of multicasting. It reworks the preceding examples by changing the string manipulation method's return type to **void**, and using a **ref** parameter to return the altered string to the caller.

```
// Demonstrate multicasting.

using System;

// Declare a delegate.
delegate void strMod(ref string str);

class StringOps {
  // Replaces spaces with hyphens.
  static void replaceSpaces(ref string a) {
    Console.WriteLine("Replaces spaces with hyphens.");
    a = a.Replace(' ', '-');
  }

  // Remove spaces.
  static void removeSpaces(ref string a) {
    string temp = "";
```

12

```
  int i;

  Console.WriteLine("Removing spaces.");
  for(i=0; i < a.Length; i++)
    if(a[i] != ' ') temp += a[i];

  a = temp;
}

// Reverse a string.
static void reverse(ref string a) {
  string temp = "";
  int i, j;

  Console.WriteLine("Reversing string.");
  for(j=0, i=a.Length-1; i >= 0; i--, j++)
    temp += a[i];

  a = temp;
}

public static void Main() {
  // Construct delegates.
  strMod strOp;
  strMod replaceSp = new strMod(replaceSpaces);
  strMod removeSp = new strMod(removeSpaces);
  strMod reverseStr = new strMod(reverse);
  string str = "This is a test";

  // set up multicast
  strOp = replaceSp;
  strOp += reverseStr;    ◄──────────────────   Create a multicast.

  // Call multicast
  strOp(ref str);
  Console.WriteLine("Resulting string: " + str);
  Console.WriteLine();

  // remove replace and add remove
  strOp -= replaceSp;
  strOp += removeSp;    ◄──────────────────   Create a different multicast.
```

```
    str = "This is a test."; // reset string

    // Call multicast
    strOp(ref str);
    Console.WriteLine("Resulting string: " + str);
    Console.WriteLine();
  }
}
```

Here is the output:

```
Replaces spaces with hyphens.
Reversing string.
Resulting string: tset-a-si-sihT

Reversing string.
Removing spaces.
Resulting string: .tsetasisihT
```

In **Main( )**, four delegate instances are created. One, **strOp**, is null. The other three refer to specific string modification methods. Next, a multicast is created that calls **removeSpaces( )** and **reverse( )**. This is accomplished via the following lines:

```
strOp = replaceSp;
strOp += reverseStr;
```

First, **strOp** is assigned a reference to **replaceSp**. Next, using **+=**, **reverseStr** is added. When **strOp** is invoked, both methods are invoked, replacing spaces with hyphens and reversing the string, as the output illustrates.

Next, **replaceSp** is removed from the chain, using this line:

```
strOp -= replaceSp;
```

and **removeSp** is added using this line:

```
strOp += removeSp;
```

Then, **StrOp** is again invoked. This time, spaces are removed and the string is reversed.

12

Why Delegates

Although the preceding examples show the "how" behind delegates, they don't really illustrate the "why." In general, delegates are useful for two main reasons. First, as the next section will show, delegates support events. Second, delegates give your program a way to execute a method at runtime without having to know precisely what that method is at compile time. This ability is quite useful when you want to create a framework that allows components to be plugged in. For example, imagine a drawing program (a bit like the standard Windows Paint accessory). Using a delegate, you could allow the user to plug in special color filters or image analyzers. Furthermore, the user could create a sequence of these filters or analyzers. Such a scheme would be easily handled using a delegate.

1-Minute Drill

- What is a delegate? What is the main benefit of using a delegate?
- How is a delegate declared?
- What is multicasting?

Events

Built upon the foundation of delegates is another important C# feature: the *event*. An event is, essentially, an automatic notification that some action has occurred. Events work like this: An object that has an interest in an event registers an event handler for that event. When the event occurs, all registered handlers are called. Event handlers are represented by delegates.

Events are members of a class and are declared using the **event** keyword. Its general form is shown here:

event *event-delegate object-name;*

- A delegate is an object that refers to a method. A delegate lets you call a method that is known only at runtime.
- A delegate is declared using the keyword **delegate**, followed by the return-type, name, and parameter list.
- Multicasting enables a chain of methods to be called from a single delegate invocation.

Here, *event-delegate* is the name of the delegate used to support the event, and *object-name* is the name of the specific event object being created.

Let's begin with a very simple example:

```
// A very simple event demonstration.

using System;

// Declare a delegate for an event
delegate void MyEventHandler();          Create a delegate for the event.

// Declare an event class.
class MyEvent {
  public event MyEventHandler activate;    Declare an event.

  // this is called to fire the event.
  public void fire() {
    if(activate != null)
      activate();                          Fire the event.
  }
}

class EventDemo {
  static void handler() {
    Console.WriteLine("Event occurred");
  }

  public static void Main() {
    MyEvent evt = new MyEvent();           Create event instance.

    // add handler() to the event list
    evt.activate += new MyEventHandler(handler);   Add handler to event chain.

    // fire the event
    evt.fire();                            Generate an event.
  }
}
```

This program displays the following output:

```
Event occurred
```

12

Although simple, this program contains all the elements essential to proper event handling. Let's look at it carefully.

The program begins by declaring a delegate for the event handler, as shown here:

```
delegate void MyEventHandler();
```

All events are activated through a delegate. Thus, the event delegate defines the signature for the event. In this case, there are no parameters, but event parameters are allowed. Because events are commonly multicast, an event should return **void**.

Next, an event class, called **MyEvent**, is created. Inside the class, an event object called **activate** is declared, using this line:

```
public event MyEventHandler activate;
```

Notice the syntax. This is the way that all types of events are declared.

Also declared inside **MyEvent** is the method **fire( )**, which is the method that a program will call to signal (or, "fire") an event. It calls an event handler, through the **activate** delegate, as shown here:

```
if(activate != null)
  activate();
```

Notice that a handler is called if and only if **activate** is not **null**. Since other parts of your program must register an interest in an event in order to receive event notifications, it is possible that **fire( )** could be called before any event handler has been registered. To prevent calling a **null** object, the event delegate must be tested to ensure that it is not **null**.

Inside **EventDemo**, an event handler called **handler( )** is created. In this simple example, the event handler simply displays a message, but other handlers could perform more meaningful actions. In **Main( )**, a **MyEvent** object is created and **handler( )** is registered as a handler for this event, as shown here:

```
MyEvent evt = new MyEvent();

// add handler() to the event list
evt.activate += new MyEventHandler(handler);
```

Notice that the handler is added using the += operator. Events support only += and – =.

Finally, the event is fired as shown here:

```
// fire the event
evt.fire();
```

Calling **fire( )** causes all registered event handlers to be called. In this case, there is only one registered handler, but there could be more, as the next section explains.

A Multicast Event Example

Events can be multicast. This enables multiple objects to respond to an event notification. Here is an event multicast example:

```
// An event multicast demonstration.

using System;

// Declare a delegate for an event.
delegate void MyEventHandler();

// Declare an event class.
class MyEvent {
  public event MyEventHandler activate;

  // this is called to fire the event.
  public void fire() {
    if(activate != null)
      activate();
  }
}

class X {
  public void Xhandler() {
    Console.WriteLine("Event received by X object");
  }
}

class Y {
  public void Yhandler() {
```

12

```
      Console.WriteLine("Event received by Y object");
  }
}

class EventDemo {
  static void handler() {
    Console.WriteLine("Event received by EventDemo");
  }

  public static void Main() {
    MyEvent evt = new MyEvent();
    X xOb = new X();
    Y yOb = new Y();

    // add handler() to the event list
    evt.activate += new MyEventHandler(handler);
    evt.activate += new MyEventHandler(xOb.Xhandler);
    evt.activate += new MyEventHandler(yOb.Yhandler);

    // fire the event
    evt.fire();
    Console.WriteLine();

    // remove a handler
    evt.activate -= new MyEventHandler(xOb.Xhandler);
    evt.fire();
  }
}
```

Create a multicast chain for events.

The output from the program is shown here:

```
Event received by EventDemo
Event received by X object
Event received by Y object

Event received by EventDemo
Event received by Y object
```

This example creates two additional classes, called **X** and **Y**, which also define event handlers compatible with **MyEventHandler**. Thus, these handlers can also become part of the event chain. Notice that the handlers in **X** and **Y** are not static. This means that objects of each must be created, and the handler linked to an object instance is added to the event chain.

Understand that events are sent to specific object instances, not generically to a class. Thus, each object of a class must register to receive an event notification. For example, the following program multicasts an event to three objects of type **X**:

```
// Objects, not classes, receive events.

using System;

// Declare a delegate for an event.
delegate void MyEventHandler();

// Declare an event class.
class MyEvent {
  public event MyEventHandler activate;

  // this is called to fire the event.
  public void fire() {
    if(activate != null)
      activate();
  }
}

class X {
  int id;

  public X(int x) { id = x; }

  public void Xhandler() {
    Console.WriteLine("Event received by object " + id);
  }
}

class EventDemo {
  public static void Main() {
    MyEvent evt = new MyEvent();
    X o1 = new X(1);
```

12

```
    X o2 = new X(2);
    X o3 = new X(3);

    evt.activate += new MyEventHandler(o1.Xhandler);
    evt.activate += new MyEventHandler(o2.Xhandler);
    evt.activate += new MyEventHandler(o3.Xhandler);

    // fire the event
    evt.fire();
  }
}
```

The output from this program is shown here:

```
Event received by object 1
Event received by object 2
Event received by object 3
```

As the output shows, each object registers its interest in an event separately, and each receives a separate notification.

Note

C# allows you to write any type of event that you desire. However, for component compatibility with the .NET Framework you will want to consult Microsoft's guidelines in this regard.

1-Minute Drill

- In C#, what is an event and what keyword is used to create one?
- How do delegates relate to events?
- Can events be multicast?

- An event is a notification of some change in a program. The keyword **event** is used to create an event.
- An event handler is specified using a delegate.
- Yes, events can be multicast.

Namespaces

The namespace was mentioned briefly in Module 1 because it is a concept fundamental to C#. In fact, every C# program makes use of a namespace in one way or another. We have not needed to examine the namespace in detail prior to now because C# automatically provides a default namespace for your program.

Let's begin by reviewing what you already know about namespaces. A *namespace* defines a declarative region that provides a way to keep one set of names separate from another. In essence, names declared in one namespace will not conflict with the same names declared in another. The namespace used by the .NET Framework library (which is the C# library) is **System**. This is why you have included

```
using System;
```

near the top of every program. As you saw in Module 11, the I/O classes are defined within a namespace subordinate to **System** called **System.IO**. There are many other namespaces subordinate to **System** that hold other parts of the C# library.

Namespaces are important because there has been an explosion of variable, method, property, and class names over the past few years. These include library routines, third-party code, and your own code. Without namespaces, all of these names would compete for slots in the global namespace and conflicts would arise. For example, if your program defined a class called **Finder**, it could conflict with another class called **Finder** supplied by a third-party library that your program uses. Fortunately, namespaces prevent this type of problem because a namespace localizes the visibility of names declared within it.

Declaring a Namespace

A namespace is declared using the **namespace** keyword. The general form of **namespace** is shown here:

```
namespace name {
  // members
}
```

12

Here, *name* is the name of the namespace. Anything defined within a **namespace** is within the scope of that **namespace**. Thus, **namespace** defines a scope. Within a namespace you can declare classes, structures, delegates, enumerations, interfaces, or another namespace.

Here is an example of a **namespace** that creates a namespace called **Counter**. It localizes the name used to implement a simple countdown counter class called **CountDown**.

```
// Declare a namespace for counters.
namespace Counter {        ←————————   Declare the Counter
  // A simple countdown counter.                  namespace.
  class CountDown {
    int val;

    public CountDown(int n) { val = n; }

    public void reset(int n) {
      val = n;
    }

    public int count() {
      if(val > 0) return val--;
      else return 0;
    }
  }
}
```

Here, the class **CountDown** is declared within the scope defined by the **Counter** namespace.

Here is a program that demonstrates the use of the **Counter** namespace.

```
// Demonstrate a namespace.
using System;

// Declare a namespace for counters.
namespace Counter {
  // A simple countdown counter.
  class CountDown {
```

```
    int val;

    public CountDown(int n) { val = n; }

    public void reset(int n) {
      val = n;
    }

    public int count() {
      if(val > 0) return val--;
      else return 0;
    }
  }
}
```

Here, **Counter** qualifies **CountDown**.

```
class NSDemo {
  public static void Main() {
    Counter.CountDown cd1 = new Counter.CountDown(10);
    int i;

    do {
      i = cd1.count();
      Console.Write(i + " ");
    } while(i > 0);
    Console.WriteLine();

    Counter.CountDown cd2 = new Counter.CountDown(20);

    do {
      i = cd2.count();
      Console.Write(i + " ");
    } while(i > 0);
    Console.WriteLine();

    cd2.reset(4);
    do {
      i = cd2.count();
      Console.Write(i + " ");
    } while(i > 0);
    Console.WriteLine();
  }
}
```

12

The output from the program is shown here:

```
10 9 8 7 6 5 4 3 2 1 0
20 19 18 17 16 15 14 13 12 11 10 9 8 7 6 5 4 3 2 1 0
4 3 2 1 0
```

Some important aspects of this program warrant close examination. First, since **CountDown** is declared within the **Counter** namespace, when an object is created, **CountDown** must be qualified with **Counter**, as shown here:

```
Counter.CountDown cd1 = new Counter.CountDown(10);
```

However, once an object of type **Counter** has been created, it is not necessary to further qualify it or any of its members with the namespace. Thus, **cd1.count( )** can be called directly without namespace qualification, as this line shows:

```
i = cd1.count();
```

using

As explained in Module 1, if your program includes frequent references to the members of a namespace, having to specify the namespace each time you need to refer to one quickly becomes tedious. The **using** directive alleviates this problem. Throughout this book you have been using **using** to bring the C# **System** namespace into view, so you are already familiar with it. As you would expect, **using** can also be used to bring namespaces that you create into view.

There are two forms of the **using** directive. The first is shown here:

using *name*;

Here, *name* specifies the name of the namespace you want to access. This is the form of **using** that you have already seen. All of the members defined within the specified namespace are brought into view (that is, they become part of the current namespace) and can be used without qualification. A **using** directive must be specified at the top of each file, prior to any other declarations.

The following program reworks the counter example from the previous section to show how you can employ **using** to bring a namespace that you create into view:

```csharp
// Demonstrate a namespace.
using System;

// Bring Counter into view.
using Counter;
```

using brings **Counter** into view.

```csharp
// Declare a namespace for counters.
namespace Counter {
  // A simple countdown counter.
  class CountDown {
    int val;

    public CountDown(int n) { val = n; }

    public void reset(int n) {
      val = n;
    }

    public int count() {
      if(val > 0) return val--;
      else return 0;
    }
  }
}

class NSDemo {
  public static void Main() {
    // now, CountDown can be used directly.
    CountDown cd1 = new CountDown(10);
    int i;

    do {
      i = cd1.count();
      Console.Write(i + " ");
    } while(i > 0);
    Console.WriteLine();

    CountDown cd2 = new CountDown(20);

    do {
      i = cd2.count();
      Console.Write(i + " ");
    } while(i > 0);
```

Now use **CountDown** directly.

12

```
    Console.WriteLine();

    cd2.reset(4);
    do {
      i = cd2.count();
      Console.Write(i + " ");
    } while(i > 0);
    Console.WriteLine();
  }
}
```

The program illustrates one other important point: Using one namespace does not override another. When you bring a namespace into view, it simply adds its names to whatever other namespaces are currently in effect. Thus, both **System** and **Counter** have been brought into view.

A Second Form of using

The **using** directive has a second form, which is shown here:

using *alias* = *name*;

Here, *alias* becomes another name for the class or namespace specified by *name*. The counting program is reworked once again here so that an alias for **Counter.CountDown** called **Count** is created.

```
// Demonstrate a using alias.
using System;

// Create an alias for Counter.CountDown.
using Count = Counter.CountDown;        ◄──── Create an alias for
                                              Counter.CountDown.
// Declare a namespace for counters.
namespace Counter {
  // A simple countdown counter.
  class CountDown {
    int val;

    public CountDown(int n) { val = n; }

    public void reset(int n) {
      val = n;
    }
```

```
      public int count() {
        if(val > 0) return val--;
        else return 0;
      }
    }
  }

class NSDemo {
  public static void Main() {
    Count cd1 = new Count(10);        ◄──────────  Use the alias.
    int i;

    do {
      i = cd1.count();
      Console.Write(i + " ");
    } while(i > 0);
    Console.WriteLine();

    Count cd2 = new Count(20);

    do {
      i = cd2.count();
      Console.Write(i + " ");
    } while(i > 0);
    Console.WriteLine();

    cd2.reset(4);
    do {
      i = cd2.count();
      Console.Write(i + " ");
    } while(i > 0);
    Console.WriteLine();
  }
}
```

Once **Count** has been specified as another name for **Counter.CountDown**, it can be used to declare objects without any further namespace qualification. For example, in the program this line

```
Count cd1 = new Count(10);
```

creates a **CountDown** object.

12

Namespaces Are Additive

There can be more than one namespace declaration of the same name. This allows a namespace to be split over several files or even separated within the same file. For example, the following program defines two **Counter** namespaces. One contains the **CountDown** class. The other contains the **CountUp** class. When compiled, the contents of both **Counter** namespaces are added together.

```csharp
// Namespaces are additive.
using System;

// Bring Counter into view.
using Counter;

// Here is one Counter namespace.
namespace Counter {                          // Declare Counter namespace twice.
  // A simple countdown counter.
  class CountDown {
    int val;

    public CountDown(int n) { val = n; }

    public void reset(int n) {
      val = n;
    }

    public int count() {
      if(val > 0) return val--;
      else return 0;
    }
  }
}

// Here is another Counter namespace.
namespace Counter {                          // Declare Counter namespace twice.
  // A simple count-Up counter.
  class CountUp {
    int val;
    int target;

    public int Target { get{ return target; } }

    public CountUp(int n) { target = n; val = 0; }

    public void reset(int n) {
```

```
        target = n;
        val = 0;
    }

    public int count() {
      if(val < target) return val++;
      else return target;
    }
  }
}

class NSDemo {
  public static void Main() {
    CountDown cd = new CountDown(10);
    CountUp cu = new CountUp(8);
    int i;

    do {
      i = cd.count();
      Console.Write(i + " ");
    } while(i > 0);
    Console.WriteLine();

    do {
      i = cu.count();
      Console.Write(i + " ");
    } while(i < cu.Target);

  }
}
```

This program produces the following output:

```
10 9 8 7 6 5 4 3 2 1 0
0 1 2 3 4 5 6 7 8
```

Notice one other thing: the statement

```
using Counter;
```

brings into view the entire contents of the **Counter** namespace. Thus, both **CountDown** and **CountUp** can be referred to directly, without namespace qualification. It doesn't matter that the **Counter** namespace was split into two parts.

12

Namespaces Can Be Nested

One namespace can be nested within another. Consider this program:

```
// Namespaces can be nested.
using System;

namespace NS1 {
  class ClassA {
    public ClassA() {
      Console.WriteLine("constructing ClassA");
    }
  }
  namespace NS2 { // a nested namespace ←———— NS2 is nested inside NS1.
    class ClassB {
      public ClassB() {
        Console.WriteLine("constructing ClassB");
      }
    }
  }
}

class NestedNSDemo {
  public static void Main() {
    NS1.ClassA a= new NS1.ClassA();

 // NS2.ClassB b = new NS2.ClassB(); // Error!!! NS2 not in view

    NS1.NS2.ClassB b = new NS1.NS2.ClassB(); // this is right
  }
}
```

This program produces the following output:

```
constructing ClassA
constructing ClassB
```

In the program, the namespace **NS2** is nested within **NS1**. Thus, to refer to **ClassB**, you must qualify it with both the **NS1** and **NS2** namespaces. **NS2** by itself is insufficient. As shown, the namespace names are separated by a period.

You can specify a nested namespace using a single **namespace** statement by separating each namespace with a period. For example:

```
namespace OuterNS {
  namespace InnerNS {
    // ...
  }
}
```

can also be specified like this:

```
namespace OuterNS.InnerNS {
  // ...
}
```

The Default Namespace

If you don't declare a namespace for your program, then the default namespace is used. This is why you have not needed to use **namespace** for the programs in the preceding modules. While the default namespace is convenient for the short, sample programs found in this book, most real-world code will be contained within a namespace. The main reason for encapsulating your code within a namespace is that it prevents name conflicts. Namespaces are another tool that you have to help you organize programs and make them viable in today's complex, networked environment.

1-Minute Drill

● A namespace defines a _____.

● What are the two forms of **using**?

● Can a namespace be split between files?

● A namespace defines a scope.
● `using name;` and `using alias = name;` are the two forms of **using**.
● Yes.

Project 12-1: Putting Set into a Namespace

In Project 7-1 you created a class that implemented a set type called **Set**. This is precisely the type of class that you should consider putting into its own namespace. One reason for this is that the name **Set** could easily conflict with other classes of the same name. By putting **Set** into its own namespace, you can avoid potential name conflicts.

Step-By-Step

1. Using the code from **SetDemo.cs** (the file from Project 7-1), move the entire **Set** class into a file called **Set.cs**. In the process, enclose the set code inside the namespace **MyTypes.Set**, as shown here:

```
/*
   Project 12-1

   Put the Set class into its own namespace.
*/
using System;

namespace MyTypes.Set {

  class Set {
    char[] members; // this array holds the set
    int len; // number of members

    // Construct a null set.
    public Set() {
      len = 0;
    }

    // Construct an empty set of a given size.
    public Set(int size) {
      members = new char[size]; // allocate memory for set
      len = 0; // no members when constructed
    }

    // Construct a set from another set.
    public Set(Set s) {
      members = new char[s.len]; // allocate memory for set
```

```csharp
    for(int i=0; i < s.len; i++) members[i] = s[i];
    len = s.len; // number of members
  }

  // Implement read-only Length property.
  public int Length {
    get{
      return len;
    }
  }

  // Implement read-only indexer.
  public char this[int idx]{
    get {
      if(idx >= 0 & idx < len) return members[idx];
      else return (char)0;
    }
  }

  /* See if an element is in the set.
     Return the index of the element
     or -1 if not found. */
  int find(char ch) {
    int i;

    for(i=0; i < len; i++)
      if(members[i] == ch) return i;

    return -1;
  }

  // Add a unique element to a set.
  public static Set operator +(Set ob, char ch) {
    Set newset = new Set(ob.len + 1);

    // copy elements
    for(int i=0; i < ob.len; i++)
      newset.members[i] = ob.members[i];

    // set len
    newset.len = ob.len;

    // see if element already exists
```

```
      if(ob.find(ch) == -1) { // if not found, then add
        // add new element to new set
        newset.members[newset.len] = ch;
        newset.len++;
      }
      return newset; // return updated set
  }

  // Remove an element from the set.
  public static Set operator -(Set ob, char ch) {
    Set newset = new Set();
    int i = ob.find(ch); // -1 if element not found

    // copy and compress the remaining elements
    for(int j=0; j < ob.len; j++)
      if(j != i) newset = newset + ob.members[j];

    return newset;
  }

  // Set union.
  public static Set operator +(Set ob1, Set ob2) {
    Set newset = new Set(ob1); // copy the first set

    // add unique elements from second set
    for(int i=0; i < ob2.len; i++)
        newset = newset + ob2[i];

    return newset; // return updated set
  }

  // Set difference.
  public static Set operator -(Set ob1, Set ob2) {
    Set newset = new Set(ob1); // copy the first set

    // subtract elements from second set
    for(int i=0; i < ob2.len; i++)
      newset = newset - ob2[i];

    return newset; // return updated set
  }
  }
}
```

2. After putting **Set** into the **MyTypes.Set** namespace, you will need to include the **MyTypes.Set** namespace in any program that uses **Set**, as shown here:

```
using MyTypes.Set;
```

3. Alternatively, you can fully qualify references to **Set**, as shown in this example:

```
MyTypes.Set.Set s1 = new MyTypes.Set.Set();
```

Conversion Operators

In some situations, you will want to use an object of a class in an expression involving other types of data. Sometimes, overloading one or more operators can provide the means of doing this. However, in other cases, what you want is a simple type conversion from the class type to the target type. To handle these cases, C# allows you to create a *conversion operator*. A conversion operator converts an object of your class into another type.

There are two forms of conversion operators, implicit and explicit. The general form for each is shown here:

public static operator implicit *target-type*(*source-type v*) { return *value*; }

public static operator explicit *target-type*(*source-type v*) { return *value*; }

Here, *target-type* is the target type that you are converting to, *source-type* is the type you are converting from, and *value* is the value of the class after conversion. The conversion operators return data of type *target-type*, and no other return type specifier is allowed.

If the conversion operator specifies **implicit**, then the conversion is invoked automatically, such as when an object is used in an expression with the target type. When the conversion operator specifies **explicit**, the conversion is invoked when a cast is used. You cannot define both an implicit and explicit conversion operator for the same target and source types.

To illustrate a conversion operator, we will use the **ThreeD** class that we created in Module 7. Recall that **ThreeD** stores three-dimensional coordinates. Suppose you want to convert an object of type **ThreeD** into an integer so it can be used in an integer expression. Further, the conversion will take place by using the product of the three dimensions. To accomplish this, you will use an implicit conversion operator that looks like this:

```
public static implicit operator int(ThreeD op1)
{
  return op1.x * op1.y * op1.z;
}
```

Here is a program that illustrates this conversion operator:

```
// An example that uses an implicit conversion operator.
using System;

// A three-dimensional coordinate class.
class ThreeD {
  int x, y, z; // 3-D coordinates

  public ThreeD() { x = y = z = 0; }
  public ThreeD(int i, int j, int k) { x = i; y = j; z = k; }

  // Overload binary +.
  public static ThreeD operator +(ThreeD op1, ThreeD op2)
  {
    ThreeD result = new ThreeD();

    result.x = op1.x + op2.x;
    result.y = op1.y + op2.y;
    result.z = op1.z + op2.z;

    return result;
  }

  // An implicit conversion from ThreeD to int.
  public static implicit operator int(ThreeD op1)
  {
    return op1.x * op1.y * op1.z;
  }

  // Show X, Y, Z coordinates.
  public void show()
  {
    Console.WriteLine(x + ", " + y + ", " + z);
```

A conversion operator from **ThreeD** to **int**

```
    }
}

class ThreeDDemo {
  public static void Main() {
    ThreeD a = new ThreeD(1, 2, 3);
    ThreeD b = new ThreeD(10, 10, 10);
    ThreeD c = new ThreeD();
    int i;

    Console.Write("Here is a: ");
    a.show();
    Console.WriteLine();
    Console.Write("Here is b: ");
    b.show();
    Console.WriteLine();

    c = a + b; // add a and b together
    Console.Write("Result of a + b: ");
    c.show();
    Console.WriteLine();

    i = a; // convert to int
    Console.WriteLine("Result of i = a: " + i);
    Console.WriteLine();

    i = a * 2 - b; // convert to int
    Console.WriteLine("result of a * 2 - b: " + i);
  }
}
```

Conversion to **int** invoked.

This program displays the output:

```
Here is a: 1, 2, 3

Here is b: 10, 10, 10

Result of a + b: 11, 12, 13

Result of i = a: 6

result of a * 2 - b: -988
```

12

As the program illustrates, when a **ThreeD** object is used in an integer expression, such as **i = a**, the conversion is applied to the object. In this specific case, the conversion returns the value 6, which is the product of the coordinates stored in **a**. However, when an expression does not require a conversion to **int**, the conversion operator is not called. This is why **c = a+b** does not invoke **operator int( )**.

Remember that you can create different conversion operators to meet different needs. You could define one that converts to **double** or **long**, for example. Each is applied automatically and independently.

An implicit conversion operator is applied automatically when a conversion is required in an expression, when passing an object to a method, in an assignment, and also when an explicit cast to the target type is used. Alternatively, you can create an explicit conversion operator that is invoked only when an explicit cast is used. An explicit conversion operator is not invoked automatically. For example, here is the previous program reworked to use an explicit conversion to **int**:

```
// Use an explicit conversion.
 using System;

// A three-dimensional coordinate class.
class ThreeD {
  int x, y, z; // 3-D coordinates

  public ThreeD() { x = y = z = 0; }
  public ThreeD(int i, int j, int k) { x = i; y = j; z = k; }

  // Overload binary +.
  public static ThreeD operator +(ThreeD op1, ThreeD op2)
  {
    ThreeD result = new ThreeD();

    result.x = op1.x + op2.x;
    result.y = op1.y + op2.y;
    result.z = op1.z + op2.z;

    return result;
  }

  // This is now explicit.
  public static explicit operator int(ThreeD op1)
  {
    return op1.x * op1.y * op1.z;
```

Conversion is now explicit.

```
    }

    // Show X, Y, Z coordinates.
    public void show()
    {
      Console.WriteLine(x + ", " + y + ", " + z);
    }
}

class ThreeDDemo {
  public static void Main() {
    ThreeD a = new ThreeD(1, 2, 3);
    ThreeD b = new ThreeD(10, 10, 10);
    ThreeD c = new ThreeD();
    int i;

    Console.Write("Here is a: ");
    a.show();
    Console.WriteLine();
    Console.Write("Here is b: ");
    b.show();
    Console.WriteLine();

    c = a + b; // add a and b together
    Console.Write("Result of a + b: ");
    c.show();
    Console.WriteLine();

    i = (int) a; // explicitly convert to int -- cast required
    Console.WriteLine("Result of i = a: " + i);
    Console.WriteLine();

    i = (int)a * 2 - (int)b; // casts required
    Console.WriteLine("result of a * 2 - b: " + i);

  }
}
```

Now, casts are required.

Because the conversion operator is now marked as explicit, conversion to **int** must be explicitly cast. For example, in this line:

```
i = (int) a; // explicitly convert to int -- cast required
```

if you remove the cast, the program will not compile.

12

Ask the Expert

Question: Since implicit conversions are invoked automatically, without the need for a cast, why would I want to create an explicit conversion?

Answer: Although convenient, implicit conversions should be used only in situations in which the conversion is inherently error-free. To ensure this, implicit conversions should be created only when two conditions are met. The first is that no loss of information, such as truncation, overflow, or loss of sign, occurs. The second is that the conversion does not throw an exception. If the conversion cannot meet these two requirements, then you should use an explicit conversion.

There are a few restrictions to conversion operators:

- You cannot create a conversion from a built-in type. For example, you cannot redefine the conversion from **double** to **int**.

- You cannot define a conversion to or from **object**.

- You cannot define both an implicit and an explicit conversion for the same source and target types.

- You cannot define a conversion from a base class to a derived class.

- You cannot define a conversion from or to an interface.

1-Minute Drill

- What is a conversion operator?
- What is the difference between implicit and explicit conversions?
- Can a conversion operator convert from a built-in type?

- A conversion operator specifies a conversion to or from a class type.
- An implicit conversion is automatically invoked. An explicit conversion must be invoked via a cast.
- No.

The Preprocessor

C# defines several *preprocessor directives,* which affect the way that your program's source file is interpreted by the compiler. These directives affect the text of the source file in which they occur, prior to the translation of the program into object code. The preprocessor directives are largely a holdover from C++. In fact, the C# preprocessor is very similar to the one defined by C++. The term *preprocessor directive* comes from the fact that these instructions were traditionally handled by a separate compilation phase called the *preprocessor.* Today's modern compiler technology no longer requires a separate preprocessing stage to handle the directives, but the name has stuck.

C# defines the following preprocessor directives:

#define	#elif	#else	#endif
#endregion	#error	#if	#line
#region	#undef	#warning	

All preprocessor directives begin with a # sign. In addition, each preprocessor directive must be on its own line.

Given C#'s modern, object-oriented architecture, there is not as much need for the preprocessor directives as there is in older languages. Nevertheless, they can be of value from time to time, especially for conditional compilation. Each directive is examined in turn.

#define

The **#define** directive defines a character sequence called a *symbol.* The existence or non-existence of a symbol can be determined by **#if** or **#elif** and is used to control compilation. Here is its general form:

```
#define symbol
```

Notice that there is no semicolon in this statement. There may be any number of spaces between the **#define** and the symbol, but once the symbol begins, it is terminated only by a newline character. For example, to define the symbol **EXPERIMENTAL**, use this directive:

```
#define EXPERIMENTAL
```

12

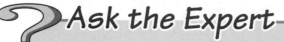

Ask the Expert

Question: In C/C++ I know that you can use #define to perform textual substitutions, such as defining a name for a value, and to create function-like macros. Does C# support these uses of #define?

Answer: No. In C#, **#define** is used only to define a symbol.

#if and #endif

The **#if** and **#endif** directives allow you to conditionally compile a sequence of code based upon whether an expression involving one or more symbols evaluates to true. A symbol is true if it is has been defined. It is false otherwise. Thus, if a symbol has been defined by a **#define** directive, it will evaluate as true.

The general form of **#if** is

```
#if symbol-expression
    statement sequence
#endif
```

If the expression following **#if** is true, the code that is between it and **#endif** is compiled. Otherwise, the intervening code is skipped. The **#endif** directive marks the end of an **#if** block.

A symbol expression can be as simple as just the name of a symbol. You can also use these operators in a symbol expression: !, = =, !=, &&, and ||. Parentheses are also allowed.

For example:

```
// Demonstrate #if, #endif, and #define.
#define EXPERIMENTAL

using System;

class Test {
  public static void Main() {

    #if EXPERIMENTAL
      Console.WriteLine("Compiled for experimental version.");
    #endif

    Console.WriteLine("This is in all versions.");
  }
}
```

Compiled only if **EXPERIMENTAL** is defined, which it is in this example.

This program displays the following:

```
Compiled for experimental version.
This is in all versions.
```

The program defines the symbol **EXPERIMENTAL**. Thus, when the #if is encountered, the symbol expression evaluates to true, and the first **WriteLine( )** statement is compiled. If you remove the definition of **EXPERIMENTAL** and recompile the program, the first **WriteLine( )** statement will not be compiled because the #if will evaluate to false. In all cases, the second **WriteLine( )** statement is compiled because it is not part of the #if block.

As explained, you can use a symbol expression in an #if. For example:

```
// Use a symbol expression.
#define EXPERIMENTAL
#define TRIAL

using System;

class Test {
  public static void Main() {

    #if EXPERIMENTAL
      Console.WriteLine("Compiled for experimental version.");
    #endif

    #if EXPERIMENTAL && TRIAL  ◀──────  A symbol expression.
      Console.Error.WriteLine("Testing experimental trial version.");
    #endif

    Console.WriteLine("This is in all versions.");
  }
}
```

The output from this program is shown here:

```
Compiled for experimental version.
Testing experimental trial version.
This is in all versions.
```

In this example, two symbols are defined, **EXPERIMENTAL** and **TRIAL**. The second **WriteLine( )** statement is compiled only if both are defined.

12

#else and #elif

The **#else** directive works much like the **else** that is part of the C# language: it establishes an alternative if **#if** fails. The previous example can be expanded as shown here:

```
// Demonstrate #else.

#define EXPERIMENTAL

using System;

class Test {
  public static void Main() {

    #if EXPERIMENTAL
      Console.WriteLine("Compiled for experimental version.");
    #else
      Console.WriteLine("Compiled for release.");
    #endif

    #if EXPERIMENTAL && TRIAL
      Console.Error.WriteLine("Testing experimental trial version.");
    #else
      Console.Error.WriteLine("Not experimental trial version.");
    #endif

    Console.WriteLine("This is in all versions.");
  }
}
```

Use the **#else**.

The output is shown here:

```
Compiled for experimental version.
Not experimental trial version.
This is in all versions.
```

Since **TRIAL** is no longer defined, the **#else** portion of the second conditional code sequence is used.

Notice that **#else** marks both the end of the **#if** block and the beginning of the **#else** block. This is necessary because there can only be one **#endif** associated with any **#if**.

The **#elif** directive means "else if" and establishes an if-else-if chain for multiple compilation options. **#elif** is followed by a symbol expression. If the expression is true, that block of code is compiled and no other **#elif** expressions are tested. Otherwise, the next block in the series is checked. The general form for **#elif** is

```
#if symbol-expression
   statement sequence
#elif symbol-expression
   statement sequence
#elif symbol-expression
   statement sequence
#elif symbol-expression
   statement sequence
#elif symbol-expression
   .
   .
   .
#endif
```

For example:

```
// Demonstrate #elif.
#define RELEASE

using System;

class Test {
  public static void Main() {                        Use #elif.

    #if EXPERIMENTAL
      Console.WriteLine("Compiled for experimental version.");
    #elif RELEASE  ←
      Console.WriteLine("Compiled for release.");
    #else
      Console.WriteLine("Compiled for internal testing.");
```

12

```
    #endif

    #if TRIAL && !RELEASE
        Console.WriteLine("Trial version.");
    #endif

    Console.WriteLine("This is in all versions.");
  }
}
```

The output is shown here:

```
Compiled for release.
This is in all versions.
```

#undef

The **#undef** directive removes a previously defined definition of the macro name that follows it. That is, it "undefines" a macro. The general form for **#undef** is

    #undef *symbol*

For example:

```
#define SMALL

#if SMALL
  // ...
#undef SMALL
// at this point SMALL is undefined.
```

After the **#undef** directive, **SMALL** is no longer defined.

    #undef is used principally to allow symbols to be localized to only those sections of code that need them.

#error

The **#error** directive forces the compiler to stop compilation. It is used for debugging. The general form of the **#error** directive is

> #error *error-message*

When the **#error** directive is encountered, the error message is displayed. For example, when the compiler encounters this line:

```
#error This is a test error!
```

compilation stops and the error message "This is a test error!" is displayed.

#warning

The **#warning** directive is similar to **#error** except that a warning rather than an error is produced. Thus, compilation is not stopped. The general form of the **#warning** directive is

> #warning *warning-message*

#line

The **#line** directive sets the line number and filename for the file that contains the **#line** directive. The number and the name are used when errors or warnings are output during compilation. The general form for **#line** is

> #line *number "filename"*

where *number* is any positive integer and becomes the new line number, and the optional *filename* is any valid file identifier, which becomes the new filename. **#line** is primarily used for debugging and special applications.

12

#region and #endregion

The **#region** and **#endregion** directives let you define a region that will be expanded or collapsed by the Visual C++ IDE when using the outlining feature. The general form is shown here:

```
#region
  // code sequence
#endregion
```

1-Minute Drill

- How do you define a symbol?
- What does **#if** do?
- What operators are allowed in an **#if** or **#elif** expression?

Attributes

C# allows you to add declarative information to a program in the form of an *attribute*. An attribute defines additional information that is associated with a class, structure, method, and so on. For example, you might define an attribute that determines the type of button that a class will display.

Attributes are specified between square brackets, preceding the item they apply to. You can define your own attribute, or use attributes defined by C#. Although creating your own attributes is a topic that is beyond the scope of this book, it is quite easy to use two of C#'s built-in attributes: **Conditional** and **Obsolete**. They are examined here.

- To define a symbol, use **#define**.
- The **#if** introduces a block of code that is compiled if the symbol expression associated with the **#if** is true. This block is terminated by a **#endif**.
- The operators allowed in an **#if** or **#elif** expression are !=, = =, &&, ||, and !

The Conditional Attribute

The attribute **Conditional** is perhaps C#'s most interesting attribute. It allows you to create *conditional methods*. A conditional method is invoked only when a specific symbol has been defined via **#define**. Otherwise, the method is bypassed. Thus, a conditional method offers an alternative to conditional compilation using **#if**. To use the **Conditional** attribute you must include the **System.Diagnostics** namespace.

Let's begin with an example:

```
// Demonstrate the Conditional attribute.
#define TRIAL

using System;
using System.Diagnostics;

class Test {

  [Conditional("TRIAL")]            trial( ) is executed only
  void trial() {                    if TRIAL is defined.
    Console.WriteLine("Trial version, not for distribution.");
  }

  [Conditional("RELEASE")]          release( ) is executed only
  void release() {                  if RELEASE is defined.
    Console.WriteLine("Final release version.");
  }

  public static void Main() {
    Test t = new Test();

    t.trial(); // call only if TRIAL is defined
    t.release(); // called only if RELEASE is defined
  }
}
```

The output from this program is shown here:

```
Trial version, not for distribution.
```

12

Let's look closely at this program to understand why this output is produced. First notice that the program defines the symbol **TRIAL**. Next, notice how the methods **trial( )** and **release( )** are coded. They are both preceded with the **Conditional** attribute, which has this general form:

    [Conditional *symbol*]

where *symbol* is the symbol that determines whether the method will be executed. This attribute can be used only on methods. If the symbol is defined, then when the method is called, it will be executed. If the symbol is not defined, then the method is not executed.

Inside **Main( )**, both **trial( )** and **release( )** are called. However, only **TRIAL** is defined. Thus, **trial( )** is executed. The call to **release( )** is ignored. If you define **RELEASE**, then **release( )** will also be called. If you remove the definition for **TRIAL**, then **trial( )** will not be called.

Conditional methods have a few restrictions: They must return **void**. They must be members of a class, not an interface. They cannot be preceded with the **override** keyword.

The Obsolete Attribute

The **System.Obsolete** attribute lets you mark a program element as obsolete. It has this general form:

    [Obsolete *"message"*]

Here, *message* is displayed when that program element is compiled. Here is a short example:

```
// Demonstrate the Obsolete attribute.
using System;

class Test {

  [Obsolete("Use myMeth2, instead.")]
  static int myMeth(int a, int b) {
    return a / b;
  }
```

Display a warning when **myMeth( )** is used.

```
// Improved version of myMeth.
static int myMeth2(int a, int b) {
  return b == 0 ? 0 : a /b;
}

public static void Main() {
 // warning displayed for this
  Console.WriteLine("4 / 3 is " + Test.myMeth(4, 3));

 // no warning here
  Console.WriteLine("4 / 3 is " + Test.myMeth2(4, 3));
 }
}
```

When the call to **myMeth( )** is encountered in **Main( )** during program compilation, a warning will be generated that tells the user to use **myMeth2( )**, instead.

1-Minute Drill

● What is an attribute?

● What is a conditional method?

● What is the purpose of the **Obsolete** attribute?

Unsafe Code

C# allows you to write what is called "unsafe" code. While this statement might seem shocking, it really isn't. Unsafe code is not code that is poorly written; it is code that does not execute under the management of the Common Language Runtime (CLR). As explained in Module 1, C# is normally used to create managed code. It is possible, however, to write code that does not execute under the

12

● An attribute is additional information associated with some item, such as a **class**, **struct**, or method.
● A conditional method is one for which the **Conditional** attribute has been specified. A conditional method is executed only if the symbol specified in the attribute is defined.
● The **Obsolete** attribute causes a warning message to be issued, indicating that an obsolete item is used.

control of the CLR. Since this unmanaged code is not subject to the same controls and constraints as managed code, it is called "unsafe" because it is impossible to verify that it won't perform some type of harmful action. Thus, the term *unsafe* does not mean that the code is inherently flawed. It just means that it is possible for the code to perform actions that are not subject to the supervision of the managed context.

Managed code, while being beneficial for the most part, prevents the use of *pointers*. If you are familiar with C or C++, then you know that pointers are variables that hold the addresses of other objects. Thus, pointers are a bit like references in C#. The main difference is that a pointer can point anywhere in memory; a reference always points to an object of its type. Since a pointer can point anywhere in memory, it is possible to misuse a pointer. It is also easy to introduce a coding error when using pointers. This is why C# does not support pointers when creating managed code. Pointers are, however, both useful and necessary for some types of programming (such as system-level utilities), and C# does allow you to create and use pointers. All pointer operations must be marked as unsafe, since they execute outside the managed environment.

In general, if you need to create code that executes outside of the CLR, then you are better off using C++. The declaration and use of pointers in C# parallels that of C/C++; if you know how to use pointers in C/C++, then you can use them in C#. But remember, the point of C# is the creation of managed code. Its ability to support unmanaged code allows it to be applied to a special class of problems. It is not for normal C# programming. In fact, to compile unmanaged code, you must use the **/unsafe** compiler option.

Working with unmanaged code is an advanced topic, and a detailed discussion is beyond the scope of this book. That said, we will briefly examine pointers and the two keywords that support unmanaged code: **unsafe** and **fixed**.

A Brief Look at Pointers

Pointers are variables that hold the addresses of other objects. For example, if **x** contains the address of **y**, then **x** is said to "point to" **y**. Pointer variables must be declared as such. The general form of a pointer variable declaration is

type* var-name;

Here, *type* is the pointer's base type; it must be a non-class type. *var-name* is the name of the pointer variable. For example, to declare **p** to be a pointer to an **int**, use this declaration:

```
int* ip;
```

For a **float** pointer, use

```
float* fp;
```

In general, in a declaration statement, preceding a variable name with an *
causes that variable to become a pointer.

The type of data that a pointer will point to is determined by its *base type*.
Thus, in the preceding examples, **ip** can be used to point to an **int**, and **fp** can
be used to point to a **float**. Understand, however, that there is nothing that
actually prevents a pointer from pointing elsewhere. This is why pointers
are potentially unsafe.

There are two operators that are used with pointers: * and &. The & is a
unary operator that returns the memory address of its operand. (Recall that
a unary operator requires only one operand.) For example:

```
int* ip;
int num = 10;

ip = &num;
```

puts into **ip** the memory address of the variable **num**. This address is the
location of the variable in the computer's internal memory. It has *nothing* to
do with the *value* of **num**. Thus, **ip** *does not* contain the value 10 (**num**'s initial
value). It contains the address at which **num** is stored. The operation of & can
be remembered as returning "the address of" the variable it precedes. Therefore,
the above assignment statement could be verbalized as "ip receives the address
of **num**."

The second operator is *, and it is the complement of &. It is a unary
operator that returns the value of the variable located at the address specified
by its operand. Continuing with the same example, if **ip** contains the memory
address of the variable **num**, then

```
int val;
val = *ip;
```

will place into **val** the value 10, which is the value of **num**, which is pointed to
by **ip**. The operation of * can be remembered as "at address." In this case, then,
the statement could be read as "**val** receives the value at address **ip**."

12

Pointers can also be used with structures. When you access a member of a structure through a pointer, you must use the arrow operator, which is ->, rather than the dot (.) operator. For example, given this structure:

```
struct MyStruct {
  public int x;
  public int y;
  public int sum() { return x + y; }
}
```

here is how you would access its members through a pointer:

```
MyStruct o = new MyStruct();
MyStruct* p; // declare a pointer

p = &o;
p->x = 10;
p->y = 20;

Console.WriteLine("Sum is " + p->sum());
```

Ask the Expert

Question: I know that when declaring a pointer in C++ that the * is not distributive over a list of variables in a declaration. Thus, this statement

```
int* p, q;
```

declares an integer pointer called p and an integer called q. It is equivalent to the following two declarations.

```
int* p;
int q;
```

Is the same also true for C#?

Answer: No. In C#, the * is distributive and the declaration

```
int* p, q;
```

creates two pointer variables. Thus, it is the same as these two declarations:

```
int* p;
int* q;
```

This is an important difference to be aware of when porting C++ code to C#.

Using unsafe

Any code that uses pointers must be marked as unsafe by using the **unsafe** keyword. You can mark an individual statement or an entire method as unsafe. For example, here is a program that uses pointers inside **Main( )**, which is marked unsafe:

```
// Demonstrate pointers and unsafe.
using System;

class UnsafeCode {
  // mark Main as unsafe
  unsafe public static void Main() {        ← Mark Main( ) as unsafe
    int count = 99;                           because it uses a pointer.
    int* p; // create an int pointer

    p = &count; // put address of count into p

    Console.WriteLine("Initial value of count is " + *p);

    *p = 10; // assign to count via p

    Console.WriteLine("New value of count is " + *p);
  }
}
```

12

The output of this program is shown here:

```
Initial value of count is 99
New value of count is 10
```

Using fixed

The **fixed** modifier prevents a managed object from being moved by the garbage collector. This is needed when a pointer refers to such an object. Since the pointer has no knowledge of the actions of the garbage collector, if the object is moved, the pointer will point to the wrong object. Here is the general form of **fixed**:

```
fixed (type *p = &fixedObj) {
    // use fixed object
}
```

Here, *p* is a pointer that is being assigned the address of an object. The object will remain in its current memory location until the block of code has executed. You can also use a single statement for the target of a **fixed** statement. The **fixed** keyword can be used only in an unsafe context.

Here is an example of **fixed**:

```
// Demonstrate unsafe code.
using System;

class Test {
  public int num;
  public Test(int i) { num = i; }
}

class UnsafeCode {
  // mark Main as unsafe
  unsafe public static void Main() {          Use fixed to fix
    Test o = new Test(19);                    location of o.

    fixed (int* p = &o.num) { // use fixed to put address of o.num into p

      Console.WriteLine("Initial value of o.num is " + *p);

      *p = 10; // assign to count via p

      Console.WriteLine("New value of o.num is " + *p);
    }
  }
}
```

The output from this program is shown here:

```
Initial value of o.num is 19
New value of o.num is 10
```

Here, **fixed** prevents **o** from being moved. Because **p** points to **o.num**, if **o** moved, then **p** would point to an invalid location.

As stated at the outset of this section, the creation and use of unsafe code is an advanced topic, and there are more issues involved with its creation than are discussed here. If writing unsafe code will be a part of your programming future, then you will need to study it further. (You will find in-depth coverage of this topic in my book *C#: The Complete Reference*, Osborne/McGraw-Hill.)

1-Minute Drill

● What is a pointer?

● When must **unsafe** be used?

● What is the purpose of **fixed**?

Runtime Type Identification

In C# it is possible to determine the type of an object at runtime. In fact, C# includes three keywords that support runtime type identification: **is**, **as**, and **typeof**. Although runtime type identification is an advanced feature that you will not use in your day-to-day programming, it is important to have a general understanding of it.

Testing a Type with is

You can determine if an object is of a certain type by using the **is** operator. Its general form is shown here:

expr is *type*

● A pointer is a variable that holds the memory address of another object.
● Any code that uses a pointer must be specified as **unsafe**.
● The **fixed** modifier prevents the garbage collector from moving an object.

Here, *expr* is an expression whose type is being tested against *type*. If the type of *expr* is the same as, or compatible with, *type,* then the outcome of this operation is true. Otherwise, it is false. Here is an example:

```
// Demonstrate is.
using System;

class A {}
class B : A {}

class UseIs {
  public static void Main() {
    A a = new A();
    B b = new B();

    if(a is A) Console.WriteLine("a is an A");
    if(b is A)
      Console.WriteLine("b is an A because it is derived from A");
    if(a is B)
      Console.WriteLine("This won't display -- a not derived from B");

    if(b is B) Console.WriteLine("B is a B");
    if(a is object) Console.WriteLine("a is an Object");
  }
}
```

> **a** is not a **B**, so this **is** is false.

> This **is** operation is true because **a** is an **A**.

The output is shown here:

```
a is an A
b is an A because it is derived from A
B is a B
a is an Object
```

Most of the **is** expressions are self-explanatory, but two may need a little discussion. First, notice this statement:

```
if(b is A)
  Console.WriteLine("b is an A because it is derived from A");
```

The **if** succeeds because **b** is an object of type **B**, which is derived from type **A**. Thus, **b** is compatible with **A**. However, the reverse is not true. When this line is executed:

```
if(a is B)
  Console.WriteLine("This won't display -- a not derived from B");
```

the **if** does not succeed because **a** is of type **A**, which is not derived from **B**. Thus, they are not compatible.

Using as

Sometimes you will want to try a cast at runtime, but not raise an exception if the cast fails. To do this, use the **as** operator, which has this general form:

> *expr* **as** *type*

Here, *expr* is the expression being cast to *type*. If the cast succeeds, then a reference to type is returned. Otherwise, a null reference is returned.

Using typeof

You can obtain a **System.Type** object for a given type by using **typeof**, which has this general form:

> **typeof**(*type*)

Here, *type* is the type being obtained. **System.Type** is a class that describes the information associated with a type. Using the obtained object, you can retrieve information about the type. For example, this program displays the complete name for the **StreamReader** class:

```
// Demonstrate typeof.
using System;
using System.IO;

class UseTypeof {
  public static void Main() {
    Type t = typeof(StreamReader);
    Console.WriteLine(t.FullName);
  }
}
```

This program outputs the following:

```
System.IO.StreamReader
```

System.Type contains many methods, fields, and properties that you will want to explore on your own.

12

1-Minute Drill

- What operator determines if an object is compatible with a type?
- What is the difference between **as** and a cast?
- What does **typeof** obtain?

Other Keywords

To conclude this book, the few remaining keywords defined by C# that have not been described elsewhere are briefly discussed.

The internal Access Modifier

In addition to the access modifiers **public**, **private**, and **protected**, which we have been using throughout this book, C# also defines **internal**. Mentioned briefly in Module 6, **internal** declares that a member is known throughout all files in an assembly, but unknown outside that assembly. An *assembly* is a file (or files) that contains all deployment and version information for a program. Thus, in simplified terms, a member marked as **internal** is known throughout a program, but not elsewhere.

sizeof

Occasionally you might find it useful to know the size, in bytes, of one of C#'s value types. To obtain this information, use the **sizeof** operator. It has this general form:

sizeof(*type*)

- The **is** operator determines if an object is compatible with a type.
- A cast throws an exception if it fails. The **as** operator returns **null** on failure.
- The **typeof** operator obtains a **System.Type** object that describes the specified type.

Here, type is the *type* whose size is being obtained. The **sizeof** operator can be used only in an unsafe context. Thus, it is intended primarily for special-case situations, especially when working with a blend of managed and unmanaged code.

lock

The **lock** keyword is used when working with *multiple threads*. In C#, a program can contain two or more *threads of execution*. When this is the case, pieces of the program are multitasked. Thus, pieces of the program execute independently, and conceptually speaking, simultaneously. This raises the prospect of a special type of problem: What if two threads try to use a resource that can be used by only one thread at a time? To solve this problem, you can create a *critical code section* that will be executed by one and only one thread at a time. This is accomplished by **lock**. Its general form is shown here:

```
lock(obj) {
  // critical section
}
```

Here, *obj* is an object that seeks to obtain the lock. If one thread has already entered the critical section, then a second thread will wait until the first thread executes. When the lock is granted, the critical section can be executed.

readonly

You can create a read-only field in a class by declaring it as **readonly**. A **readonly** field can be initialized, but not changed after that. Thus, **readonly** fields are a good way to create constants, such as array dimensions, that are used throughout a program. Both static and non-static **readonly** fields are allowed.

Here is an example that creates a **readonly** field:

```
// Demonstrate readonly.
using System;

class MyClass {
  public static readonly int SIZE = 10;   ← This essentially declares a constant.
}
```

```
class DemoReadOnly {
  public static void Main() {
    int[]nums = new int[MyClass.SIZE];

    for(int i=0; i<MyClass.SIZE; i++)
      nums[i] = i;

    foreach(int i in nums)
      Console.Write(i + " ");

    // MyClass.SIZE = 100; // Error!!! can't change
  }
}
```

Here, **MyClass.SIZE** is initialized to 10. After that, it can be used, but not changed. To prove this, try removing the comments from before the last line and then compiling the program. As you will see, an error will result.

stackalloc

You can allocate memory from the stack by using **stackalloc**. It can be used only when initializing local variables and has this general form:

type **p* = stackalloc *type*[*size*]

Here, *p* is a pointer that receives the address of the memory that is large e nough to hold *size* number of objects of *type*. **stackalloc** must be used in an unsafe context.

Normally, memory for objects is allocated from the *heap,* which is a region ssof free memory. Allocating memory from the stack is the exception. Variables allocated on the stack are not garbage collected. Rather, they exist only while the block in which they are declared is executing. The only advantage to using **stackalloc** is that you don't need to worry about the variables being moved about by the garbage collector.

The using Statement

In addition to the **using** *directive* discussed ealier, **using** has a second form which is called the **using** *statement*. It has this general form:

```
using (obj) {
  // use obj
}
```

Here, *obj* is an object that is being used inside the **using** block. When the block concludes, the **Dispose( )** method will be called. This form of **using** applies only to objects that implement the **System.IDisposable** interface.

const and volatile

The **const** modifier is used to declare variables that cannot be changed. These variables must be given initial values when they are declared. Thus, a **const** variable is essentially a constant. For example,

```
const int i = 10;
```

creates a **const** variable called **i** that has the value 10.

The **volatile** modifier tells the compiler that a variable's value may be changed in ways not explicitly specified by the program. For example, a variable that holds the current system time might be updated automatically by the operating system. In this situation, the contents of the variable are altered without any explicit assignment statement. The reason the external alteration of a variable may be important is that the C# compiler is permitted to optimize certain expressions automatically, on the assumption that the content of a variable is unchanged if it does not occur on the left side of an assignment statement. However, if factors outside the immediate code, such as a second thread of execution, change the value of the variable, this assumption is wrong. By using **volatile**, you are telling the compiler that it must obtain the value of this variable each time it is accessed.

What Next?

Congratulations! If you have read and worked through the preceding 12 modules, then you can call yourself a C# programmer. Of course, there are still many things to learn about C#, its libraries, and subsystems, but you now have a solid foundation upon which you can build your knowledge and expertise. Here are a few of the topics that you will want to learn more about:

● Using C# to create GUI-based Windows applications that use the various user interface elements, such as push buttons, menus, lists, and scroll bars

● Creating multithreaded applications

12

- Building components
- Using C#'s collections classes, which support such things as stacks, queues, and lists
- Using C#'s networking classes
- Versioning your applications

To continue your study of C#, I recommend my book *C#: The Complete Reference* (Osborne/McGraw-Hill). This book covers all of the topics just mentioned plus many more. In it you will find complete coverage of the C# language, its libraries, subsystems, and application.

 # Mastery Check

1. Show how to declare a delegate called **filter** that returns a **double** and takes one **int** argument.

2. How is multicasting accomplished using a delegate? What restrictions apply?

3. How are delegates and events related?

4. Can an event be multicast? Is an event sent to an instance or to a class?

5. What is the main benefit of namespaces?

6. Show the alias form of **using**.

7. What are the two types of conversion operators? Show their general forms.

8. Name the preprocessor directives that are used for conditional compilation.

9. Show the attribute syntax.

10. What is unsafe code?

11. How can you determine the type of an object at runtime?

12. On your own, continue to explore and experiment with C#.

Appendix A

Answers to Mastery Checks

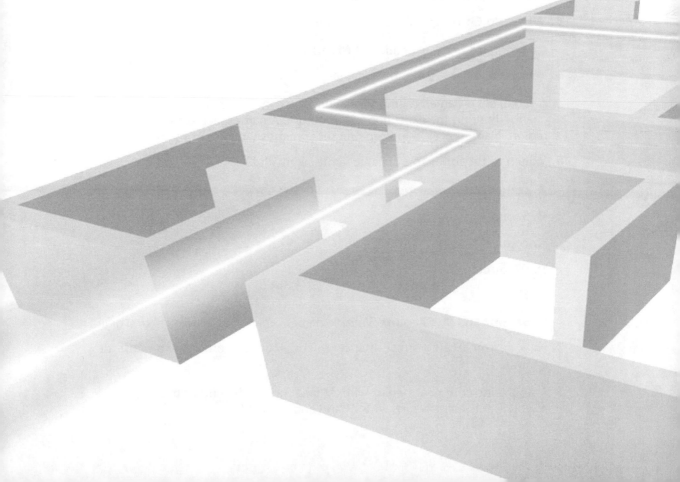

Module 1: C# Fundamentals

1. What is the MSIL and why is it important to C#?

MSIL stands for Microsoft Intermediate Language. It is an optimized, portable set of assembly language instructions that is compiled into executable code by a JIT compiler. MSIL helps C# achieve portability, security, and mixed-language compatibility.

2. What is the Common Language Runtime?

The Common Language Runtime (CLR) is the part of .NET that manages the execution of C# and other .NET-compatible programs.

3. What are the three main principles of object-oriented programming?

Encapsulation, polymorphism, and inheritance are the three main principles of object-oriented programming.

4. Where do C# programs begin execution?

C# programs begin execution at **Main( )**.

5. What is a variable? What is a namespace?

A variable is a named memory location. The contents of a variable can be changed during the execution of a program. A namespace is a declarative region. Namespaces help keep one set of names separate from another.

6. Which of the following variable names is invalid?

A. count

B. $count

C. count27

D. 67count

E. @if

B. $count and **D. 67count**. Variable names cannot begin with a $ or a digit.

7. How do you create a single-line comment? How do you create a multiline comment?

A single-line comment begins with // and ends at the end of the line. A multiline comment begins with /* and ends with */.

8. Show the general form of the **if** statement. Show the general form of the **for** loop.

The general form of the **if**:

if(*condition*) *statement*;

The general form of the **for**:

for(*initialization*; *condition*; *iteration*) *statement*;

9. How do you create a block of code?

A block of code is started with a **{** and ended with a **}**.

10. Is it necessary to start each C# program with the following statement?

```
using System;
```

No, **using System** is not necessary, but leaving it out means that you must qualify members of the **System** namespace by putting **System** in front of them.

Module 2: Introducing Data Types and Operators

1. Why does C# strictly specify the range and behavior of its simple types?

C# strictly specifies the range and behavior of its simple types to ensure portability across platforms.

2. What is C#'s character type, and how does it differ from the character type used by many other programming languages?

C#'s character type is **char**. C# characters are Unicode rather than ASCII, which is used by many other computer languages.

3. A **bool** value can have any value you like because any nonzero value is true. True or false?

False. A **bool** value must be either **true** or **false**.

4. Given this output:

```
One
Two
Three
```

A

Using a single string and escape sequence, show the **WriteLine( )** statement that produced it.

```
Console.WriteLine("One\nTwo\nThree");
```

5. What is wrong with this fragment?

```
for(i = 0; i < 10; i++) {
  int sum;

  sum = sum + i;
}
Console.WriteLine("Sum is: " + sum);
```

There are three fundamental flaws in the fragment. First, **sum** is created each time the block created by the **for** loop is entered and then destroyed on exit. Thus, it will not hold its value between iterations. Attempting to use **sum** to hold a running sum of the iterations is pointless. Second, **sum** will not be known outside of the block in which it is declared. Thus, the reference to it in the **WriteLine( )** statement is invalid. Third, **sum** has not been given an initial value.

6. Explain the difference between the prefix and postfix forms of the increment operator.

When the increment operator precedes its operand, C# will perform the corresponding operation prior to obtaining the operand's value for use by the rest of the expression. If the operator follows its operand, then C# will obtain the operand's value before incrementing.

7. Show how a short-circuit AND can be used to prevent a divide-by-zero error.

```
if((b != 0) && (val / b) ...
```

8. In an expression, what type are **byte** and **short** promoted to?

In an expression, **byte** and **short** are promoted to **int**.

9. Which of the following types cannot be mixed in an expression with a **decimal** value?

A. float

B. int

C. uint

D. byte

A. float

10. In general, when is a cast needed?

A cast is needed when converting between incompatible types or when a narrowing conversion is occurring.

11. Write a program that finds all of the prime numbers between 1 and 100.

Here is one way to find the primes between 1 and 100. There are, of course, other solutions.

```
// Find prime numbers between 1 and 100.

using System;

class Prime {
  static void Main() {
    int i, j;
    bool isprime;

    for(i=1; i < 100; i++) {
      isprime - true;

      // see if the number is evenly divisible
      for(j=2; j <= i/2; j++)
        // if it is, then it's not prime
        if((i%j) == 0) isprime = false;

      if(isprime)
        Console.WriteLine(i + " is prime.");
    }
  }
}
```

Module 3: Program Control Statements

1. Write a program that reads characters from the keyboard until a period is received. Have the program count the number of spaces. Report the total at the end of the program.

```
// Count spaces.

using System;

class Spaces {
```

```csharp
   public static void Main() {
     char ch;
     int spaces = 0;

     Console.WriteLine("Enter a period to stop.");

     do {
       ch = (char) Console.Read();
       if(ch == ' ') spaces++;
     } while(ch != '.');

     Console.WriteLine("Spaces: " + spaces);
   }
 }
```

2. In the **switch,** can the code sequence from one **case** run into the next?

No. The "no fall through" rule states that the code from one **case** label must not continue on into the next. Case statements can be "stacked," however.

3. Show the general form of the **if-else-if** ladder.

```
if(condition)
   statement;
else if(condition)
   statement;
else if(condition)
   statement;

   .

   .

   .

else
   statement;
```

4. Given

```csharp
if(x < 10)
  if(y > 100) {
    if(!done) x = z;
    else y = z;
  }
else Console.WriteLine("error"); // what if?
```

to what **if** does the last **else** associate?

The last **else** associates with **if(y > 100)**, which is the nearest **if** at the same level as the **else**.

5. Show the **for** statement for a loop that counts from 1000 to 0 by −2.

```
for(int i = 1000; i >= 0; i -= 2) // ...
```

6. Is the following fragment valid?

```
for(int i = 0; i < num; i++)
  sum += i;

count = i;
```

No, **i** is not known outside of the **for** loop in which it is declared.

7. Explain what **break** does.

A **break** causes termination of its immediately enclosing loop or **switch** statement.

8. In the following fragment, after the **break** statement executes, what is displayed?

```
for(i = 0; i < 10; i++) {
  while(running) {
    if(x<y) break;
    // ...
  }
  Console.WriteLine("after while");
}
Console.WriteLine("After for");
```

After **break** executes, "after while" is displayed.

9. What does the following fragment print?

```
for(int i = 0; i<10; i++) {
  Console.Write(i + " ");
  if((i%2) == 0) continue;
  Console.WriteLine();
}
```

```
0 1
2 3
4 5
6 7
8 9
```

A

10. The iteration expression in a **for** loop need not always alter the loop control variable by a fixed amount. Instead, the loop control variable can change in any arbitrary way. Using this concept, write a program that uses a **for** loop to generate and display the progression 1, 2, 4, 8, 16, 32, and so on.

```
/* Use a for loop to generate the progression

   1 2 4 8 16, ...
*/

using System;

class Progress {
  public static void Main() {

    for(int i = 1; i < 100; i += i)
      Console.Write(i + " ");
  }
}
```

11. The ASCII lowercase letters are separated from the uppercase letters by 32. Thus, to convert a lowercase letter to uppercase, subtract 32 from it. Use this information to write a program that reads characters from the keyboard. Have it convert all lowercase letters to uppercase, and all uppercase letters to lowercase, displaying the result. Make no changes to any other character. Have the program stop when the user presses period. At the end, have the program display the number of case changes that have taken place.

```
// Change case.

using System;

class CaseChg {
  public static void Main() {
    char ch;
    int changes = 0;

    Console.WriteLine("Enter period to stop.");

    do {
      ch = (char) Console.Read();
      if(ch >= 'a' & ch <= 'z') {
        ch -= (char) 32;
        changes++;
        Console.WriteLine(ch);
      }
```

```
    else if(ch >= 'A' & ch <= 'Z') {
      ch += (char) 32;
      changes++;
      Console.WriteLine(ch);
    }
  } while(ch != '.');
  Console.WriteLine("Case changes: " + changes);
  }
}
```

Module 4: Introducing Classes, Objects, and Methods

1. What is the difference between a class and an object?

A class is a logical abstraction that describes the form and behavior of an object. An object is a physical instance of the class.

2. How is a class defined?

A class is defined by using the keyword **class**. Inside the **class** statement, you specify the code and data that comprise the class.

3. What does each object have its own copy of?

Each object of a class has its own copy of the class' instance variables.

4. Using two separate statements, show how to declare an object called **counter** of a class called **MyCounter**.

```
MyCounter counter;
counter = new MyCounter();
```

5. Show how a method called **myMeth( )** is declared if it has a return type of **double** and has two **int** parameters called **a** and **b**.

```
double myMeth(int a, int b) { // ...
```

6. How must a method return if it returns a value?

A method that returns a value must return via the **return** statement, passing back the return value in the process.

7. What name does a constructor have?

A constructor has the same name as its class.

A

8. What does **new** do?

The **new** operator allocates memory for an object and initializes it using the object's constructor.

9. What is garbage collection and how does it work? What is a destructor?

Garbage collection is the mechanism that recycles unused objects so that their memory can be reused. A destructor is a method that is called just prior to an object being recycled.

10. What is **this**?

The **this** keyword is a reference to the object on which a method is invoked. It is automatically passed to a method.

Module 5: More Data Types and Operators

1. Show how to declare a one-dimensional array of 12 **doubles**.

```
double[] x = new double[12];
```

2. Show how to declare a 4 by 5, two-dimensional array of **ints**.

```
int[,] nums = new int[4, 5];
```

3. Show how to declare a jagged two-dimensional **int** array in which the first dimension is 5.

```
int [][] nums = new int[5][];
```

4. Show how to initialize a one-dimensional **int** array with the values 1 through 5.

```
int[] x = { 1, 2, 3, 4, 5 };
```

5. Explain **foreach**. Show its general form.

The **foreach** loop cycles through a collection, returning each element in turn. Its general form is shown here:

foreach(*type var-name* in *collection*) *statement*;

6. Write a program that uses an array to find the average of ten **double** values. Use any ten values you like.

```
// Average 10 double values.

using System;

class Avg {
  public static void Main() {
    double[] nums = { 1.1, 2.2, 3.3, 4.4, 5.5,
                      6.6, 7.7, 8.8, 9.9, 10.1 };
    double sum = 0;

    for(int i=0; i < nums.Length; i++)
      sum += nums[i];

    Console.WriteLine("Average: " + sum / nums.Length);
  }
}
```

7. Change the sort in Project 5-1 so that it sorts an array of strings. Demonstrate that it works.

```
// Demonstrate the Bubble sort with strings.

using System;

class StrBubble {
  public static void Main() {
    string[] strs = {
                      "this", "is", "a", "test",
                      "of", "a", "string", "sort"
                    };
    int a, b;
    string t;
    int size;

    size = strs.Length; // number of elements to sort

    // display original array
    Console.Write("Original array is:");
    for(int i=0; i < size; i++)
      Console.Write(" " + strs[i]);
    Console.WriteLine();

    // This is the bubble sort for strings.
    for(a=1; a < size; a++)
```

```
      for(b=size-1; b >= a; b--) {
        if(strs[b-1].CompareTo(strs[b]) > 0) { // if out of order
          // exchange elements
          t = strs[b-1];
          strs[b-1] = strs[b];
          strs[b] = t;
        }
      }

    // display sorted array
    Console.Write("Sorted array is:");
    for(int i=0; i < size; i++)
      Console.Write(" " + strs[i]);
    Console.WriteLine();
  }
}
```

8. What is the difference between the **string** methods **IndexOf( )** and **LastIndexOf( )**?

   The **IndexOf( )** method finds the first occurrence of the specified substring. **LastIndexOf( )** finds the last occurrence.

9. Expanding on the **Encode** cipher class, modify it so that it uses an 8-character string as the key.

```
// An improved XOR cipher.

using System;

class Encode {
  public static void Main() {
    string msg = "This is a test";
    string encmsg = "";
    string decmsg = "";
    string key = "abcdefgi";
    int j;

    Console.Write("Original message: ");
    Console.WriteLine(msg);

    // encode the message
    j = 0;
    for(int i=0; i < msg.Length; i++) {
      encmsg = encmsg + (char) (msg[i] ^ key[j]);
      j++;
      if(j==8) j = 0;
    }
```

```
Console.Write("Encoded message: ");
Console.WriteLine(encmsg);

// decode the message
j = 0;
for(int i=0; i < msg.Length; i++) {
  decmsg = decmsg + (char) (encmsg[i] ^ key[j]);
  j++;
  if(j==8) j = 0;
}

Console.Write("Decoded message: ");
Console.WriteLine(decmsg);

    }
}
```

10. Can the bitwise operators be applied to the **double** type?

No.

11. Show how this sequence

```
if(x < 0) y = 10;
else y = 20;
```

can be rewritten using the ? operator.

```
y = x < 0 ? 10 : 20;
```

12. In the following fragment, is the **&** a bitwise or logical operator? Why?

```
bool a, b;
// ...
if(a & b) ...
```

It is a logical operator because the operands are of type **bool**.

Module 6: A Closer Look at Methods and Classes

1. Given this fragment:

```
class X {
  int count;
```

is the following fragment correct?

```
class Y {
  public static void Main() {
    X ob = new X();

    ob.count = 10;
```

No, a private member cannot be accessed outside of its class. As explained, when no access specifier is present, a class member defaults to private access.

2. An access specifier must _____ a member's declaration.

precede

3. The complement of a queue is a stack. It uses first-in, last-out accessing and is often likened to a stack of plates. The first plate put on the table is the last plate used. Create a stack class called **Stack** that can hold characters. Call the methods that access the stack **push( )** and **pop( )**. Allow the user to specify the size of the stack when it is created. Keep all other members of the **Stack** class private. Hint: You can use the **Queue** class as a model; just change the way that the data is accessed.

```
// A stack class for characters.

using System;

class Stack {
  char[] stck; // this array holds the stack
  int tos;     // top of stack

  // Construct an empty Stack given its size.
  public Stack(int size) {
    stck = new char[size]; // allocate memory for stack
    tos = 0;
  }

  // Construct a Stack from a Stack.
  public Stack(Stack ob) {
    tos = ob.tos;
    stck = new char[ob.stck.Length];

    // copy elements
    for(int i=0; i < tos; i++)
      stck[i] = ob.stck[i];
  }
```

```
    // Construct a stack with initial values.
    public Stack(char[] a) {
      stck = new char[a.Length];

      for(int i = 0; i < a.Length; i++) {
        push(a[i]);
      }
    }


    // Push characters onto the stack.
    public void push(char ch) {
      if(tos==stck.Length) {
        Console.WriteLine(" -- Stack is full.");
        return;
      }

      stck[tos] = ch;
      tos++;
    }

    // Pop a character from the stack.
    public char pop() {
      if(tos==0) {
        Console.WriteLine(" -- Stack is empty.");
        return (char) 0;
      }

      tos--;
      return stck[tos];
    }
}

// Demonstrate the Stack class.
class SDemo {
  public static void Main() {
    // construct 10-element empty stack
    Stack stk1 = new Stack(10);

    char[] name = {'T', 'o', 'm'};

    // construct stack from array
    Stack stk2 = new Stack(name);
```

```
      char ch;
      int i;

      // put some characters into stk1
      for(i=0; i < 10; i++)
        stk1.push((char) ('A' + i));

      // construct stack from another stack
      Stack stk3 = new Stack(stk1);

      //show the stacks.
      Console.Write("Contents of stk1: ");
      for(i=0; i < 10; i++) {
        ch = stk1.pop();
        Console.Write(ch);
      }

      Console.WriteLine("\n");

      Console.Write("Contents of stk2: ");
      for(i=0; i < 3; i++) {
        ch = stk2.pop();
        Console.Write(ch);
      }

      Console.WriteLine("\n");

      Console.Write("Contents of stk3: ");
      for(i=0; i < 10; i++) {
        ch = stk3.pop();
        Console.Write(ch);
      }
    }
  }
}
```

Here is the output from the program:

```
Contents of stk1: JIHGFEDCBA

Contents of stk2: moT

Contents of stk3: JIHGFEDCBA
```

4. Given this class:

```
class Test {
  int a;
  Test(int i) { a = i; }
}
```

write a method called **swap( )** that exchanges the contents of the objects referred to by two **Test** object references.

```
void swap(Test ob1, Test ob2) {
  int t;

  t = ob1.a;
  ob1.a = ob2.a;
  ob2.a = t;
}
```

5. Is the following fragment correct?

```
class X {
  int meth(int a, int b) { ... }
  string meth(int a, int b) { ... }
```

No. Overloaded methods can have different return types, but they do not play a role in overload resolution. Overloaded methods *must* have different parameter lists.

6. Write a recursive method that displays the contents of a string backwards.

```
// Display a string backwards using recursion.

using System;

class Backwards {
  string str;

  public Backwards(string s) {
    str = s;
  }

  public void backward(int idx) {
```

A

```
      if(idx != str.Length-1) backward(idx+1);

      Console.Write(str[idx]);
   }
}

class BWDemo {
  public static void Main() {
    Backwards s = new Backwards("This is a test");

    s.backward(0);
  }
}
```

7. If all objects of a class need to share the same variable, how must you declare that variable?

   Shared variables are declared as **static**.

8. What do **ref** and **out** do? How do they differ?

   The **ref** modifier causes a parameter to be passed by reference. This allows a method to modify the contents of the calling argument. A **ref** parameter can receive information passed into the method. The **out** modifier is the same as **ref** except that it cannot be used to pass a value into a method.

9. Show the four forms of **Main( )**.

```
public static void Main()
public static void Main(string[] args)
public static int Main()
public static int Main(string[] args)
```

10. Given this fragment

```
void meth(int i, int j, params int [] args) { // ...
```

    which of the following calls are legal?

    A. meth(10, 12, 19);

    B. meth(10, 12, 19, 100);

    C. meth(10, 12, 19, 100, 200);

    D. meth(10, 12);

    They are all legal.

Module 7: Operator Overloading, Indexers, and Properties

1. Show the general form used for overloading a unary operator. Of what type must the parameter to the operator method be?

public static *ret-type* operator *op(param-type operand)*
{
  // operations
}

The operand must be of the same type as the class for which the operator is being overloaded.

2. To allow operations involving a class type and a built-in type, what must you do?

To allow the full mixing of a class type with a built-in type, you must overload an operator two ways. One way has the class type as the first operand and the built-in type as the second operand. The second way has the built-in type as the first operand and the class type as the second operand.

3. Can the ? be overloaded? Can you change the precedence of an operator?

No, the **?** cannot be overloaded. No, you cannot change the precedence of an operator.

4. What is an indexer? Show its general form.

An indexer provides array-like accessing of an object.

```
element-type this[int index] {
   // The get accessor.
   get {
      // return the value specified by index
   }

   // The set accessor.
   set {
      // set the value specified by index
   }
}
```

A

5. In an indexer, what functions must its **get** and **set** accessors perform?

The **get** and **set** accessors get the value specified by an index or set the value specified by an index, respectively.

6. What is a property? Show its general form.

A property combines a field with the methods that access it.

```
type name {
   get {
      // get accessor code
   }

   set {
      // set accessor code
   }
}
```

7. Does a property define a storage location? If not, where does a property store its value?

No, a property does not define a storage location. It manages access to a separately defined field. Thus, you must declare a field that will be managed by the property.

8. Can a property be passed as a **ref** or **out** argument?

No, a property cannot be passed as a **ref** or **out** parameter.

9. For the **Set** class developed in Project 7-1, define < and > such that they determine if one set is a subset or a superset of another set. Have < return **true** if the left set is a subset of the set on the right, and **false** otherwise. Have < return **true** if the left set is a superset of the set on the right, and **false** otherwise.

```
// Determine if one set is a subset of another.
public static bool operator <(Set ob1, Set ob2) {
  if(ob1.len > ob2.len) return false; // ob1 has more elements

  for(int i=0; i < ob1.len; i++)
    if(ob2.find(ob1[i]) == -1) return false;
  return true; //
}

// Determine if one set is a superset of another.
```

```
    public static bool operator >(Set ob1, Set ob2) {
      if(ob1.len < ob2.len) return false; // ob1 has fewer elements

      for(int i=0; i < ob2.len; i++)
        if(ob1.find(ob2[i]) == -1) return false;
      return true; //
    }
```

10. For the **Set** class, define the **&** so that it yields the intersection of two sets.

```
    // Set intersection.
    public static Set operator &(Set ob1, Set ob2) {
      Set newset = new Set();

      // add elements common to both sets
      for(int i=0; i < ob1.len; i++)
        if(ob2.find(ob1[i]) != -1) // add if element in both sets
          newset = newset + ob1[i];

      return newset; // return updated set
    }
```

Module 8: Inheritance

1. Does a base class have access to the members of a derived class? Does a derived class have access to the members of a base class?

   No, a base class has no knowledge of its derived classes. Yes, a derived class has access to all nonprivate members of its base class.

2. Create a derived class of **TwoDShape** called **Circle**. Include an **area( )** method that computes the area of the circle and a constructor that uses **base** to initialize the **TwoDShape** portion.

```
    // A subclass of TwoDShape for circles.
    class Circle : TwoDShape {
      // Construct Circle
      public Circle(double x) : base(x, "circle") { }

      // Construct an object from an object.
      public Circle(Circle ob) : base(ob) { }

      public override double area() {
```

```
        return (width / 2) * (width / 2) * 3.1416;
    }
}
```

3. How do you prevent a derived class from having access to a member of a base class?

To prevent a derived class from having access to a base class member, declare that member as **private**.

4. Describe the purpose of **base**.

The **base** keyword has two forms. The first is used to call a base class constructor. The general form of this usage is

   base(*param-list*);

The second form of **base** is used to access a base class member. It has this general form:

   base.*member*

5. Given the following hierarchy:

```
class Alpha { ...

class Beta : Alpha { ...

Class Gamma : Beta { ...
```

in what order are the constructors for these classes called when a **Gamma** object is instantiated?

Constructors are always called in order of derivation. Thus, when a **Gamma** object is created, the order is **Alpha**, **Beta**, **Gamma**.

6. A base class reference can refer to a derived class object. Explain why this is important as it relates to method overriding.

When a virtual method is called through a base class reference, it is the type of the object being referred to that determines which version of the method is called.

7. What is an abstract class?

An abstract class contains at least one abstract method.

8. How do you prevent a class from being inherited?

To prevent a class from being inherited, declare it as **sealed**.

9. Explain how inheritance, method overriding, and abstract classes are used to support polymorphism.

Inheritance, virtual methods, and abstract classes support polymorphism by enabling you to create a generalized class structure that can be implemented by a variety of classes. Thus, the abstract class defines a consistent interface that is shared by all implemented classes. This embodies the concept of "one interface, multiple methods."

10. What class is a base class of every other class?

object is a base class of every other class.

11. Explain boxing.

Boxing is the process of storing a value type in an object. Boxing occurs automatically when you assign a value to an **object** reference.

12. How can **protected** members be accessed?

A **protected** member is available for use by derived classes, but is otherwise private to its class.

Module 9: Interfaces, Structures, and Enumerations

1. "One interface, multiple methods" is a key tenet of C#. What feature best exemplifies it?

The **interface** best exemplifies the one interface, multiple methods principle of OOP.

2. How many classes can implement an interface? How many interfaces can a class implement?

An interface can be implemented by an unlimited number of classes. A class can implement as many interfaces as it chooses.

3. Can interfaces be inherited?

Yes, interfaces can be inherited.

4. Must a class implement all of the members of an interface?

Yes, a class must implement all members defined by an interface.

5. Can an interface declare a constructor?

No, an interface cannot define a constructor.

6. Create an interface for the **Vehicle** class from Module 7. Call the interface **IVehicle**.

```
interface IVehicle {
  int range();

  double fuelneeded(int miles);

  int passengers {
    get;
    set;
  }

  int fuelcap {
    get;
    set;
  }

  int mpg {
    get;
    set;
  }
}
```

7. Create an interface for safe arrays. Do this by adapting the final fail-soft array example from Module 7.

```
// Create a fail-soft interface.
using System;

// This is the fail-soft interface.
public interface IFailSoft {
  // This specifies the length property interface.
```

```csharp
  int Length {
    get;
   }

  // This specifies the indexer interface.
  int this[int index] {
    get;
    set;
  }
}

// Now, implement IFailSoft.
class FailSoftArray : IFailSoft {
  int[] a; // reference to array
  int len; // length of array

  public bool errflag; // indicates outcome of last operation

  // Construct array given its size.
  public FailSoftArray(int size) {
    a = new int[size];
    len = size;
  }

  // Read-only Length property.
  public int Length {
    get {
      return len;
    }
  }

  // This is the indexer for FailSoftArray.
  public int this[int index] {
    // This is the get accessor.
    get {
      if(ok(index)) {
        errflag = false;
        return a[index];
      } else {
        errflag = true;
        return 0;
      }
    }
```

A

```
      // This is the set accessor
      set {
        if(ok(index)) {
          a[index] = value;
          errflag = false;
        }
        else errflag = true;
      }
    }

    // Return true if index is within bounds.
    private bool ok(int index) {
     if(index >= 0 & index < Length) return true;
     return false;
    }
  }

// Demonstrate the improved fail-soft array.
class ImprovedFSDemo {
  public static void Main() {
    FailSoftArray fs = new FailSoftArray(5);
    int x;

    for(int i=0; i < (fs.Length); i++)
      fs[i] = i*10;

    for(int i=0; i < (fs.Length); i++) {
      x = fs[i];
      if(x != -1) Console.Write(x + " ");
    }
    Console.WriteLine();
  }
}
```

8. How does a **struct** differ from a **class**?

A **struct** defines a value type. A **class** defines a reference type.

9. Show how to create an enumeration for the planets. Call the enumeration **Planets**.

```
enum Planets {Mercury, Venus, Earth, Mars, Jupiter, Saturn,
               Uranus, Neptune, Pluto};
```

Module 10: Exception Handling

1. What class is at the top of the exception hierarchy?

System.Exception is at the top of the exception hierarchy.

2. Briefly explain how to use **try** and **catch**.

The **try** and **catch** statements work together. Program statements that you want to monitor for exceptions are contained within a **try** block. An exception is caught using **catch**.

3. What is wrong with this fragment?

```
// ...
vals[18] = 10;
catch (IndexOutOfRangeException exc) {
  // handle error
}
```

There is no **try** block preceding the **catch** statement.

4. What happens if an exception is not caught?

If an exception is not caught, abnormal program termination results.

5. What is wrong with this fragment?

```
class A : Exception { ...

class B : A { ...

// ...

try {
  // ...
}
catch (A exc) { ... }
catch (B exc) { ... }
```

In the fragment, a base class **catch** precedes a derived class **catch**. Since the base class **catch** will catch all derived classes, too, unreachable code is created.

A

6. Can an exception caught by an inner **catch** rethrow that exception to an outer **catch**?

Yes, an exception can be rethrown.

7. The **finally** block is the last bit of code executed before your program ends. True or false? Explain your answer.

False. The **finally** block is the code executed when a **try** block ends.

8. In Exercise 3 of the Mastery Check in Module 6 you created a **Stack** class. Add custom exceptions to your class that report stack full and stack empty conditions.

Here is one way to add exception handling to the **Stack** class.

```
// An exception for stack-full errors.
using System;

class StackFullException : ApplicationException {
  // create standard constructors
  public StackFullException() : base() { }
  public StackFullException(string str) : base(str) { }
}

// An exception for stack-empty errors.
class StackEmptyException : ApplicationException {
  // create standard constructors
  public StackEmptyException() : base() { }
  public StackEmptyException(string str) : base(str) { }
}

// A stack class for characters.
class Stack {
  char[] stck; // this array holds the stack
  int tos;  // top of stack

  // Construct an empty Stack given its size.
  public Stack(int size) {
    stck = new char[size]; // allocate memory for stack
    tos = 0;
  }

  // Construct a Stack from a Stack.
  public Stack(Stack ob) {
    tos = ob.tos;
```

```
    stck = new char[ob.stck.Length];

    // copy elements
    for(int i=0; i < tos; i++)
      stck[i] = ob.stck[i];
  }

  // Construct a stack with initial values.
  public Stack(char[] a) {
    stck = new char[a.Length];

    for(int i = 0; i < a.Length; i++) {
      try {
        push(a[i]);
      }
      catch(StackFullException exc) {
        Console.WriteLine(exc);
      }
    }
  }

  // Push characters onto the stack.
  public void push(char ch) {
    if(tos==stck.Length)
      throw new StackFullException();

    stck[tos] = ch;
    tos++;
  }

  // Pop a character from the stack.
  public char pop() {
    if(tos==0)
      throw new StackEmptyException();

    tos--;
    return stck[tos];
  }
}
```

9. Explain the purpose of **checked** and **unchecked**.

checked and **unchecked** determine if arithmetic overflow causes
an exception or not. To avoid an exception, mark the related code as
unchecked. To raise an exception on overflow, mark the related code
as **checked**.

A

10. How can all exceptions be caught?

All exceptions can be caught using one of these two forms of **catch**.

catch { }

catch(Exception exc) { }

Module 11: Using I/O

1. Why does C# define both byte and character streams?

Byte streams are useful for file I/O, especially binary file I/O, and they support random access files. The character streams are optimized for Unicode.

2. What class is at the top of the stream hierarchy?

The class at the top of the stream hierarchy is **Stream**.

3. Show how to open a file for reading bytes.

Here is one way to open a file for byte input:

```
FileStream fin = new FileStream("myfile", FileMode.Open);
```

4. Show how to open a file for reading characters.

Here is one way to open a file for reading characters:

```
StreamReader frdr_in = new StreamReader(new FileStream("myfile",
                       FileMode.Open));
```

5. What does Seek( ) do?

Seek( ) sets the current file position.

6. What classes support binary I/O for the built-in types?

Binary I/O for the C# built-in types is supported by **BinaryReader** and **BinaryWriter**.

7. What methods are used to redirect the standard streams under program control?

I/O is redirected by calling **SetIn( )**, **SetOut( )**, and **SetError( )**.

8. How do you convert a numeric string such as "123.23" into its binary equivalent?

A numeric string can be converted into its internal representation by using the **Parse( )** method defined by the .NET structure aliases.

9. Write a program that copies a text file. In the process, have it convert all spaces into hyphens. Use the byte-stream file classes.

```
/* Copy a text file, substituting hyphens for spaces.

   This version uses byte streams.

   To use this program, specify the name
   of the source file and the destination file.
   For example:

   Hyphen source target
*/

using System;
using System.IO;

class Hyphen {
  public static void Main(string[] args) {
    int i;
    FileStream fin;
    FileStream fout;

    try {
      // open input file
      try {
        fin = new FileStream(args[0], FileMode.Open);
      } catch(FileNotFoundException exc) {
        Console.WriteLine(exc.Message);
        return;
      }

      // open output file
      try {
        fout = new FileStream(args[1], FileMode.Create);
      } catch(FileNotFoundException exc) {
        Console.WriteLine(exc.Message);
        return;
      }
```

A

```
      } catch(IndexOutOfRangeException exc) {
        Console.WriteLine(exc.Message + "\nUsage: Hyphen From To");
        return;
      }

      // Copy File
      try {
        do {
          i = fin.ReadByte();
          if((char)i == ' ') i = '-';
          if(i != -1) fout.WriteByte((byte) i);
        } while(i != -1);
      } catch(IOException exc) {
        Console.WriteLine(exc.Message);
      }

      fin.Close();
      fout.Close();
    }
}
```

10. Rewrite the program in Exercise 9 so that it uses the character stream classes.

```
/* Copy a text file, substituting hyphens for spaces.

   This version uses character streams.

   To use this program, specify the name
   of the source file and the destination file.
   For example:

   Hyphen source target
*/

using System;
using System.IO;

class Hyphen {
  public static void Main(string[] args) {
    int i;
    StreamReader fin;
    StreamWriter fout;

    try {
      // open input file
```

```
   try {
     fin = new StreamReader(args[0]);
   } catch(FileNotFoundException exc) {
     Console.WriteLine(exc.Message);
     return;
   }

   // open output file
   try {
     fout = new StreamWriter(args[1]);
   } catch(FileNotFoundException exc) {
     Console.WriteLine(exc.Message);
     return;
   }
 } catch(IndexOutOfRangeException exc) {
   Console.WriteLine(exc.Message + "\nUsage: Hyphen From To");
   return;
 }

 // Copy File
 try {
   do {
     i = fin.Read();
     if((char)i == ' ') i = '-';
     if(i != -1) fout.Write((char) i);
   } while(i != -1);
 } catch(IOException exc) {
   Console.WriteLine(exc.Message);
 }

 fin.Close();
 fout.Close();
}
}
```

Module 12: Delegates, Events, Namespaces, and Advanced Topics

1. Show how to declare a delegate called **filter** that returns a **double** and takes one **int** argument.

```
delegate double filter(int i);
```

2. How is multicasting accomplished using a delegate? What restrictions apply?

A multicast is created by adding methods to a delegate chain using the **+=** operator. The return type of the delegate (and thus, the methods added to it) must be **void**.

3. How are delegates and events related?

An event requires the use of a delegate.

4. Can an event be multicast? Is an event sent to an instance or to a class?

Yes, events can be multicast. An event is always sent to a specific instance.

5. What is the main benefit of namespaces?

A namespace defines a declarative region that prevents name collisions.

6. Show the alias form of **using**.

using *alias* = *name*;

7. What are the two types of conversion operators? Show their general forms.

There are implicit and explicit conversion operators. Their general forms are shown here:

public static operator implicit *target-type*(*source-type v*) { return *value*; }

public static operator explicit *target-type*(*source-type v*) { return *value*; }

8. Name the preprocessor directives that are used for conditional compilation.

The conditional compilation directives are **#if**, **#elif**, **#else**, and **#endif**.

9. Show the attribute syntax.

Attributes are enclosed between square brackets, as shown here:

[*attribute*]

10. What is unsafe code?

Unsafe code is code that executes outside the managed context defined by the CLR.

11. How can you determine the type of an object at runtime?

To determine the type of an object at runtime, use the **is**, **as**, or **typeof** operators.

Index

&
    bitwise AND, 224-226
    logical AND, 75, 76, 80-81
    pointer operator, 567
&& (short-circuit AND), 75, 77-78, 80-81
*
    multiplication operator, 72-73
    pointer operator, 567, 568-569
@ to designate verbatim string literals, 65-66
@-qualified keywords, 44
|
    bitwise OR, 224, 225, 226-227
    logical OR, 75, 76, 80-81
|| (short-circuit OR), 75, 77-78, 80-81
[ ], 190-191, 199, 202, 203, 219, 319, 562
^
    bitwise exclusive OR, 224, 225,
      227-229
    logical exclusive OR, 75, 76
{ }, 23, 24, 38, 39, 58, 158, 159, 160
=, 28, 82
= = (relational operator), 34, 75, 76, 316,
    317, 397
    and strings, 219
!, 75, 76

!=, 34, 75, 76, 316, 317
    and strings, 219
/, 72-73
/* */, 22
//, 23
<
    I/O redirection operator, 493-494
    relational operator, 34, 75, 76, 316
<<, 225, 230-232
<=, 34, 75, 76, 316
-, 72-73
->, 568
- -, 37, 74-75, 305, 308-309
%, 72, 73
( ), 24, 85, 92, 179
. (dot operator), 149, 159, 289-290
+
    addition operator, 72-73
    used with WriteLine( ), 28
++, 37, 74-75, 305, 308-309
#, 59, 555
?, 236-238
>
    I/O redirection operator, 493-494
    relational operator, 34, 75, 76, 316

>>, 225, 230-232
>=, 34, 75, 76, 316
; (semicolon), 24, 39
~

  bitwise NOT, 224, 225, 229
  used by destructor, 181

A

Abs( ), 273
abstract type modifier, 382, 391, 392, 395, 396
Access control, 242-250
Access specifiers, 23, 147, 242, 573
Accessors
  indexer, 319-320, 323
  property, 328-329, 330
AND operator
  bitwise (&), 224-226
  logical (&), 75, 76, 80-81
  short-circuit (&&), 75, 77-78, 80-81
ApplicationException, 438, 439, 457
ArgumentException, 482
ArgumentNullException, 482
Arguments, 24, 156, 163
  command-line, 283-286
  passing, 252-254
  variable number of, using, 261-264
Arithmetic operators, 29, 72-75
Array(s), 190-213
  boundaries, 195
  implemented in C# as objects, 190, 191
  initializing, 193-194, 200-202
  jagged, 202-204
  Length property of, 206-208
  multidimensional, 198-202
  one-dimensional, 190-198
  parameter params, 261-264
  reference variables, assigning, 205-206
  sorting, 196-198
  of strings, 221
ArrayTypeMismatchException, 457
as operator, 573
ASCII character set, 55, 225-226
Assembly, 242, 574
Assignment operator(s)
  =, 28, 82
  arithmetic and logical (op=), 82-83

bitwise, 232
  and operator overloading, 317, 318
Assignments
  reference variables and, 154-155
  type conversion in, 83-85

B

Backslash character constants, 63-64
base keyword
  to access a hidden base class member,
    357, 364-366
  to call a base class constructor, 357-362
BinaryReader class, 477, 498, 499
  input methods, table of, 499-500
BinaryWriter class, 477, 498
  output methods, table of, 498
Bitwise operators, 224-235
Blocks, code, 38-39, 68
bool value type, 48, 56-57
  and relational operators, 76
break statement, 100, 107, 109, 131-133
Bubble sort, 196-198
BufferedStream class, 475
byte value type, 48, 49, 51-52, 62
Bytecode, 5, 8

C

C format specifier, 59
C, history of, 2-3
C++
  history of, 3-4
  and the .NET Framework, 10
  when to use instead of C#, 566
C#
  as a component-oriented language, 6
  history of, 2, 5-6
  and Java, 2, 6
  keywords, 42-43, 44
  and the .NET Framework, 7-8, 10
  program compilation, 8-9
  as a strongly typed language, 48, 376
Call-by-reference
  using ref to create a, 255-257
  vs. call-by-value, 252-254

CanRead property, 475
CanSeek property, 475
CanWrite property, 475
Case sensitivity and C#, 25
case statement, 107, 109-112
Casts, 85-87, 90-91
    as operator, using the, 573
    and explicit conversion operators, 549,
      13:34-554
catch statement(s), 439-443
    for catching all exceptions, 448
    and catching derived class exceptions,
      460-462
    multiple, using, 446-447
    parameter, with a, 455-457
    and rethrown exceptions, 452-453
char value type, 48, 49, 55
Character(s), 54-55
    constants (literals), 55, 62
    escape sequences, 63-64
    encoding, 493
    from keyboard, inputting, 100-101
checked statement, 466-469
Class(es), 146-152
    abstract, 391-395, 404
    base, definition of, 346
    constructor. *See* Constructor(s)
    definition of, 8, 12
    derived, definition of, 346
    general form of, 146-147, 348
    and interfaces, 404, 405-410
    library, .NET, 8, 22, 44, 535
    member. *See* Member, class
    name and program file name, 21-22
    sealed, 396
    well-designed, 147-148, 167-168
class keyword, 22, 147
Close( ), 474, 476, 477, 483, 486, 498
Code
    blocks, 38-39, 68
    managed vs. unmanaged, 9, 565-566
    section, critical, 575
    unreachable, 163
    unsafe, 565-571
Collection, 214
Comments, 22, 23, 24

Common Language Runtime (CLR), 8-9, 15,
    565-566
Common Language Specification (CLS), 9
CompareTo( ), 219, 510
Compilation, conditional, 555
Compiler
    C# command-line, 15-16
    JIT, 8, 15
Components and C#, software, 6
Conditional built-in attribute, 562-564
Console class, 24, 478, 481
Console input, 100-101
Console.Error, 473, 478, 480-481
Console.In, 473, 478-479
Console.Out, 473, 478, 480-481
const modifier, 577
Constants, 62
    named integer, 404, 432
Constructor(s), 174-178
    base to call a base class, using, 357-362
    in class hierarchy, order of calling,
      347-375
    and inheritance, 355-363, 378-381
    overloading, 275-283
continue statement, 100, 133-134
Control statements. *See* Statements, control
Conversion operators, 549-554
    implicit vs. explicit, 554
Copy( ), 219
Cross-language interoperability, 5 6
.cs file extension, 21
csc.exe command-line compiler, 15-16

D

Data type(s), 28
    casting. *See* Casts
    class as, 148-149, 154
    conversion, automatic, 83-85, 270-272
    promotion of, 88-91
    reference, 48, 154
    value (simple). *See* Value types
    See also Type
decimal value type, 48, 53-54
    literal, 62
Decrement operator (− −), 37, 74-75, 305,
    308-309

default statement, 107, 109
#define directive, 555-556
delegate keyword, 520
Delegates, 520-528
    declaring, 520-521
    instantiating, 523
    and multicasting, 525-527
Destructors, 181
DirectoryNotFoundException, 482
Dispose( ), 577
DivideByZeroException, 438-439, 457
do-while loop, 100, 125-127
Dot operator (.), 149, 289-290
double value type, 29-31, 52-53
Dynamic method dispatch, 382

E

#elif directive, 559-560
else, 101-106
#else directive, 558-559
Encapsulation, 11-12, 22, 69, 167-168, 242
#endif directive, 556-557
#endregion directive, 562
Enumerations, 404, 432-435
Equals( ), 317, 397-398, 510
#error directive, 561
Errors
    runtime, 438
    syntax, 25-26
event keyword, 528
Events, 528-534
    multicasting, 530, 531-534
Exception class, 438, 455-457
Exception handling, 438-469
    block, general form of, 439
    and creating derived class exceptions, 458-460, 469
    and uncaught exceptions, 443-445
    See also catch statement(s)
    See also try block(s)
Exceptions, standard built-in, 438, 457-458
explicit keyword, 549
Expressions, 88-92

F

false, 56, 317
File(s)
    I/O. *See* I/O, file
    position indicator, 502-503
FileAccess enumeration, 483
FileMode enumeration, 481, 482
FileNotFoundException, 481-482
FileStream class, 475, 481, 488
Finalize( ), 397
finally block, 439, 453-455
fixed keyword, using the, 570-571
float value type, 29, 31, 52
    literal, 62
Floating-point(s), 29, 31, 52-53
    literals, 62
Flush( ), 474, 477, 486, 498
for loop, 36-38, 100, 115-122, 125
    variations, 117-122
foreach loop, 100, 214-217
FormatException, 506
Frank, Ed, 4
Function, 12

G

Garbage collection, 180-181, 267
    and arrays, 190
    and fixed, 570-571
get accessor
    for indexer, 319-320, 323
    for property, 328, 330, 333
GetHashCode( ), 317, 397-398
GetType( ), 397
Gosling, James, 4, 5
goto, 100, 133, 134-136

H

Hash code, 397
Heap memory region, 576
Hejlsberg, Anders, 6
Hexadecimal literals, 63
Hierarchical classification, 13
    and inheritance, 346
Hoare, C.A.R., 293

I

Identifiers, 43-44
#if directive, 556-560
if statement, 34-36, 100, 101-106
    nested, 103-104
if-else-if ladder, 104-106
    switch statement vs., 111
implicit keyword, 549
Increment operator (++), 37, 74-75, 305,
    308-309
Indentation style, 40
Indexers, 319-328
    interface, 421-424
    multidimensional, 325-327
    one-dimensional, 319-325
    overloading, 328
    read-only or write-only, creating, 323
    virtual, 385
IndexOf( ), 219
IndexOutOfRangeException, 440, 457
Inheritance, 11, 13, 346-401
    basics of, 346-353
    and constructors, 355-363, 374-375,
      378-381
    and interfaces, 424-426
    multilevel, 371-374
    name hiding and, 363-365
    sealed to prevent, using, 396
Instance of a class, 146
    See also Object(s)
Instance variables
    accessing, 149, 159
    declaring, 148
    definition of, 12, 146
    hiding, 186
    this to access hidden, using, 186
    as unique to their object, 149, 151-153
int value type, 28, 29, 30, 49, 50, 51, 52
Integer(s), 31, 49-52
    literals, 62
    promotion, 89
Interface(s), 404-429
    explicit implementation of, 426-429
    general form of, 405
    implementing, 405-410
    indexers, 421-424

    and inheritance, 424-426
    properties, 419-421
    reference variables, 410-413
interface keyword, 404
internal access specifier, 242, 574
Internet, 2, 4
    and portability, 5
InvalidCastException, 457
I/O, 472-517
    console, 478-481
    redirection, 492-495
    streams. *See* Streams
I/O, file, 481-504
    and binary data, 498-502
    byte oriented, 481-487
    character-based, 488-492
    random access, 502-505
IOException, 474
is operator, 571-573

J

Java
    and C#, 2, 6
    features lacking in, 5-6
    history of, 4-5
Java Virtual Machine (JVM), 5
JIT compiler, 8, 15

K

Keywords, C#, 42-43, 44

L

Label, 135
LastIndexOf( ), 219
Length property
    of arrays, 206-208, 330-333
    of Stream, 475
    of strings, 219
Library, .NET Framework class, 8, 22, 44, 535
#line directive, 561
Literals, 62-66
lock, 575
Logical operators, 75-81

long value type, 49, 50-51
    literal, 62
Loops
    criteria for selecting, 125
    do-while, 100, 125-127
    for. *See* for loop
    foreach, 100, 214-217
    infinite, 120, 131-132
    nested, 141-142
    while, 100, 123-125

M

Main( ), 23-24, 25, 148, 156, 283-286, 289
    and command-line arguments, 283-286
Managed code, 19, 565-566
Math class, 52, 53
Member, class, 12, 146
    access and inheritance, 350-352,
        353-355
    controlling access to, 147, 242-250
    dot operator to access, 149
MemberwiseClone( ), 397
Memory allocation
    using new, 153-154, 179, 191
    using stackalloc, 576
MemoryStream class, 475, 517
Message property of Exception, 456-457
Metadata, 9
Method(s), 12, 155-167
    abstract, 391-395
    base to access hidden, using, 364,
        365-366
    calling, 159
    conditional, 563
    delegates and, 520-528
    dispatch, dynamic, 382
    general form of, 156
    and interfaces, 404, 405
    operator, 300-301, 309-314
    overloading, 267-274
    overriding. *See* Overriding, method
    and parameters, 156, 163-167
    passing objects to, 250-254
    recursive, 286-289
    returning object from, 265-267
    returning a value from, 159, 160-162
    returning more than one value from,
        255, 257-259
    scope defined by, 69
    signature, 274
    static, 289, 290-293
    virtual, 382-390
Microsoft Intermediate Language (MSIL), 8-9,
    15
Modulus operator (%), 72-73
Multicasting
    delegates and, 525-527
    and events, 530, 531-534
Multitasking, 575

N

Name hiding
    and code blocks, 72
    and inheritance, 363-366, 426
namespace keyword, 535
Namespace(s), 22, 26-27, 535-549
    additive characteristic of, 542-543
    declaring, 535-538
    default, 545
    nested, 544-545
Naughton, Patrick, 4
Negative numbers, representation of, 230
.NET Framework, 2, 7-9
    and C++, 10
    class library, 8, 22, 44, 535
new, 153-154, 179-180, 191, 194
    to hide base class member, 363, 366, 426
NOT operator
    bitwise unary (~), 224, 225, 229
    logical unary (!), 75, 76
NotSupportedException, 474
Null statement, 120

O

Oak, 4
Object(s), 12, 146, 151
    creating, 149, 153-154
    to methods, passing, 250-254
    returning, 265-267

object class, 396-401
    methods defined by, 397
    reference to value type, 399-401
Object initialization
    with another object, 276-277
    with constructor, 174-178
Object-oriented programming (OOP), 3-4,
    10-14
Obsolete built-in attribute, 562, 564-565
Octals, 65
One's complement (unary NOT) operator (~),
    224, 225, 229
Operator(s)
    arithmetic, 29, 72-75
    assignment, 28, 82-83, 317
    bitwise, 224-235
    conversion. *See* Conversion operators
    logical, 75-81
    parentheses and, 92
    precedence, table of, 88
    relational, 34, 75-77, 315-317
    ternary, 236-238
operator keyword, 300
Operator overloading, 300-318
    binary, 300-304
    and overloading an operator method,
        309-314
    relational, 315-317
    restrictions, 317-318
    unary, 300-301, 304-308
OR operator (|)
    bitwise, 224, 225, 226-227
    logical, 75, 76, 80-81
OR operator, short-circuit (||), 75, 77-78, 80-81
out parameter modifier, 255, 257-261, 301,
    325, 333
OutOfMemoryException, 458
OverflowException, 458
    and checked and unchecked, 466-469
Overloading
    constructors, 275-283
    indexers, 328
    methods, 267-274
    operators. *See* Operator overloading
override keyword, 382, 385
Overriding, method, 382-390
    and dynamic method dispatch, 382

P

Parameter(s), 156, 163-167
    modifiers, 255-264
    and overloaded constructors, 276
    and overloaded methods, 267, 270-272
params parameter modifier, 261-264
Parse( ) methods, 505, 506-510
Peek( ), 476
Pointers, 566-571
Polymorphism, 11, 12-13
    and overridden methods, runtime, 382,
        385-386
    and interfaces, 404
    and overloaded methods, 267, 273
Portability, 4-5, 6, 8, 49
Position property, 475
Pow( ), 93
Preprocessor directives, 555-562
private access specifier, 23, 242-250
    and inheritance, 350-352
Programming
    mixed-language, 5
    object-oriented. *See* Object-oriented
        programming (OOP)
    structured, 3, 11
Properties, 328-333
    interface, 419-421
    read-only or write-only, creating, 330
    restrictions on, 333
    virtual, 385
protected access specifier, 242, 351, 353-355
public access specifier, 23, 242-250

Q

Queue(s), 209
Quicksort algorithm, 289, 293-296

R

Random access file I/O, 502-505
Read( ), 100-101, 474, 476, 478, 483, 484, 499
ReadBlock( ), 476
ReadByte( ), 474, 483, 485, 499
ReadLine( ), 476, 478, 479
readonly field, 575-576

ReadToEnd( ), 476
Recursion, 286-289
ref parameter modifier, 255-257, 301, 325, 333
Reference variable(s)
    assigning derived class reference to base
        class, 377-381
    and assignment, 154-155
    declaring, 153
    modified by ref and out, 260-261
ReferenceEquals( ), 397
#region directive, 562
Relational operators, 34, 75-77, 315-317
Replace( ), 522
return statement, 100, 159, 160
Ritchie, Dennis, 2
Runtime type indentification, 571-573

S

sbyte value type, 48, 49, 51-52, 62
Scopes, 68-72
sealed keyword, 396
Security, 9
SecurityException, 482
Seek( ), 474, 502-503, 517
SeekOrigin enumeration, 503
Selection statements, 100, 101-115
set accessor
    for indexer, 319-320, 323
    for property, 328, 329, 330
SetError( ), 494
SetIn( ), 494
SetOut( ), 494
Sheridan, Mike, 4
Shift operators, bitwise, 225, 230-232
short value type, 49, 50, 52, 62
Sign flag, 50
Signature of a method, 274
sizeof operator, 574-575
Sqrt( ), 52-53, 290
Stack, definition of, 12, 207
stackalloc, 576
StackOverflowException, 458
StackTrace property of Exception, 456-457
Statements, 24, 39-40
    null, 120
Statements, control, 33
    iteration, 100, 115-130, 214-217

jump, 100, 131-140, 159, 160
selection, 100, 101-115
static, 24, 289-293
Stream(s)
    binary, 477
    byte, 481
    classes, byte, 475
    definition of, 472
    memory-based, 517
    predefined, 475
    redirecting standard, 492-495
    wrapper classes, character, 475-477
Stream class, 474-475
    methods, table of, 474
    properties, table of, 475
StreamReader class, 477, 488, 491-492
    and character encoding, 493
StreamWriter class, 477, 488-491
    and character encoding, 493
String(s)
    arrays of, 221
    constructing, 218
    immutability of, 222-223
    indexing, 219
    Length property of, 219
    literals, 64-66, 217
    numeric, converting, 505-510
    as objects, 217
string class, 217-223
    methods, 218-221
StringBuilder class, 223
StringReader class, 477, 517
StringWriter class, 477, 517
Stroustrup, Bjarne, 3, 4, 5
struct keyword, 430
Structures, 404, 430-432
    .NET numeric, 505-506
Subclass, 353
Substring( ), 222-223
Sun Microsystems, 4
Superclass, 353
switch statement, 100, 106-112
    and no fall-through rule, 109-110, 112
Syntax errors, 25-26
System namespace, 22, 26-27, 535
System.Diagnostics namespace, 563
System.Exception class. *See* Exception class
System.IDisposable interface, 577

System.IO namespace, 473, 481, 535
System.IO.Stream class. *See* Stream class
SystemException, 438-439, 457

T

TargetSite property of Exception, 456-457
Ternary operator (?), 236-238
TextReader class, 475-476, 477, 478, 479, 488
    methods defined by, table of, 476
TestWriter class, 475, 476-477, 488
this, 184-186, 277-279, 291
Threads, multiple, 575
throw, 439, 450-453
ToString( ), 397, 398, 456-457
true, 57, 317
True and false in C#, 57
try block(s), 439-443
    nested, 449-450
Two's complement, 50
Type
    casting. *See* Casts
    checking, 48, 376
    conversion, automatic, 83-85, 270-272
    extensibility, 300
    indentification, runtime, 571-573
    promotion, 88-91
typeof operator, 573
Types, data. *See* Data types

U

uint value type, 49, 50, 51, 52
    literal, 62
ulong value type, 49, 50
    literal, 62
unchecked statement, 466-469
#undef directive, 560
Unicode, 54-55, 225-226, 488
Unmanaged code, 9, 565-566
unsafe keyword, using, 566, 569
ushort value type, 49, 50, 52, 62
using
    directive, 22, 26-27, 538-541
    statement, 576-577

V

Value type(s), 48-49, 154
    boxing and unboxing, 399-401
    .NET numeric structures, 505-506, 510
Variable(s)
    declaration, 28, 29, 67, 70
    definition of, 27
    dynamic initialization of, 68
    initializing, 67-68, 70-71
    instance. *See* Instance variables
    local, 67
    names, rules governing, 43-44
    reference. *See* Reference variables
    scope and lifetime of, 68-72
    static, 289-291, 292
    volatile, 577
virtual keyword, 382, 385, 391
Virtual methods, 382-390
    properties, 385
Visual C++ IDE (Integrated Development
    Environment), 15, 16-21
void, 24, 156
    methods, 159-160
volatile modifier, 577

W

#warning directive, 561
Warth, Chris, 4
while loop, 100, 123-125
Windows environment, 6, 7
Write( ), 29, 474, 476, 481, 485-486, 498
WriteByte( ), 475
WriteLine( ), 24, 28, 29, 31, 398, 456, 476, 481
    formatted output version of, 58-59

X

XML comment, 24
XOR (exclusive OR) operator (^)
    bitwise, 224, 225, 227-229
    logical, 75, 76

INTERNATIONAL CONTACT INFORMATION

AUSTRALIA
McGraw-Hill Book Company Australia Pty. Ltd.
TEL +61-2-9417-9899
FAX +61-2-9417-5687
http://www.mcgraw-hill.com.au
books-it_sydney@mcgraw-hill.com

CANADA
McGraw-Hill Ryerson Ltd.
TEL +905-430-5000
FAX +905-430-5020
http://www.mcgrawhill.ca

**GREECE, MIDDLE EAST,
NORTHERN AFRICA**
McGraw-Hill Hellas
TEL +30-1-656-0990-3-4
FAX +30-1-654-5525

MEXICO (Also serving Latin America)
McGraw-Hill Interamericana Editores S.A. de C.V.
TEL +525-117-1583
FAX +525-117-1589
http://www.mcgraw-hill.com.mx
fernando_castellanos@mcgraw-hill.com

SINGAPORE (Serving Asia)
McGraw-Hill Book Company
TEL +65-863-1580
FAX +65-862-3354
http://www.mcgraw-hill.com.sg
mghasia@mcgraw-hill.com

SOUTH AFRICA
McGraw-Hill South Africa
TEL +27-11-622-7512
FAX +27-11-622-9045.
robyn_swanepoel@mcgraw-hill.com

**UNITED KINGDOM & EUROPE
(Excluding Southern Europe)**
McGraw-Hill Education Europe
TEL +44-1-628-502500
FAX +44-1-628-770224
http://www.mcgraw-hill.co.uk
computing_neurope@mcgraw-hill.com

ALL OTHER INQUIRIES Contact:
Osborne/McGraw-Hill
TEL +1-510-549-6600
FAX +1-510-883-7600
http://www.osborne.com
omg_international@mcgraw-hill.com